THE ISLAND GARDEN

ReFormations

MEDIEVAL AND EARLY MODERN

Series Editors:
David Aers, Sarah Beckwith, and James Simpson

THE ISLAND GARDEN

England's Language of Nation from Gildas to Marvell

LYNN STALEY

University of Notre Dame Press

Notre Dame, Indiana

Manufactured in the United States of America

Library of Congress Cataloging-in-Publication Data

Staley, Lynn, 1947–
The island garden : England's language of nation from Gildas to Marvell /
Lynn Staley.
p.   cm. — (ReFormations : medieval and early modern)
Includes bibliographical references and index.
ISBN 978-0-268-04140-3 (pbk. : alk. paper) —
ISBN 0-268-04140-7 (pbk. : alk. paper)
1. National characteristics, British, in literature.
2. English literature—Old English, ca. 450–1100—History and criticism.
3. English literature—Middle English, 1100–1500—History and criticism.
4. English literature—Early modern, 1500–1700—History and criticism.
5. Literature and history—Great Britain—History.   6. Islands in literature.
7. Gardens in literature.   8. Geography in literature.   9. Great Britain—
History—Anglo-Saxon period, 449–1066—Historiography.
10. Great Britain—History—1066–1687—Historiography.   I. Title.
II. Title: England's language of nation from Gildas to Marvell.
PR149.N3S83   2012
820.9'35842—dc23

2012008953

For Maxwell Johnson, my son

List of Abbreviations   ix

Introduction: The Language of Place   1

CHAPTER ONE
Writing in the Shadow of Bede: England, the Island Garden   15

CHAPTER TWO
The Island Garden and the Anxieties of Enclosure   71

CHAPTER THREE
The Fourteenth Century and Place   121

CHAPTER FOUR
Susanna and Her Garden   177

Conclusion: Island Discourse   227

Notes   243
Works Cited   301
Index   335

Figures follow p. 182

ANTS   Anglo Norman Text Society

DNB   *Oxford Dictionary of National Biography*, ed. H. C. G. Matthew and Brian Harrison (Oxford: Oxford University Press). Online edition, ed. Lawrence Goldman.

De Excidio *De Excidio Britonum*. Gildus. *The Ruin of Britain and Other Works*, ed. and trans. Michael Winterbottom (Totowa: Rowan and Littlefield, 1978).

EHR   *English Historical Review*

ELH   *English Literary History*

GRA   *William of Malmesbury. Gesta Regum Anglorum*, 2 vols., ed. and trans. R. A. B. Mynors, R. M. Thomson, and M. Winterbottom (Oxford: Clarendon Press, 1998).

HA   *Henry, Archdeacon of Huntingdon. Historia Anglorum*, ed. and trans. Diana Greenway (Oxford: Clarendon Press, 1996).

HE   *Historia Ecclesiastica Gentis Anglorum. Bede's Ecclesiastical History of the English People*, ed. and trans. Bertram Colgrave and R. A. B. Mynors (Oxford: Clarendon Press, 1969).

HRB   *Historia Regum Britanniae, Geoffrey of Monmouth. The History of the Kings of Britain,* Latin text, ed. Michael D. Reeve, trans. Neil Wright (Woodbridge, UK: Boydell Press, 2007).

JEGP   *Journal of English and Germanic Philology*

JMEMS   *Journal of Medieval and Early Modern Studies*

JWCI   *Journal of the Warburg and Courtauld Institutes*

PL   J.-P. [Jacques-Paul] Migne, *Patrologiae cursus completus. Series Latina* (Paris: [various publishers], 1844–64).

SAC   *Studies in the Age of Chaucer*

SEL   *Studies in English Literature*

SP   *Studies in Philology*

SR   *Statutes of the Realm,* 4 vols. (London, 1810–19). Searchable Text Edition (Burlington, ONT: Tanner Ritchie)

YLS   *Yearbook of Langland Studies*

INTRODUCTION

The Language of Place

In about 540 C.E. Gildas wrote his *De Excidio Britonum* in order to
deplore and explain the state of Britain. He chose a potent metaphor
for Britain whose "obstinacy, subjection, and rebellion" brought about
her present misery   the island garden, thus linking Britain's actual
geography to the biblical Eden, the garden lost through human rebellion. Eden was also the prototype for the garden of the Song of
Songs, which is linked, of course, to its bride, allegorically the soul or
the church, and for the gardens at the heart of monastic foundations.[1]
In describing Britain as "like a bride arrayed in a variety of jewelry,"
Gildas signaled the connections between Britain and these gardens
and prepared the way for his account of Britain as a postlapsarian garden whose rebellious people, like Israel, bride of God, have turned
beauty and fertility into waste and sterility. Moreover, rather than
simply produce the metaphor, Gildas joined his moral and allegorical
perspective to a physical reality, describing Britain as a geographic
entity, "virtually at the end of the world," eight hundred miles in

1

length, two hundred in width, fortified by the sea. Gildas's description of Britain, the wasted garden island or the fallen bride, was taken up by Bede in his *Historia Ecclesiastica Gentis Anglorum* two centuries later and modified in ways that illustrate the process by which one man's metaphor can become another man's differently directed mode of analytic discourse. Whereas for Gildas Britain's insularity is the source of its vulnerability, since its beauty and singularity inspire willfulness and incite desire, Bede describes *England* as permeable (not necessarily vulnerable) and inherently hospitable; as colonized (rather than victimized), thus as enriched by those who transgress its boundaries; as attached to (rather than detached from) the rest of the world; and, finally, as enriching a world now in need of the Christian culture once translated to its own shores. Bede's act of translation, and the popularity of his history, provided later writers with a language with which to construct or explore national identity. Even before there was a political community called England, there was an island called Britain, whose history could be told and explained using the language of place, a language that, from Gildas on, was associated with Christian and providential perspectives on history.

This book isolates and explores this language of England's self-definition; but, more important, it explores the ways in which the trope of the beautiful island garden became attached to, or was a sign for, the anxieties of the English nation and was reformulated at certain key moments by writers who perceived, as did Bede, its usefulness as an elastic, subtle, but nonetheless pointed discourse for historical analysis and thus for social or political critique. In fact, the trope of the island garden, used by Gildas in reference to Britain, was refocused through an Anglocentric lens that, as R. R. Davies has argued, dominated the historical tradition from the twelfth century on.[2] Though we are all aware that Britain is an island and that even now England is referred to as a garden, the image of the island garden during the medieval and early modern periods was neither simple nor stable but used variously to express those concerns and anxieties belonging to national identity and to an understanding of the nature of its community. Put simply, I suggest that the description of Britain as an island garden, which Gildas employs to describe its fall from Edenic bounty to waste and sin and Bede to suggest the processes of historical reparation of the English that he attributes to the church, catalyzed two crucial historical perspectives and thus analytic modes. The key concept attached to England's language of place is enclosure, the island enclosed by the sea, the garden enclosed by its wall, the bride enclosed by her chastity, the nation protected by its ecclesiastical foundations or by its kings, a concept fraught with anxieties of violation or of isolation that the writers of the histories, treatises, and poems discussed in this book explore.

In chapter 1 I trace England's language of place as employed by Gildas and Bede and used thereafter by the post-Conquest historians William of Malmesbury, Henry of Huntingdon, and Geoffrey of Monmouth and the sixteenth-century Tudor historians who employed the terms of Bedan history filtered through twelfth-century historians even as they struggled to reformulate them. These historians, like Gildas and Bede, are concerned with the whole of England's history rather than with the annals of specific years and therefore ground their works in introductory accounts of origins. The twelfth-century historians provide examples of the different ways in which history could be written following either Gildas or Bede. Both William of Malmesbury and Henry of Huntingdon do not simply fit their works into Bede's *Historia*, but, like him, manifest historical perspectives that suggest the processes of history, the providential reparations that succeed apparent disasters. Though England's is a history of five invasions, as both acknowledge, it is also a history of growing social, legal, and ecclesiastical cohesion. Each weaves the uncertainties and the brutalities of history into a whole cloth that serves as a testimony to an order that is inherent in the identity of the nation itself, despite the realities of personal cupidity, passion, or misfortune. Like Bede, William of Malmesbury and Henry of Huntingdon give evidence of narrating a piece of a more comprehensive history whose end they cannot see but whose providential shape they can adumbrate. I trace the historiographical perspective of Geoffrey of Monmouth to Gildas and his use of history as jeremiad wherein history is hostage to human sin and nation but a name for a truncated or unrealized concept. What is an important distinction in medieval historiography, including that to be found in the vernacular *Brut* and Higden's *Polychronicon*, becomes an urgent debate about the relationship of England to the world in Tudor histories that mark the contraction of the island garden and its increasingly beleaguered and enclosed identity. However, here, too, there is evidence of historians—among them William Camden, Ralph Hollinshed, William Lambarde, and Samuel Daniel—who do not explicitly dissent from official views but nonetheless offer intaglios that suggest their understandings of Bede's broader vision, a vision that is foreclosed by Milton in his *History of Britain*.

However, what appears a subtle but straightforward dialectic among historians who employ the language of place to debate the relationship between islands and the merits or realities of cultural isolation is complicated by literary texts, which I explore in the second chapter. A wide variety of authors make use of the trope in very different ways, creating a discourse whose themes and images are reformulated and reapplied to contemporary situations. Earlier histories tended to associate England's singular, and potentially sacral, identity either with the strength of its ecclesiastical foundations or with its anointed rulers. However, when in the mid-fourteenth century William Langland employed another enclosed space—the peasant holding, the half acre—as an image for England, he prompted a dialectic worked out in images for national identity that implied a relationship between sovereign power and the common good. From the A-text of *Piers Plowman* on, those subjects and anxieties linked to the image of the island garden became attached to alternate images for England as less a moated isle than a semienclosed garden in need of proper cultivation. Langland's translation of the metaphor for nation from a discrete and royal space into an agricultural holding had, as chapter 2 demonstrates, a long life in English literature. This dialectic, as it was expressed through the construction and exploration of enclosed spaces, is the more arresting because it predates the later country/city debate and stages a subtle probing of social status, regality, and the relationship of both to law.[3] Chaucer detaches the image of the peasant holding as a metaphor for nation from Langland's poem of spiritual pilgrimage and uses it to explore the nature of political authority and order, looking forward to the more politically explicit use of images of enclosed spaces throughout the fifteenth and sixteenth centuries, particularly in texts addressing the land-enclosure disputes. However, an image and set of concerns that can be found in agricultural manuals and parliamentary sermons is altered once more by Ben Jonson, who attaches it to the estate, and by Andrew Marvell, whose "Upon Appleton House" muses on a once ecclesiastical and now secular house, Nun Appleton, the home of Cistercian nuns until it was suppressed in the reign of Henry VIII. In the poem Marvell considers subjects like the relation of the individual to society, national origins and identity, and the nature of the sacred, issues that are likewise central to thirteenth- and fourteenth-century treatments of England as garden. With its concern for boundaries, lineage, and the processes by which sanctity is asserted, "Upon Appleton House" links what has been described as the last of the country house poems with a tradition beginning with Gildas and Bede and continuing through monastic myths of origin, the medieval chronicle tradition and their refractions in vernacular literature. Marvell's own circumstances—a Yorkshireman by birth; contemporary with the burgeoning antiquarian interests of men like Dugdale, Tanner, and Cotton; and an assiduous scholar in his own right—wrote with more than a casual knowledge of the transformation of sacred space, all too evident in a Yorkshire once the very heart of medieval ecclesiastical geography.

Chapter 3 takes as its problem Langland's employment of the image of the enclosed croft and focuses on the fourteenth century, in particular, on texts that can be associated with Edward III. Though "change" does not simply happen, there are periods that seem to hasten change or to offer new ways of imagining the present. I look to the reign of Edward III (1327–77) as such a moment.[4] In 1341, when as a youngish king he still had much to learn about the arts of governing, Edward came to verbal blows with his chancellor and archbishop of Canterbury, John Stratford, in letters that were widely distributed. The occasion was money; the subject, authority. Edward had been left high and dry on the continent, waiting for funds he had requested that would allow him to continue the conflict he had begun in 1340 when he claimed the throne of France, thus beginning a war, punctuated by periods of truce, that came to define diplomatic relations in Europe for a hundred years. Returning to England, embarrassed and furious, he began a public quarrel with Stratford, which he ostensibly lost but which he parlayed into a personal victory. Within a few years he held a court of the Round Table and initiated the Order of the Garter, by which he sought to bind the nobility to himself and to identify England with the Virgin Mary and Saint George, patron of chivalry.

England, however, was not univocal. This is also a period when parliament increasingly finds its voice, when the first outbreak of the

Black Death occurs, when a local concern with justice is manifest, and when the wages of war must be paid. I examine chronicle accounts of the period, such as those of Adam Murimuth and Robert of Avesbury, treatises such as *The Treatise of Walter de Milemete* and *De Speculo Regis*, poems like *Winner and Waster* (possibly associated with the Order of the Garter), the A-text of *Piers Plowman*, and shorter poems, arguing that it is possible to explore the competing impulses of a world not so singly or simply seen in elite images. That so many of these texts continued to be copied into later manuscripts says much about the continuing relevance of what are Edwardian texts. As I suggested in *Languages of Power in the Age of Richard II*,[5] the picture that emerges is not that to be found in France where sacrality rested with the king.[6] The present study pushes that statement even further, arguing that in England what is set apart, examined, and sacralized is the secular household, frequently figured as a garden, whose rights are, or ought to be, inviolate. The secular has not replaced the sacred; the sacred has been redefined. These primarily midcentury texts, written when Edward was centering power on himself as a figure of cultic chivalry, suggest other sets of rhetorical possibilities in the images of farmyards, forest spaces, and crofts that were sometimes used as alternate images of nation. In inserting the half-acre into his evolving poem, William Langland located himself within these contemporary concerns and offered a powerful counterimage—one rooted in the actualities of English agricultural life—to the royal isle protected by Saint George that was promulgated by Edward III. Langland's croft quickly entered vernacular culture and maintained its political vitality through the early seventeenth century.

Chapter 4 concerns the biblical Susanna, whose enclosed garden provided English writers from the thirteenth century to the seventeenth with a means of exploring place, not as a royal or peasant holding, but as a household where safety and identity are guaranteed by law. The story of Susanna, which was commonly applied to lessons of marital chastity and of faith and trust in God, received a profoundly legal emphasis in English texts, and the garden in which she is surprised by the unjust elders was used as synecdoche for the household (both ecclesiastical and lay) and its vulnerability to illegal practices. I argue that her story, as it can be read through English texts during this period, serves to underline a perspective on law, on individual rights and consciousness, and on the understanding of what constitutes sacred space that is ultimately crucial to England's self-conception, in which both the monastic foundation and the great house were described as resting on a law that even kings must serve. Significantly, Susanna and her garden are not located in regal space but in gentry space, suggesting the need to imagine a character for enclosed sanctity that, with the exception of the thirteenth-century "Tractatus metricus de Susanna," is neither ecclesiastical nor regal. English treatments of Susanna employ those terms that are key to explorations of national self-definition, particularly those that inquire into competing systems of authority. Susanna's sanctity as chaste wife is imaged in her garden, which is a mirror of her and her marriage *and* a figure for private space and its sanctity under the law and relationship to the outside world. The texts concerning Susanna provide a sometimes startling echo of concerns for privacy and communal prerogative voiced through a biblical fiction, concerns that are certainly expressed in contemporary terms but that also suggest a continual understanding of the island garden as reinforced and defined not by moats but by law.

The discourse here described is not intended as a comprehensive literary history of the medieval and early modern periods, or as a catalog of gardens in English literature, but as a specifically focused exploration of the ways in which a number of authors develop the semantics of the language of place to construct or explore England's cultural, social, and political identity. James Simpson has presented a powerful argument for the narrowing of English culture with the reign of Henry VIII and his concentration of power in the crown.[7] Although authors like Bale and Foxe certainly stand as examples of Henry's cultural revolution, this book suggests a concurrent and subtly opposing impulse, a broadening understanding of *sources* for national identity worked out using language associated with those issues of insularity and isolation that are integral to accounts of England, the island garden. If Bede suggests that England's history is the history of its church and later historians choose regnal years as defining categories for their accounts of England, this book presents other ways of reckoning history, ways to be found in the works of writers who offer pictures of spaces whose sanctities depend neither on monasteries nor on kings. The particular garden enclosed by the sea that is the subject of this book—whose historic identity cannot be understood without reference to the language of place that was associated with its geographic identity—prompted a conversation as dense and rich as any to be found in late Henry James, a concatenation of images that serve as signs of a discourse tracing out an urgent inquiry into identity. Rather than demonstrate a Darwinian trajectory by which the sacred devolves to the secular, the language of place allows for the reinscription of the sacred on the ordinary, a resacralization of national identity through the rituals of daily life, which are the laws of the household and its order. That the georgic order of the household of the realm is not necessarily to be identified with the sovereign or with the quality of sovereign power is integral to an England conceived of as a nation whose porous boundaries, including those of its households, are regulated or protected by its laws. Moreover, the discourse I identify and describe provides a *non* to the *sic* of those who insist on a break with the past occasioned by the Reformation in England. By discussing and linking those authors who offered images of nation in the farm or the great house, enclosures whose rights are guaranteed by the Great Charter and by the legal system that served to check monarchical privilege, I also offer evidence that modifies claims that the Tudors effectively refocused the imagery of nation on the crown. The Tudors may have tried to do so, but, despite Tudor propaganda, this book suggests ways in which others sketched in an England whose identity was more diverse, or robust, and hardly unifocal.[8] In my conclusion I consider ways in which those tropes that I have traced back through the Middle Ages remained in play but were necessarily altered during England's evolution from island garden to the island garden/mercantile empire and were jettisoned by those English settlers in America.

▨   The subjects related to my argument—the medieval/early modern "divide," the ideation of England as a place, and the history of England's histories—make it possible for this book to intersect with the work of many other scholars and to reflect the current interest among medievalists in understanding, or in trying to measure, the shadows cast by our thousand years on the next one hundred fifty. In *The "Shepheardes Calender,"* I probed Spenser's relationship to his medieval cultural past and the degree to which he sought to ground his poem in the traditions of those authors in whose footsteps he followed and to assert the newness of his poem and the urgencies of his own cultural and political moment.[9] Since then, there has been an increasingly sophisticated inquiry into England's and Britain's textual culture, especially into the contemporary understanding of the historic past, not in an attempt to identify medieval sources for early modern formulations, but rather to understand how authors might employ a past to explain a present, sometimes rewriting that past.[10] Medievalists like Lee Patterson and Paul Strohm have analyzed the medieval construction of its own past, particularly as it concerns Chaucer or the Lancastrian accession to the throne, and, of course, the Reformist (re-)construction of England's Romish past is well known and well studied.[11] More recently James Simpson has bridged the two periods, following out the implications of Lollard studies initiated by Anne Hudson and Margaret Aston.[12] He, like Eamon Duffy, argues for a cultural break and a consequent break between the medieval and early modern periods, though, unlike Duffy, Simpson does not romanticize medieval England as a time of intellectual plenitude.[13] Rather, Simpson underlines the degree to which Henry VIII imposed his sovereignty on English culture through the dominance of the court as a center for culture. As I have suggested elsewhere,[14] particularly in contrast to the France of Charles V, we can find no such cultural hegemony in England in the fourteenth century; instead we can find competing courts and a variety of cultures. The work presently orchestrated by David Wallace, along with the various dense microstudies by Ralph Hanna, Robert Barrett, Christopher Cannon, Sarah Beckwith, Theresa Coletti, and Gail McMurray Gibson, points up the multivocality of late medieval English culture by studying not simply texts but also the regional culture and systems of patronage and social affiliation from which they emerged.[15] Given the mobility of medieval life, especially of magnatial households, what may have had regional roots came to contribute to a national culture that Thorlac Turville-Petre has argued can be identified very early. Jocelyn Wogan-Brown and Ardis Butterfield have presented powerful arguments for the diversity of that "national culture," a culture whose three languages and literary forms cross-fertilized one another well into the Tudor period. Their insistence that any idea of nation in this period must be detached from more modern notions of nationalism or imperialism is an important distinction.[16] Instead, as this book demonstrates, it is the island itself as a geographic reality become an ideological construct that prompts an inquiry into an identity whose boundaries are not linguistic, and hardly geographic since they uneasily enclose Celtic cultures that frequently go unmentioned or were deliberately occluded by a dominant English political system and culture.[17] More often than not, to say Britain is to mean England. If I echo such acts of occlusion here, it is because I am interested in the language of place as it was used to describe Britain/England, the self-proclaimed island garden.[18]

Moreover, these studies of Yorkshire, Worcester, Cheshire, or East Anglia manifest more than regional consciousness; they manifest an early attempt to understand place as it relates to the greater place that is England. Kathy Lavezzo and Catherine A. M. Clarke have suggested ways in which ideas of place functioned as defining tropes for England and for those men or institutions that sought to ally themselves with the idea of nation as the beautiful isle or the distant island, and Virginia Blanton has placed the cult of Saint Æthelthryth, particularly as it is treated in the *Book of Ely*, within a web of concerns about national inviolability that were occasioned by the Norman Conquest.[19] Such studies of the tropes of nation, like studies of regional culture, underscore the complicated processes by which England's writers created a language of identity that served as an indicator of a particular historical perspective and thus could be used to explain or castigate or meditate on a present situation. The invaluable work of Antonia Gransden on medieval and early modern historians certainly testifies to the historical awareness of the monks and chroniclers who wrote the volumes to which I refer in this book and provides a picture of the connections between and among chroniclers throughout a thousand-year span.[20] Those connections are frequently obvious, in the sense that William of Newburgh cites Gildas and Bede or John Foxe disparages medieval historians when they offer laudatory accounts of Rome. The connections, however, are also fundamental in that the most notable writers of England's history seek to do more than recount events; they seek to locate events within a broader understanding of England's island status.

It is that understanding, or the rhetoric associated with a particular understanding of England as a place, that prompted my own work, which began, not with England, but with Susanna's garden. In tracing this garden from Alan of Melsa's use of it in his early-thirteenth-century poem to the fourteenth-century *Pistel of Susan* and on into early modern representations of it, I was struck by two interrelated points. First, English accounts of Susanna and the Elders link the garden to the household, and second, they suggest that the sanctity of both depends on the law. Where Alan of Melsa describes a garden that can be assimilated to the Cistercian language of enclosure, later accounts of it suggest its affiliation with secular holdings; however, both the thirteenth-century poem and the late medieval and early modern treatments of Susanna and her garden link the narrative to a broader concern for the rights of individuals under the law. Susanna's garden led me backward to the island garden and to a sacral identity Bede describes in his account of the growth of the English church, which links the English to the redeemed Israel. England's ecclesial identity increasingly yields to, or is joined with, a concept of sacral regality and thus to the king's potentially sacral role in respect to nation, a complex cultural process described by Paul Binski in his studies of Westminster Abbey and Palace.[21] Gardens, whether metaphoric or actual, are entrusted to gardeners, to guardians who protect them and allow them to increase. For Bede, the guardian is the church that, through conversion, education, and diplomacy, created a Christian culture that established an identity for England and maintained a fruitful relationship with Christendom. With the Norman Conquest and Angevin rule, nation may be more firmly identified with regality, but, at the same time, as medieval historians notice and record, the ancient traditions of England's laws can also be seen as defining a construction of nation. In the mid-fourteenth century the tension between those two—and potentially opposed—guardians, and consequently a dialectic about the very identity of the island garden, becomes apparent in numerous texts that employ a carefully worked out language of place. The reign of Edward III is a sort of watershed for efforts to rewrite England's myth of self-identity. Thereafter, the image of the royal island enclosed by its sea and that of the smallholding enclosed by law become signs of a serious inquiry into the very nature of national identity. It is the language in which this inquiry is cast that is my subject, the ambiguities, the struggles, and the uncertainties of "island discourse." The plan for the book moves from the broad historical narrative of England to increasingly focused studies—of the language of place as it was employed by late medieval writers to explore England as a national identity, a language then taken up and re-formed by early modern writers; of the importance of fourteenth-century constructions of England to this discourse; and finally to a single narrative, Susanna, which exemplifies a history of these uses of place and the concerns attached to them. In identifying and analyzing England's language of place, I make an implicitly bolder claim—that in rhetoric lies history or alternate histories, new perspectives on events that should be understood not as simply reflecting events but as events in their own right.

▪ At a crucial point in writing this book, I was blessed with a year's membership at the Institute for Advanced Studies as a Dilworth Fellow. There, with Carolyn Walker Bynum as professor of the School of Historical Studies, I could write and test my ideas in the bracing atmosphere of lunch table and seminar room. I was lucky to share that year with many wonderful scholars, but I think particularly of conversations with Caroline Bynum, Julia M. H. Smith, Regina Graffe, and Elisheva Baumgarten, whose offices neighbored my own. I have also been invited to speak, and thus to try out parts of this book, with audiences at the University of Rochester, at the Canada Chaucer Conference, at the University of Illinois at Urbana-Champaign, Fordham University, Columbia University, Catholic University, and Princeton University, as well as at meetings of the New Chaucer Society, the Gower Society, and the Medieval Academy of America. The two readers for the University of Notre Dame Press, David Aers and an anonymous reader, made some very astute suggestions, prompting me to sharpen and expand my argument.

I thank James Simpson and Brian Cummings for inviting me to write the essay "Enclosed Spaces" for their collection, *Cultural Reformations: Medieval and Renaissance in Literary History*, thus giving me the opportunity to conceptualize this much longer project. In earlier forms parts of chapter 4 were published as "Susanna and English Communities," in *Traditio* 62 (2007), and as "Susanna's Voice," in *Sacred and Profane in Chaucer and Late Medieval Literature: Essays in Honour of John V. Fleming*, edited by Robert Epstein and William Robins (Toronto: University of Toronto Press, 2010).

For their helpfulness I am grateful to librarians at the Society of Antiquaries, London, the National Gallery, the British Library, the

Bodleian Library, Christ Church Library, Oxford, the Brotherton Collection at Leeds University, and the Hampshire Record Office. I would also like to thank the editorial staff at the University of Notre Dame Press, in particular Stephen Little and Rebecca R. DeBoer. As always, my work would not be possible without the support of Colgate University's superb library staff. During this project, I have felt an extreme sense of privilege in my intellectual companions—the quick and the dead—and I thank them all here, generally, and, particularly, in the notes to each chapter.

CHAPTER ONE

WRITING IN THE SHADOW OF BEDE

England, the Island Garden

In the introduction to his *Collection of the History of England* (1618), Samuel Daniel excuses himself from beginning with originary myths by saying that the beginning of all peoples and states is as unknown as the heads of great rivers, that such myths are rather intended to aggrandize nations that "commonly rise from the springs of pouertie, pyracie, robberie, and violence" and "abuse the credulitie of after ages."[1] On the other hand, in book IV of *The Faerie Queene*, describing the marriage of the Thames and Medway, Edmund Spenser had done just that—traced the sources of England's rivers and thus provided a watery map of a nation whose mythic history is one of the subjects of his great poem. In the opening paragraphs of his *History of Britain*, John Milton, like Daniel, insists on the unknowability of the "beginning of Nations," falling back finally on legend to fill in facts that time has destroyed.[2] That history is inseparable from England's physical aspect, the beautiful island bounded by the sea, whose geographic distinction renders it at once desirable and vulnerable. Both Daniel and Milton, though writing very different types of histories, have origins more easily traced than the sources of rivers, and the perspectives each provides on the "pouertie, pyracie, robberie, and violence" of earlier times are grounded in those of their medieval predecessors.

Gildas and Bede provided the models for later English historians, models that are interrelated but offer radically different narrative perspectives on events. Gildas in the *De Excidio Britonum*, written in about 540, adopts the stance of the Old Testament prophet complaining of the (self-)destruction of Britain. Bede finished his *Historia Ecclesiastica Gentis Anglorum* in 731, and, while drawing on Gildas's work, moves beyond the jeremiad to offer a picture of the nation's history that also gives a foretaste of its future as Bede saw it.[3] Both works cast long shadows over the efforts of post-Conquest English writers to evolve a language of national self-description. Later monastic historians such as William of Malmesbury, Henry of Huntingdon, and William of Newburgh either cite Bede or simply begin where he left off, going on to emulate his broadly syncretic understanding of English history. Both Bede and William of Newburgh refer to Gildas, whose more somber vision underlies a number of other medieval histories. Both authors were studied in the Tudor period. Polydore Vergil was responsible for the rediscovery of Gildas, publishing an edition of the *De Excidio* in 1525, and Matthew Parker and Sir Robert Cotton, following the lead of earlier reformers like John Bale and John Leland, collected vast libraries of medieval manuscripts, and Parker published a sequence of major English historians.[4] Such genealogies trace more than the knowledge of England's past; they can be used to trace an understanding of the past and its relation to the present and the future. For example, like Augustine and Orosius, Gildas locates events within a moral framework, seeking to understand the causal relationship between human agency and belief and the history of peoples, drawing, like his sources, on the providential perspective on history articulated in Scripture. Thus in his introductory Epistle he aligns himself with Israel's prophets because he aligns the Britons with the wayward children of Israel. However, he begins the history itself with a geographic and topographic account of the island of Britain. In so doing, he marries topography to moral narrative and initiates a process by which a concept of nation would become inseparable from an ideation of place.

The description of Britain as an island garden with which Gildas, and countless historians after him, begins constitutes not a uniform way of conceiving of Britain but a trope with a set of available ideas or anxieties that include fears for safety, fears of isolation, Edenic bounty, Edenic fall, the garden, the wasteland, history as a record of rupture, history as a record of reparation—a set of ideals and anxieties that thread their way through medieval and early modern histories of England and that are expressed using the language of place. In their exploitation of the trope of the island garden England's historians suggest ways of understanding England's relationship to the ecclesiastical, civil, and cultural influences of the world outside its waters, which both offer it protection and provide means of entry into a land whose historic identity is composed through conquest.

THE MASTER NARRATIVE

Gildas, like Orosius, writes an explicitly postlapsarian history that derives its logic from its author's perspective on event as rupture. Orosius, writing at the behest of Saint Augustine, created an account of world history that begins with a verbal *mappa mundi* and continues with accounts of earliest Old Testament history, the barbarian invasions of the Roman Empire, and the gradual imposition of order through the acts of kings whose conversions to Christianity signal the beginning of a new era. Gildas composes his *De Excidio* in the shadow of the lost Eden without benefit of moments of remedial history. For Orosius's world map, wherein Britain perches on the boundary of Europe, Gildas enlarges the detail, a map of Britain, an island almost at the end of the world, stretching toward the North Pole, surrounded and maintained by the sea. Gildas's picture of Britain, isolated geographically, decorated by twenty-eight cities and a number of castles and other fortifications, yields to a description of the island, bejeweled with wide plains, flowers, clear fountains filled with snow-white pebbles, murmuring rivers, and bountiful cold lakes, like an elect and ornamented bride. Though Gildas names this island *Brittannia*, his geographic references suggest that he employs the word ambiguously. For example, just after describing Brittannia as almost at the end of the world, an island held or maintained ("tenens") by the sea, he mentions that it has two rivers like arms ("veluti brachiis"), the Thames and the Severn, through which luxuries used to pour from overseas.[5] The rivers, the Thames on the east, linking England to the North Sea, and the Severn on the west, between England and Wales, seem to concentrate his focus on the area between those two arms. Later, Gildas mentions Saint Alban of Verulam (Saint Albans) and the martyrs Aaron and Julius in Caerleon in Wales (10) but also describes the Picts and Scots as emerging after the Romans depart and seizing the extreme part of the country ("terrae") (19) up to the wall. The roughly adumbrated boundaries—the Thames, the Severn, Hadrian's Wall—seem to circumscribe an area that corresponds to Gildas's idea of Britain, the beautiful bride, decked with bounty. He announces her fall immediately thereafter, describing Britain as, from its first inhabitation, stiff of neck and mind, in constant conflict against God, against its own countrymen, and against those figures of authority set to rule over it. Gildas then proceeds to recount Britain's very early Roman and Christian history up to the battle of Badon Hill and the defeat of Roman Britain and hence of Christianity and civilization. Thereafter, he provides a prophetic commentary on the sins of Britain's kings and priests, who have led the island to its ruin. Gildas's address to Britain is inseparable from his account of it as geographically isolated, once inviolate, now violated by its own willfulness and by the pagan Saxons who have triumphed over the Britons who, lacking the protection of the Roman legions, cannot defend their own country.

Gildas, writing in a time of great upheaval, allies Britain with Israel, and thus with the pattern of salvation history articulated by Israel's prophets where sin is concomitant with misfortune and civic chaos.[6] Gildas's analysis depends on the opposition of order and chaos, the former usually linked to the Britons' acceptance of authority, whose sign is the civilization evinced in the farms, buildings, and cities of a peaceful and prosperous nation. For Gildas, the sign of chaos is the wasteland, the ruined garden. Diocletian's nine-year persecution of Christians destroys a civilization that Gildas describes as renewed and rebuilt afterward. He notes that those who had fled into forests, desert places, and caves (11) return and rebuild churches and chapels and observe the ceremonies of the church. However, with the Arian heresy, which Gildas describes as an invasion by venomous snakes and beasts from abroad, the country returns to its wickedness, preferring novelties to settled ways. With the rise of Maximus, whom Gildas describes as a shoot ("germen") from the savage forests of Britain's own "tyrant thickets" ("tyrannorum virgultis") (13), Britain marches against Rome, with the result that its young men are lost and it is vulnerable to the invasions of Picts and Scots, increasingly so as Rome's patience and might weakens. The barbarian Saxons Gildas describes as wolves and lions (23) and the state of Britain as a wasteland containing only deserted cities and a dissipated people (23, 26).

If Gildas establishes the analogy between Britain and the errant Israel and between himself and the prophets foretelling Israel's doom, Bede chooses the broader perspective inherent in Orosius's and Eusebius's histories and produces a narrative that depicts rupture as the inevitable catalyst for growth. Like Gildas, Bede employs the term *Brittannia;* however, he focuses on an area that is England, the geography for the *Ecclesiastical History of the English People.* In describing England as an insular *locus amoenus,* Bede at once nods to Gildas's earlier description of it as a fallen garden or bride, provides a new perspective on England's history, and sets the terms later chroniclers and monastic historians would use to describe England and its institutions.[7] Like Gildas, Bede describes the island as beautiful and fertile; however, where Gildas claims for himself the role of Balaam's ass, warning the stiff-necked bride, Israel, of her disobedience, infidelity, and consequent barbarism, Bede begins with a picture of the fertile island, whose seas and land provide it with bounty, then moves immediately to list its five languages that are unified by the last, Latin, the language of Christian belief and culture. This is a crucial move, for Bede thereby signals two fundamental and interrelated themes of the *Ecclesiastical History,* the ongoing and the collaborative nature of the narrative called *historia.* Thus Bede says at the present time ("in praesenti") there are as many languages belonging to peoples in the island as books composing the law or the Pentateuch, books that concern a search for the same truth and wisdom (16/17). He then names those languages, English, British, Irish, Pictish, and Latin, only one of which (*Brettonum,* belonging to the ancient Britons) might be described as a native tongue. The languages are those of invaders, and his phrase *in praesenti* opens up the possibility of other languages and peoples, an ongoing process of rupture and renewal. The first twenty chapters of Bede, which correspond to Gildas's historical narrative, adumbrate an identity for

England that is built not on its isolation and waywardness but on its centrality to world history.[8]

Bede achieves this more syncretic perspective by locating England and its history in a broader geographic and historical context. For example, immediately after listing the five languages, Bede attaches each to those peoples who spoke them. He notes the origin of the Picts, their encounters with the Britons, and their migration throughout Britain to Ireland, where they are refused settlement and move finally to the north of the island Britain. The Irish themselves come to Britain and settle among the Picts. Bede then describes Ireland, its milder weather, its healthy air and soil, its abundance of game. He proceeds to the Roman invasions of the island, which he describes very differently from Gildas. Gildas's account of the Roman conquest emphasizes the Britons' fecklessness, their lack of resistance, but, at the same time, their only nominal obedience to Roman edicts (5–7). At once cowardly and treasonable, the Britons are depicted as necessitating the sort of servitude Rome imposed. Bede's is an account of a gradual process of invasion, battle, and conquest, with the less sophisticated Britons falling to Rome's superior military skills. Moreover, his account of this process links England's history to Rome's, noting the various emperors and their impact on England's history. Thus, when he comes to the persecutions of Diocletian and the martyrdom of Alban, both are contextualized within the broader perspective of world or Roman history, and events taking place in England imaginatively occur on a world stage, not simply within the confines of Gildas's chill and distant island (8). Bede designates Alban as one whose suffering brought England into the company of those throughout the world who attained glory by confessing their faith during the ten-year persecutions enacted by Diocletian in the east and Maximianus Herculius in the west (i.6, 7). The story of England's first martyr, which is a founding story for the English church, whose identity for Bede is inseparable from that of the nation, assumes its place within a greater narrative of providential world history.[9] Bede continues to move back and forth between England and the world, placing the local within a global field of vision. His narrative perspective mitigates England's geographic and metaphoric isolation while at the same time providing a providential understanding of England's lapses and weaknesses that must be understood as events within a variegated and constantly changing history. Bede, of course, had the benefits of hindsight, allowing him to move past both the Arian and Pelagian heresies, as well as the widespread godlessness and waste with which Gildas ends his history. Or, more specifically, Bede had the benefit of Gregory the Great, at whose direction the mission to England under Augustine was sent.

For Bede, England's people, including its formerly invading Angles and Saxons, "whom he foreknew" (quam praesciuit) are God's *people* ("plebem suam") (68/69). From book I, chapter 22, on, these English come to stand for Britain, just as the history Bede recounts is that of the English church. He thus singles out the *gens Anglorum* as elect, as the object of the Gregorian mission (68/69, 78/79), whose salvation alters the history of the island, Britain, and signifies its geographic and cultural identity.[10] At the same time, Bede's use of a singular (and humble) noun, *people*, rather than *peoples*, suggests unity rather than multiplicity, not invaders and native inhabitants but a people foreknown by God and awaiting yet another Roman invasion that will link England with world Christianity. The *Libellus Responsionum*, containing Gregory's answers to Augustine regarding Catholic practice among the English, which Bede inserts at the end of book I, followed by his account of the gifts and letter Gregory sent to the newly converted king of Kent, Æthelbert, shorten the mental and physical distance between England and the rest of the world. In urging Æthelbert to use Constantine as a model and in letting him know that the end of the world is at hand (i.32), Gregory implicitly allows the king to locate himself within a global set of examples and concerns. Similarly, Bede's account of Augustine's mission is an account of Christianity's reestablishment in England: Augustine, with Æthelbert's aid, restores a church in Canterbury that had once been founded by earlier Roman believers (i.33). Bede's first book, though it certainly chronicles invasions, conflicts, and lapses, constructs from Gildas's account of rupture and loss a history of continual reformation, of the conversion of a people who now dominate an island of many tongues and whose spiritual election marks both their identification with nation, Britain/England, and their participation in world history.

The stories of significant ecclesiastical figures like Augustine, Aidan, Cuthbert, Wilfrid, Hild, and Theodore all work against any sense of isolation as a good. Bede consistently outlines a Christian practice of leadership that breaks down the sort of insularity that, in the end, he assigns to the Irish and their adherents. Aidan (III.3, 5, 15–17) and Cuthbert (IV.27–32) each leave monastic island communities, Iona and Lindisfarne, to take up their very active lives as bishops. Hild's life (IV.23–24), as Bede says, falls into two halves, one in the world and one as a very capable abbess. When she originally took on the monastic life, she wished to remove herself to Gaul but was called first to Hartlepol and finally to Whitby. Hild's rule of both monasteries was energetic and devoted to establishing the Rule and to increasing the knowledge of those within her cure. Bede commends her for sending on five members of Whitby to episcopal appointments. And, of course, Hild served as Caedmon's spiritual patron, advising him to take holy orders and having him instructed in sacred history. Bede's account of Theodore of Tarsus, archbishop of Canterbury (668–90), in the opening chapters of book IV, powerfully illustrates England's connections to the world. When an English candidate for the see is carried off by the plague while he is in Rome, Pope Vitalian first names the African Hadrian, who demurs out of humility but suggests Theodore, a native of Tarsus living in Rome. Before coming to England, Theodore must grow out his eastern tonsure in favor of the western, but when he comes he brings Hadrian with him as well. They bring to England great learning, the intellectual habits and expectations of a sophisticated Mediterranean civilization, including knowledge of Greek and sacred music. In one economically told story, Bede links England to Rome, Africa, and Turkey. In fact, his account of the journey from Rome to England—by ship to Marseilles, by land to Arles, to Paris, and to England by slow stages, entertained at each stopping place for long periods—draws a map of the Christian world wherein distance is eclipsed by hospitality and familiarity.[11]

Bede's interest in redrawing the world map to keep England well within the orbit of the center is encapsulated by his handling of the controversy over the date of Easter and the priestly tonsure. Both are issues with geographic implications, and both preoccupy Bede throughout the *History*. The celebration of Easter first comes up in book II after Augustine has begun his mission and received Pope Gregory's answers to his questions about Christian practice in England. In the second chapter Bede recounts Augustine's failed attempt to persuade the Briton bishops to join with him and his monks in celebrating Easter according to Roman calculation, thus preserving the unity of the church and working together to evangelize the island.[12] Two chapters later, Lawrence, successor to Augustine, again tries to persuade the Irish and the Britons to join together in Roman Catholic practice. In chapter 19, in 634 Pope Honorius writes to the Irish, urging them to join with the churches of Christ throughout the world rather than persist in their own practice, placed as they were on the "extreme ends of the earth." In book III Bede narrates England's geographic shift of allegiance. King Oswald of Northumbria, on coming to the throne, seeks to restore the faith to the kingdom and sends to Ireland, where he had experienced conversion during his exile, for a bishop. The Irish send Aidan of Iona, whose zeal and holiness are without question but who observes the northern Irish date for Easter (III.3). Bede's account of Aidan is respectful of his holiness and humility, his love of peace, and his great charity, but he also notes Aidan's mistaken (or ignorant) celebration of Easter, a miscalculation that severs England from unity with Christendom (III.17). Aidan is succeeded by another Irish bishop. It is at this point that Bede gives an account of what has become a controversy between those from Gaul and Kent and those from Ireland about the celebration of Easter. He places his account almost at the center of the *History* as the point to which and from which England's ecclesiastical history moves.

The council held at Whitby, which was attended by King Oswiu and his son and by bishops and clergy from both sides, serves as a marker of Britain's geographic divide (III.25), since those on each side ("pars") trace their conversions and religious educations to either Rome or Ireland. What Bede has King Oswiu describe as the need for unity ("those who served one God should observe one rule of life") is a council about national identity, about the direction England should face, toward Ireland and the ends of the earth or toward Europe. While Bishop Colman, speaking for the Irish date, traces his method of calculation to that supposedly established by the apostle John, Wilfrid, speaking for Rome, counters with a picture of the world and its observance of the Roman date established by the saints Peter and Paul. Wilfrid says that this date is in use in Italy, Gaul, Africa, Asia, Egypt, Greece, "et omnem orbem," wherever is scattered the church of Christ. He goes on, "The only exceptions are these men and their accomplices in obstinacy, I mean the Picts and the Britons, who in these, the two remotest islands of the Ocean, and only in some parts of them, foolishly attempt to fight against the whole world." Wilfrid then explains that John, fearing to alienate his fellow Jews, assigned a date to Easter "in accordance with the law" on the fourteenth day of the first month. However, Peter and Paul, remembering that Christ rose on the first day of the week, celebrated Easter on the first day after the fourteenth day if the fourteenth day was not the first. After these two points, the first geographic, the second historical, Wilfrid points out that Colman follows neither John nor Peter and Paul, since he always celebrates Easter on a Sunday, which, according to him, John did not do. It is King Oswiu who decides, choosing to follow Peter; and Colman and his disciples return to Ireland, refusing both the Roman dating for Easter and the Roman tonsure in the form of a crown (III.26). Bede ends his discussion of the Irish episcopate by remarking on their simplicity and piety. They came from one island, Iona, on Britain's western shore to inhabit Lindisfarne on its eastern. They leave Lindisfarne as bare as they found it: not having money, they did not erect new buildings. They preached, prayed, and baptized. Bede, in other words, does not accuse them of spiritual laxity; but in leaving Lindisfarne and Britain/England, which are now pointed east, toward Europe and the world, they return to another island that has cut itself off from predominant Christian practice.

Bede's subsequent remarks about the English church and its place in the world should be seen as expanding on his earlier geographic pointers.[13] First, Archbishop Theodore must grow out his hair before he can be consecrated and come to England: "waiting for four months until his hair grew, in order that he might receive the tonsure in the shape of a crown; for he had received the tonsure of the holy apostle Paul, after the Eastern manner." He comes to England with the African, Abbot Hadrian. Both men enrich the island with their learning, but it is worth noting that the island draws both men to itself: imaginatively Africa and Asia come to England and not before the new archbishop grows out his hair in order to be acceptable to Roman Catholic practice. The picture of the English church that predominates in the remainder of this fourth book of the *History* is, under Theodore's episcopate, of regular and uniform observance, of theological probity, and of cultural vitality. Civil conflict certainly continues, but this is the book containing the accounts of Benedict Biscop, of Æthethryth, and of Caedmon, as well as of Theodore's preemptive strike against the threat of the Monophysite heresy making its way from Constantinople to England. The book ends with Bede's account of Cuthbert, whose movements out of cenobitic and then eremetic isolation to the episcopate and back into isolation on the isle of Farne near the end of his life dramatize the permeability of the boundaries he chooses for himself. Bede's depictions of spiritual isolation could thus also be described as depictions of spiritual community, or as intaglios of islands whose strengths lie both in their singularity and in their proximity. England no longer seems on the edge of the world but, if not at its center, well within reach of the center and its insular identity not so much breached as enhanced by its congress with the world to the east and south.

Book V of the *History* returns to those concerns adumbrated in the first book and completes those issues embedded in the council at Whitby recounted in the third book, as well as looking onward to a new future for England, a future in which England fully participates in the affairs of the world. The promise of earlier accounts of its fecundity—of its early martyr, Alban; of its kings converting to the faith brought by Augustine—are more than fulfilled by the florescence everywhere manifest in this fifth book. If Bede follows Gildas in describing Britain's natural fertility in book I, in book V he describes a Britain now identified with England and rich in holy figures such as Oethelwald of Farne and John, bishop of Hexham, who were known for miracles during their lifetimes (1–6). Where book I relates the invasion of England by Roman legions and then by Roman missionaries, book V narrates the accounts of English kings such as Cædwalla of the West Saxons, his successor Ine (7), and Cenred of Mercia and with him Offa, a prince of the West Saxons (V.19), who become pilgrims to Rome, imaginatively joining ecclesiastical travelers like Benedict Biscop and Wilfrid.[14] Where in book I England is the destination of missionaries, now the English seek to become missionaries. Egbert, living a life of exile in Ireland, wishes to go to Germany where he hopes to find many peoples "from whom the Angles and Saxons, who now live in Britain, derive their origin" (V.9). Though Egbert does not achieve his desire, Wihtberht goes from his own exile in Ireland unsuccessfully to Frisia. Willibrord and eleven others are more successful, and two English priests go to the kingdom of the Old Saxons, where they find martyrdom, which bears its own fruit in the miracles that attend their passions. Where once the English could only consecrate a bishop in Gaul, now, when in need of a bishop for the Frisians, the missionaries send a chosen brother to England for consecration (V.11). Where book I ends with Pope Gregory's letter to Augustine, giving him precepts for maintaining Christian practice in England, near the end of book V England becomes the means by which the northern Irish, the Picts, and even the monks of Iona adopt the Roman date for Easter and the Roman tonsure (V.15). In fact, Abbot Ceolfrith of Jarrow, at the request of Nechtan, king of the Picts, sends a long letter outlining the reasons for celebrating Easter and adopting the tonsure in accordance with Rome (V.21).

It is in this letter that Bede most explicitly links the English to the children of Israel. Gildas's identification of the Britons with the children of Israel is designed to underline their willfulness and shortsightedness. Bede's vision is broader, and his insertion of Ceolfrith's letter into the *History* suggests an identification with an Israel as chosen and as historically bound to the revelations of the new law in Christ.[15] The letter is painstaking in its attention to the dating of the observance of Passover to be found in Exodus and the likely dating for the exodus from Egypt.[16] Moreover, the writer notes, since Christ is our Passover, the first day of the week, the day of his resurrection, the day for Easter is calculated according to the precepts of the law (the first lunar month of the year after the vernal equinox and the evening of the fourteenth day) and, according to the new law, on the Sunday that precedes that fourteenth day:

> So at last we duly celebrate our Easter feast to show that we are not, with the ancients, celebrating the throwing off of the yoke of Egyptian bondage but, with devout faith and love, venerating the redemption of the whole world, which, being prefigured by the liberation of the ancient people of God, is completed in the resurrection of Christ. (544/545)

The proper dating, then, typologically links those who observe it to the redeemed Israel, whose flight from Egypt is fulfilled in Christ's resurrection from death. The writer thus provides a temporal perspective that goes beyond a history of Israel's failures and gathers the English into the new covenant, made in completion of the old. Similarly, with the tonsure, which the writer admits has several forms, among them those attributed to Job and to Joseph (546/547). However, though other forms of the tonsure are not evil, and certainly not as important as the proper date for Easter, the writer encourages the Picts to adopt the tonsure of Saint Peter, in the likeness of the crown of thorns, and thereby to signal their unity with the rest of the Christian world. The king responds to this letter by thanking God "for having made him worthy to receive such a gift from the land of the English" (de terra Anglorum) (552/553), going on to thank them for instructing him. The English, like the earlier Roman Pope Gregory, thus teach (and write letters) in order to draw the hinterlands toward themselves and into a greater unity. With the conversion of the monks at Iona in the next chapter, Britain's own unity is assured. Only the Britons still maintain their ways, but they are checked by the English who rule over them.

The final two chapters of the *History* return to the preoccupations of the first two, offering a picture of England as having at present fulfilled its early promise but as also poised in the insecurities of history. Bede enumerates the bishops of England, offering a new geography, a new map of England as the English church. He describes a thriving and settled land but not an isolated one. He notes the Saracen threat to Gaul and the two comets of 729, which portended worldwide calamities. He also mitigates any sense that England should relax in its own times of peace and fair weather by saying that now

> many of the Northumbrian race, both noble and simple, have laid aside their weapons and taken the tonsure, preferring that they and their children should take monastic vows rather than train themselves in the art of war. What the result will be, a later generation will discover. (560/561)[17]

What is at stake here is a return to isolation, to the insularity with which Bede begins his *History*, an insularity broken down by waves of invaders of many persuasions until England becomes the means of illuminating others and a land of proper Christian observance, music, education, all possible only by virtue of those centuries of invasions. As Bede's final chapter suggests, the monastery is not a retreat from the world but a strategic engagement with it. After providing his readers with a synopsis of England's history, he inserts himself into this history—a native Northumbrian, whose life has been lived between the monasteries of Wearmouth and Jarrow but whose intellectual and religious life has been focused on the labors of teaching and of commenting on the works of the Fathers. About himself, he says, as Chaucer would many centuries later say of his Clerk, that he delights in learning, teaching, and writing ("discere aut docere aut scribere"). He lists these patristic commentaries, thus signing himself as heir of two traditions, one belonging to one region of England, the other to a greater Christian culture whose boundaries now include England without erasing the island's insular and privileged identity. As a Saxon and an educated monk, he embodies the unity of the five languages he lists in his opening chapter. Bede also here provides a picture of those ideals of Benedictine monasticism that have much in common with the picture he has drawn of his own land, thus implying a distinction between what is insular and distinct and what is isolated and ignorant of the knowledge necessary for participation in Christian civilization.

Bede's concern with the goods of Christian unity, and particularly with England's place in that unity, is apparent in Thomas Stapleton's translation of the *History* into English in 1569. Stapleton was a Catholic who left England for the Low Countries and died in Louvain. His translation of Bede was published in Antwerp, but he dedicated it to his queen, Elizabeth I. In his dedicatory letter he urges her to return England to its history and traditions, to reunite the English with the greater world of Catholic Christendom. In his apology for England's originary identity and for Bede as its historian, he suggests the rupture with the past England has enacted, characterizing the present as "these perilous times of schisme."[18] Schism, of course, concerns the breaking apart of a whole, a whole that for Stapleton is depicted in Bede's history of England's conversion and union with Roman practice. By extension, having broken with Rome, England has broken with history and with the world. He thus points out to Elizabeth the "misse information" of the few, the fact that these "pretended refourmers of the church . . . haue departed from the patern of that sounde and catholike faith planted first among Englishemen by holy S. Augustin our Apostle" (3r). Stapleton's subsequent account of Christian history consigns England to the margins of the world should Elizabeth maintain "her dominion" in heresy and thereby sever it from world Christendom, its history, and England's own history. Stapleton clearly did not simply translate Bede; he read Bede and understood Bede's concern with isolation. He also comprehended the ways in which Bede anchored history in geography, since near the end of his Letter to the Reader Stapleton notes that his translation will give Bede's place-names as they are now called. What he produced was not antiquarian tract or simple translation but Bede's history, meant as a living and relevant account of England's identity as rooted in its fundamental relationship with Roman Catholicism and hence with the history of the world. What is noteworthy about Stapleton's argument is its language of rupture and its hints of England's likely isolation, his warning that in its "pretended" reform, England has unmade Bede, the author of its master narrative.

WRITING ENGLAND AFTER BEDE: WILLIAM OF MALMESBURY, HENRY OF HUNTINGDON, AND GEOFFREY OF MONMOUTH

Bede's account of England as a bountiful and beautiful island that is also characterized by an ethnic diversity unified and dignified by its inclusion in mainstream Christian practice and culture is not simply a conventional beginning point for later English historians but an identifying trope for the English nation.[19] In contradistinction, Gregory of Tours nests his history of the Franks within salvation history, beginning with Adam and going on to chart the spread of Christianity from Rome, a history validated by his accounts of the early martyrs whose acts are mingled with the deeds of kings. William of Jumiéges's *Gesta Normannorum Ducum* begins with the weaknesses of the Franks and the Viking invasions. Orderic Vitalis (1075–ca. 1142), though English by birth, who certainly used Bede's history, in his *Historia Ecclesiastica* written in St. Evroul, the Norman monastery where he was sent as a boy, follows the spirit of Gregory and William in focusing on the deeds of the Normans and their character as a people as it can be deduced from events in both France and England. Orderic, like Bede, is concerned with place, or with the geography of his particular place, the Pays d'Ouche, and its connections to the world, and at the beginning of the third book uses the founding stories of monasteries to map Normandy as God's vineyard, planted and fertilized by means of these religious foundations. He also has a clear sense of the boundary, and hence the difference, between Normandy and England, in book 8 describing the Normans' awareness of their divided loyalties to Norman and English dukes, as well as the distinction between the English, who define Albion, and the Welsh.[20] However, the subject of geographic boundaries as they might define a national identity is not apposite to the aims of William or Orderic; rather they emphasize the civilizing effects of Roman Christianity on a formerly ferocious people and those subsequent deeds that signify character and shape history. They, like Gregory of Tours, use the category *gens* to articulate a concept of nation.[21]

For the post-Conquest English historians William of Malmesbury (1080–1143) and Henry of Huntingdon (1080–1160) the history of England is a history instituted by Bede, who established the foundations of an English nation whose boundaries enclosed people or peoples, thus an island of marvels and beauties, a place that is the site of the struggles between individuals and of individuals. Their Anglocentric perspective designates the rest of the British Isles as containing peoples, primarily the Welsh and the Scots who are invaded, subjugated, or otherwise controlled by the English.[22] On the other hand, both historians suggest their understanding of Bedan historiography with its attentiveness to England's fruitful relationship to Europe and, consequently, its tendency to see national boundaries less as lines of defensive isolation than as borders that provide means of egress and access. In contradistinction, their contemporary Geoffrey of Monmouth (ca. 1100–ca. 1154), whose largely fictional *Historia Regum Britanniae* enjoyed enormous popularity, takes his direction from Gildas's more insular perspective on Britain and its history. Bede used and incorporated the work of Gildas; William and Geoffrey also refer to Gildas; all three later authors used Bede, in addition to drawing on other common sources. However, Gildas and Bede inaugurated two very different ways of writing England's history, ways that have profound implications for these three twelfth-century historians who likewise have a decided impact on later historians and their efforts to write history that accords with political affiliations.[23]

The importance of Bede to both William of Malmesbury and Henry of Huntingdon is apparent in the beginnings of both histories. Both cite Bede in their opening remarks, describing him as the one true historian of England's early days.[24] William, as he does in his *Gesta Pontificum Anglorum*, uses England's geography as the organizing principle for his first book, saying that he will describe the growth of the four kingdoms of Kent, Wessex, Northumbria, and Mercia in turn, thus overlaying his history with a map of the land that is the nation of the English (*GRA* 14/15–16/17). Henry's opening reproduces the description of Britain as a beautiful and bountiful island that Bede himself incorporated from Gildas. He then identifies England as Britain (*HA* 12/13), saying that the island was once called Albion, "later Britain, and now England." He next amplifies Bede's account of the island by naming in English and Latin the twenty-eight noble cities for which England was famous that Bede mentions (without naming) in his first chapter. He also echoes Bede's account of England's five languages by saying that divine vengeance has sent five plagues, through the Romans, the Picts and the Scots, the English, the Danes, and the Normans, substituting a perspective more congenial to Gildas's account of God's judgment on the unfaithful than to Bede's syncretic picture of England's history.[25] Like William of Malmesbury, Henry of Huntingdon casts a map over his narrative, describing the acts of naming by which the Saxon (or English) conquerors dominated the land, dividing it into seven kingdoms, these into shires and bishoprics. He pauses to lament that the names of the twenty-eight cities have fallen from fame and those of the shires that now predominate may with time become "incognita et incredibilia" (*HA* 16/17). Henry then continues his account of the actual island—its weather, wonders (such as Cheddar Gorge and Stonehenge), its main roads, and, returning to Bede, its five languages. More important than these obvious references to Bede's *Historia Ecclesiastica Gentis Anglorum* are those underlying assumptions of that work that are present in both the *Gesta Regum Anglorum* and the *Historia Anglorum*: a sense of England as a distinct geographic place with ties to Europe, a recognition that history is a narrative in process, and an awareness that all history looks toward a future that is bound to but not necessarily in bondage to a past. Bede's achievement, of creating a history where localism gained global significance, where barbarism became civilization, and where individual piety and insight moved from the cloister or the court outward, is present in both William's and Henry's handling of certain aspects of the segments of England's story they recount.

William of Malmesbury, of both English and Norman lineage, begins with Bede, who told the history of the English from their arrival in England to his own time (*GRA* 14/5), summarizing Bede's history, then augmenting it with events from Bede's death to 1127. Like Bede he emphasizes the ethnic diversity of England but also the goods of unity among the four kingdoms of the English and, later, between English and Danes and Normans.[26] Thus, while England's insularity is an inevitable aspect of its identity as a nation, that same insularity is constantly penetrated by peoples from the Continent and Scandinavia who are, in turn, Christianized and educated. William's account of the conversion of Æthelbert differs from Bede's by slightly mitigating the picture of England as isolated. In place of Bede's well-known account of Pope Gregory's encounter with the boys in the Roman slave market as the impetus for conversion, William begins with King Æthelbert's marriage to a daughter of the king of the Franks and the bishop who accompanied her to England. By the purity of his life, Bishop Luidhard, according to William, invited the king to learn about Christ, thus making the job of Augustine of Canterbury easy when he arrived with the Roman missionaries.[27] Himself half Norman, William might be expected to write favorably of the relations between the two kingdoms; however, his account also suggests England's early and ongoing involvement with continental affairs.

William of Malmesbury's treatment of Bede, as well as his account of Alcuin, underlines the relationship between the island and the world with which it is affiliated. In book I he gives a loving account of Bede that does not simply praise Bede's piety or learning, but his status within and service to a world community. In fact, at the end of his encomium he disparagingly remarks on Bede's successors as, even if somewhat learned, spending their lives in ungrateful silence (*GRA* 94/95), while most remained unlearned, slothful, and idle, and the fervor of learning declined in the entire island. He then quotes an epitaph for Bede, which he calls shameful, that praises him only for his wisdom. In contrast, William describes Bede as one born in the farthest part of the world whose learning shone in all lands (*GRA* 82/83). William continues to link the local with the global by affirming that even in remote England one can find the location of Bede's birth and education, a place he describes as formerly a garden fragrant with monasteries and cities but now ravaged by both the Danes and the

Normans. What follows is an account of the environs of Wearmouth/ Jarrow: the river Wear, the gentle breezes, the monasteries built and enriched with books, windows filled with translucent glass, and masterful stonework commissioned by Benedict Biscop. He quotes Bede's modest account of himself at the end of the *Historia* and follows it with lavish praise for the esteem Bede and his learning enjoyed throughout the world and for the piety and charity that characterized Bede even at the end of his life. Similarly with Alcuin, William describes an English monk and scholar whose "labor" is in the world. Alcuin, sent by royal commission to Charlemagne, sends back to England for books "such as I had in my own country" (*GRA* 96/97–98/99) in order to bring back to France the flowers of Britain ("reuehant in Frantiam flores Britanniae"), so that if there is an enclosed garden in York, there may also be in Tours "rays from paradise" (emissiones paradisi). Alcuin's elegant allusion here to the enclosed garden of the Song of Songs, which was conflated with the paradises of England and the monastery, refuses to conflate enclosure and isolation, suggesting, as Bede suggests throughout the *Historia*, that what is enclosed can also be transplanted and made newly fruitful. William then describes Alcuin as educating Charlemagne in dialectic, rhetoric, and astronomy and as putting his own talents to the test by writing many books. After Alcuin, William recounts the history of the Frankish kings, returning finally to Alcuin and his warnings about the importance of education as a remedy against the vices Gildas ascribed to national collapse. After the "interlude" praising Bede and Alcuin and describing the Franks, William picks up the thread of England's own history. However, the "interlude" does its own significant work in drawing the enclosed island into the world by means of the industry manifested in learning and writing. The stories of Alcuin and Bede remind William's readers that England's children, too, can leave its boundaries and invade the world.

Later, in his account of King Alfred, William continues to blur the boundaries of the island whose history he recounts. He points out that Alfred sent envoys to India (*GRA* 190/191) and Armenia. During conflicts with the Danes, Alfred hides with his mother on the island of Athelney (*GRA* 182/183–184/185), where he is fortified by visions of the indigenous Saint Cuthbert.[28] Not long after that vision, Alfred leaves the island in disguise as a minstrel and infiltrates the camp of the Danish king, where he learns information allowing him to triumph over his enemies. Isolated and yet accessible, Athleney is the site of both his refuge from the Danes and his base of operations against them. Restored to power, Alfred goes on to establish treaties with the invaders, send out envoys to other lands, and translate the learning of Christian culture into the native tongue. Like Alfred's seclusion on Athelney, England's island status serves William not as a trope of isolation, but of syncretism, a means of underlining the wisdom of maintaining the nation as at once distinct and accessible, as stronger because of its carefully determined status. Such a perspective, of course, clears the way for William's account of the Norman Conquest, not as conquest but as triumphal progress. William's depiction of triumph obtains until Yorkshire, when the story of the struggles between barbarism and civilization, between waste and bounty that characterizes England's written history is reprised as a regional narrative. William describes Yorkshire as a refuge for Scots and Danes and as caught between the machinations and barbarism of Malcolm, king of the Scots, and the necessary ferocity of Duke William, who subjects York to famine and orders the region devastated, its fruit and grain ruined by fire and water, the once fruitful province become a barren wasteland. Alcuin's "enclosed garden," the learning and civilization of Yorkshire, becomes unrecognizable waste (iii.249).[29]

Henry of Huntingdon breaks down Bede's synthetic and syncretic history into localities, thus focusing his history on the kingdoms of England, their kings and their conflicts but, ultimately, on a resolution emerging from conflict.[30] Henry's localism privileges geography as a historical category, maintaining the significance of the physical island as an indicator of national identity. From the multitudinous and local, he draws broader moral lessons pertinent to his understanding of history as process, an understanding he shares with Bede, whose history ends with the unity of Roman observance. Henry further organizes his local histories under the broader rubrics of those major periods of England's history he refers to in his opening chapter: the Romans yield to the English, who are succeeded by the Danes, then by the Normans, the rulers of England in Henry's own day. The rubrics afford him his overarching moral understanding of the process by which weakness yields to greater strength. Thus at the beginning of book V, which considers the Danish wars, he characterizes England's invaders according to the effect each had on the land, and, though he describes them as "plagues," his accounts seem less to describe desolation than evolution. For example, the Romans subjugated *but* ruled splendidly by right of conquest ("lege dominantium splendide rexerunt") (*HA* 272/273). The Picts and Scots he describes as destructive but repulsed and of brief duration. For the Saxons he has more respect, since they gained possession through warfare but built on their gains and, having built, ruled by law. The Normans subdued the land but by right of kingship ("regni iure") granted the conquered their "life, liberty, and ancient law" (*HA* 272/273). Though he describes the Danes' incursions as destructive, unpredictable, and inevitable, the wars are the occasion for Alfred's valor and leadership as king of Wessex (*HA* v.6–13), and under the Danish Cnut England achieves a unity and peace previously elusive. Moreover, Alfred, by defeating and capturing Danish hostages in Devonshire, reaps the conversion of the Danish king Guthrum as one of the conditions of their release. In the midst of a relentless account of battles between English and Danes, Henry links events in England to world history, first by sketching in the threats the Norsemen posed to England and to Europe (274/275) and second by noting in 885 the deaths of the Frankish king Charles and Pope Marinus, along with the Danish army's siege of Paris. Alfred's twenty-eight-year reign, which was never free from warfare with the Danes, is praised by Henry in one of the poems he inserts into his history. With Cnut, the story of conflict evolves into one of compromise when he and Edmund strike a deal that Edmund shall rule Wessex and Cnut Mercia; when Edmund is treacherously killed, Cnut punishes the traitor and, as "king of the English," marries Emma, the Norman princess and former wife of the dead King Æthelred II. When in Cnut's fifteenth year Robert, duke of Normandy, dies and is succeeded by his bastard son, William, and Cnut dies five years later, the history of the Normans in England is inevitable. However, Henry pauses to praise Cnut for his supreme authority and for his humility in the face of God's greater power (*HA* 366/367–368/369). Though it can seem that Henry tells the same story again and again, instances of recurrent chaos are superseded by ever more significant triumphs of order. This order is concentrated in the rule of law and thus in those figures of authority who make just laws and act according to them. The close-ups Henry provides of significant figures, frequently emphasized by his poetic encomiums, serve as moral examples of good authority: Cnut benefits by comparison with Æthelred, and the Norman kings William I and Henry I, despite their violence, are drawn as complicated and capable sovereigns of a nation whose strength depends on a strong monarchy.[31]

Bede writes with the unity of the English church and people as his end; both William of Malmesbury and Henry of Huntingdon write with the coming ("adventum") of the Normans as their ends, though this "end" is conceived of as the beginning of a new period of England's history. William of Malmesbury dedicates the *Gesta Regum Anglorum* to Robert, earl of Gloucester, illegitimate son of Henry I and a major figure in the political events and struggles of the time. In the dedicatory letter and at the end of the *Gesta*, William praises Earl Robert's patronage of the liberal arts. In the letter, William describes his history as a mirror in which Earl Robert can see himself, and in the closing chapters he describes Earl Robert as a mirror in which William can see the virtues of many men and can also detect in him the virtues of the Normans, Flemings, and French combined into a single exemplary figure. Such language, of course, reflects the *topoi* of compliment, but it also reinforces William's own emphasis as a historian. In going on to praise Earl Robert for his devotion to literature, for his reputation for justice, for his generosity and aversion to avarice, he adumbrates the components for national unity, a unity potential in the goods he perceives in the reign of Henry I. The *Gesta* begins with two other letters, to David of Scotland and to David's niece, Matilda, daughter of Henry I, whose wars with Stephen, her cousin, for the English throne (1135–54) would only be resolved with the accession of her son, Henry II, when the Anarchy ended with Stephen's death. William ends his history in 1126 but continued to revise it until about 1134, and in the *Historia Novella* he wrote annalistically of contemporary history.[32] In other words, the *Gesta Regum Anglorum* ends at a point where the coming of the Normans can be described in terms that allow for progress. Even Yorkshire, wasted by William I, William describes as revived by the coming of the Cistercians, whose order offers the "high road of supreme progress to Heaven" (*GRA* 576/577). The account of the Cistercian order (*GRA* 576/577–584/585) is described, like accounts of the coming of Gregory's missionaries to England, as a return, thus as one more instance wherein England's boundaries seem both to seclude and to invite. Where the mission under Augustine came to convert a land that already had (forgotten) Christian martyrs and thus to restore it to renewed order and civilization, so the Cistercians, founded in Burgundy by the Englishman Stephen Harding, seek out the wasteland as sites for their abbeys. William spends several pages on Harding "our countryman" and the rigor and purity of Cistercian observance, which implicitly helps to restore England to itself. More central to the language of England's identity, the Cistercians restore the garden of Yorkshire, a story best told later by William of Newburgh.

Henry of Huntingdon likewise evinces a concept of history as process, potentially as progress when he ends book X of the *Historia Anglorum* by addressing the not-yet-crowned Henry II in hexameters, hailing him as a light that warms England's mortal chill, speaking of the king's coming as a new incarnation in which the "flesh" of England is entered and restored by the "spirit," the new king. In book VI, which records the coming of the Normans, Henry describes William as redefining England's geography through the Domesday Book in the eighteenth year of his reign. William sent out justices through every shire, recording the dimensions of every village, the number of animals in every village, and the productivity of every "city, castle, village, farm, river, marsh, and wood." Not only do they measure and record, but they convert records to charters, which are kept in the treasury "until today" (*HA* 400/401). Disenfranchising the English and redistributing lands to his nobles, "farming out" with an aim to acquire more and more wealth, William is described as ravenous but also as powerful and worthy of praise (*HA* 404/405–406/407). He protects the beasts of the chase, turns villages into wasteland for hunting, and subjugates Scotland and Wales, as well as England. Henry also stresses that in William's lands the rule of law protects the weak and innocent, and he founds a new abbey, Battle. William's death brings a return of instability to England (see book VII), but Henry balances this by sketching in the clashes in Europe between "pagans" and Christians in Spain and between Danes in Denmark. Despite the conflicts of the years after William's death and the anarchy of Stephen's reign, Henry hints at a broader narrative whose end is not necessarily the present chaos. This is not to say that either William or Henry is writing a variety of Darwinian history in which humankind steadily improves and evolves toward majesty. Both are Christians and churchmen, writing history, as Bede does, with full awareness of the coming apocalypse, and all three convey a belief that history illustrates ways in which heavenly justice falls on the unrighteous.[33] However, these historians nonetheless depict England as bound up with European history, thus as not isolated, and as participating in a process by which unity and consequently national strength emerge from faction and weakness. Central to this unity is the church and its freight of literature, education, and culture, the education and skill all three writers manifest in their allusions to classical authors, to world history, and, in Henry's case, in the encomiastic hexameters that stud his narrative. What conversion—of the English, the Danes, the Normans—represents is a type of invasion that transforms waste into garden space and into a fruitfulness that can, in turn, be exported, a process possible only if those boundaries that define national space are porous.

The concept of place, or the anxieties that attend that composition of place, are differently composed in Geoffrey of Monmouth's *History of the Kings of Britain (Historia Regum Britanniae)*.[34] Francis Ingledew has recently analyzed Geoffrey's *Historia* in relation to Virgil's *Aeneid* and its inherent and dynastic historiography to which he assigns three related categories of meaning—genealogical, prophetic, and erotic—saying that, simply by virtue of its popularity, the *Historia* sapped the Augustinian theology of the history of Orosius and his successors.[35] Ingledew focuses on the Arthurian history that Geoffrey creates and its ultimate relationship to subsequent retellings, notably in the *Brut*, and the chivalric history promulgated by Edward III in his creation of the Order of the Garter. Without discounting the importance of Virgilian epic to Geoffrey and his mythic account of Britain's history as in direct line of descent from Brutus, a history to some extent presided over by Merlin as the English sibyl, it is crucial to place Geoffrey in relation to both Gildas and Bede who provided Geoffrey with the components of the master narrative with which he had to work. Diana Greenway describes Henry of Huntingdon as writing around extracts from Bede.[36] Geoffrey, likewise, writes around the edges of his predecessors, as he admits in the prologue in which he claims to have found an old book containing untold stories of the history of the kings of Britain before the Incarnation. His "translation" of this book derives its "veracity" from the parent text and, inevitably, is intended to provide a new perspective on the greater history of Britain. He thus rewrites Britain's history as insular but also as fixed in recurrent cycles of chaos and violence.

In the first four books of the *Historia*, Geoffrey, drawing on the *Historia Brittonum*, extends Gildas's history into a distant past; in so doing he appropriates Gildas's characterization of Britain as a fallen garden and the Britons as prone to fighting. Geoffrey begins with the description of Britain, the beautiful, distant, and fertile island, that he found in both Gildas and Bede. He then moves to the Trojan origins of Brutus, Brutus's history, and his discovery of Britain, which Geoffrey, like Henry of Huntingdon, found in the *Historia Brittonum*.[37] Though the direction of this first book is toward order, there are also hints of the theme of political conflict that pervades Geoffrey's history: Brutus founds the city, New Troy, giving it citizens and laws by which they could live in peace, but Geoffrey, citing Gildas, reminds his readers that New Troy will be renamed by King Lud, whose desire to call the city by his own name prompts conflict with his brother. Book II plunges into war, intrigue, and passion and contains accounts of Brutus's lineage, the story of Lear and his daughters, and attempts by subsequent kings to establish peace through law. Despite such efforts—the building of roads, the creation of cities and legal codes—the history is dominated by a picture of human nature as self-interested, shortsighted, violent, and unscrupulous, restrained only temporarily by the power of those kings who rule by law. Book IV fleshes out and fictionalizes the account of the Roman conquest of Britain to be found in the *Historia Brittonum*, describing the effort it took for Caesar to win Britain and the strategies of King Cassibellaunus to evade Roman dominion, creating a narrative whose "truth" lies in its vivacity, its vision of history as character-driven. Where the *Historia Brittonum* contains a stripped-down account of Caesar's tripartite effort to conquer Britain, ruled then by the legendary king Belinus (*HB*19–20), Geoffrey turns what is already an improbable account into a struggle between "Cassibellaunus king of the Britons" (*HRB* IV.55) and Julius Caesar, played out with accounts of battles, of ceremonies of thanksgiving, and, finally, of Cassibellaunus's defeat through the treachery of one of his dukes. Where Gildas briefly describes the Britons' treachery and cowardice in relation to their Roman rulers, Geoffrey invents a prehistory of Britain's conflict with Rome in the invasion of Rome by the two brothers King Belinus and Brennius, whose own conflicts are played out with great drama before they unite to ravage Gaul and Italy (book III). After he recounts Caesar's conquest of Britain, Geoffrey continues to dramatize the valorous efforts of some kings of Britain to break free from Roman oppression.[38]

By the time Geoffrey arrives at Arthurian matter, he has created a pattern of history for Britain that moves between temporary concord and treachery and conflict, a history that reflects the impulses of an irredeemable human nature. Both Gildas and the *Historia Brittonum* mention Arthur as mounting a last campaign against the Saxons invited into Britain by King Vortigern.[39] Geoffrey famously inaugurates an elaborate history for Arthur that is inserted into a history already authenticated by Gildas and Bede, who link the coming of the Saxons into Britain to the invitation of an English king, for whom Bede supplies the name Vortigern.[40] Geoffrey takes the story of Merlin from the *Historia Brittonum* and elaborates on it so as to create in Merlin a figure of prophecy and magic who helps Vortigern, Uther, and Arthur in their efforts against the Saxons and in their efforts to create peace in Britain.

The history of the reign of King Arthur in Geoffrey's *Historia*, though it is longer than his account of any other reign and became the nucleus for the matter of Arthur that was composed subsequently, is, nonetheless, an epitome of the perspective on history that drives Geoffrey's work and, to some extent, makes the most sense when seen in that context. Discounting for the moment the magical elements that belong to the role of Merlin, the story of Arthur reprises other significant tales within the *Historia* and is fitted into the pattern of order and chaos that is the history of Britain. Briefly, Arthur's reign *in Britain* is a moment between Uther's war with the Saxons (and Uther's own passion for another man's wife) and his own refusal to pay Roman tribute and five-year sojourn in Gaul, fighting the forces of the emperor Lucius, an absence that results in Mordred's seizure of the throne and Arthur's queen, more debilitating civil war, and the deaths of the principals. Arthur's moment of order is his coronation, which Geoffrey describes as succeeding Arthur's conquest of Ireland, Norway, Denmark, and Gaul and thus as a celebration of his might and wealth, both in the eyes of Britons and in the eyes of all other nations (*HRB* IX). The celebration, with its elaborate rituals of churchgoing, feasting, and tourneying, is punctuated by the entry of twelve ambassadors from Emperor Lucius, who carry a letter ordering Arthur to pay the tribute to Rome first initiated by Julius Caesar. The letter is the impetus for Arthur—with the unanimous support of his nobles—to muster forces from Britain and all other countries attending the coronation and to advance with a vast army on Roman power. Arthur's victorious march to Autun and victory over Lucius is described in book X, and in book XI we see the unraveling of Arthur's enormous power with the news of treachery at home and the civil war he must return to fight, with the result that almost all the men both in his and in Mordred's armies are killed. Arthur himself is mortally wounded and "taken away to the island of Avalon to have his wounds tended and, in the year of Our Lord 542 handed over Britain's crown to his relative Constantinus" (XI.178).

In the escalating chaos that follows, which Geoffrey interpolates with some events from Bedan history such as the coming of Augustine to England, he pauses to allow Gormundus, an African king ravaging Britain whom he found in a chanson de geste, to castigate the Britons for their self-destructive violence:[41] "Your kingdom is divided against itself, lust for civil strife and a cloud of envy has blunted your mind, your pride has prevented you from obeying a single king, and so your country has been laid waste before your eyes by most wicked barbarians, and its houses fall one upon another."[42] More war is followed by famine, plague, and depopulation as the Britons flee into Cornwall, Brittany, and Wales. A final attempt by Cadualadrus to retake control of Britain is nullified by an "angelic voice," which warns that "God did not want the Britons to rule over the island of Britain any longer, until the time came which Merlin had foretold to Arthur" (XI.205). The demise of the "noble Britons" into the degenerate Welsh opens the way for the histories of the Saxon kings Geoffrey deeds to William of Malmesbury and Henry of Huntingdon, reserving the history of the kings of the Britons to himself, since only he possesses the book containing this information. As a writer, Geoffrey invents a space where he can insert the fabulous history he recounts, which takes place in that shadowy period from before the Romans to the ultimate establishment of Saxon kingdoms, creating a story of the Britons as noble but flawed by their own divisiveness, as producing the conditions for the triumph of the English and thus the triumph of England the nation.

However, Geoffrey passes on more than legend pieced into fact: he offers a historiography more indebted to Gildas than to Bede and consequently constructs a counternarrative to those composed within the traditions of Bedan history. Where Bede's history takes pains to characterize England as an island distinct from Europe but fully involved in European civilization and, later, as both drawing the world to itself in the person of Archbishop Theodore and as knitting Ireland, Scotland, and parts of Germany to Europe through the efforts of English churchmen, Geoffrey enhances the distance between the island and the main by writing continual conflict into his history. His accounts of the kings of Britain who hold off or attack Roman armies elaborate on Gildas's view of the Britons as prone to fighting among themselves, to at once repulsing Roman power and needing its protection, and thus as powerless to deal with the Picts, the Scots, or the Saxons (*De Excidio*, 14–22). Geoffrey strengthens the sense of conflict, and thus of distance, depicting conflict as a battle of personalities: Belinus and Brennius, Casibellaunus, and Arthur emerge from the murk of the past with vividly realized goals, strengths, and weaknesses. This makes for good reading, but as "history" it reduces the narrative of history to segments that can be lifted out, as, indeed, many were by later writers, segments that underline Britain's unevolved and nonproductive relations with the larger world. The pictures Bede offers of people entering and leaving England and of the gradual spread of Christian culture weave his own segments into a narrative whole whose fundamental order reflects his plan in the *Historia Ecclesiastica*. Bede's narrative moves to the final account of himself, "servant of Christ and priest of the monastery of Peter and Paul which is at Wearmouth and Jarrow," linking the local and personal with the broader world of Benedictine monasticism, the conduit for the many books and commentaries he has made. He thus signals his and England's mutually nourishing ties to Christendom; those northern places, Wearmouth and Jarrow, seem attached to Europe, not distant from it in "an island numb with chill ice and far removed as in a remote nook of the world, from the visible sun" (*De Excidio*, 8).

Because frozen in a perpetual cycle of personal conflict, Geoffrey's Britain cannot yield any idea of historical process. Like Gildas, he begins with the beautiful island whose fall is repeated continuously. Gildas employs the jeremiad in order to establish his perspective for the reader, in the preface quoting Jeremiah's lament for the city sitting solitary and bereaved, once mighty and peopled, now subservient and empty ("solam sedisse urbem viduam, antea populis plenam, gentium dominam, principem provinciarum, sub tributo fuisse factam"). Britain's history in the *De Excidio* is a parenthesis between jeremiadical complaints, for the final section castigates the sins of Britain's kings and clergy, employing the language of Old Testament prophecy to foretell a coming punishment, ending with a brief prayer for good pastors. Whatever process might be possible in terms of Gildas's bleak perspective on his own time lies in the future, which like the future of lost Israel depends on the grace of God. Bede, who of course had his own life as evidence for historical process, eschews jeremiad for a historical narrative whose end grows out of its beginning and will extend beyond into a future whose shape might be affected by an understanding of events set within time and place. Geoffrey, on the other hand, begins with fiction, with the secret source, the "librum uetustissimum," a ploy Chaucer slyly uses in *Troilus and Criseyde* by referring to a source for his own history as "myn auctour . . . Lollius" (*T&C* I.394). Directly after the prologue, Geoffrey describes Britain, using the familiar trope of the beautiful island and capping it with a reference to the five peoples who inhabit it. Where the five languages and peoples are for Bede a sign of a potential unity to be wrung from diversity, Geoffrey concentrates on the Britons, whose pride brings divine vengeance ("ultione diuina") upon them. Geoffrey thus writes a narrative whose major figures are connected only by genealogy or race and not by any shared perspective on either history or nation.

Nation in the *Historia Regum Britanniae* is threatened by the world outside its boundaries and consequently aggressive in its attempts to extend its own power or defend itself from invasion. Insular and isolated, Britain begins as the beautiful isle and ends as a wasteland scoured by war, famine, and pestilence, conditions that the Old Testament prophets used to foresee the possibilities of new life springing from dereliction. Gildas's final section, in which he adopts the stance of the Old Testament prophet addressing bad kings and churchmen, derives whatever hope it has from its assumption that the prophet's voice might not fall on entirely deaf ears; Geoffrey places his hope in magic, in the statement that Arthur has only been taken to Avalon, another island, this one inaccessible, that times may change when Merlin's prophecies are fulfilled (*HRB* XI.178, 205). The angelic voice that warns Cadualadrus not to attempt to return to Britain tells him, instead, to go to Rome and do penance, where he will die. It then says that the Britons will one day recover the island, but, first, Cadualadrus's body will have to be removed from Rome to Britain and the bodies of other saints, which had been hidden from the Saxons, discovered. This is the world of the quest, where the timing of wondrous events happens only when certain conditions have been fulfilled, often by those who have no knowledge that the bodies (or rings or swords) have any meaning whatsoever. Agency defers to prophecy, and a concept of a future that might owe something to an understanding of the past recedes into the mists of mystery.

Geoffrey's achievement, though different in kind, should be taken as seriously as those of his contemporaries William of Malmesbury and Henry of Huntingdon. All three seek to find a way to write in the shadow of significant English historians and to make sense of a confusing narrative of events that will certainly be altered when Henry II accedes to the throne of England. Both William and Henry adapt Bedan historiography to their own times, weaving the Danes and the Normans into what is a Bedan narrative. Geoffrey writes fiction in the guise of history and provides another, and a more insular, perspective on history as a record of loss, in which Britain is at odds with the world beyond its boundaries, enmeshed in personal conflicts, and awaiting a semimagical release from its self-imposed wasteland.[43]

Though William of Newburgh, a canon in the Augustinian priory in Newburgh, Yorkshire, who was closely associated with the important network of Cistercian abbeys throughout the north, cites both Gildas and Bede in the opening sentences of his *Historia Rerum Anglicarum*, which begins in 1066 and ends abruptly in 1198, just before his death, his account of Yorkshire in the period just after the Conquest is an extension of the traditions of Bedan history that also invigorate his sources.[44] For example, William's account of the Cistercian foundations in the north powerfully suggests the ways in which this order, at once indigenous and foreign, restores the fecundity of a region laid waste by war. Up to 1132, the date he assigns to the founding of Fountains Abbey, the narrative is one of relentless strife between Stephen and Matilda, the two claimants to the throne of England, between churchmen, between the church and the crown, and between

the English and the Scots. This period in England was certainly difficult, but William shapes his narrative in a way that underlines the potential renewal offered by the foundings of Fountains, then Rievaulx,
and Byland and Newburgh, his own priory, which enjoyed amicable
relations with its Cistercian neighbors. What he recounts is a story
that elides the conflicts associated with the origins of Fountains, presenting this event as a point when the fount of salvation begins to
flow in England (50).[45] For William, these abbeys, built in remote and
isolated Yorkshire, transplant the pure observance of the Benedictine
rule instituted by Stephen Harding and practiced by Saint Bernard to
all of England; he calls Rievaulx, Fountains, and Byland the three
lights of "our province" (53). What William does not mention, or cannot know, is that the Cistercians' skills as farmers, engineers, and managers helped to restore to plenty a wasted space, the space Alcuin once
described as a garden.[46]

Like Bede's, William of Newburgh's account of ecclesiastical foundations is an account of victory over barbarism—the barbarism of the
Scots and the barbarism of England's own civil war (see I.xxii–xxiv).
When later in book I he tells the story of the two green children, curiously translated from the land of Saint Martin who appear in ditches
in East Anglia at harvest time, William, unlike Ralph of Coggeshall,
assigns the event to the chaotic reign of Stephen.[47] These children
eventually lose their green color when fed English food and prove
"like us" (similes nobis effecti) (83), learn the use of "our" speech, and
are christened. The boy, who seemed younger, dies shortly thereafter,
but the girl grows up indistinguishable from other women and later
marries in Lynn. The story, like those of religious incursions from
abroad, the Cistercians or the Savigniacs, underlines the power of England itself, its food, its language, its landscape, to absorb and alter
the initially alien. Just as Hengist and Horsa and their followers become the English, so those persons or institutions imported into England seem to increase the vigor of the indigenous. Furthermore, as
England's historians imply, in England, there is nothing indigenous,
or, to put it another way, the indigenous people, the Britons, are those
who dwell in the barbarism of Celtic regions, in an isolation far more
profound than that of any island paradise.[48] Like his predecessors, William associates the nation with the English church, whose sanctity
is underwritten both by geographic distinctiveness and by cultural

inclusiveness. In such vignettes, William evinces his understanding that England's language of self-identity is more than purely descriptive and reveals an underlying anxiety belonging to its geographic condition.

Perhaps one of the most compelling aspects of the roughly contemporary Cistercian language of identity is its affinity with those terms, and accompanying anxieties, of England's self-description that can be found in writers such as William of Newburgh. The Cistercian effect on the landscape of England was as profound, and as invasive, as were those earlier Christian foundations that altered the world of Anglo-Saxon England.[49] With their abilities to reshape their immediate environments, diverting rivers, creating water mills and early plumbing systems, breeding animals, and making advances in farming and land management, the Cistercians did more than bring a metaphoric garden to England; they created real gardens. From the earliest days of the monastic movement, pastoral language *and* actual gardens were associated with the cloistered life. In England, with its textual focus on Christian culture and its taming of barbarism, what Æthelwulf in the first quarter of the ninth century called the "fruitful cell" was more than a metaphor for prayerful isolation but also for those beacons of civilization established by the early monks.[50] As Paul Meyvaert has noted, for the Cistercians the garden represented the whole monastic setting.[51] Such a setting was at once intensely private, an enclosed garden theoretically apart from the world, and a communal space joined, by necessity, to the exigencies of the world, its commerce, land claims, gifts, and politics.[52] Charles Quest-Ritson has pointed out that, with the Dissolution, England lost some of the pleasures of its table: "before 1500 even the poorest had access to apples, pears, plums, and cherries, and often damson, medlars, and service trees, too." The monks' knowledge of horticulture was lost with their abbeys.[53] That very set of issues encapsulated in descriptions of England as both isolated from and open to the world likewise characterizes Cistercian texts dealing with the vowed life and its relation to the world outside the cloister. Unlike the Carthusians, another post-Conquest order, for whom the cell was the garden and the communal life "the desert," the Cistercians were apart from the world but lived their cloistered lives in community.[54] Though there were certainly scholars and writers among the English Cistercians, they lived in dormitories and lived a far more public existence than did the Carthusians, whose lives in their cells were divided between prayer and either reading or writing. On the other hand, the increasing desire of Cistercians in the later medieval period for privacy, for private cubicles or chambers, or gardens, suggests ways in which they reflected contemporary ways of thinking about the self and its individual needs and were forced to create language that justified an individual solitude originally alien to the order.[55]

Those needs, or the nature of those needs, underlie earlier Cistercian accounts of vocation, which, again, seem especially resonant in relation to England's own pastoral language of self-definition. The early Cistercians employed the pastoral language inherent in the language of monasticism, which owes its vitality to that of Scripture, especially to texts like the Song of Songs, as a means of heightening the purity of their rule, seen as a return to the ideals of Saint Benedict himself.[56] Thus the verse prologue to the *Exordium Magnum* of the order describes Clairvaux as the entryway to the garden of the Canticles, language that recurs throughout Cistercian self-descriptions, in which the cultivation of the heart is likened to the cultivation of the earth.[57] In Sermon 35 on the enclosed garden of the Canticle, Gilbert of Hoyland (d. 1172)—abbot of Swineshead in Lincolnshire, friend of Roger of Byland (Furness was the mother house of both Byland and Swineshead), and one of the continuators of Bernard's sermons on the Canticle— dwells on the good of enclosure, stressing the need for unity in the order. In Sermon 38 he refers to the Bride as the garden, a garden threatened by the winds of oppression that can crush the monks.[58] Since Cistercian houses are dedicated to the Virgin, who was also frequently seen as the Bride of the Song of Songs described in the lush language of the Canticle, accounts of Cistercian foundations sometimes were praised as sites of nurture, fertility, and seclusion befitting Mary, their patron.[59] Alluding to Saint Bernard's Sermon 30 on the Canticle, the *Narratio de Fundatione Fontanis Monasterii* describes Fountains as a vine in a barren place, which grew and expanded to extend its branches to the sea and to propagate the earth, later on describing Clairvaux as a "domo aromatum in operibus pietatis matris suae ungenta redolebant." In contrast, St. Mary's of York, the Benedictine abbey that the monks left to establish Fountains, has no fame and no Marian odor of sanctity.[60] Walter Daniel's *Life of Aelred of Rievaulx* describes Aelred's original view of the abbey: "High hills surround the valley, encircling it like a crown. These are clothed by trees of various sorts and maintain in pleasant retreats the privacy of the vale, providing for the monks a kind of second paradise of wooded delight." To visual delight is added aural, for the water tumbling down from the rocks made a melody, that, along with the rustling branches of the trees, formed a "jubilee of harmonious sound, music whose every diverse note is equal to the rest."[61] Aelred was ravished by the beauty of Rievaulx and by its purity of rule, going on to seek a vocation there but a vocation that left him little time to enjoy his own abbey as a place of peace. Such accounts do more than evoke the natural beauty of Cistercian sitings or the language of Clairvaux and its great abbot. In most cases written decades after the foundations themselves and by authors certainly aware of the language of England's own founding narratives, they capture the tension between the secluded, the protected, the feminine, and the active world outside the cloister (or the island), whose members are drawn to a seclusion that is inevitably altered and must continue to alter in its dealings with the outside world.[62] What are anxieties fundamental to the order's ideals are likewise those belonging to the description of England as the beautiful island.

The inherently opposed perspectives on England as a place that guide Gildas and Bede to write geography as narrative and that are epitomized in texts such as those of English Cistercians can be seen in the two most important histories of the later Middle Ages, the fabulous prose *Brut*, which, like Geoffrey of Monmouth's *Historia* might better be called a romance, and Ranulf of Higden's *Polychronicon*, which sets the history of England within a universal history. Both texts were widely copied and circulated in the late Middle Ages and then printed, thus extending their historical influence well into the sixteenth century.[63] The author of the *Brut* follows Gildas in inscribing the fallen garden onto the map of England. The *Brut* begins with the story of Dioclisian's thirty-three daughters, who murder their husbands and flee to England, where they lie with devils and engender giants; their new land is called Albion after the eldest daughter, Albina (3–4).[64] The first ninety-five chapters recount the ancient history of the Britons, including the history of Arthur. Chapter 96 describes the triumph of the Saxons, who change the name of the land to England:

but fram þe tyme þat Brut come ferst into Engeland, þis land was callede Britaigne, & þe folc Britons, til þe tyme þat þis Gurmond eftesones conquerede hit & ȝaf it vnto Saxonius, and þai anone riȝt chaunged þe name. (95)

The subsequent history of Britain/England, like that of Britain, is dominated by violence. The narrative continues to emphasize the monstrous as it affects the nation, whether through outbreaks of extreme barbarism or as barbarism is subdued or, at best, harnessed by key figures, the mythic Brutus and Arthur, and the kings of England. As Ingledew has suggested, the *Brut* is driven by its emphasis on personality, in particular the noble or royal personality.[65] The *Brut*'s account of the reign of King John (chaps. 146–55) is thus filled with drama, all of which is a manifestation of John himself: his intransigence, cruelty, showdown with the church, destruction of the Cistercians, and humiliation by Innocent III and his legate Pandulf who force him to agree to a "Letter of Obligation to the Court of Rome" and by the barons who force him to sign the Magna Carta, and his murder when a Cistercian from Swineshead slips toad venom into a wassail he shares with him. The author goes so far as to describe the extraction of the toad venom, from a great (female) toad. John's life encapsulates the *Brut*'s account of the tumult of English history, with its familial treacheries, outbreaks of greed and lust, and ongoing violence; that the toad is female comes as no surprise in a history introduced by the story of Albina and her sisters and fleshed out by those of Lear, Uther, and Arthur, all of whom are betrayed by the feminine. The few points of stability reside in the princes and nobles who triumph briefly over the passions of themselves and others.

If the *Brut* fills in and amplifies the fiction of history as established by Geoffrey of Monmouth, Higden's *Polychronicon* anchors itself in the expansiveness of England's ecclesiastical histories. Higden, a monk and scholar of St. Werburgh's Abbey in Chester, locates his history of England within a comprehensive account of world history. Higden generally downplays or ignores England's legendary history, thereby avoiding the picture of nation as a violated garden and the rhetoric of loss that is attached to that image. The first book is a *mappa mundi*, describing the parts of the earth, oceans, seas, rivers, mountains, the different countries, ending with Britain. Like Bede, whom he cites, Higden emphasizes Britain's plenty, going on to describe its marvels, such as hot wells and Stonehenge, then its rivers, regions, shires, islands, provinces, and episcopal sees, creating an orderly *accessus* for his account of England's history, whose origins he locates not in the appetites of Albina and her monstrous sisters but in the Britons, who first inhabited it in the time of Eli and Silvius Posthumus, king of the Latins, thirty- two years before the founding of Rome. The monstrous indeed exists but to the north in Scotland, in the Picts, those ancient threats to England's civilization. For Higden, England's original name, Albion, signifies its white cliffs, not a grotesque progenitrix. Higden alludes to Brutus as Albion's conqueror and hence to its new name, Britain, but the references are relatively terse and do not serve to privilege the mythic and fantastic elements found in Geoffrey of Monmouth and the *Brut* but rather to underline the orderly progress of history: the founding of cities, the creation of laws, and the coming of Christianity in the reign of King Lucius. Higden includes the histories of Uther and his son Arthur, but briefly, pausing to point out certain improbabilities in the stories.[66]

Once Higden writes himself into real time, the *Polychronicon* maintains its perspective on history as a struggle against disorder in which the church, frequently in conflict with kings, serves as a stabilizing force. For example, Higden's chapter on the coming of the Cistercians to England (VII.10) begins with Stephen Harding, "Anglicus natione," who, perceiving that God made the world by reason, can find no reason or authority (398) for the elaborations to the Benedictine rule practiced by the monastery in Molesme to which he attached himself. His decision to found an order devoted to the purity of the rule is thus described as a rational, not an ecstatic, act. In 1135 Walter Espec brought a group of those monks to England and founded an abbey at Rievaulx. Higden details the severity of their clothing and lifestyle, saying that the order increased so that it was a mirror of zeal for all monks and a reproof to the indolent. In his account of King John (VII.33), who seized church property, refused to accept Stephen Langton as archbishop of Canterbury, and brought interdict upon England, Higden intimates the deleterious shift in the balance of power from king to church, a shift that was John's own doing. He mentions John's offenses against his brother and sister, the evil weather and portents that accompanied his reign, his hostilities with the monks of Canterbury, the presence of Albigensians in England, troubles in Normandy, and, finally, the papal legate Pandulf, who brokered the deal between Innocent III and John whereby England became a feodary of the church of Rome, and John's brutal murder of a holy man who had warned him of the consequences of his cruelty. He ends with the story told in more detail by the *Brut* author ("vulgata fama") (196) that John was poisoned by a Cistercian lay brother of Swineshead, who drank of the same cup he offered the king and died with him. Higden does not comment on it, merely passes it along, saying that the monk did take the sacrament before he drank the poison. His account is far less sensational than the *Brut*'s, far less focused on John's personality, allowing the events themselves to suggest the lessons of history.

While Higden's narrative is focused on English history, it does not lose its wide-angle perspective on England as one nation in a greater world peopled by popes, other sovereigns, and world conflicts, such as the Crusades. In so doing, Higden works against the mythic and personality-driven narrative of insular romance-history, implicitly subsuming England into a more inclusive world order, that of Catholic Europe.[67] In book I, chapter 10, Higden describes Paradise as a *hortus*, a place of wholesome air and all beauty, securely closed by the ring of fire guarded by the Cherubin. Higden's England, like Bede's, is paradisal, enclosed, beautiful, bountiful, and wholesome, but it is not closed. It is vulnerable to human passions and barbarity but nonetheless potential—a landscape whose permeability opens it to restorers, seeking to bring order out of chaos.

RE-FORMING ENGLAND'S HISTORY

The histories of England written during and after the reign of Henry VIII suggest an attempt to grapple with the legacy of Bedan history, frequently by privileging historical perspectives stemming from Gildas or Geoffrey of Monmouth. In providing a picture of England as insular but linked to continental issues and institutions and as participating in cultural interchanges with the Continent, Bede, like his successors, locates the beautiful island in a larger geographic space that was not necessarily threatening to the island's proclaimed identity. In the traditions of these histories, and, in fact, of medieval English histories in general, there was room for a good deal of criticism, of both royal power and papal power, that suggested other sources of civil authority like the laws of the land or the king's council.[68] Such critiques offer a broader view of the complexities of nation, since they bring other sets of needs into a picture that necessarily must now contain more than the figure of the sovereign. Tudor histories certainly participate in the traditions of medieval history but also suggest a narrowing of focus on the sovereign and a more pronounced polemical tone not as congenial to political critique. There are markers that can be used to understand what are carefully defined ways of conceptualizing England as a place in these later Tudor texts: accounts of King John and King Arthur provide a sense of the sorts of anxieties embedded in attempts to describe this nation, the island garden, and its relationship to the world outside its shores.

The marked difference in accounts of the reign of King John underlines the degree to which histories written in the shadow of Henry VIII are without the broad view and potentially analytic mode of earlier medieval histories. The harsh views of John to be found in the works of contemporary historians are passed on to Ranulf Higden and the author of the English *Brut*, as well as to Robert Fabyan (d. 1512), writing for Henry VII, not for his son or his son's counselor, Thomas Cromwell.[69] The Henrician John is, as Carol Levin has pointed out, a "good prince," whose struggles with English churchmen and with the pope provided historical precedent for the reformers' views about the dangers Rome posed to English liberties.[70] Both Simon Fish and John Bale, who was one of Cromwell's propagandists, linked Henry to King John, thus, as Levin notes, making it dangerous to write critically of John's reign. Since medieval historians had underlined John's rapaciousness, his incredible cruelty, lechery, and self-indulgence, these early Tudor accounts of him present only the terms of his quarrel with Innocent III over Stephen Langton and, in fact, as does John Foxe later, ignore his conflict with his barons that ended with the signing of the Magna Carta.[71]

What is especially significant about these Tudor treatments of King John is the picture they provide of England as threatened by the foreign; they create an enemy without and thereby ignore the realities of a political situation whereby John was forced by his barons' rebellion to sign the Great Charter. Admittedly, since Matthew Paris there had been confusion about the dating of the Charter and thus about the identity of the king who signed it—John or his son Henry III. As J. C. Holt notes, Matthew Parker's edition of Matthew Paris made the erroneous date available.[72] The only English edition of the "selected" statutes (1534) until the reign of Elizabeth, when a statute book was published in 1583, presents the Charter as signed by Henry III in his ninth year.[73] On the other hand, Foxe's version of the end of John's reign suggests his awareness of John's difficulties with the barons, and Bale's *Kynge Johan* makes Nobylyte friends with Sedition, who, once John is without recourse, proclaims, "Englande is our owne whych is the most pleasaunte grounde/ In all the rounde worlde" (65). At the end of the play Bale presents a scene of penance and forgiveness where all profess sorrow for rejecting an anointed king and affirm the principle of royal supremacy: "in his owne realme a kynge is judge over all, / By Gods appoyntment, and none maye hym judge agayne, / But the Lorde hymself" (p. 90). Bale's emphasis on baronial opposition to King John as seditious collusion with the church to usurp the power of the crown is possible only if Bale does not include the Magna Carta in the play, which he does not.[74] Instead, he underlines the semipriestly power of the prince, who "of God a magistrate appoynted/ To the governaunce of thys same noble regyon, / To see mayntayned the true faythe and relygyon" (pp. 42–43), presenting John as Moses and Henry VIII as, like Joshua, completing the journey into the Promised Land. In this scheme, the church, in the person of Pandulf, the papal legate sent by Innocent III to England to oversee John's capitulation, becomes the invader. Bale here opposes his history to that of Polydore Vergil, who, following his medieval sources, had described John as earning the wrath of God for his impious behavior.[75]

The Tudor King John was a potentially more useful figure even than Thomas Beckett, since accounts of John could explore both the issue of royal power and the dangers to England from abroad.[76] Bale's *Kynge Johan* was first staged in 1538 at Archbishop Cranmer's house at Christmastide and was drawn from information in William Tyndale's *Obedience of a Christian Man*, published in Antwerp in 1528 at about the same time that Simon Fish had published in Antwerp his *Supplicacyon for the Beggers*.[77] Fish's treatise was available in England by 1529 for the opening of the November parliament and provides a short and memorable argument for the supremacy of the king that is rooted in a construction of England as an "oppressed commonwealth" vulnerable to invasion and of its history as fissured by the "spiritual kingdom" whose land and power rival that of the sovereign.[78] Fish's ostensible subject is the number of beggars and the lack of alms to support them. He then advances a cause:

> And this most pestilent mischief is comen vppon youre saide poore beedmen by the reason that there is yn the tymes of youre noble predecessours passed craftily crept ynto this your realme an other sort (not of impotent but) of strong puissaunt and counterfeit holy and ydell beggers and vacabundes, whiche syns the tyme of theyre first entre by all the craft and wilinesse of Satan are nowe encreased vnder your sight, not onely into a great nombre but also ynto a kingdome. (1)

Fish here describes an invasion as momentous as that of the Saxon settlement in England—invited by Vortigern to settle and help defend England from the northern barbarians, Hengist, Horsa, and their confederates stayed to conquer. Similarly, these idle churchmen fill the land. A few pages later, he remarks that neither the Danes nor the Saxons "shulde neuer haue ben abill to haue brought theire armies from so farre hither ynto your lond, to haue conquered it," if they had had such idle gluttons at home; nor would Arthur have been able to resist Emperor Lucius if such "yerely exactions had ben taken of his people" (2v–3r). His references to significant invasions of England and to Arthur's legendary invasion of the Continent remind Henry of the vulnerable island that is his realm, the history of which is epitomized by the question, "whate tongue is abill to tell that euer there was eny comon welth so sore oppressed sins the worlde first began?"(3r). Fish then moves to the effects of this invasion, which has translated lordship from the king to the invaders. He uses King John, Henry's "nobill predecessour," as an example of a king beset by traitors, who then made England "tributary" to Rome (3v). Thus the "one" kingdom is divided ("made tweyne") into "the spirituall kyngdome (as they call it) for they wyll be named first, And your temporall kindgome" (5v). Fish's argument about the idleness of the monastic orders is, of course, drawn from earlier Lollard satire, and his advocacy of regal power likewise has Wycliffite precedent. However, his remarks, which are directed to Henry, offer the king a historical precedent for reclaiming England from these invaders by exerting his sovereign power to "Set these sturdy lobies a brode in the worlde, to get theim wiues of theire owne, to get theire liuing with their laboure in the swete of theire faces according to the commaundement of god" (8r). Fish thus seeks to replace intercessory prayer with manual labor, idleness with activity, thereby freeing up funds for the truly poor and restoring the king's power to himself: "Then shall not youre swerde, power, crowne, dignite, and obedience of your people, be translated from you. Then shall you haue full obedience of your people" (8r).

The emphasis in *A Supplicacyon for the Beggers* on sovereign power looks forward to William Marshall's translation of Marsilius of Padua's *The Defender of Peace* in 1535. William Marshall was one of Thomas Cromwell's propagandists, and his translation, *The Defence of peace: lately translated out of laten into englysshe*, which he admits does not contain all of Marsilius's text, is explicitly antipapal, thus following the spirit of Marsilius's polemic against papal plenitude. However, as Alan Gewirth has pointed out, Marsilius, whom he describes as looking forward to the idea of a sovereign state, espoused a popular sovereignty devoted to the common benefit from which law and government derive their authority.[79] Marshall's translation, like its source, specifies tranquillity or peace as the chief good of a community, which is itself evidence of a society's evolution into a "commune weale," but Marshall concentrates all power in the sovereign. Marshall thus removes the principle of ecclesiastical power but at the same time avoids the issue of popular power: "that in the lawes of man: onely the prynce or els some other man by his auctoryte, may dyspence" (138).

At about this time, the November parliament of 1534 had as its first statute made the king the supreme head of the Church of England, granting the sovereign not simply the title, but all honors, jurisdictions, privileges, and dignities belonging to that head, as well as the power and authority to "visite represse redresse reforme ordre correct restrayne and amende all suche errours heresies abuses offenses contemptes and enormyties what so ever they be," which may "lawfullye" be reformed.[80] The second statute specified the oath of allegiance to Henry and his heirs by Anne Boleyn; allowed by that granting the king the first fruits each year, thus stripping the church of a significant

source of income. Hall's *Chronicle* notes the parliament's business, saying that one "special" statute was authorized, making the king supreme
head of the Church of England, "by which the Pope with all his College of Cardinalles with all their Pardons and Indulgences was vtterly
abolished out of this realme."[81] Hall records that two years previously,
on 11 May 1532, Henry sent for the Speaker and twelve men from
Commons, having already with him eight lords, in order to raise the
issue of the clergy's divided allegiance. The king's language is entirely
personal, suggesting that a subject who is also a prelate must owe all
his allegiance to his sovereign:

> we thought that the clergie of our realme had been our subiectes
> wholy, but now wee haue well perceiued that they bee but halfe
> our subiectes, yea, and scace our subiectes: for all the Prelates in
> their consecracion, make an othe to the Pope, clene contrary to the
> othe that they make to vs, so that they seme to be his subiectes,
> and not ours. (788–89)

For the oath a bishop or abbot took promising fidelity and obedience to Rome, Henry mandated one in which the prelate forswore his
allegiance to the pope if it should be hurtful or prejudicial to the sovereign, acknowledging that he held his office from the king only.[82]
Later, in 1539, when Henry had grown more conservative, Hall describes him as endorsing the Six Articles, though their rigor "brought
many an honest and simple persone to there deathes." He then goes
on to describe a beleaguered England:

> The kynges highnes whiche neuer ceased to stody and take payne
> both for the auauncement of the common wealth of this his Realme
> of England, of the which he was the only supreme gouernour and
> hed, and also for the defence of al thesame, was lately enfourmed
> by his trustie & faithfull frendes the cankerd & cruel serpent the
> bishop of rome . . . had moued and stirred diuerse great princes and
> potentates of Christendome to inuade the Realme of England, and
> vtterlie to destroy the whole nacion of thesame. (828)

Henry's fears of invasion from France or Spain were justifiable and
influenced both the diplomacy of the next few years and the muster of

troops and readying of defenses that Hall describes as following the king's announcement. More important in relation to the idea of nation Hall insinuates, the above language identifies the nation's safety with the care and power of its prince, underlining the isolation and vulnerability of England in the face of the "great princes and potentates of Christendome." The evils of invasions that Tudor historians ascribed to Roman Christianity during earlier centuries reappear in sixteenth-century polemic as threats of invasions by continental Catholics, thus reifying the perspectives of Gildas and Geoffrey of Monmouth that any island nation must constantly attend to its boundaries and reinforcing an insularity by which the island detached itself from the threat of the foreign, consequently focusing on the personal might of the king.

The Tudor devotion to the legend of King Arthur (translated by Spenser into *Prince* Arthur unblemished by the fall of Camelot) captures the need to focus the nation around a singularly magnificent figure. Polydore Vergil's skepticism about the historicity of Arthur, which echoes the similarly skeptical views of William of Malmesbury, William of Newburgh, and Ranulf Higden, was excoriated by John Leland in his *Assertio Inclytissimi Arturii* (1544). Leland's text was translated and published in 1582 by Richard Robinson and, significantly, dedicated to Lord Arthur Gray, baron of Wilton and lord deputy of Ireland, to whom Edmund Spenser served as secretary after Spenser left London for Ireland in 1580.[83] Leland presents an Arthur largely drawn from the pages of Geoffrey of Monmouth: Mordred, his nephew, takes both the queen and the kingdom while Arthur is at war in France; Lancelot is there, as he is not in Geoffrey, but as Arthur's faithful friend who, after his king's death, befriends the sinful but repentant Guinevere and accompanies her into the vowed life. This imperial Arthur is, like Geoffrey's, betrayed and besieged both at home and abroad. Like the corresponding dismantling of the cult of Saint Thomas Becket, as well as the rehabilitation of King John, these reformations of English history work to elide the sins of princes and magnify the personalities of sovereigns. Similarly, the carefully designed cult of Queen Elizabeth, which adapted the encomiums and festivities devoted to England's former patroness, the Virgin Mary, to celebrate the mysteries of England's new Virgin Queen, was designed to reaffirm the centrality of the sovereign to national identity.[84] In

1522 Henry VIII had chastised Martin Luther for ignoring the general councils of Christ's church and the judgment of the pope and the church at Rome, warning him that he may find himself as "poor and bare of friends as ye be of grace and goodness."[85] Henry's interest in aligning himself and his country with Roman Christendom waned shortly thereafter, prompting a sense of nation as isolated and threatened by potential European invasion.

Polydore Vergil's account of Henry's divorce and consequent split with Rome and reorganization of the English church certainly underlines the rupture with the past but also hints at England's growing isolation. Vergil first notes that Henry married Anne Boleyn, by whom he had a daughter, then: "Meanwhile a parliament was held in London, in which the English church assumed a political organization never seen in former ages" (in quo ecclesia Anglicana formam potestatis nullis ante temporibus uisam induit).[86] As Vergil says, by making himself head of the English church, Henry allocated to himself the first fruits of all vacant livings and the annual tenth of these livings, but he also reorganized the system of ecclesiastical justice whereby the defendant first appealed to his bishop, then to his archbishop, finally to the king "so thus there was absolutely no need of the authority of the pope in the administration of any matters concerning the church." Vergil suggests his own thoughts about the situation by swiftly recounting the deaths of John Fisher and Thomas More, whom he describes as preferring their convictions to their lives, thus as acting in opposition to the king. He then notes that Henry went on to decree new religious rites ("nouos religionis ritus") that made the worship of God different in England and, at the same time, reduced monastic establishments.[87] Vergil returns to his account of Catherine's exile and subsequent death from illness, including a final letter Catherine sent to the king, with a quick mention of Ann Boleyn's execution, Henry's marriage to Jane Seymour, and Seymour's death in childbirth. Vergil ends his history in 1538 with the birth of Edward VI.[88] Considering the opening sections of the *Anglica Historia*, drawn from Gildas and Bede, which lovingly catalog England's topographic beauty and wealth, the seemliness of its people, its proximity to the Continent, and its early embrace of "the loove and worshipping of Christe . . . soe that the Christian relligion . . . was alwayse extante in som parte of the Ilond, untill that at the lengthe bie Saint Gregory it was cleane delivered from confusion,"[89] the closing section, terse and fraught with decrees, executions, and deaths, suggests rupture rather than continuance, isolation rather than singularity.

Polydore Vergil's sketch of the beautiful island as wasted and wrenched from its ancient identity as a nation separate from but bound to Western Christendom by the ambitions of its prince becomes for Protestant Tudor historians the vulnerable island, in danger of reliving a history of spoil and conquest.[90] Foxe's *Acts and Monuments* explicitly provides a picture of England as vulnerable to incursions from abroad. In his account in book II of the reigns of Constantine and Maximus, both of whom took large armies out of the island, Foxe laments, "Thus poor Britain, being left naked and destitute on every side, as a maimed body, without might or strength, was left open to its enemies." If what is "open" is naked and destitute, what is closed is safe, a status Foxe ascribes to King Arthur's Britain. Though he doubts Arthur's continental victories, he praises Arthur's wars against the resident Saxons because they "gave to the Britons some stay and quietness during his life." Later, following but emending Bede, Foxe describes Archbishop Theodore's episcopate as a type of invasion since he brought to England the influences of Italy and displaced the native with foreign personages and standards. He describes William the Conqueror as severe and cruel, substituting his own laws for those of Edward the Confessor, the "true-bred Englishman," and the Conquest as a punishment for England's sins.[91] Like Foxe, Grafton emphasizes the idea of conquest and thus of foreign dominion as supplanting indigenous rights, rights traduced by William I in the nineteenth year of his reign with his land survey and Domesday Book "that afterward turned this land to sundry griefes and plagues, as after shall apere." Grafton emphasizes the perfidy of the monks in his account of King John, turning John into a champion of the nation in its struggle with the church.[92]

The first volume of Holinshed's *Chronicles*, which contains the three-book "Historicall Description of the Islande of Britayne" by William Harrison, as well as Holinshed's "Preface to the Reader," reflects those anxieties attendant on island status, a geographic identity that had become a powerful metaphor for national identity.[93] In *Reading Holinshed's "Chronicles,"* Annabel Patterson argues that Holinshed builds multivocality into the *Chronicles* as an ideology of historical writing, a principle or methodology to which she gives much credit. The multiple voices that Holinshed employs to recount England's history, which he lists in the "Names of Authors" section directly after the "Preface to the Reader," serve as a catholic list of medieval sources, both English and continental that at once validate his own project and suggest the ancient and historical relationship between the island and the world beyond its waters. However, even as the *Chronicles* manifests its compiler's broad knowledge and ambitious vision, it also suggests ways in which the sixteenth-century historian found it hard to escape the view of a beleaguered and potentially vulnerable island garden. Harrison, in particular, describes England's history as one of conquest and subjection. In section 1, chapter 3, of "An Historicall Description," "What sundry Nations have inhabited in this Islande," Harrison, as does Henry of Huntingdon, enumerates the series of invasions to which England has been subject, ending with the Norman Conquest. While his 1577 "Historicall Description" refers to the "importable loade" the Normans were to "our surburdoned shoulders," the much-expanded 1587 version states, "English and British were made slaues and bondmen, and bought and sold as oxen in open market!" In both versions Harrison sums up his account of English subjugation by saying that foreign princes are "lured" by the island's "manifolde commodities." The relatively mild sexual innuendo of *lured* is heightened when he follows it up by describing "this Islande" as a "praye" and a "common receptacle for straungers." His language here echoes and expands Gildas's description of Britain as the bride-turned-whore, who for Harrison becomes the "common receptacle" for all men's ambitions. The loving and detailed catalog of the island's topographic features, regional wonders, and riches that makes up the three books of Harrison's "Historicall Description" underlines just how alluring England is. Its waterways, which attracted both Edmund Spenser and Samuel Daniel in their accounts of England, its hot springs, its fairs and markets, castles, cities, marvels, livestock, minerals, habits, laws, and breeds of dog all serve as pendants, elaborating on Gildas's account of the decked bride and creating of England a work of art whose beauty and wealth are only merchandise for the common trader.

Holinshed's "Preface to the Reader," which was shortened and relegated to the sixth volume in the 1587 edition of the *Chronicles*, offers a prefatory and mitigating perspective on what Harrison describes as a history of conquest.[94] Though Holinshed admits the effects of each conquest, he also suggests the degree of order that succeeded chaos. Thus the Saxons overthrew and exiled the Britons and destroyed the Christian religion of early England but divided and governed the island. Weakened by their own dissension, the Saxons were conquered by the Danes and the Danes by the Saxons until the Saxon leaders' contempt for law caused them to be delivered into the hands of "a stranger," Duke William of Normandy. Holinshed concludes:

> And herewith altering the whole state, hee planted lawes and or-
> dinaunces as stoode moste for his auayle and suretie, which being
> after qualified with more milde and gentle lawes, tooke suche effect,
> that the state hath euer sithence continued whole and vnbroken
> by wise and politike gouernement, although disquieted, sometime
> by ciuill dissention, to the ruyne commonly of the firste mouers,
> as by the sequele of the historie ye may see. (*Chronicles* [1577] I.4)

Significantly, the 1587 edition ends its truncated "Letter to the Reader" with the Saxon destruction of Christian religion, thus deleting Holinshed's suggestion in the portion quoted above that history is process. Moreover, as he says in his account of the unnamed William the Conqueror, William altered the "whole state" and planted laws that served his own interests; *however,* those laws were "after qualified," and the state has "ever since continued whole and unbroken by wise and politic government." In this carefully balanced sentence, Holinshed indicates both the inequities of conquest and the likelihood that harshness will give way to mildness. More important, he emphasizes not the personalities of sovereigns or conquerors but the wise and politic government that is the fruit of well-planted laws. In ending with the term "sequele of the historie," he hints at a view of history harmonious with that of William of Malmesbury, who is cited in his list of authorities for the *Chronicles.*

Both William Camden's *Britannia* and Samuel Daniel's *Collection of the Historie of England* offer even more syncretic perspectives that, like those of Bede and later medieval authors, suggest the degree to which England exists in a mutually nourishing relation to a greater whole.[95] Camden published the *Britannia* in 1586, dedicating it to

William Cecil, Lord Burghley; it went through five more editions by 1607 and a translation into English by Philemon Holland in 1610. Camden's wide circle of friends included the collector Robert Cotton, and he and Camden provided Daniel with access to texts he needed for his histories. In the *Britannia* Camden offers a monumental survey of Britain that, as he admits, draws on a wide variety of sources that he employs to describe the mongrel but vigorous nature of its people.[96] For example, he comments that, through long association, the Romans and the Britons could be counted "one stock" (83); though he admits the paganism and harshness of the Saxons, he also suggests their abilities as leaders and settlers (132) and the alacrity of their acceptance of Christianity (136–37). In his account of the Gregorian mission to England, he follows Bede in recounting a "bringing in" of arts and sciences to an island too long separated from European culture and then stresses the degree to which communities in Europe became the beneficiaries of England's renewed learning. Of the Normans, he writes, "And eversince their comming, England as well for martiall honour as civil behaviour, hath among the most florishing Kingdoms of Christiandome flourished with the best" (154). He follows this brief account of the early period of England's history with a leisurely and detailed account of its regions, each of which is introduced by a map that allows him to use topography as the grid for an account of customs, cities, episcopates, and geographic and architectural details.[97] Camden's regional focus enables his broader, syncretic understanding of history. In his description of Ripon in Yorkshire, he notes the beautiful church, and, like William of Malmesbury and William of Newburgh, praises the renascence brought to the area by the many monasteries situated throughout. Nor does he neglect Fountains Abbey, a rich prize for Henry and Cromwell and by Camden's time a ruin, noting the strictness of its rule, Saint Bernard's praise for the house, and the daughter houses to which it was "mother" (700). What Camden offers, here and elsewhere, is a national identity that incorporates the past by continually noting the network of relationships among persons, countries, and cultures that comprise the island he so lovingly describes. In his *Remaines concerning Britain*, Camden remarks, "King Henry the 8 who subuerted so many churches monuments and tombes, lyeth inglorious at Windsor," powerfully suggesting that by attempting to wipe out the past, Henry did not reap the glory attributed to him by the Reformist historians. It is this rupture that Camden and his fellow antiquarians and book collectors implicitly repair, offering a picture of an island nation whose insularity need not be a source of fear and xenophobia.[98]

▓   To end with Samuel Daniel's *The Collection of the History of England* (1612, 1618) and John Milton's *History of Britain* (1648?–71) is not to suggest there was or is an end to the making of history but to pause at texts whose affiliations with earlier efforts to define England or Britain as an island garden are fundamental to their rhetorical stances and historical perspectives.[99] Both Daniel and Milton were deeply read, and both refer to the long list of historians and chroniclers that precede them: in his "Letter to the Reader," Daniel cites what is, in effect, a full library, and Milton frequently acknowledges his reliance, especially, on William of Malmesbury and his knowledge of and low regard for Florence of Worcester, Henry of Huntingdon, Roger Hovedon, and others.[100] However, though both employ a similar set of sources, they do not emerge with similar points of view. Daniel, like William of Malmesbury and Camden, his friend, describes a history of rupture and reparation. For example, Daniel's "The Life and Reigne of William the first" opens with an account of radical change:

> I come to write of a time, wherein the State of England receiued an alteration of Lawes, Customes, Fashion, manner of liuing, Language-writing, with new formes of Fights, Fortifications, Buildings, and generally an innouation in most things, but Religion. So that from this mutation, which was the greatest it euer had, we are to begin, with a new accompt of an England, more in dominion abroad, more in State, and ability at home, and of more honour and name in the world, then heretofore: which by being thus vndone, was made, as if it were, in the fate therof to get more by loosing, then otherwise. For as first, the Conquest of the Danes; brought it to the intyrest Gouerment it euer possest at home . . . so did this of the Norman by comming in vpon it, make a way to let out, and stretch the mighty armes therof ouer the Seas, into the goodly prouinces of the South. (22)

Though Daniel divides history in terms of regnal years, he offers a perspective on sovereigns that is less interested in personality than in ability, hence in a sovereign's impact on England's history. Thus, in the above passage, Daniel takes radical change and the ruptures that accompany it as points where nations can become stronger through loss, later referring to William as "this busie new State-building King" (42). He offers an intelligent analysis of the reign of King John, including an account of John's signing of the Magna Carta at the insistence of his barons, who threaten that if John "refused to confirme and restore vnto them those liberties" they would make war on him (120). Daniel then focuses on the provision in the Charter for baronial counsel as a check on royal power (121).[101] He praises Edward III in businesslike terms: "To be short, hee was a Prince who knew his worke, and did it; and therefore was hee better obeyed, better respected and serued then any of his Predecessors" (220). Daniel ends his *Collection* by proclaiming his focus on the kingdom whose medieval history he writes:

> Thus farre haue I brought this Collection, of our History, and am now come to the highest exaltation of this Kingdome, to a State full built, to a Gouernment reared vp with all those maine Couplements of Forme and Order, as haue held it together euer since: notwithstanding those dilapidations made by our ciuile Discord, by the Nonage or negligence of Princes, by the alterations of Religion, by all those corruptions which Tyme hath brought forth to fret and canker-eate the same. (222)

Those "Couplements of Forme and Order" that hold the kingdom together have been forged from the change Daniel celebrates either implicitly or explicitly as growth in his accounts of the arrival of the Romans, the Saxons, the Danes, and the Normans to an island that seemed "secluded . . . out of the knowledge of the world" so that "we shall shew the passage of things the better" (2).

If Daniel eschews and seems to work against those anxieties of vulnerability that frequently accompanied accounts of the history of England, the island garden, Milton does not. As Nicholas von Maltzahn has emphasized, in Gildas Milton found a voice and a prophetic mode that connected his republican discontent with his countrymen to the moral weaknesses of the ancient Britons.[102] In fact, Milton begins with the assumption of weakness: despite his acknowledgment that the early history of Britain is obscure, he recounts the "absurd" and "gross" (6) legend of Albina, as well as that of Brutus who discovers Britain: "The Iland not yet Britain but Albion, was in a manner desert and inhospitable, kept only by a remnant of Giants; whose excessive Force and Tyranie had consum'd the rest" (16). He goes on to mention Brutus's destruction of the giants and division and naming of the land, which in the rocks and caves of Cornwall still contained giants and monsters. Milton's decision to recount Galfredian history through book I of the *History* accords with his choice of Gildas as mentor, for it underscores the emphasis in the subsequent books on the decline and decay of the island garden, which even by Brutus's time was "kept" in bestiality. Where Daniel begins with the obscurity of the beginnings of nations, nods briefly to the unverifiable Brutus, and moves immediately to Caesar and Roman England, Milton begins by recognizing decay, violence, and destruction as facts of the histories of nations and continues to describe an island isolated by geography and the rule of giants and maintained in order only tenuously thereafter.

Milton's emphasis on civil disorder and decay as endemic to England, its history and the records of that history, frames each of the six books, which are organized around the invasions to which England was subject. In the long first paragraph of book II, where he recounts the Roman conquest, Milton admits the destruction that comes with war but also holds up the need for a man of "valour" to "use the necessity of Warr and Dominion, not to destroy, but to prevent destruction," to "bring in" liberty and civility, warning that when "the esteem of Science and liberal study waxes low in the commonwealth," eloquence decreases and historians lack style (39–40). He thus links national virtue and learning and both with the writing of history, at once excusing himself for his reliance on Gildas and Roman historians and suggesting the continued chaos and isolation of England itself, since it lacks a full tradition of capable and creditable historical authors. The opening of book III offers a more serious critique of England, past and present; he links the desperate state of England during the departure of the Roman legions and the incursions of the Picts and Scots from the north with the "confused Anarchy" produced by the civil wars of his own time (129). He goes on to tell the familiar story of Vortigern's embassy to the Saxons, asking for protection from the northerners, drawing on Nennius and Henry of Huntingdon for an account of Arthur and of the gradual stabilization of England under the Saxons. Though book IV opens with the admission that the Saxons created seven kingdoms, Milton moves quickly to stress the growing dissension among them (185), then to the Gregorian mission prompted by the sight of Northumbrian children for sale in the Roman slave market and the Christianization of England. Book IV, however, ends with the decline into luxury and division ("all the same vices which Gildas alleg'd of old to have ruined the Britans") (256) and the growing chaos of the Danish invasions. Book V continues to emphasize the wickednesses of the Saxons ("now full as wicked as the Britans were at their arrival") (259), the strength of the Danes, and the gradual decline of England, which culminates at the end of book VI with the "Yoke of an out-landish Conqueror"(402). Milton's "out-landish" translates William of Malmesbury's "alienum," as his editor, French Fogle notes, but the word conveys more than the sense of foreign conquest. What is "out-land" is not "in-land" or *island*, thus playing on the vulnerabilities of an island whose churchmen "had fitted themselves for this servitude" by abandoning the study of Latin, literature, and religion and whose leaders had dissolved into drunkenness, lechery, and "other Vices which effeminate mens minds"(402). Milton thus metaphorically ends where he began, with a reference to Belina and the bestial giants Brutus found on his arrival. The end draws a lame moral from the relentlessly circular account of decay:

> If these were the Causes of such misery and thraldom to those our Ancestors, with what better close can be concluded, then here in fit season to remember this Age in the midst of her security, to fear from like Vices without amendment the Revolution of like Calamities. (403)

"Revolution" underlines the shape of the *History of Britain*, the periodic shift from chaos to relative order to chaos again, without benefit of the providential and linear shape that can be traced in Bede and his successors. For Milton, as for Gildas and Geoffrey of Monmouth, those endemic weaknesses of the English should produce no false sense of security but only the remembrance of "thraldom" and the fear of vice, which historically summons conquerors to island shores.

BOUNTIFUL LAND

The bounty of the island garden is finally both the subject of attempts to write its history and the point of the historian's perspective on his task. In drawing on but amplifying Gildas's account of the bride arrayed in cities, wide plains, hills, mountains, flowers, fountains, rivers, and lakes (3), Bede also shifts the emphasis from the ingratitude and haughtiness (4) of this bountifully decked bride—and hence her vulnerability to the outside world—to a hospitality that sanctions, protects, and incorporates the alien. For example, Bede in his accounts of the conversions of Alban and Æthelbert uses the word *hospitio*. Alban, though still a pagan, guarantees hospitality, meaning lodging, for a priest fleeing from persecution ("clericum quendam persecutores fugientem hospitio recepit") (1.7). Converted through grace by his reverence for the priest's faith and devotion, Alban offers himself rather than his guest ("hospite") and becomes Britain's first martyr. Quoting Fortunatus, Bede links Alban's fame with the fruitfulness of Britain: "Albanum egregium fecunda Britania profert." Thus fertile Britain brings forth illustrious Alban, just as his conversion and martyrdom proceed from the grace that comes to him when he receives the Christian priest with hospitality. Bede uses the same wording when describing Æthelbert's offer to receive Augustine and his fellow monks with hospitality ("quin potius benigno uos *hospitio recipere*"; emphasis added), despite his own unwillingness to give up the old beliefs for the new (1.25). The monks' imitation of the primitive church (1.26)—their simplicity, faith, and devotion—prompt the conversions of the king and many others.

These two—and, for Bede, twinned—accounts link conversion, or creative change, with hospitality to the foreign. William of Malmesbury, who does not recount England's Roman history and thus omits the story of Alban, provides his own version of the story of Æthelbert, one that captures the sense of Bede's narrative.[103] Citing both Bede and the *Anglo Saxon Chronicle* for the reign of Æthelbert, he describes the king as feckless in his youth but acquiring military skill with age and, finally, as becoming civilized through marriage to a Frank: "Then it was that, by intercourse with the Franks, a nation hitherto barbarous and now united in one way of life daily 'unlearnt its woodland wildness' and turned to more civilized ways" (*GRA* 28/29).[104] William attributes Æthelbert's later conversion to the softening of heart ("animus iam emollitus") already accomplished by his exposure to Frankish civilization and to the purity of life of Bishop Luidhard, who had accompanied the queen to England. Henry of Huntingdon employs Bede's wording for both incidents. Foxe does not. Foxe's account of Alban is indebted to Bede, and though he does not use the word *hospitality*, the gloss reads, "Fruit of hospitality to be noted" (*A&M* I:257). Foxe pays great attention to Alban's martyrdom but discounts as superstitions the miracles attributed to him that Bede includes, thus creating a story of individual conversion and faith in the face of great adversity rather than a celebration of England's fecundity in the splendid Alban, whose death, as Gildas and Bede attest, opened up a way through a deep river and caused a spring to bubble up in a hilly plateau, the miraculous pendants for the martyr's crown. Foxe's record of Æthelbert's conversion (II:330) makes no reference to hospitality, or to the civilizing effects of the Franks, though he admits, with Bede, that Queen Bertha's Christianity had made Æthelbert more receptive to Augustine's preaching. Rather than offer Augustine and his monks hospitality, Æthelbert offers them a deal, promising not to mistreat them ("ye shall not be molested by me, but shall be right well entreated, having all things to you ministered necessary for your supportation") and giving them leave to preach. Foxe's choice of *entreated* suggests that Æthelbert is either promising to deal with them "right well" or negotiating with them for the terms of their stay. His unwillingness to suggest that these Roman missionaries were received with hospitality is adumbrated in the rest of the book, where, following Bede's *History*, including the questions of Augustine to Pope Gregory, he adds remarks about the growing (and dangerous) supremacy of Rome and about the follies of Roman Christianity, saying that later history will "comprehend" the "declining time of the church, and of true religion" (II: 385). Milton's language is softer than Foxe's: "Nevertheless because ye are strangers, and have endur'd so long a journey . . . ye may be sure we shall not recompence you with any molestation, but shall provide rather how we may friendliest entertain ye" (188). The suggestion of friendly entertainment is a reference to hospitality, or to the duties of hosts to guests, as Heal has described them in *Hospitality in Early Modern England.*[105]

Both William Camden and William Lambarde, friends, and, with Cotton and others, founders of the Society of Antiquaries, subtly link England's bounty with the issue of hospitality and both as directly related to national identity. For example, Camden's account of Kent in *Britannia* describes the bounty of its natural resources while at the same time linking the abundant fruit trees to an earlier transplantation: "Howbeit everie where almost it is full of meadowes, pastures, and cornfields: abounding wonderfully in apple-trees, and cherrie-trees also, which being brought out of Pontus into Italie, in the 608. yeere after the foundation of Rome, and in the 120. yeere after, translated from thence into Britaine, prosper heere exceeding well, and take up many plots of land." Camden then goes on to commend the "civilitie and courtesie" of the inhabitants, likewise commended by Caesar (324). He thus celebrates a *translatio,* not of culture or learning or power, but of fertility, from Greece to Italy to Kent in England, where the stocks of these ancient apple and cherry trees flourish and mark a region whose hospitality was likewise noted by Caesar. In *A Perambulation of Kent,* Lambarde specifically links the issue of hospitality to that of national identity, saying that he wishes to have "guests and strangers" who visit England "fynde such courtesie and intertainment" so that England shall no longer be called inhospitable, employing a term he derives from Horace, "hospitibus feros," to describe England's reputation with other nations.[106] Such ferocity or wildness, is of course the very quality William of Malmesbury considers tamed in Æthelbert by companionship or cohabitation ("contubernio") with the Frankish Christians.

Such excerpts from the histories capture an ongoing awareness of the anxieties belonging to a nation conceived of, first, as a geographic entity, distinct but inherently open to invasion or incursion. Other considerations of England's identity figure such concerns as isolation, insularity, hospitality or courtesy, and safety by offering pictures of spaces—gardens, forests, monasteries, estates—that are intertwined with these perspectives on a history that must always begin with bounty and beauty and its relation to the alien. However, gardens demand guardians, and either explicitly or implicitly these texts that I

explore in later chapters are concerned with the question of guardian-
ship, offering finely tuned debates that locate authority not always in
the crown. Thus John Stow mitigates the grim fact that after the Normans *all* were "made subiecte vnto the perpetuall bondage of the Normans" by offering a stirring account of the men of Kent standing up
to Duke William for their ancient liberties and saving the "laws and
customs of country."[107] Strikingly here and elsewhere, nation is a place
possessed of laws and liberties worked out and passed down to princes
lest they identify place with lordship.

CHAPTER TWO

THE ISLAND GARDEN AND THE
ANXIETIES OF ENCLOSURE

Those anxieties of national identity, attached as they were to the to-pography of a distinct and enclosed space, that were examined and refined by historians are refigured in poems, treatises, sermons, and addresses throughout the medieval and early modern periods. In fact, they are the essential subjects of England's literature of place, which offers its own subtle commentary on the processes of national self-definition. The concatenation of competing images of England that Shakespeare embeds in *Richard II* can be traced to the rich traditions of medieval writers. John of Gaunt, prince of the blood, defines his nation as

> This royal throne of kings, this sceptred isle,
> This earth of majesty, this seat of Mars,
> This other Eden, demi-paradise,
> This fortress built by Nature for herself
> Against infection and the hand of war,

This happy breed of men, this little world,
This precious stone set in the silver sea,
Which serves it in the office of a wall
Or as a moat defensive to a house
Against the envy of less happier lands,
This blessed plot, this earth, this realm, this England[1]

In the next act the gardeners describe the nation as Richard's un-lucky and unweeded garden in which "law and form and due propor-tion" have been ignored (3.4.41). Gaunt's encomium defines England's majestic earth in relation to noble identifying traits: fortresses, moated homes, and scepters. These are "farmed out" by Richard's profligacy and greed, the blessed plot become a tenement, rented to the highest bidder. On the other hand, the gardeners speak for law as restrain-ing majesty, as maintaining a "firm estate" in *our* sea-walled garden" (3.4.42–43; my emphasis). The gardeners' easy analogy between *their* garden and the realm, between unruly plants and ambitious men, as well as their casual assumption that the state of the garden concerns them, substitutes another image for the "precious stone set in the sil-ver sea" and offers a vastly different way of conceptualizing England.

Such a depiction of England as set apart by virtue of geography and sacral kingship is central to the Wilton Diptych, which shows a young Richard II presented by John the Baptist and the English saints, Edward and Edmund, to the Virgin and Child. The angels flanking the Virgin on the right-hand panel wear Richard's badge of the White Hart; one of the angels carries a banner with a red cross, the banner of Saint George.[2] In 1993 it was discovered that the orb (which is one centimeter in diameter) of the banner contains a miniature of an is-land on which are a white castle and trees, surrounded by a sea with a boat in sail and, above, a blue sky (see figs. 1 and 2). Dillian Gordon has argued that the orb represents England as the *dos Mariae*, the dowry of the Virgin.[3] That the idea of England as Mary's dowry was current is clear from Thomas Arundel's remarks to that effect in 1400, sug-gesting that at least by the reign of Richard II England claimed a spe-cial relationship with Mary.[4] Depicting England enclosed by the sea, as Mary by her chastity, donated to the Virgin, and ruled by the young king, the Wilton Diptych, which is a portable altar, offers itself as an icon of sacred kingship and sacred geography.[5] As an icon, the beautiful and mysterious diptych offers an image of England that rests on stasis protected by privilege. However, as Shakespeare's gardeners indicate, there are other ways of imaging the island garden: as girded by law that must be internalized and executed for the good of all in a realm set within necessity or change.

The tension between the two images, differentiated by the social status of the speakers and set in counterpoise with one another, can be traced to the mid-fourteenth century and the artistry of William Langland, who exploited another sort of discrete space, the peasant holding, making of it, in effect, a counterimage for England. In so doing he offered another way of thinking about the nature of the common good as a component of national identity. Langland's use of the peasant holding depends on his ability to infuse a literal space with a set of meanings that allow it to continue life as a trope whose significance does not depend on abstraction but on the concrete and the commonplace.[6] Langland's image both participates in and alters a discourse about national identity expressed as topographic description. In seeking to reconcile England's status as the beautiful island with a relationship to the world outside it, that discourse, originating in Bede's refitting of Gildas's trope and diatribe, reified the goods of experience, discipline, and discretion but not of isolation. The recurring images were elite—monasteries, castles garnished against incursion—and bespoke the power to be found in islands and their surrounding waters.

In 1352, returning to England after a truce in the war, Edward III met rough weather and lost men to the sea. His remarks are among the last bits of history Ranulf Higden records: "My goode lady seynt Marye, what is it, and what bodeþ it, þat in my wendynge into Fraunce I wynde have and weder and al þing at my wille, and in my comynge aʒen toward Engelond I have tempest and many hard happes."[7] The king here complains as suitor to lady, as knight to patron, and certainly Mary served as patroness to the Order of the Garter, which was bound to her and to the king in chivalry. Edward's self-characterization as mobile and manly, moving between England and France while hoping for the goodwill of his "lady" Mary, evinces his appropriation and mastery of the island's distinction. Like Mary, England is enclosed, but as king he comes and goes, all at the behest of his noble lady. If Edward's chivalric language, like the elaborately conceived Wilton Diptych at which Richard must have gazed (and at himself kneeling, vested, and hailed by the Christ child) while in prayer, seems endlessly self-reflexive, Langland provides a way of thinking about space as less elite, certainly less narcissistic, but nonetheless exalted.

In Passus 7 of the A-text of *Piers Plowman*, which responds to an Edwardian scene of royal panoply and a set of fiscal concerns outlined in the earlier *Wynnere and Wastoure*, Langland transplants the language of national identity to the field of peasant labor. Chaucer and the author of the early-fifteenth-century *Mum and the Sothseggar* at once exploit Langland's use of the agricultural landscape as a metaphor for nation and detach it from Langland's poem, to some extent from its allusive relation to Christian allegory. The use of the agricultural holding as a sign for England's secular-but-sacred identity becomes more explicitly political in the literature relating to land enclosure from the late fifteenth century on and is further enriched and altered by authors of both agricultural manuals and encomiums to great houses, such as Thomas Tusser, Ben Jonson, and Andrew Marvell. The lines of influence between and among the texts making up this discourse are certainly there, but more interesting than simple influence is the discourse itself and its persistent focus on the configuration of place or space—the island or an analogous boundaried space—as expressive of an understanding of the common good that is subtly at odds with an identification of island with sovereign power.

PIERS'S CROFT

In his first text of *Piers Plowman* (ca. 1362–70), Langland placed into circulation an image, a semienclosed space, Piers's half acre, close by his croft. In so doing, Langland drew on its biblical and parabolic, as well as legal and agricultural, associations, creating an image whereby allegory, agriculture, and nation combine in ways that were to become inextricable in English literature.[8] Both the half acre and the croft are based in English rural life. The half acre was the average area of the strip, separated by narrow unplowed strips, into which open fields were plowed, those half acres then allotted to individuals; the croft designated an enclosed small parcel of land, frequently adjoining a house.[9] Langland uses both terms as concepts in which the language of tropology coexists with that of topography. He employs the

term *croft* in two ways in the *Visio*, first as part of an image that David
Aers has called a type of the preacher's "picturing model" in Piers's
directions to the dwelling of Truth, which are unchanged in all three
writings of the poem:[10]

> Þanne shalt þou come be a croft, ac come þou nought þereinne;
> Þ[e] croft hattiþ coveite-nouȝt-menis-catel-ne-here-wyues,
> Ne-none-of-here-seruauntis-þat noiȝe-hem-miȝte;
> Loke þou breke no bowis þere but it be þin owene. (A: 6.59–62)

Since Piers has just told the pilgrims that they must first wade in a
brook and not swear, the croft, which they are not to enter or pillage,
serves as a spiritual way station offered by the Law, codified in the Ten
Commandments, a stage preceding their arrival at the court of Mercy.

However, his second use of *croft* places it in relation to the half
acre, which he invites the pilgrims to help him work (A: 7.4). He assigns the croft to the Knight's protection as part of an idealized social
covenant:

> I shal swynken & sweten & sowe for vs boþe,
> A[nd] ek laboure for þi loue al my lif tyme,
> In couenaunt þat þou kepe holy [k]ir[k]e and myself
> Fro wastours [and wikkide men] þat wolde me destroye,
> And go hunte hardily [to] har[is] & [to] fox[is],
> And [to] boris & [to] bukkes þat breken myn heggis,
> And fecche þe hom fauconis þe foulis to kille,
> For þise comiþ to my croft & croppiþ my whete. (A: 7.27–34)

Piers's language here comes from the countryside, from the parcels
enclosed by hedges held by individual tenants and worked for private
profit but usually subject to communal control or censure when the
subject was common grazing.

Langland uses this croft as synecdoche for all peasant holdings,
which depend on a covenant between knights and laborers. The foxes
that enter into the croft and threaten his livelihood evoke the foxes, the
temptations or heretics, of Canticle 2.15, that spoil the grapes within
the vineyard of the church or wreck the work within the field of the
spirit, and initially suggest that we simply see the croft as a symbol

for the church. However, he complicates the image by having Piers go on to mention hares, boars, and bucks, those animals whose very existence was guaranteed by the Law of the Forest, which prevented the peasant from ridding himself of huntable beasts.[11] The sequence, which begins in seemingly uncomplicated allegory, ends in the realm of England and the law governing the use of the land. Langland has not only substituted a rural scene for a tropological pictogram; he here, and briefly, provides another sort of picture, idealized but nonetheless intended as an image of a realm wherein peasant and knight are bound through the land and where the scene of rural labor is not one pageant within a program depicting the laborer as an appendage to the noble household. Thus the laborers in the Luttrell Psalter take their reality from the family and its myths manifested in the Psalter, and the peasants in the *Tres Riches Heures* exist in relation to the castles in the background.[12] Langland's foregrounding of the peasant holding and its needs offers an image of potentially subversive power that he quickly reinserts into another pictogram by naming Piers's wife and children: "Dame werche-whanne-tyme-is," "do-riȝt-[so]-or þi damme-shal-þe bete," "suffre-þi-souereynes-to-hauen-here-wille / And-deme-hem-nouȝt-for-ȝif-þou-dost-þou-shalt-it-dere-abiggen, / Let-god-worþe-wiþal-for-so-his-woord-techiþ" (A: 7.70−74). Here, we return to a tropology designed to reify adages fitting the laborer into the necessary strictures of time and power.

    Piers's reference in the above passage to "wastours" who threaten him does not so much place the croft, the peasant household, within the concerns of the household of the realm as substitute the croft for the noble household as a countersymbol for England, the nation.[13] The word, which appears ten times in Passus 7, was used to indicate one who destroys or marauds but more immediately one who consumes improvidently, who wastes resources, who spends but does not either produce or save. Its currency as a social or political category extends well beyond the mid-fourteenth century. In *A Game of the Chese*, which assimilates monarchic rule to the chessboard and game, Wasters are the eighth type of pawn, to whom the king must assign tutors to teach them not to waste and to labor.[14] The most explicit account of wasters in relation to their effects on community occurs in the alliterative poem titled "Here begynnes a tretys and god schorte refreyte by-

twixe Wynnere and Wastoure." Though the single manuscript in which
the debate ("refreyte") appears was compiled by Robert Thornton of
East Newton in Yorkshire about 1450, the poem itself is usually dated
to around 1352, at least a decade earlier than the A-text of *Piers Plowman*. Thornton seems to have drawn on the collections of his friends
and associates in Yorkshire for the exemplars he copied, suggesting
that though there is now only one copy of *Wynnere and Wastoure*, it
might well have been known to Langland.[15] Passus 7 certainly seems
to express his familiarity with the poem and its arguments. However,
what is presented as debate between two landowners before the king
in *Wynnere and Wastoure* Langland transforms into a picture of Waster
and his effect on a society organized around a concept of labor as fundamental to the common good.

Langland thereby moves into a different register in Passus 7.
Though Passus 6, in which Piers describes the pathway to Truth is
consistently tropological, Passus 7, with its account of the work of
the land, slips tellingly between the actual and the abstract. In Passus 6, Piers describes his labor in relation to his service to Truth:

> I haue ben his folewere al þis fourty wynter;
> Boþe sowen his secd, & sewide hise bestis,
> And kepide his corn, & cariede it to house,
> Dyke[d] & d[o]luen & do what he hiȝte,
> Wiþinne & wiþoute waytide his profit. (A: 6.30–34)

The pronoun *his* designating the seed and the beasts and the corn and
the profit as belonging to Truth marks the passage as an allegorical
description of spiritual labor described as though it were physical. In
Passus 7, after Piers has agreed to lead the pilgrims to Truth if they
will help him cultivate his half acre, the account is subtly different:

> "I wile worsshipe þerewiþ treuþe in my lyue,
> And ben his pilgrym at þe plouȝ for pore menis sake.
> My plouȝpote shal be my pyk & putte at þe rotis,
> And helpe my cultir to kerue & close þe forewis."
> Now is peris & þe pilgrimes to þe plouȝ faren;
> To erien þis half akir helpen hym manye;

Dikeris & delueres dy[gg]eþ vp þe balkis.
Þerewiþ was perkyn payed, and preisid hem ȝerne.
Oþere werkmen þere were [þat] wrouȝte ful faste,
Eche man on his maner made hymself to done,
And summe to plese perkyn pykide vp þe wedis. (A: 7.93−103)

This passage adds a layer to Pier's earlier account of himself. First, the pronouns have changed to first person. Second, Piers suggests that Truth might be found in the ordinary, in laboring for poor men's sake. In the C-text, Langland heightens the social ramifications of this line by having Piers say that he will be a pilgrim at the plow "for profit to pore and ryche" (C: 8.111). In A, rather than the pike or staff of the pilgrim, he will wield the plow.[16] He and those who wish to be pilgrims are diking, digging, and delving Piers's half acre, the others working to please Piers. Langland has not suggested that Piers is to be understood as Truth; instead, he presents a scene of harmonious labor, each man working according to his manner. The half acre is a half acre, revealing a profit to be gained in social harmony. This is not to say that Langland is no longer concerned with Truth, but the truth here is that of the orderly community, where working has as its end communal "winning." In *Wynnere and Wastoure*, Wynnere is described as hoarding for himself, as deleterious to the communal good because he produces but does not share. The poem, which Ralph Hanna has called a *"jeu d'esprit*, a debate between two equally powerful imperatives for magnates" (262), to manage and expropriate or to spend sumptuously, locates both wasting and winning within the household of the king or magnate.[17] Where *Wynnere* is focused on lordship, Langland transfers those same concerns to the smallholding, to the place where what is to be either hoarded or consumed is actually produced. He describes those acts of production as productive of harmony because they take place in the half acre, a distinct but communal space. Directly after this idyllic picture of well-directed labor, Piers takes a break to see "whoso best wrouȝte." He finds wasters.

Langland's depiction of wasters echoes but, again, reformulates the depiction of waste to be found in *Wynnere and Wastoure*. Thus Wynnere describes Wastoure as living richly and unthriftily, consuming but not contributing. He offers Wastoure a warning about the effects of his mode of living:

Teche thy men for to tille and tynen thyn feldes;
Rayse up thi rent-howses, ryme up thi yerdes,
Owthere hafe as thou haste done and hope aftir werse—
That es firste the faylynge of fode, and than the fire aftir,
To brene the alle at a birre for thi bale dedis.
The more colde es to come, als me a clerke tolde. (288–93)

Langland vivifies Wynnere's warning in the picture he provides of the want and panic occasioned by the Hunger Piers summons to punish his own wasters. However, Langland transforms the depictions of waste in *Wynnere and Wastoure* by concentrating not on landlords but their laborers, "their men." Rather than the injunction to teach *thy* men to till *thy* fields, those who do the tilling are told:

Ac treuþe shal teche ȝow his tem for to dryue,
Boþe to setten & to sowen, & sauen his telþe,
[Cacche cowes] from his corn, [and] kepen hise bestis,
Or ȝe shuln ete barly bred & of þe bro[k] drynke;
But he be blynd, or brokesshankid, or beddrede ligge:
Þei shuln ete as good as I, so me god helpe,
Til god of his grace garc h[e]m to arise. (A: 7.126–32)

   Piers's warning echoes that of Wynnere but slips curiously between the abstract and the concrete. The truth implied by Wynnere's statement that there is more cold to come becomes a proper noun, Truth, who will teach us how to drive *his* team. However, the inherent allegoresis of this statement, which echoes Piers's description of his own labor in Passus 6, along with the immediacy of Piers's imperative second-person address, is attached to the list of concrete jobs Truth will teach, not simply driving his team, but sowing, cow-catching, and animal tending, and by the plain peasant fare, barley bread and brook water, any waster shall eat. In other words, Langland has balanced this scene somewhere between allegory and actuality by anchoring Truth to a rural landscape of bread, cows, and corn and, more important, to the truth of hunger that threatens those who do not work for the common good.
   Similarly, the depiction of Hunger that follows shows the effects of actual physical hunger for a reading public that likely understood

all too well what years of dearth might produce. Again, Langland locates hunger in peasant space, with the food that is available before
the croft is harvested (A: 7.264—75), beans, herbs, cabbage, milk, in
contradistinction to the rich food Wastoure is said to eat:

> The bores-hede schall be broghte with plontes appon lofte,
> Buk-tayles full brode in brothes there besyde,
> Venyson with the frumentee, and fesanttes full riche,
> Baken mete therby one the burde sett,
> Chewettes of choppede flesche, charbiande fewlis,
> And iche a segge that I see has sexe mens doke.
> If this were nedles note, anothir comes aftir,
> Roste with the riche sewes and the ryalle spyces,
> Kiddes cloven by the rigge, quarterd swannes,
> Tartes of ten ynche, that tenys myn hert
> To see the borde overbrade with blasande disches,
> Als it were a rayled rode with rynges and stones. (332—43)

Wynnere here suggests the importance of luxury to Wastoure by the
list of rich foods that decorate Wastoure's table as gems embellish a
cross, thus linking the excesses of ecclesiastical and secular life, as well
as suggesting Wastoure's fetishization of his table. Langland, in describing what the "pore peple" (276) fetch to stave off hunger, enumerates the fruits of the English countryside as they were stored in peasant larders: peascods, beans, black apples, cherries, pears, green wheat.
Whereas the first list belongs to the satire of wealth and excess and
could describe the table of King Arthur in *Sir Gawain and the Green
Knight* or of Chaucer's Franklin, the second depicts a place characterized by agricultural labor, removed from the tables of the privileged,
though shadowed in Wastoure's replies to Wynnere that he should not
hoard but provide for the poor:

> The bemys benden at the rofe, siche bakone there hynges,
> Stuffed are sterlynges undere stelen bowndes—
> What scholde worthe of that wele if no waste come?
> Some rote, some ruste, some ratons fede.
> Let be thy cramynge of thi kystes for Cristis lufe of heven!
> Late the peple and the pore hafe parte of thi silvere;

For if thou wydwhare scholde walke and waytten the sothe,
Thou scholdeste reme for rewthe, in siche ryfe bene the pore.
 (251–58)

In Wastoure's picture of Wynnere's home, groaning with stored
food and valuables, the poet provides the obverse of Wynnere's picture
of Wastoure's overlaid table. Langland transforms magnatial store-
houses and elaborate banquet boards into the annual contingencies of
the peasant's diet, before and after the croft is harvested, and sets them
against the realities of hunger, either the short-term hunger at the end
of the agricultural cycle or the specter of long-term hunger should
the harvest fail.[18] Piers here preaches labor as remedial for the common good.

Though in the next passus Langland returns to allegory, to the
pardon Truth grants to Piers, Passus 7, with some exceptions, takes
place in the countryside as a peasant might experience it—its contingencies, its less than ideal workers and working conditions, its food,
and its clothing. When he and the Knight strike a bargain for the
benefit of the common good, Piers is not dressed like the Christologi-
cal figure he will appear as near the end of both the B- and C-texts but
as a peasant ready to work:

He caste on his cloþis, ycloutid & hole,
Hise cokeris & his cuffis for cold of his nailes,
And heng his hoper at his hals in stede of a scrippe (A: 7.54–56)

Piers's simplicity certainly stands in contrast to Wastoure's extrava-
gance:

Thou ledis renkes in thy rowte wele rychely attyrede;
Some hafe girdills of golde that more gude coste
Than alle the faire fre londe that ye byfore haden. (270–72)

Wastoure's men wear their land (or its value) as their clothing; in contrast, Piers puts on his dirty clothes and his leggings and exchanges
a pilgrim's scrip for a seed container in order to work his land. In relation to the B- and C-texts of the poem, Piers's clothing fits into
Langland's lengthy preoccupation with clothing as a sign of inward

identity and, in Piers's specific case, with the reality of Incarnation since in those texts Christ jousts wearing Piers's armor. But now Piers appears as any English peasant on a cold day, preparing to sow wheat.

Langland's subtlety here is hard to overstate. He has done more than substitute Piers's agricultural stability for the restless "rowte" of Wastoure's affinity group. He has defined Piers in relation to the half-acre, to the *croft*, and created an image that had a potential national significance that neither Wynnere nor Wastoure, as spokesmen for particular economic philosophies, ever did. The author of *Wynnere and Wastoure* has clearly located his poem in England's landscape and economy; there are references to England, to English coats of arms, and to English money, and, near the end of the poem, a description of London's neighborhoods. He has also indicated the broad social implications of espousing either production or consumption as economic principles, relating both Wynnere and Wastoure to the effect each has on the social fabric and on the poor in particular.[19] While responding to descriptions and opinions prominent in *Wynnere*, Langland broadens the scope of his poem by at once shifting the focus away from landlords and toward laborers (whose "job" is production) and suggesting that the croft that Piers farms serves as an image for England, whose productivity depends on the acceptance of a philosophy of the common good as guaranteed by Truth. Langland did not invent the croft as a legal reality, nor did he first use the term metaphorically, but he employed language denoting agricultural space in ways that became eminently usable by those seeking images for quizzing or establishing a national identity.

The word *croft*, denoting "a piece of enclosed ground used for tillage or pasture," shows up early in English legal documents.[20] The word, with the same meaning, continued to be used well into the modern period, usually in relation to the small landholder or peasant tenant and frequently in wills or deeds where a specific piece of land was passed down or on. The croft's humble nature was expressed in the *South English Legendary* (ca. 1300) in the legend of Mary Magdalene, when the priest who makes Mary a dwelling realizes that she is nourished by angels: "He hadde wunder for that he saigh that the aungles comen ofte/ Aboute onderne eche daye, ase he stod in is crofte, / And hou huy beren the Maudeleyne an hei opon lofte, / And also hou huy broughten hire agein and setten hire adoun wel softe."[21] Later, in the fifteenth century, the word's association with possession is underlined when the devil in the Towneley Judgment pageant says, "Com to my crofte . . . All harlottys and horres . . . Welcom to me see!"[22] Bishops, of course, have sees, and devils crofts, but leave it to a devil to conflate the two. In the *Castle of Perseverance*, the devil boasts, "I clymbe fro þis croftc, with Mankynde, o, to syttyn on lofte." In the *The Book of the Vices and Virtues* (ca. 1450), rich men are said to "benymeþ here neiȝe-bores wiþ strengþe, londe or croft or hous or rente, and takeþ on þe riȝt side and on þe lefte syde; so þat no þyng may ouer-sterte hem."[23] These are references only to the anxieties and delusions of owner-ship, but the *Northern Homily Cycle* (ca.1350) uses the word to describe Mary's fecundity:

> Þat o greyne won al vr wele
> Whon greyne on grounde was sowe
> In Marie lond, þat Mylde croft
> Þer-in com Crist feire and soft
> Out of heuene, þe heiȝe loft,
> And greuh in grounde ful lowe.[24]

The author here draws on the same rhyme words, *croft, loft, soft*, used by the author of the life of Mary Magdalene, which, in turn, look forward to the inflated language of later devils who wish to abandon crofts for lofts. These are obvious (and easy) rhymes, but they also rest on the physical and tropological contrast between high and low that is at the heart of Christian thought, as well as central to Lang-land's use of agricultural space as a defining image. Thus Mary's land, her body, is the mild and welcoming field into which Christ fell from on high, growing in low ground so that humankind might be raised. By this point, Edward III was already joking about his intimate rela-tion to the Virgin and had established her as patroness of the Order of the Garter a few years before. The chain of association between Mary and England is hinted at by Edward and made much more ex-plicit in Ricardian culture: Mary's land, Mary's womb, or her dower, her *dos*, the fair isle enclosed by the sea. But Langland employs an-other word denoting enclosure, the croft, not the noble island, but the patch of ground tilled and watched over by Piers, who for a few lines in Passus 7 turns himself and his fellows to mutually productive labor on the half acre, which becomes an idealized picture of England as a discrete but common agricultural space.

I am here drawing a distinction between Langland's exploitation of the figure of the Plowman and his use of the croft as an image. That the two are related goes without saying. The literature of Middle English social complaint contained plowmen before Langland began to write, and he took what was a powerful figure linked to the language of social injustice or to the poetry of poverty and transformed it, over the course of the poem, into a figure for Christ.[25] Piers continued to have a long symbolic existence in late medieval and early modern culture, particularly in Lollard or reformist circles. Langland's handling of the croft, or the half acre, has its roots in an even older chronicle tradition, which embedded the meaning of England's identity in explorations of its insularity. But the island was, to some extent, noble space, as the orb in the Wilton Diptych microscopically manifests. The spaces belonging to laborers, periodically enclosed and then opened for common grazing, exist in a different register though they might well yield similar sorts of preoccupations.

This is not to read *Piers Plowman* as simply a social document but to pull one image from an early scene, an image in subtle contrast to those courts, monasteries, and castles that proliferate in earlier accounts of England's insular and sacred geography, that suggests a potential critique of those images used to articulate social order. However, lest he be accused of populism, Langland is careful to place the peasant in relation to the knight through the covenant each has sworn—the one to "swynk and swete," to labor "for þi love al my lif tyme," the other to protect church and layman from destructive forces. The social order is not questioned; rather, Piers underlines the bonds holding society in place. But his picture of that society in this section of the poem is a rural one that at once draws on the agricultural metaphors of the prophets and of Jesus' parables and is grounded in England's literal agricultural topography. Langland's image of the peasant croft was appropriated in suggestive and subtle ways by Chaucer and the author of *Mum and the Sothseggar* and passed on in the sixteenth- and seventeenth-century literature of the agricultural landscape that, enclosed but permeable, was used to signify or to question a national identity.

THE AGRICULTURAL LANDSCAPE
AND ENCLOSURE

In the *Canterbury Tales*, Chaucer depicts a number of peasant house-holds. Some are in varying states of internal disorder, such as those in the Miller's and the Reeve's tales; some, however, are not so much dis-ordered as threatened by figures who misuse their own power, such as the Summoner in the Friar's tale and Walter in the Clerk's. In the de-scriptions of both the widow's household and Griselda's, Chaucer em-phasizes their poverty and simple thriftiness. The widow's appears to be enclosed, since the Summoner "clappeth at the wydwes gate."[26] The account of Griselda's circumstances is fuller (*CT* 4: 197–203, 223–31): her father's house is in a village, within which poor folk keep their ani-mals and their lodgings. Griselda spins, keeps a few sheep, and has one field that is apart from the house; when she returns home each night, she brings cabbages or herbs for supper. As in the French translation but not Petrarch's account, Walter watches Griselda at her labors when he rides out hunting. Chaucer thus composes a scene that is faithful to his sources while also recalling the scene in *Piers Plowman* and Piers's advice to the knight standing beside him—to hunt in order to pro-tect Piers's croft—but Walter hunts for pleasure. Griselda seems to act out the advice encoded in Piers's son's name.[27] If we read the ac-count of Griselda and of the widow in terms of their *literal* circum-stances, the questions asked through both scenes concern civil and ec-clesiastical power as it touches the lives of the rural poor. Though such questions are compelling for Langland and Chaucer, it is in the Nun's Priest's tale that Chaucer fully and daringly exploits the potential la-tent in Langland's reference to Piers's croft.

Two of Chaucer's sources for the Nun's Priest's tale contain fairly detailed accounts of enclosed yards that would have been recognizable as crofts in England.[28] *Le Roman de Renart* describes the household of a very wealthy peasant, whose well-stocked house is close by the farm-yard, the whole property "enclosed with stout, pointed oak stakes reinforced with hawthorn bushes." Renart enters through a broken stake, though Chantecler proclaims the enclosure safe. Similarly in *Le Roman de Renart le Contrefait*, a wealthy peasant has enclosed his prop-erty with walls and hedges "because he feared for himself a great deal, lest someone should take his possessions or do him grief"; his rooster, Chantecler, feels himself safe because his lord is a rich man. Both D. W. Robertson and Larry Scanlon have pointed out the anti-fraternal satire of the Renart fables, where the smooth-talking fox/friar baffles and captures the foolish rooster/priest, who, lulled by his apparent safety, is easily flattered and almost brought to ruin.[29]

Chaucer alters the design in order to suggest a potential relationship between croft and nation. The tale begins, not with a wealthy, greedy peasant, but with a poor widow, a dairywoman, whose hall is sooty and whose diet is as simple as Griselda's. She has a cottage near a wood, in a valley, and "a yeerd . . . enclosed al aboute/ With stikkes, and a drye dych withoute" (7: 2847–48), in which she has her rooster, Chauntecleer. Chaucer's description of the rooster (7: 2850–64) has no counterpart in his sources. After praising his crowing, the Nun's Priest goes on:

> His coomb was redder than the fyn coral,
> And batailled as it were a castel wal;
> His byle was blak, and as the jeet it shoon;
> Lyk asure were his legges and his toon;
> His nayles whitter than the lylye flour,
> And lyk the burned gold was his colour. (*CT* 7: 2859–64)

With red comb, black shiny beak, azure legs and toes, white nails, and burnt gold color, Chauntecleer is the very image of a royal rooster ("Real he was, . . . Thus roial, as a prince is in his halle" [*CT* 7: 3176, 3184]), as splendid as any figure in the Wilton Diptych, as splendid as Richard himself sitting enthroned in his hall.[30] What we see is not a rooster but the icon of a rooster inserted into a barnyard fable and at a time when Richard began to adapt some of the Valois mannerisms of regality to his public appearances in his own hall.[31]

This poor widow's yard, hedged and ditched, containing a regal rooster, is not invulnerable to the likes of foxes; nor is the rooster impervious to flattery. The fox "brast / Into the yerd ther Chauntecleer the faire / Was wont, and eek his wyves, to repaire" (7: 3218–20). The courtly epithet and the verb *repaire* describe not chickens but courtiers and, like the apostrophe comparing the fox to Ganelon, Judas, and Sinon and the simile likening the upset of the hens when Chauntecleer is captured to women's cries when Troy, Carthage, or Rome burned (7: 3355–73), assimilate the barnyard disaster to national. The reference a few lines later comparing the chaos—bees out of the hive, geese honking, dogs barking, people shouting—to the noise during the Rising of 1381 serves to locate the analogies, not in the realm of mythic history, but in England's history, its own instance of discord and failure of authority.[32] Langland follows up the account of the half acre with its gradual dissolution because of greed, wasting, laziness, or chicanery. In B: 19 and C: 21, the half acre and its Plowman return but this time as an allegory wherein the Plowman sows the seed of charity with the help of the four Evangelists, who are the oxen hauling his plow. Chaucer maintains the careful connection between the widow's croft and the commonwealth, depicting a rooster who now recognizes the dangers of the courtly speech practiced by foxes and a henyard now safer, not because of its hedge, but because of its chastened prince.

The image here stands in subtle contrast to the tiny icon on the orb of the banner in the Wilton Diptych, the noble island with its castle surrounded by the sea, given to Mary and returned to the vested young king as his cure. The Nun's Priest provides something more complicated, a poor widow's holding, a *dos* poor, indeed, hedged and ditched, ruled by a rooster, permeable to foxes who speak with oiled phrases, restored through wit, provisionally guaranteed through experience. Langland's choice of the half acre, the croft, as a sign allowing him to think about nation or national order, is startling when juxtaposed to Edward's decision to found the Order of the Garter several years before. In exchange for the noble order, with its sumptuous chivalric ideals and furnishings, devoted to the Blessed Virgin, and focused on the king, Langland proffers the peasant's holding, whose need for knightly protection is explicit but which is not identified with or seen as an appendage to noble privilege. Langland then quickly assimilates that image (which stands as a corrective to tournament fields, battlefields, and aristocratic excess) to the spiritual demands of Will's quest for understanding and meaning. The A-text ends, apparently unfinished, with the assertion that none are further from right belief than clerks who know many books, and

> Ne none sonnere ysauid, ne saddere of consience,
> Þanne pore peple, as plouȝmen, and pastours of bestis,

Souteris & seweris; suche lewide iottis
Percen wiþ a *paternoster* þe paleis of heuene
Wiþoute penaunce at here partyng, into [þe] heiȝe blisse.
　　(A: 11.309–13)

Passus 12, added on to the A-text, as well as the rewritings of this
scene in the B- and C-texts of the poem point up the dangers in Will's
assumption that it is easier to get to heaven without learning and thus
blur the picture A provides of plowmen, shepherds, shoemakers, and
sewers piercing the palace of heaven with the Our Father.[33] In the
B- and C-texts of *Piers Plowman*, Langland allows the agricultural references to plowmen and shepherds to assume their full spiritual significance only after Will's apprehension of the Passion and its meaning
for earthly systems of order.[34] The half acre becomes a way of seeing
the Christian society, whose order acquires meaning from the seed that
Piers, the Plowman/Preacher, sows with the four Evangelists.

In taking a fable linked to ecclesiastical satire and focusing it on
regal authority, employing the homely image, the barnyard, as the
landscape for royal chastening, Chaucer seems to offer both a shrewd
reading of Langland's text(s) and a careful critique of the thinking
that inspired the Wilton Diptych, if not the diptych itself, which he
might well have seen. Chauntecleer may look like a king, but he lives
in a croft, and he stays there. At no point does Chaucer suggest we
should see the croft as belonging to the rooster or as a gift of his office,
though his folly jeopardizes its order. Chauntecleer's office takes meaning from the croft and its residents, not the other way around; he serves
his hens and the poor widow, as the coronation service for English
kings suggests. As a rooster, he must abide by the laws of nature; as
a king, by the laws of the land.

In *Mum and the Sothseggar*, the substitution of the croft for the
noble island as a suitable image for England is even more apparent.[35]
The poem belongs to the reign of Henry IV and describes the narrator's efforts to understand the conditions of a good society. Like *Piers
Plowman*, which it imitates, it describes a search, but this is a search
not for theological but moral and civil understanding. After much confusion about the merits of staying mum about wrong (and thus profit-
ing from his silence) or speaking the truth (and possibly jeopardizing
himself in the name of common profit), the narrator falls asleep. In his

dream the narrator moves first through an abundant landscape of laden fields, trees, and bushes, where hares play and hounds chase, where there are sheep and cows and their young, stallions, and an abundance of all sorts of deer—"Foure hunthrid on a herde yheedid ful faire, / Layen lowe in a launde along by the pale, / A swete sight for souvrayns, so me God helpe" (929–31). After the sight of such plenty, including the promise of good hunting, the narrator moves down into a valley, among hedges filled with nesting birds, then sights a "faire hous with halles and chambres, / A frankeleynis freholde" (945–46). Though the humble croft, the half acre, has disappeared, the Franklin's freehold has an enclosed garden ("the gladdest gardyn that gome ever had" [948]), into which the narrator goes. The poet uses this garden and its ancient, wise gardener, whose exposition on apiculture links the order of the bees to that of the state, as a figure for nation. The upper landscape, woods and fields filled with delights for ladies (905) and sovereigns, is anchored by the freehold, which contains the secret of the good society, wherein drones who waste the honey that nourishes the hive are identified and destroyed and the order and thrift of the wise king of the bees is maintained in a strictly hierarchical society "ygouverned/ Yn lowlynes and labour and in lawe eeke" (997–98). The gardener himself seems the personification of that law, for it is he who destroys the drones, he who maintains the king's order, and he who urges the narrator to seek out Truth, to write something that may "amende many men of thaire misdeedes" (1279). The old man thus links the picture of the common good, figured in an enclosed georgic space, to the art of making a book, copied and clasped, that lays out Truth for knights to copy and read (1286–87). The narrator then wakes and begins again his search in a world where many are mum and few are true. The freehold, which serves as an image for an idealized England, suggests how securely the enclosed and working garden has been embedded in the political imagination—not the ecclesiastical garden, but the peasant or the franklin or the gentry garden, maintained by discernment, by truth, by law.

The noble island certainly does not disappear as a national trope, but the croft and its analogues allow for new sets of questions about that island. In 1436 the author of the *Libelle of Englyshe Polycye*, in which Henry V is praised as a "master Mariner," describes the sea as a wall around England, guaranteeing its peace and prosperity, but that sea is also the highway of its commercial power and thus both a wall and a means of access.[36] Both the image and the epithet have obvious affinities with language associated with Edward III and employ the island as an extension of regal power and protection. If the king is master of the sea, he controls access to and egress from England. As "master Mariner," the king maintains England and, in fact, extends its power into France. On the other hand, both Chaucer and the author of *Mum* employ the croft or the enclosed agricultural space to explore the relationship between isolation, experience, the limitations of lordship, and the common good. The trope of the island garden, which Langland, Chaucer, and the author of *Mum* translate into humbler enclosures, is developed as a more explicit metaphor in the late fifteenth century when the picture of England as an island *of* gardens acquires another valence, nostalgia, which potentially aligns the terms of national topography with a rhetoric of loss and carries over into political and poetic treatments of landscape well beyond the scope of this chapter. Nostalgia for a lost ideal is built into England's historiography through Gildas's postlapsarian perspective, expressed through topographic description. In linking England to the lost Edenic garden, Gildas established a way of thinking about nation in relation to landscape and geography. Bede's more compensatory vision of rupture and reparation is less nostalgic than forward-looking.

ENCLOSURE'S LANDSCAPE OF LOSS

Fourteenth-century accounts of the effects of the pestilence sometimes describe England's landscape as altered by the disease of its people. Uncultivated fields, crumbling abbeys, famine, and empty cities and towns are used to mark the devastation.[37] The chroniclers acknowledge that the plague is universal, frequently describing its progress from the Middle East to England, but what they speak of is an unmaking of those elements by which England signified its insular identity, an invasion without any remedial effect. These are accounts of acute conditions and are less nostalgic than catastrophic, providing word pictures of specific events that are horrific because they rupture the patterns of life by which we reckon order. They do not necessarily intend to suggest a change in England's fundamental identity but an affront to it. The Statute of Laborers passed in 1351, following up the Ordinance of Laborers of 1349, was an attempt to deal with the immediate agricultural shortages of the Black Death by freezing wages at preplague levels.[38] Later, in 1376–77, the fiftieth year of Edward III's reign, the "Pardon in Time of Jubilee" was entered in the statutes. Its language addresses that perception of a national catastrophe— "considering the great Charges and Losses which his said People have had and suffered in Times past, as well by the Wars, as otherwise by the Pestilence of the People, Murrain of Beasts, and the Fruits of the Land commonly failed by Evil Years in Times past"—and proclaims a general pardon from 13 October to 1 January.[39]

More serious or far-reaching are those accounts of England's landscape that intentionally provide pictures of a present that has or threatens to have changed the very nature of its understanding of community and thus of law. Unlike twentieth-century nostalgia for the disappearance of the great house as a sign of the changes in England's post–World War I landscape and social structure, late medieval and early modern writers thought in terms of a primarily agricultural landscape whose enclosure was seen as damaging an ideal of communal cooperation. Theirs was no lament for the noble life but for the town or village supported by the husbandman, in other words, for an England of semienclosed spaces—crofts, villages, towns—that replicated the greater whole, the island garden. The discourse of insularity, its anxieties and dangers, that is fundamental to accounts of England the island garden is likewise central to accounts of England's internal landscape, both agricultural and urban.

England's landscape is completely man-made, its wastes tamed, fens drained, trees cut down, fields measured, hedgerows constructed.[40] Any late medieval nostalgia for a primordial world was as misplaced as is a contemporary lament for primordial hedgerows. Despite their intricacy and their benefit to birds and to the ecology of the fields, they are not originary. It is these hedgerows, the means by which land was enclosed for private use, that were the occasion for the complaints about enclosure that become more prominent from the fifteenth century on. Though there were tensions about enclosure as early as the thirteenth century and the process of enclosure happened very gradually and was not necessarily driven only by the greed of lords, the rhetoric in which these outcries was cast creates a picture of a vanished England of crofts and common fields where prosperity depended on a set of shared values, on a set of pictures of England dominated not by castles but by smallholders whose rights were upheld by the law personified in the sovereign. Though complaints about enclosure charge it with the destruction of village life and speak of it as a new and ominous challenge, scholarly studies suggest otherwise.[41] However, at stake was an idea of the landscape that stood for the identity of the realm and whose enclosure created pockets of isolation that altered the topography and hence the character of an island garden enclosed but permeable.

In sermons prepared for Parliament, John Russell, bishop of Lincoln and chancellor during the reign of Richard III, exploited the metaphors of topography in ways that suggest his familiarity with England's written history and his awareness of issues and language pertinent to social hierarchy at the time.[42] The first sermon was prepared for the parliament of Edward V, the second for that of Richard III. Both exist in draft and are preserved in the Cotton manuscript, Vitellius E.x. In the first, Russell takes as his text Isaiah 49:1: "Audite insulae, Et attendite populi de longe, Dominus ab utero vocavit me." He specifies that he intends these should be the words of the king, the young Edward V. He goes on to liken the islands to the temporal and spiritual Lords, the people from far away to the Commons, and the one who had been called "in my tendire age to be yowre kynge and soverayne" (xxxix). He then explains his use of metaphor by reference to cosmography:

> The cosmagraphers whyche have left to us in ther wrytynges the descripcion of the rounde worlde descendynge from above downeword principally to the habitable regions and navigable sees and flodes here benethe, have hade grete respecte unto the emergence and swellynge up of londes compassed abowt with waters, whose propre denominacion is to be called Isles. . . . yf there be any suerte or fermenesse here yn thys worlde, such as may be fownde oute of hevyn, hyt ys rathyr in the Isles and londes envirounde with water. . . . And therefor the noble persons of the worlde, whych some for the merites of ther auncesturs, some for ther owne vertues, bene endued whyth grete havours, possessions and Richesses, may more conveniently be resembled un to the ferme grounde that men see in Isle londes then the lower peuple . . . livynge by ther

casuelle labours, be not withowte cause likkened un to the un-
stabille and waverynge rennynge water. (xxxix–xl)

In likening nobles who stand out by virtue of pedigree or virtue
to islands, which are the "swelling up" of landmasses in the midst of
water, Russell implicitly identifies his own island with the nobility and
the "lower people" with the unstable sea constantly threatening the
land. Russell argues that islands must stabilize themselves against
the changing and potentially destructive sea, more explicitly warning
the nobles, "Who so herkenethe not uppon the commyn voyce . . . but
bydythe hys affayres and doyngcs in ymagination of hys owne ple-
saunce" has not learned the lesson of "drede" (xlii). In the latter part
of the sermon he abandons his topographic trope and becomes more
explicitly parliamentary, urging the lords (whom he compares to the
Roman senate) to good council and the commons to obedience and at-
tendance. Though Russell illustrates his initial metaphor by reference
to Roman writers and water-bound Italian cities, the island of which
he speaks is England, "remembryng what fluctuacion and changynge
amonges the nobles hath fallen in thys Reme, he may lyghtly see that
alle owre grownd ys sett with yn the see, alle subjecte to Ebbe and
flowe, to wyndes, blastes and stormes" (xli). Since that island *is* its
noble persons, laborers, as unstable as water, may rim and test it, but
they are not its signifiers. It is then imperative that nobles do not behave with the instability of "lower peuple." The island, set with noble
embellishments, must hold back the circling sea.

Russell makes further topographic allusions in two fragments,
drafts that were probably brought together in his speech for the opening Parliament of Richard III.[43] He employs a standard corporeal figure
for the political community, which is maintained in health by law:

There be alle wey ordeigned officers to oversee, and not to permit
any owner to abuse the possession of hys own thynge, *Ne civitas
defloretur ruinis*, lest that by the severalle slouthe and neglygence of
the land lordes, citees and townes schuld [fall to extreme decay]
and ruine. Iff thys lawe be not so well accepted yn thys londe as ly-
bertee, yt ys lyghte to se what ys growen therof, by the decay of
well nyghe alle the citees and borghows of the same. (l–li)[44]

He here addresses, not islands, which need to maintain stability, but landlords, who spoil what is in their trust. His primary image is the city, the town, as it defines England's topography. In what is now the second fragment of this sermon, Russell follows the above passage with an analogy between the woman in Luke 15 who has lost a coin whose worth Jesus compares to the Kingdom of Heaven. He says, "Owre woman that hathe loste oon of here x. besauntes ys *nostra res publica*, whyche ys ferre fallen from her perfeccion," suggesting how long it may be before "we can fynde agayne the auncenne prosperyte whyche semethe now loste" (lxiii).

In the first draft of this same sermon, Russell succeeds his analogy between the woman and the realm with a more explicitly moral statement about the state of the realm:

> Wolde God that owre peuple of Englond, where every manne nowe severally studethe to hys owen singular advayle, and to thaccomplysshynge of hys own perticuler affeccion, wold thenke uppon hys owne body, the comon and public body of the Realme. . . . And yet, be he never so gret, yff by hys doynge thys body fallethe yn decaye, as we see dayly hyt doothe by closures and enparkynge, by dryvynge a wey of tenauntes and lattyng downe of tenauntries. (li–lii)

Though in the next sentence he says that unlawful assemblies (which harm both the nobles and the people) are as deleterious as the decay that comes from enclosures, his focus is on the ways in which those who own land are causing its ruin by pursuing personal advantages and ignoring the common good, which ought to be protected by law. The fragments seem to indicate that Russell ended by calling Parliament's attention to the common good: "alle the termes and lymitees of owre thoughtes and affeccions we oughte to referre to oo singular poynt, that ys to sey, to the avauncynge of the comen wele. We be yn the place where thys schuld be tretyd. Thys tyme ys prefixed for the same entente" (lvi). The place is clearly Parliament; the time is that allotted for its deliberations.

The passages I have quoted from Russell's sermons suggest his learning and rhetorical polish, but they also indicate his sense that what is sacrosanct about the realm is not so much its piety, or its ecclesiastical foundations, but its political order and its "ancient" but now lost "prosperity." He speaks of a realm that used to be, with populous and prosperous cities and towns, and of a body politic wherein the doctrine of the commonweal underwrote the administration of the law, lamenting not a lost pastoral ideal but a communal one. What is more, his political or moral diagnosis of the state of the realm is topographic. The sermon prepared for Edward V's Parliament inscribes the noble isle on the gathering. The sermon he delivered before Richard III is less soothing, and he presents pictures not of castellated islands and dangerous seas but of a wasted and empty landscape, spoiled by the greed of those who enclose common land for their own profits and pleasures and create private islands. A few years later, in the fourth year of Henry VII (1488–89), Statute 19, the "Acte agaynst pullyng doun of Tounes," is even more graphic, sketching a picture of waste: where there used to be towns of two hundred, now there are a few shepherds; churches are destroyed and bodies buried there not prayed for.[45] The words describe a frayed and fragile social fabric, certainly not anything like "ancient prosperity" but rather a few shepherds guarding someone's private wealth. Both the sermons and the statute underline the dangers of insularity: if islands need to be mindful of greedy seas, landlords should take care for the commonweal lest England lose forever the coin representing her ancient identity.

In that same decade, the fifteenth-century antiquarian and churchman John Rous produced his *Historia Regum Angliae*.[46] Rous was an opponent of enclosures and had petitioned the Coventry Parliament of 1459, as well as later ones, against them.[47] The *Historia* contains three sections that concern enclosure. In the first (37–43), Rous presents a philosophical argument based on the idea of the common good that is necessary for a single body to function. He employs the corporal analogy, with much space given to the importance of the sovereign, to support the need to maintain the whole in concord and prosperity. Thus when villages disappear to enclosure, there is less agricultural productivity and more poverty because agricultural laborers lose their livelihoods. In his second section on enclosure (87–96), Rous focuses on the idea of law, which is designed to preserve the body politic and is subverted by those who enclose lands and destroy towns and thus communal life. He cites the biblical story of Ahab and Jezebel who seize the vineyard of Naboth and are punished for their greed, along with

examples from European history that illustrate the need for sovereigns to uphold the law for the good of all. In relation to England's
history, Rous praises King Alfred for his love of learning and his attention to the law. In the third section (112–37), Rous concentrates
on England, its history and its geography. He first raises the issue of
William the Conqueror's creation of the New Forest, which resulted
in the destruction of towns and churches (112), suggesting that the
deaths of the Conqueror's sons may have been instances of God's punishment for a violation of community. He moves to contemporary time,
insisting that the destruction of towns is a sign of the avarice infect-
ing "modern times," undergirding his remarks about the threat cupidity poses to a body politic with citations from Avicenna and Albert
the Great. He refers to Jesus' sorrow over the imminent destruction
of Jeruslem by Titus and Vespasian, along with the ruptures England
has suffered at the hands of Danes and the Normans (117).

Rous then begins to move into relatively new territory for a po-
lemicist, possibly even for a historian, by linking towns to a concept
of national memory. He does so, first, by saying that destroyers of
cities are decried by the prophets, quoting Isaiah, but that builders
of cities are remembered, naming Remus and Romulus, Constantine,
Brutus, Leir, Claudius, Coil, and Cyrus. After linking England's builders with those of the ancient and biblical world, Rous turns to his own
time, stating that builders of cities and founders of monasteries are
praised perpetually, are the subjects of books, and inhabit the imagi-
nations of their noble successors. Their tombs and memorials serve
as images of their names, which are blotted out when towns are destroyed. He returns to England's history, wherein the names of towns
have disappeared, and with them a portion of national memory. Rous
next does something with a good deal of historic value for our understanding of medieval England; he names the lost villages of his own
Warwickshire (122). This list is a valuable record and certainly a testament to his field studies, but it should also be seen as an elegy set
within a history, in which real villages are named; he intones words
that would otherwise be lost. The list recalls the past, its nostalgia for
an earlier England now gone, not an act of reclamation, but a reminder
of a landscape now destroyed. He continues by listing the numbers of
households belonging to each village, the churches, the rectories, all
lost not to invaders but to the desire for economic gain that erects

walls and hedgerows to hold in sheep and shut out people. By creating vast spaces for sheep, landlords have created waste spaces made newly dangerous because of wolves and other wild animals and of men who live outside the reach of law. He here raises the specter that looms large over the master narrative of England's history, waste, barbarity, the formlessness that towns and villages and ecclesiastical foundations transform into community and consciousness. However, he has created a record of actual destruction and consequent waste and has done so with the precision of a compiler of a fifteenth-century Domesday Book.[48] For Rous, the systems of topographic organization by which nations are reckoned are undone by enclosure, and it remains to enumerate the lost. Rous begins his history of England with the expulsion from Eden, and he returns his reader to the fallen world, but a world that owes its empty spaces not to a clash between Mordred's and Arthur's legendary forces but to sheep.

The language late medieval and early modern writers used to describe alterations in the nation's landscape identifies the nation with the town as a node of interdependencies, thus with a particular ideal of communal relation in which the guarantor of the town is the plowed field, testimony to the agricultural worker. This sentence could also be turned around to read, the language late medieval and early modern writers used to describe national identity was topographic or reflected an intense awareness of England's landscape as reflective of its history. The two cannot be separated, nor can that language be separated from its early medieval origins in a rhetoric that probed the relationship between enclosure and isolation. However, the advent of print culture broadened the scope of individual or regional critique and made available in legal books, treatises, ballads, and pamphlets what otherwise remained in manuscript, available only to the scholar or the antiquary. What is striking about these topographic accounts of identity is the degree to which each is designed to make a didactic point by creating an image for the reader. The written word becomes a mnemonic picture. For example, in 7 Henry VIII, in 1515, Statute 1, against the pulling down of towns, is essentially the same as Statute 19, made in the reign of Henry VII, in 1488/9. However, where the earlier statute creates a picture of the effects of enclosure as fracturing community by saying that churches are destroyed, services are withdrawn, and the bodies buried therein not prayed for, the later statute describes a much

more arresting and elegiac picture. It begins by noting that the shift
from tillage to pastureland has resulted in the destruction of homes
and towns, which, in turn, has brought an increase of idleness:

> for where in some oon towne CC psons men and women and
> childern and their auncestours oute of tyme of mynde were dayly
> occupied and lyved by sowyng of corne and greynes bredyng of
> catell and other encrease necessarye for manys susten'nce, and
> now the seid psons and their pgnyes be mynysshed and decreasyd,
> whereby the husbandry which is the greatyst commodite of this
> realme for susten'nce of man ys greatly decayed, churches de-
> strued, the s[er]vyce of God withdrawen, Chrysten people their
> buryed, nott prayed for, the Patrons and Curate wronged, Cities
> Markett Townes brought to greate ruyne and decaie, necessaries
> for mannys susten'nce made scarse and dere, the people sore
> mynysshed in the realme, whereby the poure & defence therof ys
> febled and enpayrid, to the high dyspleasure of God and agenst his
> lawes and to the subv[er]syon of the cōmon weale of this realme
> and desolacion of the same.[49]

The phrasing here deliberately expands on the sketch provided
by the earlier statute, which stated that in some towns where there
were two hundred persons, now there are two or three herdsmen.
However, in 1515 the honest labor of the village community is made
visually available and is anchored to past practice—not simply two
hundred persons, but men, women, children, and ancestors, *oute of tyme
of mynde*, were daily occupied with specific agrarian tasks. It is that
picture of communal and agrarian labor that is lamented as having
disappeared from England's countryside, a communal labor that maintained churches, market towns, and prayers for the dead and a labor
that is linked to an ancient idea of the commonweal, semienclosed but
not isolated.

Later discussions of enclosure employ pictures of a landscape that
serves as a trope for a broader set of issues related to profit, which, in
turn, is linked to the ideal of the common profit or to national identity. For example, the early-sixteenth-century lyric, "Gode Spede the
Plough," opens with a scene of rural labor:

As I me walked over feldis wide
When men began to ere and to sowe,
I behelde husbondys howe faste they hide,
With their bestis and plowes all on a rowe.
I stode and behelde the bestis well drawe
To ere the londe that was so tough;
Than to an husbond I sed this sawe,
"I pray to God, spede wele the plough."[50]

The narrator creates a panoramic view of England, consisting
of wide fields that need sowing and husbandmen lined up with their
plows. The husbandmen go on to describe how hard pressed they are
to survive in the face of the king's purveyors, the greedy orders of the
church, and the taxmen. The poem achieves its satire by locating national identity in the fields, in the land plowed and planted by husbandmen and overharvested by those who work against the common good.
The emphasis here is on work and work on the land, not on grazing
sheep on land described as fields meant for cultivation.

The sheep and their enclosed fields were used as signs of a nation
in which landlords chose an isolation or insularity that threatened to
return England to an ancient barbarity. In book I of the *Utopia*, England's sheep are famously charged with cannibalism:

> your shepe that were wont to be so meke and tame, & so smal eat-
> ers, now, as I heare saye, be become so great deuowerers and so
> wylde, that they eate up, and swallow downe the very men them
> selfes. They consume, destroye, & deuoure whole fieldes, howses,
> and cities.[51]

The ferocious sheep are, of course, agents of the rapaciousness of
landlords who "inclose al into pastures: thei throw doune houses:
they plucke downe townes, and leaue nothing standynge, but only the
churche to to [*sic*] be made a shepehowse" (15).[52] As More and Robynson, his translator, well knew, the church was a sheep house, but
not for the devouring kind. These same charges, whereby cannibal
sheep herald incipient barbarism in England, show up in later ballads,
epigrams, and petitions, some of which cite More for his views.[53] The

commonwealth is described as decayed, as captive to profit, because land that was rightfully open has been closed, or enclosed.

In 1523 John Fitzherbert, a wealthy landowner, published his *Boke of Surueyinge*, rooting his argument for agrarian profitability, which included carefully superintended enclosure, in a topographic picture that has reference to earlier images of nation but at the same time provides a new image meant to associate a landscape of private enclosures with the common profit.[54] In the "Prologue of the author," he begins by admitting that society has degrees, that some have great possessions and great wealth, but that out of his love for the farmers and tenants he has written a book, a sequel to his *Book of Husbandry*, that will allow them to "profitably encrease and sustayne their pore hous hold." He then notes that the wealth of great landowners comes from their rents and from the profits from their manors; for that reason, both landowners and landholders and tenants need careful surveys, all land "bounded and valued in euery parte," documents specifying these boundaries, the parcels of each freeholder and tenant, along with what "rentes, customes, and seruice" the landowner "ought to haue of them." What follows is a meticulous blueprint for the measuring and valuation of different types of land found on an estate: meadow, pasture, park, wood, moor, heath, water, and so on. Fitzherbert also offers advice on the amendment of the different types of land and on the building of mills, each recommendation directed to the large landowner and his increased profit. However, in the final chapters of the book he turns to the subject of enclosure and its benefits to the smallholder.

He speaks of individual profit as necessary to common profit. Thus the man with many cattle will benefit more from common grazing ground than the man with three. If a smallholding is enclosed, it can be manured and "amended" far better than common ground. Land properly surveyed and enclosed is worth far more than open ground. He answers those who object to enclosure because it creates empty waste and dangerous lanes by arguing for widening and maintenance of the "kinges hyeway" (lv) and the creation of good lanes to closes. For Fitzherbert, the *close*, the enclosed agricultural space, is the most desirable, allowing tenants to consolidate their holdings by exchanging the many parcels they now have for one. What ensues is a picture of England's agrarian landscape wherein private profit has become a public good:

tenauntes shulde exchaunge their landes one with another & the
sayd exchaunge to stande and endure forcuer. For doute them nat
but they knowe it beste, and euery tenaunt for his owne aduaun-
tage wyll do it indifferently and the curate of the same parysshe
for his parte. and euery lordes bayly to be indyfferent to se these
closes lotted and assigned to euery mannes case so that euery man
may haue one lytell crofte or close next to his owne house if it
maye be thoughe he haue no lande of his owne. (lv)

Fitzherbert follows this idyllic vision of each man creating his
own close next to his house with advice to landlords that they have
leases drawn up that last not longer than three generations, promising
that the labor of surveying and rearranging land and drawing up new
legal agreements will be "light where winnyng foloweth" (lvi). Almost
two centuries later, Wynnere wins the argument, and profit triumphs,
at least in this book, as the sign of the happy nation. Langland's brief
vision of Piers and his neighbors working the half acre in harmony
has become one of Piers and his neighbors dividing up land for individual profit and settling down in the hope of "winning." Fitzherbert's
practical set of recommendations, which belongs in the category of
handbooks of estate management, proceeds from an acknowledgment
of self-interest not as a divisive but as a cohesive force in communities.
If educated in the benefits of certain practices like surveying and land
management and improvement, men will act "indifferently" for their
own advantage, and the private enclosures, whose leases are entered
in the bailiff's book, though transforming the landscape, nonetheless
maintain the common good.

The model of the commonweal as characterized by a particular
type of landscape remained a feature of sixteenth-century political
rhetoric. In the anonymous pamphlet *Certayne causes gathered together
wherein shewed the decaye of England* (1552), the author squarely
places the blame on sheep, on the amount of land turned over to pasturage:

The more shepe, the dearer is the woll.
The more shepe, the dearer is the motton.
The more shepe, the dearer is the beffe.
The more shepe, the dearer is the corne.

The more shepe, the skanter is the whit meate.
The more shepe, the fewer egges for a peny.[55]

The complaint is local, aimed at landlords in Oxfordshire, Bucking-hamshire, and Northamptonshire, and provides a picture of those shires as without the plows "vsed, occupied and mainteyned . . . as was in Kynge Henry the Seuenth tyme" (98). According to the author, each plow served six households, and now those "twelve score" persons be-longing to those households are without sustenance. He multiplies the social dislocation caused by the change in the agricultural landscape, asking the king "that there might be in euery shyre & hundred as many plows" as in the time of Henry VII (100). He, too, raises the issue of vanished towns:

> this Realme doeth decaye by thys meanes: It is to vnderstande and knowen, that there is in England, townes and villages to the nomber of fifty thousand & vpward, & for euery towne and vyllage,—take them one with an other throughout all,—there is one plowe decayed sens the fyrste yeare of the raigne of kynge Henry the Seuenth. (101)

The plow, the symbol of community, is likewise the symbol of the nation's prosperity. Now, rootless people "goeth about in England from dore to dore, and axe theyr almose for Goddes sake" (102). Lacking money, some steal and are hanged, "and thus the Realme doeth decay" (102). While the author does not have the dispassionate and practical tone of Fitzherbert, he, too, is anxious to provide documentation for his argument, which concerns the nation's prosperity, identity, and topography.

The author of the pamphlet offers one side of an argument about national prosperity, or the lack thereof, that is presented as a debate between a merchant, a knight, a husbandman, and a doctor by Thomas Smith in *A Discourse of the Common Weal of this Realm of England*.[56] The same notes are sounded about England—the decay of towns, high-ways, and bridges, the dearth of merchandise, and the cost of living. Not unexpectedly, the Husbandman says that the sheep are the cause of the mischief (20), arguing that the land was healthier when there were oxen, cattle, pigs, geese, and capons, as well as butter, eggs, bread, corn, and malt, in other words, when there were households rather than agribusinesses. The doctor emerges as the real analyst, recommending a hard look at price controls and market conditions, or taking a close look not at the land but at the economy and understanding how husbandry might become more profitable, in which case it will no longer be feasible to turn all to pasturage. The doctor, of course, is the voice of the future, and the knight and husbandman speak from traditional positions. Like Fitzherbert, Smith accepts the good inherent in the concept of profit and offers ideas that underline a theory of enlightened self-interest: men will do what profits them; so goes the realm.

A similar preoccupation with landscape and community is apparent in Robert Aske's defense of the monasteries when in April 1537 he was examined about his role in the Pilgrimage of Grace of late autumn, 1536.[57] His account is a description of the northern landscape—Yorkshire, Lancashire, Kendall, Westmoreland—whose "montaignes & desert places, wher the & peple be rud of condyccions & not well taught the law of God" (561), were civilized by the abbeys. Lacking them, the people lack the divine service and the sacraments, as well as the hospitality offered by the monks. Now, the profits of those places go out of the "contrey" to the king; what were local communities are now decayed. He ends with another consideration, the desecration of the landscape caused by the Dissolution:

> Also the abbeys was on of the bewties of this realme to al men & strangers passing threw the same; also al gentilmen much socored in ther nedes with money, ther yong sons ther socored, & in nonries ther doughters brought vp in vertuee; & also ther euidenses & mony left to the vsses of infantes in abbeys handes, alwas sure ther; & such abbeys as wer ner the danger of see bankes, great mayntenors of see wals & dykes, mayntenours & bilders of briges & heghwais, such other thinges for the comyn welth. (562)[58]

Aske describes the realm; its abbeys are features of its topography. His account of the effect of the monks on the north is not unlike those of medieval monastic historians, such as William of Newburgh, who describe monastic foundations, particularly those of the Cistercians, as taming the waste. Aske serves as an early witness to the visual appeal of these foundations, remarks noticeably absent from any of the letters passing between Thomas Cromwell and his henchmen as they recount the dismantling of the abbeys.[59] (Later, Donne, too, though no longer Roman Catholic, marked the Dissolution as taking beauty from the landscape: "All former comelynesse / Fledd in a minute when the Soule was gone / And having lost that beauty would have none / So fell our Monasteryes in an instant growne / Not to lesse houses, but to heapes of stone.")[60] Aske's remarks about beauty are woven into a picture of landscape as community, or as a particular idea of community. Thus, for him, the abbeys nourished those who lived in their vicinity and *maintained* the land against the sea, built bridges and highways, created the structures that allow for a commonwealth.

Aske's assertions about the communal value of the abbeys were echoed a little over ten years later, in 1548, in the "Bill on Decay of Tillage" presented to Edward VI. The bill begins by recalling the "disordre, self loue and pryvat profytt being vnyuersally growen in all the membres of the bodie of the Realme" that has resulted in the decay and diminishment of that body.[61] It thanks the king for inquiring into the plight of cities, begging him to consider "the destruction and desolacion of the Townshippes and villages in the countreie" (xlvi), as well as the scarcity and dearth of commodities. The bill accuses the nobility of forgetting they are shepherds to the people, rather than "grasiers" and "shepemasters," tearing down towns and villages and houses of husbandry in order to convert tillage into pasture. As though the spirit of Bishop Russell were presiding over this Parliament almost a century after his warning to mountains not to forget the seas that surround them, nor England to lose sight of its ancient heritage, the authors of the bill warn of the dangers of insularity or isolation. However, they also remind the king of his father's statute wherein "the dissolucion & suppression of Monasteries, priouryes and religious houses of monkes, Chanons an fryers, of the yerelye value of cc li and vnder, it was emong other thinges enacted and ordeyned and establisshed by thauctorite of the same parliament," that all who were granted those lands

> shulde be bounden by thauctorite of that acte . . . to kepe or cause to be kepte an honest contynuall house & housholde in the same site or precyncte and occupie yerelie asmoche of the same de-

> measnes in plowing and tillage . . . which hathe ben comenly vsed
> and kepte in tillage by the governours abbottes or priours of the
> same houses monasteries or priouries or by their farmours . . .
> within the tyme of twentie yeres next before the making of that
> acte. (xlix)

The bill does not replay the Pilgrimage of Grace and ask for these estates to be dissolved; instead, it backs the crown and demands reparation to the king according to a certain sum. However, its authors draw
a line connecting the decay of the agricultural landscape, the consequent decay of the realm, and the redistribution of land in the process
of the Dissolution that has resulted in visible alteration to England's
appearance.[62]

Two texts printed during the reign of Elizabeth are particularly
important to this discourse, Michael Sherbrook's *The Fall of Religious
Houses* (ca. 1590) and Francis Trigge's *An Apologie or Defence of Our
Dayes* (1589).[63] Both works echo arguments from the early 1530s concerning the value of monasteries that swirled around Cardinal Woolsey's suppression of twenty-nine houses in order to fund his new college at Oxford, including fears that abbeys would be converted into
cathedral churches. As Greg Walker notes in his reading of the early
Tudor interlude *Godly Queene Hester,* where the Jews stand in for the
religious orders in that they are described as going on pilgrimage,
dispensing hospitality to the poor, and praying for the community,
the play "provides a carefully thought-out apology for monasticism
based upon the social utility of the monastic houses."[64] Sherbrook
(1535–1610) was not a Catholic but an unobjectionable Elizabethan
Anglican priest, for forty-three years rector of Wickersley, about five
miles west of Roche Abbey in Yorkshire. His *Falle of Religious Houses*
is a strong defense of the goods afforded by these houses, as well as
a critique of the social evils caused by their dissolution. In addition
to offering a virtual view of the dismantling of Roche Abbey in which
his own uncle played a part, Sherbrook praises the monasteries for
their relief of the poor. But they offered a tempting purse for the king
(107), and, once dissolved, were dismantled by those who had formerly
enjoyed their benefits but who, like their neighbors, took away doors
and stones, locks and shackles for their own houses (123). Sherbrook
characterizes the world without the abbeys in terms of high rents,

enclosed fields, dearth, high prices, poverty, beggars, and "untempera-
ture of the weather" (128–30).

Francis Trigge's *An Apologie or Defence of Our Dayes* might well
be a point-by-point rebuttal of Sherbrook. Since Sherbrook did not
publish his treatise, however, we can assume that both men are responding to a conversation about the effects of dissolution on the nation, effects also echoed in one recusant text published in Antwerp in
1596 that says that in England "the heate of Charitie [is] exiled" and
"the fluds of almes and hospitalitie . . . are frosen with imputative Ius-
tice" and the "churches are hoary white without Image, Taper, Alter,
priest, sacrifyce, piety or deuotion."[65] This "reformed" England freezes
in a sort of nuclear winter. Trigge, also an Anglican priest and from
Lincolnshire, repeats the list of social ills commonly linked to the Dissolution, going on to describe the age and barrenness of the present
world, a time of great "dear-ness" when prices are high, food scarce,
and the world worn like an old man's garment, "chaunged suddenly
from their olde glorie, fruitfulnesse, and fertilitie" (8). He says that "it
pitieth many" to see the ruins of the abbeys, admitting the violence
that created those ruins, but likening them to the ruins of Sodom or
the errant Jerusalem. He notes that many, especially women, lament
the bare walls in churches, which are now without "their golden Images . . . their sweet frankinsence . . . their gilded chalices . . . & be-
wayle of this spoyling and laying waste of the Church" (24). To balance waste, Trigge offers the living word that now enlivens churches,
the injunction that those who mourn are like Israel, lamenting the lost
goods of their Egyptian captivity.

Complaints for a lost England that are expressed as complaints for
its altered agrarian landscape, which begin in the late fifteenth century
and continue well into the eighteenth and nineteenth centuries, center on the ideals of community as goods that ameliorate the insular
impulses of the private self. The waste perceived to threaten England is
used as a sign of lost community, a community that is, in turn, the expression of a concept of the common good. Early modern complaints
about land enclosure echo the language of medieval complaints, and
early modern reactions to the Dissolution likewise evoke the specter
of waste as a way of describing the dislocation of a nation recalled as
a community lost to similar impulses that enclosed common ground.
The conflicts given expression in such complaints are expressed in a

language of national identity whereby England is the island garden and therefore vulnerable to those forces that destroy or impinge on garden spaces. That language is also apparent in the *Second Shepherds' Play* in the Towneley manuscript. The manuscript has been identified as Marian, most likely a compilation of plays that were written earlier from Yorkshire, Lancashire, and Westmoreland, a rich area for monasteries, churches, and households and consequently for actors, minstrels, and other traveling entertainers.[66] Such a manuscript belonging to one northern recusant family evidences the continued vitality of "medieval" systems of thought and concerns.[67] The landscape adumbrated in the *Second Shepherds' Play* resonates with Aske's description of northwestern England as wild and lonely. Both of the Towneley shepherds' plays make reference to the quarrels prompted by extensive sheep farming.[68] In the first play, two shepherds argue about grazing rights. The second play is more explicit about the source of social conflict. Coll, the first shepherd, opens the play with a complaint about the conditions of contemporary life; not only is the weather bad, but "we sely husbandys" (p. 127, l. 14) are poor because "the tylthe of oure landys / Lyys falow as the floore"(p. 127, ll. 20−21). He elaborates on this shift from husbandman to shepherd, saying that the bailiffs or estate managers "cause the ploghe tary; / That, men say, is for the best— / We find it contrary. / Thus ar husbandys opprest"(p. 127, ll. 30−33).[69] Given these difficulties, the burdens of taxation and purveyance by which the king requisitioned provisions, the husbandman, whose plow is stationary, can only work as a herdsman. Coll's words do more than underline the economic difficulties he feels; they suggest his loneliness, his sense that he has no control over his immediate environment. His perception that he lacks agency will change during the course of the play, a change made visible in the shepherds' decision to offer mercy to the sheep thief, Mak, their willingness to go and see the newborn child, their newfound ability to speak graciously and lovingly around the manger. However, the opening scene of the play presents pre-Nativity darkness in terms that link that darkness to a landscape where plows sit still. But the playwright goes beyond simple description of a plowless landscape; in the pre-Nativity scenes of the discordant community and inhospitable environment that the shepherds perceive around them and that they replicate in their own fractured relationships, he dramatizes the wasteland. What is broken

down (and only momentarily) by the Nativity and by their willingness to see it and to return joyously from their visit, is the isolation or
insularity with which the wasteland is affiliated. Community is temporarily achieved, first, by merciful adjudication, the agreement among
the shepherds that they will toss Mak in a blanket rather than offer
him up for hanging for stealing their sheep, and, second, by the grace
that becomes available to them with the angels' song. Their transformation is spiritual, not social, but the playwright's exploitation of the
conditions of agrarian tension in the late medieval and/or early modern period relates the wasteland, which is the result of new agricultural
policies, to the barbarism cultivation was intended to transform. The
plays are not "about" these policies, nor do they offer any pragmatic
or lasting solutions to poverty, thievery, or displacement, but they do
present pictures of a world whose "wastelands" call for restoration.
Moreover, the author draws on a language that resonates with England's language of self-description and especially with its fears for the
state of the island garden. That that language was clearly relevant for a
post-Dissolution reader or audience suggests ways in which fears for
community were expressed through descriptions of a landscape turned
to waste and ruin by greed or violence.

THE ISLAND REFIGURED

The language of horticulture translated easily into that of statecraft,
particularly in the sixteenth century when those monastic gardens
and enclosures that had earlier helped to define the geography of
England were opened and sold to a rising nobility. Carried over from
medieval horticultural tropes, that early modern political rhetoric reflects a similar (and sometimes conflicting) set of interests in insularity and in law as they help to provide focus for a conception of the
identity of the realm. This rhetoric falls roughly into two categories,
husbandry and aristocratic landscape architecture.[70] Both are employed
by Shakespeare in *Richard II*, and both are predicated on a recognition of loss that is attached to the geography of England from the
late Middle Ages on and becomes even more pointed with the Dissolution.[71] For example, John Bale's epistle to the reader that prefaces
John Leland's *Laboryouse Journey* cites Gildas and goes on to lament

England's fall from learning and hence civilization, saying "neyther the Brytaynes under the Romanes & Saxons, nor yet the Englyshe people under the Danes and Normanes, had euer suche damage of their lerned monuments, as we haue seane in our time."[72] Bale speaks of lost books, the histories that are monuments to the past. Less than a century later Gervase Markham notes, "Although . . . the nature of this worst part of this last age hath converted all things to such wildnesse that whatsoever is truely good is now esteemed most vitious, learning being derided, fortitude drawne into so many definitions that it consisteth in meere words onely, and although nothing is happy or prosperous, but meere fashion & ostentation, a tedious fustian tale at a great man's table." He then defines a husbandman as "a good man," "turning sterrilitie and barrainenesse into fruitfulnesse and increase, whereby all common wealths are maintained," giving liberty to all vocations, "Arts, misteries and trades."[73] If this were the twelfth century, Markham might be introducing the Cistercians, those good husbandmen who turned waste and wildness into order and plenty, as Langland's plowman would attempt to create an image of national order from a half acre and Hugh Latimer's plowmen/preachers were urged to till the waiting soil of barren hearts.[74]

That same sense of loss and need for reparation invigorated the group around the reformer Samuel Hartlib in the mid-seventeenth century, which included Ralph Austen, Cressy Dimock, and John Beale, all of whom studied agriculture as an "experimental science to be disseminated for the public good."[75] Ralph Austen in *A Treatise of Fruit Trees* (1653) drew on the trope *anglia hortus*, what Andrew McRae has described as the new agricultural rhetoric of improvement and profit, in his efforts to promote the planting of fruit trees:

> An eminent person once said of this Nation, that it is a very Garden of delights, and a Well that cannot be exhausted: What then would it be, did it abound with goodly Fruit-trees, & other Profits, where now are barren Wastes: Might it not then be called another Canaan, flowing with Milke and hony, of which it is recorded that there were Fruit-trees in abundance. (Neh. 9.25)[76]

Austen does not link the dearth of fruit trees to the Dissolution, through which the monks' horticultural knowledge was lost, but rather emphasizes the benefits to the "commonwealth" and to the poor that enclosed orchards would provide.

But before Markham and Austen, there was Thomas Tusser, whose *Five Hundred Points of Good Husbandry* defined the market for husbandry books for at least fifty years after its first publication as *A Hundreth Good Pointes of Husbandrie* in 1557.[77] Tusser, himself not a very successful farmer, turned agricultural advice into doggerel verse, packaged the whole into a small, easily hand-held volume ostensibly directed at every husbandman and housewife, and provided a pocket book for a nation apparently in need of advice. He makes no apology for the rudeness of the verse in his "Preface to the buier of this booke": "What looke ye, I pray you shew what?/ Termes painted with Rhetorike fine?/ Good husbandrie seeketh not that, / Nor ist anie meaning of mine."[78] Tusser here positions himself squarely in the literary marketplace, averring his artlessness but also, by addressing not the reader but the buyer, signifying his awareness that writing about husbandry has as its end profits, just as the farmer expects to profit from his labor. In the many short poems that make up the *Five Hundred Pointes*, Tusser espouses the virtues of thrift and hard work, describes the annual cycle of a farmer's life and diet and the agricultural labors that accompany each month, provides rich lists of plants to be sown and cultivated at the proper times, and ends with verses of a more general nature. He recommends enclosure, making many of the same points Fitzherbert makes in the *Boke of Surveying*, warns about envious neighbors and slanderous tongues, presents a debate between two bachelors about "wiving and thriving," offers advice to the "housewife," and ends with one poem cataloging his own religious beliefs and another narrating his life. As McRae has noted, Tusser deserves more attention, not because he was a good poet, but because the *Five Hundred Pointes* is intended to offer images of good husbandry and housewifery that resonate with an ideal of virtuous profit.[79] Tusser, like the fourteenth-century Wynnere, advises thrift, but, like Wastoure, he links winning to a concept of community.

That concept, allied to agriculture as remedial, also underlies what is described as the first of the "great house poems," "To Penshurst," by Ben Jonson.[80] Though written in praise of the Sidney family estate, Jonson's praise, which is also a critique of the new ostentation, follows a pattern established by Tusser, who wrote for the smallholder.

Where Tusser begins by telling the buyer that he will not find rhetorical colors in this book, Jonson begins by asserting another variety
of simplicity, "Thou art not, Penshurst, built to envious show,"[81] asserting its ancient integrity and, what is more, its "better marks, of
soil, of air, / Of wood, of water" (7–8). Where Tusser describes husbandry, praises thrift, and offers a calendar of the months, beginning
with September, when holdings were newly leased, Jonson describes
the health and bounty of the grounds of the estate, the game abounding, and the gardens, which yield a variety of fruits "each in his time"
(42), embedding the pentimento of an agricultural calendar in his description. Near the end of the poem, we move into the house itself,
which is presided over, not by a country housewife, but by Lady Sidney,
who is described in terms remarkably similar to Tusser's good housewife. Tusser's fulsome advice to attend to all duties of the household—
brewing, baking, candle making, the needs of the laborers, the man-
ners of servants, the instruction of the children, the comfort of her
husband—is neatly epitomized by Jonson in his praise of Lady Sidney for her sumptuous welcome of King James:

> And what praise was heaped
> On thy good lady, then! Who, therein reaped
> The just reward of her high huswifery;
> To have her linen, plate, and all things nigh,
> When she was far; and not a room, but dressed
> As if it had expected such a guest! (83–88)

Clearly, a sluttish housewife would not have fresh linens ready, her silver polished, and each room freshly prepared. The subsequent praise
for her married chastity, her well-taught children, and her pious home
link her to a long line of virtuous women, beginning with Proverbs 31,
but more immediately to Tusser's "huswife," who keeps her home in
thrift, readiness, and submissive relation.

The concept of hierarchical order fundamental to both works reflects an idealized picture of England, the island paradise, as at once
enclosed and permeable. Tusser locates himself in relation to God
and to his patrons; Jonson locates each member of the extended Sidney family in relation to another—tenants to landlords, children to
parents, wife to husband, family to king, and all to God. Like Tusser's

smallholding, Penshurst is enclosed. However, Jonson uses its walls to suggest relation, not exclusion. He asserts of Penshurst that fruit that "every child may reach" hangs upon its walls, walls that are "reared with no man's ruin, no man's groan," and provide not a barrier but a point of entry for all, "the farmer, and the clown" (ll. 44, 46, 48). Set apart and within its land, maintained by its owner, who is its steward, who is, in turn, placed in relation to his king and his God, "To Penshurst," reminds its readers, including a royal reader, of the ideals undergirding the island garden of England in an age of excess where houses are built for show and walls are signs of exclusion, envy, and hatred. The abundance that Jonson describes Penshurst as boasting evokes earlier public tributes to Richard II and Elizabeth I, whose accessions to the throne were heralded with sprouting trees and gushing fountains and, indeed, were described as producing green leaves and wine where there had been only waste.[82] The garden thus stood as a sign of privilege or special favor, a space at once private and bound within a network of communal concerns. Thomas More's wife, Dame Alice, warned him when he was in the Tower that he would lose his garden, one of the eight magnificent gardens along the Thames that bespoke the social position of their owners, a garden in which he had walked and talked intimately with Henry in happier times.[83] Such spaces do not demand agrarian improvement in the name of profit but stand as tokens of the bonds of hierarchical ordering. In Book I of the 1587 edition of *Holinshed's Chronicles*, William Harrison notes what is a shift in approaches to the common good by noting a change in the use of the land: for the landlords now have the "commoditie and gaine" of the "large commons, laid out heretofore by the lords of the soiles for the benefit of such poore, as inhabit within the compasse of their manors."[84] By assimilating Penshurst to the smallholding and by stressing its ordered inclusiveness, Jonson remakes privilege as community because, though insular, it does not privilege isolation.

Jonson, with his erudition and his outsider social status, was able both to observe his world and to observe it in relation to other composed worlds. In "To Penshurst" he creates a poem that at once praises the Sidney family, observes the social vulgarities of his own age in relation to the harmonies of a past, and draws on the contemporary language of agriculture to write a stately poem that evokes classical estate poetry by way of eloquently identifying Penshurst as a type of ideal England. His aims are quite different from Aemelia Lanyer's "Description of Cooke-ham" (1611), another poem addressed to a country house.[85] Lanyer gives her account of Cookham through a first-person narrator whose subjective response to place constitutes one of the poem's subjects. Her description of the beauty and the friendship she enjoyed there is placed in perspective from the opening lines, in which she says her farewell to the Countess of Cumberland, its mistress. Cookham is also the site of Lanyers' religious conversion, so she describes the grounds and the house as a place of even greater personal and historical significance, enlivened by the Countess and the truth manifested through her. Lanyer thus handles the theme of patronage in a way very different from Jonson, who uses it to assert his independent vision of the necessary interdependence of the community that is England. Implicit in Jonson's praise for the Sidneys is the unspoken warning that to enclose Penshurst as a place of private pleasure is to alter its fundamental identity as a little England.

The suggestion that the hallowed examples of sixteenth- and seventeenth-century pastoral ought to be thought about in relation to the polysemous topographic language that was used to describe England is not meant to sever English pastoral from its classical roots but to add another layer to a rich set of associations. Lanyer, by implying that Cookham is England and the Holy Land and the garden of delights, allows it to reside within a range of interlinked meanings. Similarly, the author of the Towneley *Second Shepherds' Play* places Horbery Shrogs and Bethlehem within hailing distance of one another, just as English shepherds in poems like *The Shepheardes Calender* and "Lycidas" inhabit both a classical and an English landscape.[86] However, Jonson employs landscape as a *topos* in a way that evokes Tusser, which, in turn, speaks to the issues and controversies of national identity embedded in agrarian treatises. That Jonson intended "To Penshurst" to praise a type of community whose hierarchical ordering at once privileged those at its upper reaches and demanded their active participation in the quotidian *and* that his intention was fathomed by at least one sharp reader is clear from the opening stanza of "The Garden," in which Andrew Marvell's speaker begins where "Penshurst" left off:

> How vainly men themselves amaze
> To win the palm, the oak, or bays;
> And their uncessant labours see
> Crowned from some single herb or tree
> Whose short and narrow vergèd shade
> Does prudently their toils upbraid.[87]

Marvell's speaker's language here is deliberately provocative: *vainly*, *uncessant*, and *narrow* undercut *win*, *labours*, and *crowned*, words describing the virtues and rewards of the active life of civic virtue. Moreover, by suggesting that men amaze themselves by pursuing the honors for military, civic, and poetic distinction, the speaker transfers a garden's maze to the mind, proclaiming the self-delusions of those who seek recognition in the public arena. As the opening stanza for a poem whose speaker asserts the greater pleasures of contemplative solitude, the lines establish the boundaries of an argument that ends with characteristic Marvellian ambiguity. The sun dial of herbs and flowers that marks time in this garden nonetheless marks time, a computation whose end is, in agricultural or garden manuals, reckoned in terms of productivity. Marvell's opening, however, is rooted in the ground of English verse, a ground laid out by Jonson in his praise for the very active life the speaker in "The Garden" disdains. Jonson describes the Sidney children:

> Each morn, and even, they are taught to pray,
> With the whole household, and may, every day,
> Read, in their virtuous parents' noble parts,
> The mysteries of manners, arms, and arts. (95–98)

The books that are their parents teach them about civic responsibility, military duty, and the liberal arts. In describing such achievements as delusive and those who labor for them as prudent toilers, Marvell's speaker takes aim at that concept of community encoded in Jonson's enclosed but unenclosed garden, that, in providing a means of entry for all, is at once nourished and self-sustaining. So Bede had described England.

When in "Upon Appleton House" Marvell describes the estate of Thomas Fairfax as a place sanctified by nature, history, and design, as at once accessible and discreet, as ambiguously poised between the ways of action and contemplation, and as both a sign of civilization and a reminder of inherent barbarism, he is at once stating the plain facts about the estate (once the site of a Cistercian nunnery) bound within the exigencies of English law and aligning his long and delib-erately irresolute meditation with a still living concern with the out-lines and identity of England itself. With its concern for boundaries, lineage, and the processes by which sanctity is asserted, "Upon Apple-ton House" links what has been described as the last of the country house poems with that tradition beginning with Gildas and Bede and continuing through monastic myths of origin, the medieval chronicle tradition, and their refractions in a vernacular literature that comes, finally, to celebrate the secular realm as sacred. Those pre-Conquest texts and traditions that underlie later identifying texts such as Cis-tercian founding stories and the Wilton Diptych link the nation in the person of the sovereign to the church, suggesting the boundaries afforded by both geography and *ecclesia*. However, as I have suggested, it is the permeability of those boundaries that frequently preoccupies efforts to describe or celebrate England, the garden whose inviola-bility is constantly at risk and with it the very identity of England it-self. The efforts at self-understanding that are adumbrated in such texts, as well as in texts relating to enclosure and agriculture, to some extent authorize Marvell's poem, which sets Appleton House within a history and a set of concerns that take geographic distinction as their trope.

In "Upon Appleton House" Marvell did not simply inherit these images of national identity, he employed them in ways that suggest he understood them as lenses through which to view and perhaps com-pose a history of England.[88] To say Marvell employed images drawn from medieval accounts of England is to suggest that he knew them as belonging to a historiographical language. He was certainly in the right time and place for such a venture. By the time he became tutor to Maria Fairfax (late 1650–late 1652) at Appleton House in York-shire, where he wrote the poem in 1651, he would have had ample op-portunity to investigate the monuments of England's history. Born in Hull, in the East Riding of Yorkshire, he had been educated at Cam-bridge and studied law in London. Yorkshire was dense with the ruins of medieval ecclesiastical foundations, both near Hull and farther west, near Fairfax's properties. Many of these ruins were Cistercian, as was Nun Appleton, become Appleton House by Marvell's time. Sir Robert Cotton's library in London drew on the wealth of despoiled books and manuscripts to be found in Yorkshire.[89] Cotton was a friend of William Camden's, both of the generation previous to Marvell's and both catalysts for the antiquarian energy represented by Sir William Dugdale, who sought to preserve the knowledge of the past in the face of rising antiepiscopal pressures and, with Roger Dodsworth, the author of the *Monasticon Anglicanum*, the first volume of which appeared in 1655. The *Monasticon* marks the beginning of monastic history after the Dissolution. Dugdale was also close to Elias Ashmole, who from the 1650s devoted his antiquarian interests to the history of the Order of the Garter.[90] Martin Dzelzainis and Annabel Patterson have convincingly argued that Marvell had access to and used the library belonging to the earl of Anglesey in London; it is unlikely he ignored the books containing history, natural history, and English literature in Thomas Fairfax's library or those in that of Henry Fairfax, Thomas's uncle and rector of Bolton Priory, which had once been an Augustinian foundation.[91] Moreover, by this time there are contemporary references to the Wilton Diptych, which was in the collection of Charles I, as well as antiquarian interest in Edward III and his founding of the Order of the Garter.[92] While "Upon Appleton House" certainly can be read within the traditions of the pastoral and/or the georgic address, it can also be described as a secret history of England, poised somewhere between hope and regret, a continuation of those medieval attempts to use the tropes of the past to sacralize the present.

There was precedent for Marvell's deployment of pastoral address in the service of history. Both Ben Jonson, to whose "Penshurst" he alludes in the opening stanzas of "Upon Appleton House," and John Denham, whose "Cooper's Hill" was published in 1642, construct their historically rooted critiques of the present in pastoral description. Both Jonson and Denham draw on tropes of insularity to explore the nature of the geographies they describe. Jonson uses Penshurst, its bounty, its proportion, its inclusive insularity, as a type of little England, focused by its devotion to sovereign and God, bound within a chain of private and public virtues whose very simplicity is a reproach to present excess and a reminder of a lost age. Denham surveys London from Cooper's

Hill and, finding it sooty from business and vain labor (ll. 29–31), turns to Windsor where he recalls the history of Edward III and the founding of the Order of the Garter. The encircling blue garter imaginatively expands to become the encircling sea, joined to England by the Thames, which reaches around the world, at once protecting England and bringing to her tributes from other countries (101–86).[93] Denham's account of place is inevitably an account of the history of the place, but he also uses landscape, the river constrained by the greedy husbandman, the greedy water impatient with its narrow channel, to comment on the need for royal measure and popular obedience in ways Bishop John Russell would have found congenial.

Marvell is less resolute, certainly less forthright, than either Jonson or Denham, channeling history through landscape, suggesting the delights and temptations of insularity, the renewals of the present that are built on the "demolishings" of the past, the need for those in the present to invent a sacred myth to give meaning to their own rebuilt ruins. He builds into his account of the Fairfax estate two key tropes that link it to ancient histories of a sacralized England—the island garden and the *dos Mariae*.

That the two are joined as identifying features of Appleton House is apparent from stanza 10, which moves the poem away from its careful nod to Jonson in the first nine stanzas emphasizing the relatively modest and proportioned character of the house and anchors it in myths of England. Stanza 10 points up the natural beauty of Appleton House, what Nature has "laid so sweetly waste;/ In fragrant gardens, shady woods, / Deep meadows, and transparent floods." This beautiful land, like the *Brut*'s legend of national origins, can trace its history to Amazonian unnaturalness, which Marvell recounts in the mini-history of Isabel Thwaites and William Fairfax, whose kidnapping of her in 1518 rescued her from the nuns' grasp and is embedded in the poem at stanzas 11–35: "A nunnery first gave it birth." Those nuns serve as crude reminders of England's Catholic past, which is conceived of as isolating rather than as expansively insular. Marvell's nuns are self-described "virgin Amazons" (106), who desire Thwaites for her fortune and her beauty, which they promise will be cherished each night, when she will lie chastely with another nun, "All night embracing arm in arm, / Like crystal pure with cotton warm" (191–92). The suggestion links the nuns to the Amazonian Albina and her sisters, whose unnatural dominance and sexuality produced the grotesque giants that Brutus must kill. In Isabel Thwaites, the nuns claim to see the Virgin's face, which would allow them to embroider the likeness of Mary by using their prospective nun as a model:

> 'But much it to our work would add
> If here your hand, your face we had:
> By it we would Our Lady touch;
> Yet thus She you resembles much.
> Some of your features, as we sewed,
> Through every shrine should be bestowed.
> And in one beauty we would take
> Enough a thousand saints to make.' (17: 129−36)

Line 132, which suggests that the Virgin resembles the girl, rather than vice versa, underlines the nuns' inordinate desire or idolatry of the sensual; moreover, they offer her the temptations of Narcissus, whereby she should see her face multiplied throughout the convent, as though it were a pool reflecting her beauty.

However, the convent, the consecrated site of beauty and falsely directed desire, becomes reconsecrated when Fairfax carries Isabel away to marriage. Marvell thus reworks the traditions of Bedan history whereby invasion becomes reconstitution:

> At the demolishing, this seat
> To Fairfax fell as by escheat.
> And what both nuns and founders willed
> 'Tis likely better thus fulfilled.
> For if the virgin proved not their's,
> The cloister yet remainèd her's.
> Though many a nun there made her vow,
> 'Twas no religious house till now. (35: 273−80)

Marvell's irony here cuts both ways. He refers not to the Dissolution, a term commonly used to describe the dissolving of the monasteries, but to the "demolishing," thus underlining the violence visited upon these virgin buildings. He then proclaims that the nuns' wish to give her the convent was ironically fulfilled and ends with "'Twas no religious house till now," asserting the sacrality of chaste marriage over their monstrous chastity. Since Isabel resembles the Virgin, Appleton House remains in the Virgin's gift.

Marvell's treatment of Maria Fairfax, Thomas's daughter and only heir, links her to both Isabel and the Virgin, patron of England's island garden. He describes her as a virgin nymph, "with the flowers a flower to be" (301–2), and as the ordering principle for the estate's natural beauty (stanzas 82–94), which nourishes her as she grows to her own destiny. In these stanzas, Marvell presents Maria, or Mary, as she was called in the Epistle Dedicatory to Thomas Fairfax's *Short Memorials*, as the source of beauty: "'Tis she that to these gardens gave / That wondrous beauty which they have" (689–90).[94] Maria is also, like the Virgin, the source of evening peace and stillness, "Maria such, and so doth hush / The world" (681–82), the figure to whom the estate returns its own gifts:

> Therefore what first she on them spent,
> They gratefully again present:
> The meadow carpets where to tread;
> The garden flowers to crown her head;
> And for a glass the limpid brook
> Where she may all her beauties look,
> But, since she would not have them seen,
> The wood about her draws a screen. (88; 697–704)

Maria refuses the solipsistic delights the brook offers her, but the chain of giving Marvell describes, like that belonging to the Graces, is one in which she is gladly bound, for she gives beauty only to receive it back, and return it once more. Marvell's description of Appleton House and its beauty as being in the gift of Maria backs a poet's fancy with a father's care, for Thomas Fairfax had broken the terms of the entail to settle the estate on his only child.[95] It was literally the *dos Mariae*. This old name for England was current in the seventeenth century, and if Marvell had ever seen the Wilton Diptych his account of Maria as the source for vernal beauty might be even more pointed;

for, where Richard kneels in a wasteland, Mary and her vanguard stand in flowers, offering a picture of garden loveliness that resonates with Bede's account of this beautiful, bountiful land.[96]

Marvell describes Appleton House as though it were England, surrounded by a "sea" when the sluice gates of Denton, Fairfax's higher estate, are opened, abounding with loveliness tempting the narrator (and possibly Fairfax) to solipsistic monastic repose, patronized by the young Maria, whose virgin beauty protects and vivifies it. Like England, the landscape contains evidence of violence, the mowers who bloody the rails in leveling the meadows (stanzas 50–53), the royal oak weakened by the traitor worm (554) and then hacked down, the power of time itself that may make of it a pilgrimage site in the future and that signals the end of day, the end of the poem. In fact, the final stanza, with its salmon fishermen coming to shore, their shapes now unclear in the dark, ends the poem, not with Ben Jonson's acclamation, "thy lord dwells," but with the irresolution of darkness, with the impression that the panorama the poet has offered derives whatever meaning it has from its relation to a past that is shadowed in the poem's present. Maria's future is only potential and set within a landscape that is a testimony to "demolishing." Jonson's visiting king has been written out, sovereign power devolving to those individuals like Fairfax who must decide their own relations to England's community, thus the degree to which enclosure becomes isolation. As to Appleton House, it epitomizes those attempts to construe identity from circumstance and need, to name as sacred a space whose security can only be contingent, locating Marvell within the company of those who wrote England's history through its geography.

CHAPTER THREE

THE FOURTEENTH CENTURY
AND PLACE

If Langland's identification of nation with agrarian space looks forward to a long literature that quizzes and reconstructs national identity as located less in sovereignty than in a concept of community, his pointing to the half acre, Piers's croft, emerges from and indeed is a reconstruction of earlier fourteenth-century attempts to define nation in terms of a particular type of space. The reign of Edward III, particularly in the years after Edward made his claim for the French crown, is a period when efforts to define the outlines of that space are most clearly articulated. The texts that were copied into mid-fourteenth-century manuscripts, the political conflicts that accompanied the beginning of the war, and the literature of social satire and complaint from the same time provide a rich atmosphere of contestation and debate for Edward's bid to define nation in terms of his own exclusive chivalric identity as they do for Langland's deft substitution of croft for castle.[1]

As a young man, Edward received a good deal of advice about the duties of kingship. When he came to the throne, he was presented with manuscripts designed to educate a young prince about his duties and the nature of his authority. One of these, *De nobilitatibus, sapientiis et prudentiis*, written by Walter Milemete and presented to Edward in January 1327, was lavishly illustrated. As M. A. Michael has argued, the treatise contains an iconography of kingship wherein Saint George is depicted as the patron saint of England, interceding for Edward, and Edward is depicted as crowned by God. However, as Michael points out, Edward is also depicted in relation to bishops and magnates, and the king's power is figuratively balanced by them.[2] Edward had of course come to the throne in circumstances that owed a good deal to the desires of both churchmen and magnates to dislodge Roger Mortimer from the usurped power Mortimer and Isabella, Edward's mother, had wrested from Edward II.[3] The young Edward III was thus both hailed as England's true king and reminded of those limits on his own reach. Lucy Freeman Sandler has suggested a similar program of praise, advice, and censure in the iconography for the Bohun psalters, executed from the 1350s to the late 1380s or 1390s, the earliest of which, the Vienna Psalter, identifies Edward with King David by way of praising his regality and censuring his sins.[4] Sandler describes the manuscripts made for the Bohun family over a number of decades by artists, two of whom were Augustinian friars, who worked for the Bohun family and lived in their castle, Pleshey, in Essex, as complex responses to the events of the late fourteenth century and as examples of aristocratic image making. Thus they present members of the Bohun family as loyal servants of the king and as able to comment on the crown even as they supported it.

The issue of national image making is at the heart of this chapter. Edward himself certainly understood the need for image making, but he was hardly alone. He was well matched, not simply by magnates, but by clerics, poets, and chroniclers, who sought a way to offer an image of nation whose elements could be used (or rearranged) to provide perspectives as models. In the previous two chapters, I focused on England the island garden and the ways in which England's internal topography could be assimilated to the historic understanding of its status as an island, distinct but not isolated, capable of absorbing and being nourished by incursions from other peoples or orders. Later fourteenth-century writers like Langland, Chaucer, and Hoccleve also evince an awareness that space could be used to explore an under-

standing or refiguring of nation. They are heirs to those who, in the
first half of Edward's reign, attempted to define that space as concentrated in the crown, but they also extend and reformulate the efforts
of alternate Edwardian voices to envision a more ambiguously defined
and porous national space and hence audience. This is not to say that
these later writers should be seen as antiroyal or as populist but rather
that each depicts the space that is England in terms that do not so
much remove the king from the picture as let in other figures whose
impulses complicate the subject of agency that is fundamental to the
genre of literature associated with kingly advice.

ADVICE TO KINGS

The manuscripts presented to the young Edward III and Hoccleve's
Regiment of Princes bracket a period that saw a fundamental shift in
the construction of English space offered up for a king's perspective.
The manuscripts prepared for Edward between 1325 and 1327 and
Hoccleve's poem written for Henry V around 1411 are carefully "sited"
in English space, containing either direct references to specific locales
or illustrations whose heraldic detail links them to England. Such
siting can be found in other manuals of instruction. Richard Fitz
Nigel begins *The Dialogue of the Exchequer* by locating his book about
the complexities of the exchequer in English time and space: "In the
twenty-third year of the reign of King Henry II, while I was sitting
by the window of a tower next to the river Thames, suddenly someone
spoke to me, saying urgently, 'Sir, haven't you read that both knowledge
and treasure, if hidden, are useless?'"[5] Fitz Nigel plants his Boethian
opening in 1176/77 and by the Thames, a tactic also used by John
Gower in his book of princely advice, the *Confessio Amantis*, which begins in a boat on the Thames in the sixteenth year of King Richard's
reign. A similar impulse to anchor instruction in English space can
be found in Andrew Horn's creation of a library for the city of London, which included an anglicized version of Brunetto Latini's *Tresor*,
the Statutes of England, a listing of the provinces and counties of England, Henry of Huntington's history of England, and a description
of the city of London.[6] Horn was compiling his collection about the
time manuscripts were being prepared for Edward III, but Horn's

focus was the city and its liberties, the instruction of counselors rather than princes.

The three manuscripts presented to Edward all contain versions of the pseudo-Aristotelian *Secreta Secretorum* and are designed to teach a prince about the practice of authority.[7] One manuscript, Paris, Bibliothèque Nationale MS fr.571, which was made for the marriage of Edward to Philippa of Hainault, in addition to a French translation of the *Secreta*, contains *Livre du Tresor*, a prayer for a departing knight, two motets for Ludowic, king of the Franks, and Raoul le Petit's *Roman de Fauvain*, based on the harshly satiric *Roman de Fauvel*, which provides graphic pictures of falsehood operating within the court. To Fauvel/Fauvain, the hybrid horse/man or horse/woman, nothing is sacred, everything for hire. The *Roman de Fauvain*, like its model, is densely illustrated, offering pictures of Fauvain on hind legs drinking from a cup, Fauvain enthroned, Fauvain manipulating figures of church and state. In addition to these texts, BN fr. 571 once also contained a book by Julius Caesar, another on the governance of kings, the English Statutes, a French coronation *ordo*, and a glossed Lord's Prayer. As Jane H. M. Taylor has argued, the compilation has its own coherence, both teaching and admonishing, or advising in the arts of orderly rule and dramatizing the results of misrule.[8]

Michael has traced an "iconography of kingship" in the second of the manuscripts, *De nobilitatis, sapientiis, et prudenciis*, presented to Edward by Walter of Milemete, a king's clerk. There are fifteen half-page and six full-page miniatures that depict Edward's knighting and coronation: Edward seated with a falcon, Edward receiving the shield of England from Saint George, Edward seated by his mother, Isabella, angels giving Edward his arms before a Throne of Grace Trinity, and God placing the crown on Edward's head, as well as miniatures augmenting the special relation between Edward and Saint George, the divine right of English kings, and the need to surround the king with fit counselors, both ecclesiastical and lay. Michael reads these in the context of the immediate history of Edward's coronation as expressing a politics of rule that Queen Isabella sought to impart to her son.[9] Moreover, the specifically topical miniatures, which relate directly to Edward's history and status, are surrounded by borders containing grotesques—monkeys, fools, hybrid creatures—who become more prevalent in the latter parts of the manuscript. These figures fight one another in an increasing spiral of violence and contrast sharply with the miniatures depicting Edward, his valor, piety, and nobility. On folio 5a, which is the Trinity page in which Edward receives his arms, a draped and saddled horse stands beside an unarmed young man (see fig. 3). One hoof extends into the margin, and the head of the horse looks out toward the reader. Though there are many horses depicted in the scenes of battle between knights that come near the end of the manuscript, this horse resembles them less than it does pictures of either Fauvel or Fauvain, who masquerades as royalty in French manuscripts. Its quizzical gaze and placement beside the leisurely young man provide a contrast to the text, which invokes the Trinity and specifies the necessity of Christ as the foundation of every work and to Edward, who kneels before the Trinity awaiting his arms. Whether or not the horse is meant to suggest Fauvel/Fauvain, the grotesques that abound in the manuscript suggest those impulses that threaten any system of order. In the Milemete manuscript, the monstrous is contained within borders and along margins; their violations of form and stability do not threaten the central miniatures of Edwardian chivalry. On the other hand, they demand our attention because they are so graphically present in the manuscript, just as the misrule of the *Roman de Fauvain* is graphically present in another manuscript presented to Edward during the same period, where, as Michael Camille has noted, hybridity and monstrosity occupy not the margins but the center.[10]

Almost a century later, Hoccleve makes explicit what is implicit in these Edwardian manuscripts of kingly advice, creating a handbook far more innovative than anything previously done or than Lydgate's book of princely advice, *Secrees of Old Philisoffres*, which was begun by Lydgate late in his life and completed by Benedict Burgh, an Essex clergyman, several decades after Hoccleve's *Regiment. Secrees* consciously avoids those fissures that are intrinsic to Hoccleve's text and seems a return to a fairly unexceptional handbook of princely advice. It describes itself as a translation of the text by Aristotle for Alexander, which was later translated from Greek into Arabic, then into Latin and the vernacular languages of medieval Europe.[11] Addressed to Henry VI and apparently commissioned either by the king or one of his counselors, the *Secrees* nods to earlier advisers like Chaucer, Gower, and Hoccleve but maintains a steadily laudatory tone toward the prince. Nor, in contradistinction to these authors, do Lydgate and Burgh anchor the poem in identifiably English space. Lydgate embeds his own authorial self-description in the several prologues to the text, recounting his searches for wisdom, which include a fanciful trip to India and many forays into libraries. He describes his encounter with a "solytare/ Syttyng alloone with lokkys hore and gray" (257–58), who shows him the right way, the book, on whose translation he begins. Lydgate's account sets the text within the traditions of wisdom literature and its author/translator within an elaborate modesty *topos*, whereby he is baffled by his search until enlightened by an aged solitary who points him in the right metaphysical direction. The conventionality of Lydgate's opening is more pronounced when compared to Hoccleve's *Regiment*, where princely advice is set within an English space that contains not simply princes, but citizens whose appearance and conversation manifest the dis-ease of a nation where Fauvel appears to be alive and well.

Hoccleve's stark opening captures both place and narrative disruption:

> Musynge upon the restlees bysynesse
> Which that this troubly world hath ay on honde,
> That othir thyng than fruyt of bittirnesse
> Ne yildith naght, as I can undirstonde,
> At Chestres In, right faste by the Stronde,
> As I lay in my bed upon a nyght,
> Thoght me byrefte of sleep the force and might.[12]

As Charles Blyth notes of these lines, Hoccleve superimposes an identifiable locale and what will become a named and particular person, Thomas Hoccleve, on a traditional dream-vision prologue with the inevitable disquiet that will be redressed by the experience the poem recounts.[13] Even more startling are the subsequent stanzas describing the narrator's memory of recent political unrest and his certainty of worldly instability. His own unrest, which is related directly to his fear of national disorder, prompted by his memory of recent Ricardian history, drives sleep away and him out for a long walk after daylight has come. Hoccleve then joins the image of London by the Strand with one of the countryside surrounding the city. The narrator walks through the fields for what might have been an hour or more, until "A poore old hoor man cam walkynge by me" (122). Where the narrator of the *Secrees* simply learns the right way from his old solitary, Hoccleve rudely tells the hermit not to speak to him; he prefers to be alone. In these opening stanzas, Hoccleve plays with narrative traditions reworked and handed down by Langland, Chaucer, and Gower wherein restless dreamers encounter solitary figures (as in the *Book of the Duchess*) or figures of wisdom (as does Will with Holy Church or Amans with Genius) within dream landscapes that are recognizably English. But Hoccleve depicts a narrator whose problem is the state of the nation as he sees it from his tormented perspective. What is more, his version of the *Secreta Secretorum* falls into two halves, the first, a 2,016-line "prologue" that details the conversation between Hoccleve and the hermit, and the second, a 3,423-line regimen for the prince. Both present the nation as a place that includes far more than regal magnificence and that is not necessarily centered on the court.

One of the subjects included in the *Secreta Secretorum* is health, or the need to maintain the body's health. Though discussions of health, nutrition, and medicine are directed to the prince, implicitly the health of the king's body cannot be separated from that of the body politic, where imbalances or bad customs can have equally disastrous results. Hoccleve includes advice to Henry about health in the second part of the *Regiment*, but the first part offers a picture of ill health that has a good deal of political resonance. In this first section of the poem Hoccleve provides a perspective on nation   its court, its administrative offices, its clergy, and its commoners—that is striking because both the hermit and Hoccleve himself are the ones doing the seeing. The poem offers no omniscient and disembodied narrator but, in this section, a conversation between two figures who are to some extent victims of the circumstances into which they have placed themselves. Hoccleve can thus use their dialogue as confessional while at the same time using it to describe a nation's ill health. For example, in urging Hoccleve to display the source of his depression, the hermit remarks that the beggar by the road, blind, crooked, lame, and sunk in poverty (248–59), receives help because he is willing to display himself rather than "keepe him cloos and holde his pees" (253). The counsel to reveal the source of sorrow certainly echoes the advice the narrator gives the Black Knight in the *Book of the Duchess*, but it also suggests that concern with community that invigorates so much of England's literature of self-description. Moreover, what the beggar displays is his poverty, which is an illness striking at the heart of the doctrine of the common good. The beggar displays the sores of the body politic, just as the returning soldiers fallen into poverty mentioned later (920–24) are tokens of a lack of pity in their fellow soldiers. Similarly, the hermit's description of the elaborate fashions worn by young men comes after his own commendation of the wisdom that can lie under poor cloth (414–17) and his remarks about the evils of plurality after he inquires whether Hoccleve is himself beneficed (1401–2). His discussion of the errors of Lollardy emerges from his warning that Hoccleve should not isolate himself in his own thoughts and anxieties, which will lead to despair and confusion (267–371). Poverty, pride, and heresy become diseases within a nation whose people here receive almost as much scrutiny as does the crown.

In their personal remarks, both the hermit and Hoccleve reveal their own less than perfect self-governance. The hermit uses his confession of a misspent youth as the basis for his advice to Hoccleve: his own experience, which has resulted in his poverty, is the ground of his wisdom. The account itself (610–749) is conventional, in the sense that he confesses to youthful follies of pride, women, riotous living, and inordinate spending, but it is introduced by a term familiar to any reader of *Piers Plowman*, where Rechelessness becomes the spokesman for carelessness, for a willed ignorance of consequence.[14] The ability to see the self in relation to consequence and to the common good is the subject of the hermit's advice to Hoccleve, but it is also the subject of the many versions of the *Secreta Secretorum* offered to princes, as the second part of the *Regiment* illustrates. The hermit's account of himself, "Whan I was yong, I was ful rechelees" (610), serves as a parallel to Hoccleve's own *rechelessness*, or his unwillingness to move beyond his bitterness and depression over his promised and unpaid royal annuity. Like Will in Passus 5 of the C-text of *Piers Plowman*, Hoccleve grapples with the concept of labor when applied to the writer's life but with a good deal more assurance.[15] Rather than question the seriousness or value of his own work in the Privy Seal, he admits that he cannot work with plow or harrow, nor does he know what to sow in a field or how to fill a cart or a barrow (981–83), but he labors nonetheless (988–1029). His tired back, cramped fingers, and bad eyesight are testimony to the difficulties of his labor:

What man that three and twenti yeer and more
In wrytynge hath continued, as have I,
I dar wel seyn, it smertith him ful sore
In every veyne and place of his body;
And yen moost it greeveth, treewely,
Of any craft that man can ymagyne.
Fadir, in feith, it spilt hath wel ny myne. (1023–29)

By prefacing his account of a writer's work with an allusion to
Piers Plowman C: 5.12–31 where Reason asks Will just what agricultural work he can do and ending with a description of the tired body
of the "white collar laborer," Hoccleve inserts the clerical worker into
the "field" of the nation. The integrity of that labor is reinforced by
the end of the first part of the *Regiment*, when the hermit tells him to
write to the king about his unpaid annuity, or write *for* the king and
expect a reward (1905–11). He then goes on to offer Hoccleve advice
about princely address, telling him to avoid flattery, or deceit, so that
he does not become a Favel like the many Favels that frequent court
and are, in effect, treasonous because they encourage vice.[16] Instead,
"Looke if thow fynde canst any tretice/ Growndid on his estates hol-
sumnesse" (1949–50). Hoccleve takes the lesson, the hermit going off
to the Carmelite refectory and Hoccleve home, where the next morning he sits down with pen and parchment to write to his prince. So
ends the first part of the *Regiment of Princes*, not simply an *accessus*
to the *Secreta*, but a regimen for laborers, for citizens who are under
the rule of princes but who must also learn to rule themselves.[17] Presumably, in taking "penne and ynke and parchemeyn" (2013), Hoccleve must rule the pages before he writes the rule those pages will
contain. Though the book is addressed to Henry and indeed contains
a rule for him, it also locates the prince in relation to a city in which
disgruntled workers labor, to fields outside the city where there can
be found poor men and beggars, and to a poet who has just demonstrated his ability to see city, field, and prince as part of a single landscape. Neither the writer, the hermit, the beggar, nor the poor soldiers
inhabit the margins of the book; rather, they occupy the space within
the first part. The only recognizable grotesque is Fauvel, that hybrid
horse/man from the time of Edward III, and Fauvel is, as he was then,
a courtier.

In the first of the two prologues to the second part of the *Regiment*, Hoccleve continues to suggest the new national geography adumbrated in the first part. He begins conventionally enough, locating himself humbly and obediently in relation to his prince, and indeed MS Arundel 38 contains a page depicting a figure giving the book to Henry V, or receiving the book from the king.[18] In tracing the lineage of books of princely advice, such as the one he is presenting, Hoccleve locates himself in relation to Aristotle and Giles of Rome (2038–58) but contrasts his own lack of wit with their much greater wisdom. He goes on to Chaucer, whom he calls his "deere maister" and "fadir," in comparison to whom Hoccleve describes himself as "dul" (207–79). In lamenting Chaucer's death, Hoccleve recenters the map of England on the poet rather than the prince:

> Allas, my worthy maister honurable,
> This landes verray tresor and richesse,
> Deeth by thy deeth hath harm irreparable
> Unto us doon; hir vengeable duresse
> Despoillid hath this land of the swetnesse
> Of rethorik, for unto Tullius
> Was nevere man so lyk amonges us. (2080–86)

The encomium certainly allows Hoccleve to trace his own genealogy, or what he sees as his poetic genealogy, thus linking himself to Chaucer and to Cicero and thus to the "sweetness" of rhetoric, but it also suggests that "this land's" treasure and wealth are concentrated in Chaucer, that Death, by claiming him, has "despoiled" the land. The land is, of course, England, deprived and wasted not simply of rhetoric, but, as he asserts in the following stanza, of philosophy and poetry, signified in Aristotle and Virgil. Hoccleve turns back to his prince, referring to Jacob de Cessolis's *Chessbook* and ending with another reference to his own ignorance and humility.

This prologue serves as a bridge between the two parts of the *Regiment* in several ways. First, its opening address to Henry shifts attention from the blight and distress apparent in the first part to the order of social hierarchy. However, Hoccleve fissures this prologue, as indeed the entire poem is fissured, by a reminder that poets or wise men have their own perspectives on princely behavior, that, in fact,

Aristotle, Giles, Cicero, Chaucer, or Virgil are among those who articulate rules for princes. He imaginatively creates a "land" filled with eyes, voices, and pens who serve as true mirrors of princes and who can be described as a nation's real treasure. The second part of the *Regiment* translates the concerns of the *Secreta Secretorum* into English poetry, reminding Henry of the need for truth, justice, piety, mercy, patience, chastity, magnanimity, largess, prudence, counsel, and peace. Hoccleve also includes several telling references to Favel, warning Henry about ways in which Favel can undermine justice (2939) and piety (3050 ff.) and promote avarice (1475, 5253, 5258, 5268, 5275). Where Paris, Bibliothèque Nationale MS fr.571, made for the young Edward III, contains a *Secreta*, a *Tresor*, and the romance of Fauvel, Hoccleve puts Fauvel directly into his own *Secreta*, weaving allusions to hybridity and moral grotesquerie into the sage advice attributed to Aristotle. Moreover, he goes beyond those earlier manuscripts by focusing, in the first part of the *Regiment*, on figures who are not the subjects of kingly manuscripts, implying that the nation, the "land," is far more than royal demesne. Thus, in the closing stanzas, where Hoccleve speaks of peace, he reminds Henry of the "sorwe lamentable" (5329) caused by "your werres sharpe shoures" (5330):

> Allas, what peple hath your werre slayn!
> What cornes waastid and doun trode and shent!
> How many a wyf and mayde hath be bylayn
> Castels doun bete, and tymbred howses brent
> And drawen doun and al totore and rent!
> The harm ne may nat rekned be ne told;
> This werre wexith al to hoor and old. (5335–41)

The power of this stanza (aside from its adroit craftsmanship) lies in Hoccleve's linkage of prince and pauper. He begins with the spondaic exclamation, "how many people has *your war* slain" and goes on to provide graphic and metrically pointed pictures of waste: fields trampled and destroyed, women raped, castles pulled down, timbered houses burned. He focuses his lens not on the knight in battle but on the common person, the victim of noblesse oblige, going on to quote Saint Bridget of Sweden and her words urging peace between France and England.[19] Saint Bridget and her eloquence notwithstanding, it is

Hoccleve's eloquent depiction of the waste of war that focuses the passage by reminding Henry once more that he is not the only figure in the landscape and is directly responsible for the destruction of the countryside, of homes and of the people who live on and work the land. At other points in the second part of the *Regiment*, Hoccleve reminds Henry of the commons, the "tylere with his poore cote and land" (4418), and, of course, of Hoccleve himself, who lacks "My yeerly guerdon, myn annuitee" (4383), encouraging him to be generous to the poor rather than lavish in display and favors for the rich as Favel would have him be. At no point does Hoccleve imply that Henry should cede power to the populace; rather, his references to noncourtly subjects broaden the scope of princely address without resorting to satire. He insinuates that subjects are, in fact, subjects in their own right, that, while they are subject to the king, they speak from within their own set of concerns and out of their own perspectives. Next to destroyed villages, wasted fields, and raped women, Hoccleve's plea for his annuity seems bathetic, but in the first part of the poem he has demonstrated the internal waste his own poverty and depression have produced. In effect, he puts himself in the picture, a picture of nation that brings together court, city, and countryside in a mapping whose irresolutions serve as a mirror for a prince willing to look in it.

In providing for the *Regiment* two different fields of vision, Hoccleve signs himself as heir to Gower and Chaucer, both of whom he mentions, but also to William Langland. Langland's careful foregrounding of Piers in his croft was exploited by Chaucer in ways that seem fundamental to his poetic vision and nature. Not only did Chaucer exploit the croft as an image for nation in the Nun's Priest's tale, as noted in chapter 2, but both the *Parliament of Fowls* and the *Canterbury Tales* suggest Chaucer's interest in topographic perspective as it can be used to suggest the altered outlines of national identity. In two of his adaptations of Boccaccio's *Teseida*, the Temple of Venus in the *Parliament of Fowls* and the Knight's tale, Chaucer's handling of space suggests his interest in the problem Langland had posed. The enclosed garden in the *Parliament* seems at first a conventional lover's garden whose original can be found in the *Roman de la Rose*. The garden, an earthly paradise, contains at its heart a Temple of Venus, whose description, as Robert A. Pratt noted, is an almost literal translation from Boccaccio.[20] However, what begins in a garden that owes its details to

courtly pleasures enlarges to include a far noisier and certainly more
contemporary scene, the bird parliament, which closely resembles England's own in its hierarchical and spatial layout.[21] By putting the bird
parliament within the bounds of the same landscape that contains the
Temple of Venus, Chaucer implicitly links Venerian desire to the politics of the common good, as the birds themselves make clear in their
clamor and debate. The orderly arrangement of the birds is contingent on their willingness to observe degree and to leash desire by obedience to natural law. The posturing of the tercel eagles and the self-
interested noise of the lesser birds is held in check by Dame Nature,
who at the end of poem "To every foul Nature yaf his make" (*PF* 667).
However, the images that abound within the Temple of Venus suggest
that measure is more elusive in the realm of human behavior:

> Semyramis, Candace, and Hercules,
> Biblis, Dido, Thisbe, and Piramus,
> Tristram, Isaude, Paris, and Achilles,
> Eleyne, Cleopatre, and Troylus,
> Silla, and ek the moder of Romulus:
> Alle these were peynted on that other syde,
> And al here love, and in what plyt they dyde. (*PF* 288–94)

The eagles' hyperbole translates these stories of destructive love
into chivalric bird talk. The royal tercel, who wants not a mate but a
"soverayn lady," says that he will die if he does not receive her "mercy,"
going on to say that if he is ever found unfaithful may he be torn apart
by the other birds (416–41). The second tercel meets what are already
high stakes by saying that if he is ever "unkynde" to his lady, may he
be hanged by the neck (450–62). The third asserts his long love for
the formel eagle, adding that he could well die of sorrow. To these
morbid protestations of fidelity and desire, the lower birds ring out,
"Have don, and let us wende!" (492). Chaucer pairs the noble with the
ignoble—Paris, Achilles, Helen, and Dido with eagles, ducks, doves,
and cuckoos—in a landscape that itself joins the aristocratic garden to
the parliamentary arrangement around Dame Nature within a dream
where Scipio begins by advising the narrator to work for "commune
profit" (75). Chaucer's manipulation of space in this poem is painterly,
in the sense that our understanding of the poem depends upon our

willingness to move through the landscape sequentially with the narrator, who tells us what he "saw" or was "showed" to him, his progression allowing the scenes to gloss one another, or to be translated as related scenes as we "see" what he "sees." If he literally translates Boccaccio into English in the account of the Temple of Venus, he transliterates Boccaccio's iconographic and classical scene into Englishness in the bird parliament. Submerged within the political irony of attributing noble affect to eagles and sentimentality and practicality to the lower birds is a more serious point, one that Chaucer explores in the *Canterbury Tales*: Nature restrains the birds, but what constrains men? What keeps the frieze on the walls of the Temple of Venus a frieze and not the chaos of the unbridled will that threatens the order of the birds? What happens when those impulses and postures safely housed in birds are lodged (as they are) in people?

In the Knight's tale Chaucer also turns to the *Teseida* and locates it in relation to an even more potentially disruptive landscape, England, whose pilgrims come "from every shires ende" to ride from London to Canterbury. In casting the outlines of a map on the opening lines of the *General Prologue*, Chaucer certainly indicates his interest in and awareness of nation as landscape, and in the descriptions of the pilgrims in the *General Prologue* he indicates a corresponding awareness of the various points of view to be found in those shires. However, he chose to begin the tales with one he probably worked on earlier, possibly about the same time he worked on the *Parliament*.[22] Here, he does more than translate sections of the *Teseida*; he translates the tale of Theseus and Emily into English poetry. In the *Canterbury Tales*, he gives the tale to the Knight, where our understanding of Theseus's attempt to contain the impulses of the unbridled will (desire, violence, grief, vengeance, competition) is mediated through the narrator but also by the tales that succeed the Knight's and which serve as various commentaries on Theseus's efforts. As Robert Pratt noted some years ago, Chaucer does not simply translate Boccaccio; he abridged the *Teseida* by trimming it of its epic pretensions in order to sharpen the rivalry between Palamon and Arcite and concentrated the action on Theseus's palace and its immediate neighborhood.[23] In particular, Chaucer located the three oratories to Mars, Venus, and Diana in the amphitheater Theseus builds for the tournament, containing them and the desires they signify within a structure that is built to contain the destructive passions of Palamon and Arcite.

The passions depicted on the walls of the oratories, which are thereby frozen into allegorical art, useful as *exempla* refashioned from Boccaccio, Guillaume de Lorris, Fulgentius, Ovid, and others, Chaucer then inserts into the English landscape in the tales that follow the Knight's. His move is dazzling, for the passions made distant on the walls of oratories where Palamon, Arcite, and Emilia pray to triumph over the circumstances in which they find themselves become lust, greed, and humiliation in Oxford; vengeance, theft, and rape in Cambridge; gambling, rioting, and prostitution in London—all in the first fragment of the *Canterbury* book. All tales except the Knight's in the first three fragments are located in English space and make reference to local custom or place-names. Of the remaining tales, those of the Nun's Priest and the Canon's Yeoman depend on an English locale, and the Parson continually stresses the relevance of the sins by referring to contemporary trends. What is more, figures that might well have inhabited the margins of deluxe manuscripts like the Luttrell Psalter—the Miller with his red hair, prominent wart, and bagpipes; the shorn, skinny, shifty-eyed Reeve; the Cook with the sore on his leg—inhabit the body of the manuscript as narrators. Chaucer thus populates a nation, whose geography he evokes in the opening lines of the *General Prologue*, allowing his characters to define themselves in relation to others and to speak in ways that more often promote discord and indicate the elusiveness of an ideal of the common good. What is closed or contained in the Knight's tale, Chaucer opens in the tales that follow.

Similarly, he suggests through the several gardens that dot the tales the illusions that lurk in enclosures. The garden where Emilye walks at dawn singing and capturing the attention of Palamon and Arcite reappears in less noble guise in the tales of the Merchant, the Franklin, and the Shipman. Though the Merchant and the Franklin seek to put aristocratic tags on their gardens—Januarie is a knight, and Dorigen and her noble friends find a garden where they dance and sing—neither narrator is himself noble, and, in fact, both infect their gardens with the realities of commerce, as does the Shipman, who positions the merchant's counting house in proximity to his garden.

Thus the love garden of the Knight's tale, which fosters its own conventional lover's madness, is appropriated by other narrators who indicate their own worldly experience. It is in his carefully enclosed garden, penetrated now by Damian, that Januarie tells May that if she is true to him she will win "al my heritage, toun and tour . . . maketh chartres as yow leste" (IV.2172–73), then saying, "I prey yow first, in covenant ye me kisse" (IV.2176). It is in another garden that Aurelius laments to Dorigen that he did not accompany her husband over the sea, since "For wel I woot my servyce is in vayn;/ My gerdon is but brestyng of myn herte" (V.972–73), and, by his declaration of passion, sets in motion an elaborate series of exchanges that inevitably suggest trade: rocks for Dorigen, cash for the rocks, honor for discretion. Though the Franklin lards his tale with reminders that his is a noble tale, the vigorous exchange of goods for service imagined by his characters bespeaks his less noble origins. The garden in the Shipman's tale is even more explicitly mercantile, an emphasis that resonates with the preoccupations of its probable original narrator, the Wife of Bath, who describes herself as the merchant of her own body and sexuality throughout her prologue. Not only does the merchant's garden neighbor his "countour-hous" (VII.77), but it is the setting for a hard-eyed exchange between his friend, the monk, and his wife as they barter for money and sex. The affiliations among gardens in the *Canterbury Tales* suggest ways in which aristocratic garden scenes can elide the ignobility of desire, but Chaucer's narrators also people those gardens with more than knights and gentle ladies. In allowing the Merchant, the Franklin, and the Shipman/Wife of Bath to adapt the noble garden to mercantile purposes, Chaucer pushes out its boundaries in ways that parallel his broader understanding of the nation, England, whose shires yield pilgrims of all varieties. By moving in the *Parliament of Fowls* from classical to English space, Chaucer began to explore questions made more immediate and more difficult in the *Canterbury Tales* with its many speakers and positions. Questions posed through quacks and chirps inevitably seem less urgent than those posed by human subjects, each endowed with intent and frequently with the intent to push out of their marginal positions, to take up space of their own.

It is that concept of intent applied to all within the boundaries of nation that invigorates Langland's work, an emphasis he would cer-

tainly have found vivified in vernacular sermon literature.[24] By use of
exempla, of satire and complaint, and of narrative, the medieval vernacular sermon sought to use the pulpit for instruction in doctrine
and in the arts of self-scrutiny. In other words and reading beyond
the obvious praise for order and hierarchy, it is here that we can find a
recognition of agency somewhat detached from the concept of social
degree and thus a way of conceiving of space as including more than
the noble soul.

In contradistinction, the advice Edward received was focused on
the king as agent, though it reminded him of his duties to his people.
In addition to the manuscripts Edward received when he came to the
throne, in 1331 he received some rather stiff advice from William of
Pagula, directed specifically at the evils of purveyance but in the broad-
est sense a look at what being king of England entailed. There are two
related texts, *Epistola ad Regem Edwardum III* and the *Speculum Regis*,
which L. E. Boyle has demonstrated are both by William of Pagula, the
former a letter to Edward about purveyance, the latter, written a little
later, a slightly more general meditation on royal prerogative. There
are ten manuscripts of the two texts, which seem to have circulated
separately.[25] The manuscripts Edward received earlier belong to a European or French tradition of princely advice and could easily be given
to a non-English prince. The illustrations, not the treatises themselves,
link them to Edward and to England. William of Pagula writes to Edward as an English king and thus heir to a set of historic conditions and
to a particular understanding of royal power. In so doing, he sketches in
a picture of England as a space apart from the court.

The letter, written before the *Speculum*, is a more obviously English production, though both contain allusions to English history.
Though William's examples of good and bad kings are drawn from
the Old Testament, he makes it clear that England and its people should
be understood as a type of Israel, whose kings owe their power and
obedience to God. The phrase "domine, mi rex," is the primary mode
of address in both works, thus underlining William's loyalty but also
his ability to speak directly to his prince, to offer, as it were, counsel.
Thus he begins the *Epistola* by reminding his king that the governance
of the "respublica" has been committed to him; he should therefore rule
to the honor of God, to the advantage of the kingdom, seeking to

acquire the love of the people. The principle William holds up is justice, justice that becomes peace, stability, the joy of all. After his general and fairly gentle opening, William begins to discuss Edward and the lack of justice William sees in the country around Windsor, where he serves as vicar of Winkfield. There are four specific references to Windsor in the letter (102, 103, 106, 117); William deletes the place-name in the *Speculum* but retains the substance of his remarks. In addition, in the *Epistola*, William reminds Edward of the vows he took at his coronation by which he vowed to uphold the Magna Carta (89), of the feelings about him held by the English people (96, 112, 122), of his ancestors Henry III and Edward I (115), of the histories of Piers Gaveston and Hugh Despenser, who brought shame to his father's reign (116, 119), and of the sterling example set for English kingship by Edward the Confessor (117). The *Speculum* makes a number of references to the "people of England" (129, 131, 144, 164), as well as referring to Henry of Lancaster (128); to Edward I, who first introduced the diabolical practice of purveyance (167); and to Edward the Confessor as a model for Edward III (137). The *Epistola* also reminds Edward that England is "in feodo ab ecclesia Romano" (112), since John gave the nation to Rome and received again his kingship from the pope in the person of Pandulf; Edward is thus bound by the authority of the laws of England and of God.[26]

Both texts have a richness that comes from William's willingness to describe the agrarian households that are preyed on by Edward's purveyors and those of his family; he offers pictures of the English countryside—and especially the countryside around Windsor—as a plundered and wasted garden. The word that reverberates throughout both texts is *rapina*—robbery, plunder, rape—a word denoting violent seizure of what belongs to another or of another.[27] The word occurs early in the *Epistola*, when William, who begins by praising justice as a kingly virtue and by describing kings as custodians of justice, says that purveyors who do not give a fair price for what they take are engaged in extortion, not trade, *in rapina* rather than justice, in iniquity rather than equity (84). He lists what these purveyors take from villages—straw, bread, beer, hens—telling Edward that he feasts in gladness and the people mourn (94). When royal agents *(raptores)* seize sheep, oxen, cattle, and pigs, the poor are not compensated (99,

103). Not only is Edward not beloved by the poor (96), but William accuses him of eating and drinking the poor (85). Since William assimilates England to Israel, Edward becomes like Ahab (*Epis.*, 114) and the Pharoah (*Speculum*, 165), the oppressor of God's people. In the *Epistola*, William mentions Nathan, who told David the story of the rich man who stole a poor man's ewe lamb, quoting Nathan's devastating remark when David excoriates the plunder, "Tu est ille vir" (100). In other words, *you are the man* who is responsible for the fear in the villages, for the hunger after your agents have departed, for the poverty in households not compensated for the loss of animals and grain.

There is a detail in the *Epistola* that William embellishes in the *Speculum* that marks him as a gifted narrator. Directly after telling Edward that he is the man, that "tu, domine rex," who has many sheep and oxen, roosters and hens, he alludes to one poor woman who has but one hen and that hen taken from her for the king, a man with innumerable animals. The accusation becomes a story in the *Speculum*, where William expands it into an entire subsection. He describes a royal agent who came to a village and seized from one poor woman a hen, a hen whose four or five weekly eggs sustained her and her children. For the hen, the purveyor gave her one denarius and a small coin, a hen she would not have sold for three denarii. William goes on: This hen, who was fat, was prepared for "your" mouth. You killed and ate the hen; the poor woman mourned. You laugh, she weeps. You acquired the hen unjustly. She desires food and begs her bread (*Speculum*, 159). William continues, describing the king with his sumptuous clothing, the poor woman in rags, the king well housed, the woman poorly, with tears for her bread. He then exclaims, "From what audacity, what temerity, what instinct, did you dare to eat that hen?" He ends by quoting Amos 8:10, Job 21:12–14, and Isaiah 31:1, all of which warn the rich and improvident of coming judgment. William ends the section by saying, "Vide quid accidit patri tuo" (160). Edward, of course, knew well what had befallen Edward II, at the hands of his own nobles. William's technique here and in the *Epistola* is designed to locate advice in English time and space, but it is also intended to vivify the "gens anglicana" whom he so often evokes in both works. To say "the English people" is to remind Edward of the coronation ceremony and the promises he made to uphold and protect the laws and customs of England. But to describe a poor woman with children and a hen, their sustenance, is to clothe the people in hunger and rags, to describe dearth, and to call the king a raptor, a plunderer, who has cannibalized his own garden, eaten in one thoughtless meal what should have sustained a family for many days and weeks. The story he tells, of a prince's irresponsibility and a widow's sorrow, is one Chaucer would echo in his fabliau of Chauntecleer decades later, but, for Chaucer, the prince would be a rooster and the hen only a hen.

In using the reference to Nathan and David as the prelude for his account of the widow and her hen, William of Pagula does more than place Edward in David's guilty shoes. Cary J. Nederman has argued that we should see William as articulating a concept of individual rights, or, more specifically, a concept of the subjective human right to property, "regardless of class or even gender," thus of the "inviolability of the rights of subjects" and of "royal accountability" to them.[28] This is, of course, the burden of Nathan's message to David: his seduction of Bathsheba was like that of the king who seized a poor man's lamb. For Nathan, sex is less the issue than wrongful use of power, rooted in a false idea of dominion. The Penitential Psalms were thought to be the result of David's consequent despair after the death of the child Bathsheba bears and his new understanding of lordship, and they were sometimes used or cited to chasten abuses of royal power.[29] William of Pagula's implicit reading of the story of David as exhibiting a sense of erroneous *dominion* places the *Speculum* at the beginning of a series of Edwardian texts linking Edward to David. The Bohun manuscripts, which Lucy Freeman Sandler has described as containing a consistent program of Davidic references, were begun probably twenty years later, as were the Bridlington Prophecies and their gloss, which likewise see Edward as England's David.[30] Where some of these later references are focused on sexual immoderation, William of Pagula is preoccupied by a concept of property, and hence of nation, that places the king on the same terms as the peasant. The impassioned tone and careful use of *exempla* in both his letter and his treatise are radically different from the message imparted through the courtly codes to be found in the manuscripts prepared for a younger Edward. In seeking to educate Edward, William offers him a mirror of his kingdom, whose bounty and people are ravaged by royal purveyors and, hence, by the king's wrongful usurpation of power over the property of his subjects. For William, the cow, the ox, the hen represent actual property seized without benefit of fair price, thus his constant use of the word *rapina* to indicate the rupture to the commonweal inherent in royal purveyance.

William of Pagula writes both letter and treatise from within the conventions, first, of private advice to kings still young enough to be given advice from older churchmen, and, second, of more formally inscribed texts such as the *Tresor* and the *Secreta Secretorum*. The apparatus of the *Speculum Regis*, its chapter and section markings, as well as its more formal tone of address, suggests a broader range for its theorization of kingship. However, William focuses his mirror by means of England's laws, customs, people, and places, anchoring it in the *quotidian* as the continental texts of kingly advice are not. Hoccleve, writing to Henry V, realizes the true potential of the continental tradition by dismantling it and re-dressing it in English garb. If many versions of the *Secreta* begin with advice about the king's person—his health, diet, habits—and go on to include lessons in physiognomy before turning to discussions of justice, prudence, and good and bad rulers, Hoccleve begins with himself as representative of the body politic. That self claims its lack of fair compensation, thus its poverty and depression, just as the conversation between Hoccleve and the old hermit provides a corresponding picture of the body politic. If London is its center, beyond the nation's center is countryside where the old, the dispossessed, and the disenfranchised cross paths and talk. For the widow who lost her hen, William speaks. Hoccleve speaks for himself from a place identifiable as England but certainly not as noble or magnatial England. Similarly, in *Mum and the Sothseggar*, the meadow suited for courtly pleasures is anchored by the franklin's holding, where the beekeeper speaks and offers advice to kings and civil servants. William's specific audience for both the letter and the treatise is the king and those around him; however, his *implied* audience is broader. He certainly cannot and did not expect the widow to read his argument, but his representation of England contains hints of an audience beyond the king's ken. Certainly John of Salisbury had warned that without his subjects' love a king might well face rebellion, but William, in presenting the subjects as belonging to particular times and contingencies, sketches an outline of a nation later authors would fill in vividly.

FIELDS OF VISION

The distinction between audience and implied audience, which serves to adumbrate a concept of national space, is submerged in some of the key events and texts from this early Edwardian period, a period when Edward's war with France was increasing pressures on taxation and when Edward seems to have sought to create an image for himself at some remove from that proffered by William of Pagula. The political crisis of 1341 when Edward III came to verbal blows with his archbishop of Canterbury, John Stratford, in letters that were widely distributed, along with Edward's founding of the new Order of the Garter during the same decade suggest what was perceived as at stake for the crown and the nation. The two most important codices assembled during the middle years of the fourteenth century (ca. 1330–40), the Auchinleck manuscript, and BL MS Harley 2253 likewise evince an awareness of nation as a geographic unit composed of a variegated and hardly subservient or silent people. In 1348 England had its first experience of the pestilence, which had an enormous social, political, and economic impact, a date Langland uses to mark a period for England's writers. Nonetheless, it is the preplague years that provided those writers with the material out of which they fashioned a picture of the nation as an island where insularity was another name for incipient barbarism.

The occasion for the public quarrel between Edward and his archbishop was money; the subject, authority. Edward had been left high and dry on the Continent, waiting for funds he had requested that would allow him to continue the conflict he had begun in 1340. Abandoning what looked to be a successful siege of Tournai and returning secretly to England at midnight on 30 November 1340, embarrassed and furious, Edward summoned justices and clerks, arresting and confining many, looking for Stratford to accuse him of malpractice. Stratford took refuge in the cathedral monastery at Canterbury, from which he was summoned without success. Edward's altercation with Stratford, which he ostensibly lost but which he parlayed into a personal victory, has been ably studied by many historians, among them T. F. Tout, G. L. Harriss, and Roy Haines, in terms of its relationship to Edward's political understanding, to Parliament's articulation of its role in government, and to the shape of Stratford's political life.[31] However, the quarrel, or the texts that document it, also evidence public

communication through texts whose audiences are ambiguously defined but whose relevance to a perception of what constitutes the
commonwealth is implicit in the process of publication, whether oral
or written.

There are several key documents providing written evidence for
the nature of the quarrel. Roy Haines has called it a "pamphlet war," a
term that nicely captures its semipublic arena. The documents themselves are available, though not all in a single place, in the Canterbury
Life of Stratford collected by Wharton, in Robert Avesbury's chronicle,
in the *Foedera*, and in the Parliament Rolls.[32] During the first month
after Edward's return, he attempted, without success, to extricate Stratford from Canterbury. On 29 December, on the Feast of St. Thomas à
Becket, Stratford preached on Ecclesiasticus 48:12, "In his day, he did
not fear the prince," which refers to Elisha, who along with Elijah and
Isaiah are the subjects of the chapter, all of whom are praised for their
zeal and courage in the face of princely power.[33] At the end of the
sermon, and speaking in English *(lingua materna)*, Stratford admitted
his own compliance with worldly power, which had resulted in the oppression of the church and of the community of England. He spoke
of his neglect with tears in his eyes, asking the people for pardon.
The archbishop then accused his enemies, or those who were around
the king, of violating the Magna Carta and pronounced sentences of
excommunication, for which act his Canterbury biographer uses the
verb *publicavit*, thus made public.[34] On 31 December Stratford sent a
letter in French to the king defending both himself and ecclesiastical
liberties.[35] His letter, like that sent much earlier by William of Pagula,
speaks from the position of age and wisdom formally addressing a
younger king in need of wisdom. Stratford begins by reminding Edward of the need for good counsel, citing Solomon's wisdom in choosing good counselors and his son Rehoboam's folly, by which he lost
most of the land of Israel. He then moves closer to home and reminds
Edward of the bad counselors on whom his own father depended
(which he says Edward may not remember) and of some of his own
bad advisers. Stratford says that these advisers have encouraged him
to act in ways contrary to his coronation oath and to the Magna Carta,
which he swore to uphold, and have assured him that his actions will
be pleasing "a vostre comune people." Stratford says this is not so, that
bad advisers have made the king abandon Tournais and could help

him lose his honor, his land, and the hearts of his people. He urges Edward to gather around him good counselors, better than those Stratford has just excommunicated. He ends by asking for judgment by peers after a full inquiry, signing himself "primat de tout Engleterre et vostre piere espirituel," asking the Holy Spirit to grant Edward good counsel and victory over his enemies.

Stratford's letter was circulated among the bishops and elicited a sharp reply from Edward on 10 or 11 February, denying Stratford's request to appear before Parliament. In his letter, which Stratford referred to as the Libellus Famosus, Edward denounced Stratford's career in harsh terms, accusing him of ingratitude, of attempting to subvert his reign, of bad administration, of the subversion of justice, of corruption, of having defamed his ministers, and of having kindled sedition in "our people." He took issue with Stratford's very public handling of his grievances and compared him to a mouse in a satchel, a serpent in the womb, a fire in the bosom to indicate the degree of secret treachery Edward perceived in Stratford's failure to deliver the funds Edward had requested for the war. He demanded that Stratford come to London.[36] Three days later, on Ash Wednesday, Stratford, still in Canterbury, preached on Joel 11, "Turn to me with your whole heart." At the end of the sermon he read aloud the Libellus, translating it from its Latin into *lingua materna*, thereby making it public in English, proclaiming his innocence of the charges against him. He then called for prayers for the king and the queen.[37] Stratford wrote a long reply in Latin to the Libellus, defending himself against the charges and emphasizing the concept of two types of power, the secular power vested in kings by God and the ecclesiastical authority vested in churchmen to excommunicate persons they deem guilty of moral crimes. He underlined the clergy's exemption from secular justice, an exemption written into the Magna Carta.[38] The king sent two more letters, one to the pope denouncing Stratford and another, even more outspoken, on 31 March, to the archbishop, accusing the archbishop of pride, and took issue with his use of public preaching, of having made public his views.[39] This letter ended the pamphlet war, a war conducted in three languages and before a variety of audiences. Shortly thereafter, Stratford was given the protection he demanded to go to London, where eventually, after much skirmishing, he came before the king, along with some bishops, barons, and ministers (not a full Parliament after all) and was reconciled with the king, a reconciliation that was more formally enacted in October at Westminster. As Haines notes, as late as 1346, Edward issued letters patent asserting Stratford's innocence of the charges brought against him.[40]

Both the king and Stratford played to a public. A. K. McHardy has explored Edward's use of those prayers sent to the bishops for public distribution, as well as Edward's use of English for political purposes.[41] Stratford's strategic use of the mother tongue and of the stage he commanded in Canterbury and, a few months later, before the doors of Parliament as he waited to be admitted underline his own understanding of the uses of language, of various registers, of historic references, such as his frequent appeal to the Great Charter, and of the semiotics of gesture. The events also point up an incipient sense of parliamentary privilege in Stratford's appeal to the concept of full parliament and in item 15 of the Statutes of 1341 whereby the king would have been required to appoint his ministers in Parliament, thus giving Parliament an implicit power to choose the king's ministers, which Adam Murimuth says the king would not concede, although he did agree to have the ministers swear *in* Parliament that they would uphold justice.[42] The king soon thereafter, in consultation with his magnates, revoked the statute. I would not so much like to pinpoint 1341 as a single and fairly dramatic moment but as a dramatic moment within a narrative that is increasingly available and made available to a more widely composed audience, evidenced by the use of England's three languages. In his appeal to Parliament, which many historians have traced back to the Lancastrian resistance to Edward II of which Stratford was a part, Stratford offered a brief glimpse of a nation composed of alternate sources of power, just as his use of the "pulpit" Canterbury and of English suggests his own awareness of a greater English audience.

That audience, as it could be used to define the outlines of nation, can be detected in romances like *King Horn* and *Havelok the Dane*, both late-thirteenth-century romances with French or Anglo-Norman source texts, which were reshaped and written in Middle English and copied into later manuscript anthologies containing works of popular, or gentry, appeal. Both romances pay close attention to England's geography.[43] The action in *King Horn* occurs between South Devon, the Wirral peninsula, and Ireland; and in *Horn Childe and Maiden Rimnild*, the version of the romance copied into the Auchinleck manuscript, the place-names belong to northeastern England (north of the Humber, Teseside, Pikering). In *King Horn*, which Diane Speed has linked to the conventions of the chansons de geste, Saracens are the enemy from outside; in *Horn Childe and Maiden Rimnild*, the attackers are Danes and Irish.[44] *Havelok*, the action of which moves back and forth between England and Denmark, contains references to and descriptions of specific places, so specific that it immortalizes the northeastern town of Grimsby, whose seal depicts the main figures in the romance.[45] The romances explore in different ways the nature of kingship by mapping their narratives onto an island nation whose history and identity are inextricable from its geography.

The maps embedded in each romance suggest a particular historical perspective, since both romances depict acts of invasion and play out the narrative of England's own history of conquest and re-formation. In localizing conventions to be found in the chansons, where Saracens are frequently the enemies, *King Horn* does not depict a historical Saracen invasion of England but adapts a literary convention to a poem concerned with the process of invasion and assimilation. The process here is twofold. The poet first describes the Saracen invasion of Horn's own territory, Suddene, possibly Cornwall or South Devon, where fifteen ships filled with "Sarazins kene" (42) arrive and announce to the king that they will kill him and all his people. They kill all who will not forsake their religion and destroy the churches. Horn is released in a boat with his companions, and his mother, Godhild, goes into hiding, living a secret Christian life. By the first seventy lines, the poem establishes the dangers invasion by pagans (another word used to describe the Saracens) poses not simply to life, but to communal identity. Shortly thereafter, Horn and his companions become another species of invaders. Their boat lands in Westernesse, where King Aylmar welcomes them:

> 'Whannes beo ye, faire gumes,
> That her to londe beoth icume,
> Alle throttene,
> Of bodie swithe kene?
> Bi God that me makede,
> A swich fair verade
> Ne saugh ich in none stunde,

Bi westene londe:
Seie me wat ye seche.' (165—73)

Here King Murry's earlier question to the Saracens who approach
his shores ("He axede what hi soghte" [43]), is expanded into Aylmar's
question to Horn and his companions. The poet, in effect, has added
adjectives that underline Aylmar's welcome because these invaders
are "faire" (repeated twice) and "kene." If the first invasion led to car-
nage and sacrilege, the second results in hospitality, Horn's induction
into Aylmar's court, education, knighting, betrothal to his daughter
Rymenhild, and eventual reclamation of his dead father's throne. Horn
triumphs through self-control, even to the point of behaving ration-
ally and honorably in the face of Rymenhild's wild passion for him.
If the poem depicts a young man's education in kingship, including
his education into the falsehood and treachery of vassals, at the same
time it depicts a process by which Horn willingly assimilates himself
to the codes and culture of Westernesse without losing his identity as
Murry's son. At the end, he is able to defeat the Saracens in his own
land and restore it to itself:

Horn let wurche
Chapeles and chirche;
He let belles ringe
And masses let singe.
He com to his moder halle
In a roche walle.
Corn he let serie,
And makede feste merie (1393—1400)

As a good king, he restores churches, causes bells to ring and
masses to be celebrated; as a good son and heir to his father, he restores
his mother and feasts with her. The poem ends with Horn dealing out
land and responsibility to vassals, establishing rulers who are indebted
and loyal to him and thus creating a network of alliances between England and Ireland (where he has defeated Saracens for the king), and
arranging a marriage with the king of Ireland's daughter for his closest
and most loyal friend. The peace established by the end of the poem is a
peace grounded in reason and justice, in fair dealing between king and

vassal, and a peace that takes the shape of a map linking England's north and south to Ireland. The insularity that makes England vulnerable to invaders contains also the potential for communication, for assimilation and alliance. Correspondingly, King Aylmar's own isolation, which makes him vulnerable to the gossip and falsehood that has imperiled Horn's standing in that court from the beginning, contrasts with Horn's growing ability to detect and outwit treacherous men. Horn's triumph at the end of the poem is also a triumph of experience, a testament to a truly educated prince.[46]

As Susan Crane has noted, *Havelok* resembles *Horn* in its concern with inheritance rights, legality, and social order, but *Havelok* also shares *Horn*'s picture of England as open to invasion and thereby to enrichment.[47] Like Horn, Havelok has to make his way without his father, and his life traces a journey from Denmark to England, where he was brought as a child by Grim the fisherman who saves the young prince instead of drowning him as the false Earl Godard ordered him to do. In the poem, violence comes not from incursion but from the false stewards Godard and Godrich, both of whom have sworn to protect royal children on the deaths of their fathers. Godard has Havelok's two young sisters murdered before planning to drown Havelok, and Godrich imprisons Goldeboru, then marries her to a supposed churl, who turns out to be the Danish prince in exile. Possibly for this reason, the *Havelok*-poet omits the account in the French versions of Havelok's father as destroyed by King Arthur's conquest of Denmark and instead describes Birkabeyn as aware of his impending death and anxious to try to preserve the inheritances of his three children.[48] Thus, rather than tie the story of Havelok to an aggressive imperialistic Arthur springing from the pages of Geoffrey of Monmouth, the *Havelok*-poet focuses his poem on the twinned stories of Havelok and Goldeboru, both of whom change as they advance toward regaining their lost sovereign inheritances, Denmark and England.

In imaginatively joining the two countries, the poet does more than invoke the actual history of Cnut, who succeeds to an England where years before King Alfred had created a peace founded on law so that "even on public highways he would order bracelets of gold to be hung up at crossroads to mock the greed of passers-by, for no one dared to steal them."[49] If that peace was fractured by subsequent conflict, in 1017 Cnut, king of Denmark, Norway, and parts of Sweden, began his twenty-year reign. As William of Malmesbury says, "Ita cum omnis Anglia pareret uni" (*GRA* ii:181). The many, who are the English, obey one man. *Havelok*, after its minstrel opening, begins with a description of England under Athelwold, Goldeboru's father, that resonates with the Alfredian peace of the wise and strong ruler where the roads are safe from "wrobberes" (39):

> In that time a man that bore
> Wel fifty pund, I wot, or more,
> Of red gold upon hiis bac,
> In a male with or blac,
> Ne funde he non that him misseyde,
> Ne with ivele on hond leyde. (45–49)

Only at the end of the poem does peace return to England and to Denmark with Havelok's coronation and his gifts of vassalages to those who were faithful to him in his former misfortune.

The union he effects of a widespread and diverse geography is forecast in the dream he has on his wedding night as his English bride also receives assurance from an angel that her new husband is no church but "a kinges sone and kinges eyr" (1268). Havelok dreams of his body as spanning the two countries:

> Me thouthe I was in Denemark set,
> But on on the moste hil
> That evere yete cam I til.
> It was so hey that I wel mouthe
> Al the werd se, als me thouthe.
> Als I sat upon that lowe
> I bigan Denemark for to awe,
> The borwes and the castles stronge;
> And mine armes weren so longe
> That I fadmede al at ones,
> Denemark with mine longe bones;
> And thanne I wolde mine armes drawe
> Til me and hom for to have,
> Al that evere in Denemark liveden
> On mine armes faste clyveden;

And the stronge castles alle
On knes bigunnen for to falle—
The keyes fellen at mine fet.
Another drem dremede me ek:
That ich fley over the salte se
Til Engeland, and al with me
That evere was in Denemark lyves
But bondemen and here wives;
And that ich com til Engelond—
Al closede it intil min hond,
And, Goldeborw, I gaf thee. (1287–1312)

The language in which this passage is cast embodies nation as a king's encircling body, and by means of that body collapses distance or geographic boundary into union and order on the evening of the marital union between the English princess and the Danish prince.[50] Moreover, in compressing what in the French versions is a sequence of scenes belonging to the wedding night and shifting the dream from Goldeboru to Havelok, the poet foregrounds the dream and underlines the degree to which the yet-to-be king understands his own destiny and his responsibility to those countries he will rule.[51] Thus Havelok describes himself as embracing *(fadmede)* all Denmark with his long bones and as flying over the sea to England with all the Danes except serfs and enclosing England in his hand to make a gift of it for Goldboru. The poet here transforms an idea otherwise terrifying and repugnant—a Danish host flying over the sea to claim England—by turning invasion into return, since they are in Grimsby in Lincolnshire at the time, with the final line, "And, Goldeborw, I gaf thee." That gift, of course, returns to Havelok as Goldeboru's husband, king of both Denmark and England, and the single body with the long bones, the embracing arms, and the enclosing hand encompasses lands and the dividing sea in a sixty-year reign characterized by peace and by the great love between the English queen and the Danish king. The poet's use of verbs of enclosure in conjunction with descriptions of England's porous boundaries and Havelok's gifts of land and titles to his retainers depicts nation not as isolated by its surrounding sea but as bound to and by a variety of relationships—marriages, oaths of homage, gifts of office, political alliances—that increase its strength and the stability of Havelok's reign. The picture the poem offers of a nation composed by means of law, loyalty, and love is as powerful as the corresponding picture of a king whose right to rule is signed on his body in the light that issues from his mouth when he sleeps and the "kynmark" on his right shoulder (590–95, 605, 1252–58, 1263) and whose capacity for good rule is guaranteed by his triumphant return from exile, poverty, and labor. *Havelok* and *Horn*, copied by the same hand, appear in Bodleian MS Laud Misc. 108 (ca. 1300–1325), possibly suggesting ways in which each offers a compelling picture of nation or kingship during the difficult reign of Edward II (1307–27); certainly both English versions testify not so much to the translation of French texts as to their reformulation and thus to the continuing vitality of what are older legends and poems.[52]

King Horn, of which there are more copies and more versions, also appears in British Library MS Harley 2253 (ca. 1340), a manuscript anthology that, along with the Auchinleck manuscript, is a superb and intriguing witness to the reading habits of the mid-fourteenth century.[53] The contents of both manuscripts are a blend of devotional and moral treatises and lives, romance, popular verse, and social comment and critique. Where the Auchinleck manuscript is almost self-consciously English in its choice of language and texts, Harley 2253 contains works in England's three languages. Both manuscripts anthologize works that not only comment on social problems but also people England's space with figures of real need. The poems of social and political complaint in both manuscripts have received a good deal of scrutiny for their relationship to Langland's use of complaint, as well as for the ways in which they serve as "performative" texts, texts imaginatively directed to the king that offer pictures of England as in crisis and that can be assimilated to judicial complaint.[54] These poems indeed suggest ways in which Langland responded to an earlier or a contemporary literature of complaint, but, more important, they embody nation as a land whose geographic identity is marked by poverty and injustice, not the garden but the garden wasted by its guardians. In so doing they do not so much argue against elitism as refuse to idealize any benefit that issues from exclusivity or isolation, which are the prior conditions of elitism.

"The Simonie" (ca.1321), which exists in the Auchinleck manuscript, is a sharp critique of the ways in which greed for money has infiltrated all levels of society and of the church, plunging the land into war, famine, and dearth, physical and spiritual.[55] The narrator presents himself as speaking to an audience—"Ye that wolen abide, listneth and ye mowen here/ The skile./ I nelle liyen for no man, herkne who so wile" (4–6)—and implicitly as a voice for those without. Among the voiceless poor are those left unshriven or unburied by greedy friars, parishioners at the mercy of those who buy and sell ecclesiastical livings, beggars turned away by rich abbeys, households left uncared for by lazy priests, and inhabitants of town and country at the mercy of knights more interested in clothes than valor, justices more concerned with gain than law, tax collectors who deceive both people and king, as well as bailiffs, beadles, accountants, attorneys, and merchants, all intent on individual profit. The narrator warns that God sends "derthe" (392) to punish the world's pride, but when a good year comes, "Tho were we also muchele shrewes, as we were beforn, / Or more" (406–7). In speaking for the poor man, the narrator imaginatively speaks to those in authority, including the king, or to those who have the ability to redress what he describes as a national crisis of greed. "The Simonie" is the last text in the Auchinleck manuscript as it now exists and comes after a number of romances, the Battle Abbey Roll, and devotional texts in a codex thought to be the product of a professional London workshop and intended for a wealthy household. Its appearance in Auchinleck, as well as its versions in two later manuscripts, one from the late fourteenth century, the other from the first quarter of the fifteenth, evinces its relevance to readers far removed from the times of Edward II. Moreover, in the 1330s, when the Auchinleck manuscript was produced, the concerns of "The Simonie" were also the subjects of poems from earlier periods copied into Harley 2253. "Song of the Husbandman" and "Trailbaston," both in Harley 2253, are anchored in a sense of England as land in ways that look forward to Langland's use of Piers's croft as symbolic space.[56] Both poems depend on an evocation of place for their effects. As in "The Simonie," the "Song of the Husbandman" is voiced by a narrator who "hears" the complaint of "men upo mold" and conveys it to the audience. The poem itself is more immediate than "The Simonie" because after the opening "Ich herde," the first-person pronouns belong to the husbandmen themselves, the third-person pronouns to those who rob and threaten. Thus the "hayward heteth us harm" (15), the "bailif bockneth us bale"

(16), the "wodeward waiteth us wo" (17). The final lines link personal complaint to national:

> Ruls ys oure ruye and roted in the stre,
>   For wickede wederes by broke and by brynke.
> Thus wakeneth in the world wondred and wee
>   Asc god is swynden anon as so forte swynke. (69–72)

Our rye and straw spoiled and rotted is the result of bad weather, itself a sign of woe in the world. The final despairing remark that it is as good to die right now than to work so hard (and die later) ends the poem with a voice from the land that does not take refuge in pious sentiments but speaks from within the harsh realities of those who till the soil.

"Trailbaston" is even more immediate. It is one of many Anglo-Norman poems in Harley 2253 and is dated to the reign of Edward II. The poem begins with its narrator saying, "Desire seizes me to rhyme and make a story about an ordinance that is enacted in the land," that is, Trailbaston, by which commissions of justices visited each county, inquiring into statements of offense, which they would then try, either fining or imprisoning the offenders. The speaker describes himself as falsely accused and therefore in hiding in the forest.[57] The commissions were intended to deal with local acts of violence but produced violent reactions in counties where they were seen as invasive and unjust. The narrator describes a breakdown of community wherein charges brought by neighbors could lead to indictment by Trailbaston judges and to prison or stiff fines. To what he describes as a corrupt system of justice, the narrator counterposes the forest where he lives. He describes the woods in idyllic terms:

> Pur ce me tendroi antre bois, suz le jolyf umbray;
> La n'y a fauceté ne nulle male lay,
> En le bois de Belregard, ou vole le jay
> E chaunte russinole touz jours santz delay. (17–20)

His description of the woods where there is beautiful shade, no falseness, no bad law, and where the jay flies and the nightingale sings all day is repeated a few stanzas later. There (lines 53–56), he says that in the forest there is no plea except the wild beast and the beautiful shade, juxtaposing the perils of natural law with England's common law and that it is better to live "with me" in the woods than in the bishop's prison (65–66).

In the final stanza, the narrator describes the forest as a type of England:

> Cest rym fust fet al bois, desouz un lorer,
> La chaunte merle, russinole e eyre l'esperver;
> Escrit estoit en perchemeyn pur mout remenbrer
> E gitté en haut chemyn qe um le dust trover. (97–100)

> [This rhyme was made in the wood, beneath a laurel tree,
> there sing the blackbird and the nightingale and hovers the
> sparrowhawk; it was written on a parchment to keep it
> the more in remembrance, and thrown on the high road
> that people should find it.]

The first line falls back on the picture of the idyllic wood where the poem was made. However, in the second line, which appears equally careless, the poet uses the word *eyre* to describe the movements of the sparrowhawk. Hawks, of course, fly to hunt and hover over their prey. What is more, they fly on a circuit, just as justices travel on law circuits, and the word *eire* was commonly used to describe both the circuit of judges and the circuit court. In the third line the poet stresses the need for documents: they keep complaints in remembrance. By throwing his poem on the road, the poet publishes it, makes it available to whoever finds and reads it. The stanza is less artless than it appears. The first two lines begin by stressing difference and end by suggesting similarities between the law of the forest and the law of England. In the last two lines, the narrator no longer poses as an artless storyteller but as an author writing on parchment, sending his poem into a world of travelers, all regulated by the very common law he has decried. The woods that at first seemed an isolated space have, by the end of the poem, been drawn into a broader realm where the very road onto which the parchment is thrown is also the road by which judges travel their circuits. In other words, the implied map embedded in the poem includes a section called "le bois de Belregard" through which or around which roads trace their ways. What the much later Gough map of Britain (ca. 1360) depicts with its careful delineation of waterways, roads, cities, and distances, "Trailbaston" implies with its subtle picture of the refugee from society nonetheless depending on society to read his rhyme because he has access to parchment, pen, and roadway.

The obvious correlative to "Trailbaston" is the legend of Robin Hood.[58] Though the two earliest of the Robin Hood texts, *Robin Hood and the Monk* and *Robin Hood and the Potter*, are copied into mid-fifteenth-century manuscripts, there were references to tales of Robin Hood much earlier.[59] In the B-text of *Piers Plowman*, Gloton says he does not know his Paternoster or stories of "oure lord ne of oure lady" but does know "rymes of Robyn hode" (*Piers Plowman*, B: 5.394–96), and in *Troilus* Pandarus seems to allude to Robin Hood when he refers to the "haselwode, there joly Robyn pleyde" (V:1174). Such references suggest, as J. R. Maddicott has argued, that the tales must have begun circulating very early to have made sense in offhand remarks. A good deal of attention has been devoted to Robin Hood, with scholars seeking to date his origins anywhere from the late thirteenth to the mid-fourteenth century. Where Maddicott used *A Geste of Robyn Hode* as the focus for his dating the text to the 1330s, describing it as evincing a much earlier language and range of reference, Stephen Knight and Thomas Ohlgren identify the ballads *Robin Hood and the Potter* and *Robin Hood and the Monk* as the earliest examples of the Robin Hood ballads that were later compiled by the author of the *Gest*, probably in the mid-fifteenth century, though the *Gest* survives only in a printed edition.[60]

Like "Trailbaston," both *Robin Hood and the Monk* and *Robin Hood and the Potter* depict, in Robin's forest hideaway, an alternative to an officially socialized world that nonetheless is linked to and, to some extent, depends on that world. Just as the narrator of "Trailbaston" must leave his *jolyf umbray* in order to publish his rhyme, so in *Robin Hood and the Monk* Robin must leave his own "feyre foreste" (4) in order to go to church:

'Ye, on thyng greves me,' seid Robyn,
'And does my hert mych woo:

That I may not no solem day
To mas nor matyns goo.

Hit is a fourtnet and more,' seid he,
'Syn I my Savyour see . . . ' (21–26)

Robin's language here is thoroughly orthodox: he wishes to attend
Mass on solemn days and to "see" his Savior in the Eucharist. He re-
solves to go to Nottingham anyway "With the myght of mylde Marye"
(28), to whom he is especially devoted. In *Robin Hood and the Potter*, it is
a "prowd potter" who crosses Robin's territory and who has long refused "On peney of pawage to pay" (20). Though he lives in the forest
among his "mery maney" (14), he adopts the ways of the world outside
the forest in expecting travelers to pay a road toll on a path he considers his own. By challenging the potter and trading places with him for
a day, Robin enters a world stamped by mercantile exchange and rivalry, a world at once removed from and similar to his own forest realm.

Both the forest and the town are monetized. Robin wagers with
his men in both ballads, and in *Robin Hood and the Monk* the wager he
makes with Little John and that Little John wins is a cause of strife between them that sets the plot of the ballad in motion. *Robin Hood and
the Potter* is built around an elaborate monetary scheme wherein Robin
changes places with the Potter and takes the load of pots to town, sell-
ing pots worth five pence for three and starting a stampede among the
townspeople who snap them up. The five pots he is left with he gives
to the sheriff's wife. Later he has dinner with the sheriff and his wife,
wins a shooting match with a prize of forty shillings, fools the sheriff
and takes his horse, but says he will send a palfrey to town for the sheriff's wife. Robin may live in the forest, but the author of the ballad has a
shrewd townsman's eye for exchange as pots become pennies, arrows
prizes, and horses tokens of pots sold cheap. Robin soothes the Potter's
complaint that he could have made two nobles from those pots by giving him a princely sum in exchange, ten pounds, what he might earn
in a year. Robin seems to infiltrate the town only to mock its conceptions of value, but, as the ballad indicates, the town and its money cir-
culate through the forest, and Robin and his men wager with all the
enthusiasm of townsfolk.[61]

Like "Trailbaston," the two Robin Hood ballads seem most intent on raising issues relating to law and sovereignty. The narrator of "Trailbaston" questions the justice of the articles of Trailbaston and the very nature of his relationship to a legal and political hierarchy he deems corrupt while still avowing his loyalty to the king:

Ce sunt les articles de Truyllebastoun.
Salve le roi meismes, de Dieu eit maleysoun
Qe a de primes graunta tiel commissioun:
Quar en ascuns des pointz n'est mie resoun. (5–8)

[These are the articles of Trailbaston. Saving the king
himself, may he have God's curse who first of all granted such a
commission; for there is no sense of right in some of its points.]

The speaker thus distinguishes between the king and the law, thereby empowering himself to say that some of its points are unreasonable, as he seeks to demonstrate in the rest of the poem. *Robin Hood and the Monk* is a carefully worked out—if not daring—critique of the basis for social hierarchy.

The author uses the relationship between Robin and Little John and Little John and a king, who might be Edward III, to probe the ways in which the concept of sovereignty can be understood and applied.[62] The poem begins with strife between Robin and Little John because Robin has ordained that Little John shall bear his bow when he goes into town for Mass. Little John's answer restates the terms of a relationship that Robin had misunderstood:

'Thou shall beyre thin own,' seid Litull Jon,
'Maister, and I wyl beyre myne,
And we well shete a peny,' seid Litul Jon,
'Under the grene wode lyne.' (39–42)

Little John calls Robin "Maister," but he also asserts his freedom: he will bear his own bow, as will Robin. He then initiates a contest whereby they will shoot arrows and bet pennies. Robin gets angry and says he will wager three pennies to one of Little John's. Little John goes on to

win five shillings "of his maister" (49). Robin strikes Little John, and
Little John pulls his sword:

> 'Were thou not my maister,' seid Litull John,
> 'Thou shuldis by hit ful sore;
> Get the a man wher thou wille,
> For thou getis me no more.' (59–62)

In this sequence of exchanges, the word *maister* predominates, but
clearly Robin and John express different understandings of what mastery consists of. John is the one who uses and subtly offers a definition
of the word as a relationship rooted not in power but in an individual's
recognition of authority. John also suggests that he understands authority as having some relation to equity: you bear your bow, and I bear
mine. More startling is his statement that he will no longer be Robin's
"man," thus that the bond between master and man can be broken by
either party. On the other hand, once Robin has been captured, impris-
oned, and given a death penalty, John still refers to Robin as "maister"
(129) and is the one who saves him by a combination of strength and
stealth. John refers to the king, to whom he later delivers the letters
about Robin that the Monk was bearing, as "my lege lorde" and "my
lege kyng" (213, 215), and the king makes John a "yeman of the crown"
(229). John then goes on to redefine his relationship with both masters.
When he rescues Robin, he tells him, "I have done the a gode turne for
an ill / Quit me whan thou may" (305–6). Robin then says that he will
make John "maister. . . . Of alle my men and me" (313–14). John responds by refusing:

> 'Nay, be my trouth,' seid Litull John,
> 'So shalle hit never be;
> But lat me be a felow,' seid Litull John,
> 'No noder kepe I be.' (315–18)

In choosing Robin, John deserts the king, whose first reaction
is outrage: "I made hem yemen of the crowne, / And gaf hem fee with
my hond" (339–40). He then reconsiders, "He is trew to his maister . . .
He lovys better Robyn Hode/ Then he dose us ychon" (347, 349–50).
The king here serves as the ballad's explicator. He recognizes that

Robin Hood will always be "bond" (351) to Little John and that those bonds are ones of obligation on Robin's part and love on John's. The obligations that tie together king and townsman, monk and king, king and sheriff are inherently less binding than those that tie Robin to his men. And yet through Robin, whose assumption of limitless sovereignty at the beginning of the ballad brought his own life into the balance, the ballad also offers a sly lesson on bad kingship. What the king in the ballad understands as the lesson of the tale, does the king himself understand? In affirming its loyalty to that king, the ballad makes a space to instruct regality and, in so doing, uses the green world as a parallel to the world of town and crown. The forest is not a separate space within England but, like the island of Britain, a distinct space that nonetheless is related to and indebted to its neighboring communities. Moreover, by suggesting the interrelatedness of forest and town, the ballad's author, like that of "Trailbaston," peoples another portion of the map of England, Barnstable in Yorkshire, and provides voices that are not spoken about but that speak and act with a good deal of social understanding.

If, indeed, the early traditions of Robin Hood belong to the period when MS Harley 2253 was being assembled, they share much with some of the poems in that anthology. The Robin Hood tales are firmly located in the north and have long fascinated historians with their place-names and with the possible identities of Robin and the sheriff. "Trailbaston," written between 1305 and 1307, like another poem in Harley 2253, "Against the King's Taxes," is carefully linked to actual persons and situations in England. Though the Forest Belregard is fanciful, the judges named in stanza nine of "Trailbaston" are not and can be used to date the poem. "Against the King's Taxes," has, by its most recent editor, been linked to the late 1330s and to the financial crisis in which Stratford played such an important part. The skill with which it is put together—it is macaronic, in Anglo-Norman and Latin—makes it likely that it was intended for an educated reader.[63] If the poem was not written during the 1330s, it was certainly copied into an anthology then and belongs to a decade in which princely advice sometimes took the form of complaint. The speaker complains about the king waging war out of the country and urges on the king the need to not act without counsel, "For si la commune de sa terre velint consentire" (7). The community or the commons of the realm are just those persons elevated throughout the 1330s and held before the king's eyes as demanding his attention. The speaker complains in great detail about taxes, about the shortage of coins in the country, suggesting that the king might melt down his silver for coins and eat from wooden vessels, noting that the realm is potentially dangerous with too much poverty and lack and too little cash.

The quarrel with Stratford—or the terms in which it was cast by both sides—might be described as evidence for a nation whose outlines were being drawn to accommodate more than castles. Insular romance and baronial opposition to the crown, codified in the Magna Carta and underlined by the Barons' War of 1264–67 and the poetry that marked it and the death of its leader, Simon de Montfort, combined with the growing power of gentry and merchants, all bear witness to the process of England's increasing multivocality. Certainly William of Pagula, Stratford, the anonymous authors of poems and ballads, and the compiler of Harley 2253 did not arrive sui generis in the 1330s.[64] One of the poems from early in the fourteenth century included in Harley 2253 is a lament for Simon de Montfort, who had been defeated by Henry III's eldest son, later Edward I, which, like *The Song of Lewes*, opposes baronial to royal power. The author states that through his death, the earl Montfort conquered, comparing him to Thomas à Becket, who also set himself against unlimited royal power.[65] "The Elegy on the Death of Edward I," also in Harley 2253, laments Edward's death while at the same time advising his son:

> Nou is Edward of Carnarvan
> > King of Engelond al aplyht,
> God lete him ner be worse man
> > Then is fader, ne lasse of myht
> > To holden is pore-men to ryht,
> Ant understonde good consail,
> > Al Engelond for te wisse and diht;
> Of gode knyhtes darh him nout fail.[66]

The last two wishes—that Edward will care for the poor and accept good counsel—qualify might with right, implicitly linking the ability to guide or instruct and to rule England with the ability to understand good counsel. The inherently constitutional subtext of this literature can certainly be traced back to Bracton, who begins the *De Legibus* by identifying England with its laws. After saying that a realm needs two things, arms and laws, he explains that England's laws are different from those of other nations:

> Though in almost all lands use is made of the *leges* and the *jus scriptum*, England alone uses unwritten law and custom. There law derives from nothing written [but] from what usage has approved. Nevertheless, it will not be absurd to call English laws *leges*, though they are unwritten, since whatever has been rightly decided and approved with the counsel and consent of the magnates and the general agreement of the *res publica*, the authority of the king or prince having first been added thereto, has the force of law.[67]

Bracton's language here is somewhat elastic. His phrasing seems to privilege the consensus of the magnates and the solemn promise of the *res publica*. However, in using *praecedente*, he places the king's authority as a prior condition, the force of law then a triple force, king, magnates, and body politic. He does not deny the authority of the crown, but he places it within the concerns of the law of England, which has a triune origin. Later, he expands on the relationship of the king to law by comparing the king to the Virgin Mary, who, like Jesus, was privileged to be above the law but chose to be under the law in the interests of reason, justice, and humility. He concludes this analogy by saying, "Let the king therefore do the same lest his power remain unbridled."[68] Bracton continues this knotty and carefully worded argument by saying that there can be no writ against the king, nor can anyone presume to question or contravene his acts, but it is possible to petition the king, giving him the opportunity to amend an act. If the king does not amend, he awaits God's vengeance. Here Bracton gives no room for revolt against the king or for questioning the king, and yet is not a petition a form of questioning an act whose consequences seem unfortunate or unjust? The king's relationship to law may be analogous to those of Jesus and Mary, but he is neither.[69] He should emulate them and choose to observe the law. His citizens may not question him, but there are nonetheless official means to do so. Bracton says at the beginning of *De Legibus* that because England's law is unwritten and is a law of custom he writes to instruct judges in that law, compiling a *summa* of the judgments of the past. However, a written *summa* is also potentially available to anyone who can read it. It thus becomes more than a record for judges; it is implicitly a record of every man's rights under the laws of England, which constitute a bridle to unchecked regal power.

ROYAL ENCLOSURES

If, as I have suggested, Stratford's acts of publication belong to a much longer historical narrative, the narrative does not end with Stratford's apparent victory, nor does the narrative belong only to him and to those who sought to describe England as bound within a set of obligations and contingencies that did not allow for the isolation privilege might convey. Edward and those around him had a keen sense of nation and sought to define it through prayers meant for public reading, through tournaments, and through the attempt to create a concept of sacred kingship, whose official manifestation was the Order of the Garter. Edward, like the authors, manuscript compilers, and political figures of the 1330s, was engaged in a definition of space, but a space made exclusive by blood and by a religion of chivalry.

Edward III's use of propaganda, as A. K. McHardy has noted, was not as textually sophisticated as that of the French kings; however, Edward's understanding of the uses of place suggests his keen awareness that images could be made with more than words.[70] As McHardy also notes, however, Edward fully understood the tradition of asking for prayers for the king and frequently requested prayers for the success of his military campaigns. The "space" of prayers for the king, like that for his quarrel with Archbishop Stratford, was public, as was the space allotted for tournaments. The list of the tournaments of Edward III that Juliet Vale provides as Appendix 12 of *Edward III and Chivalry* suggests Edward's attention to English geography, since there are tournaments in York, Exeter, Coventry, Bristol, Hereford, and Lincoln, as well as in London and its suburbs.[71] Tournaments certainly allowed for public displays of chivalry and skill and promoted the images of king and knights and were used strategically by sovereigns and nobles, as in 1329 Mortimer had sought to use his tournament of the

Round Table to promote his own claims to the lineage of Arthur.[72] That the young Edward understood the rhetorical gesture in tournament cloth is clear from his persistent orders from 1327 on forbidding tournaments in places that were to become the sites of his own tournaments.[73] His own tournaments and hastiludes, with their mummings, prizes, and dangers, subsumed potentially random violence under the rubric of royal patronage and imprinted the king's sanction on the ritual of public displays. Just as Stratford managed to create his own public arena for verbal swordplay and the anonymous poets for social critique, in his efforts to control space Edward demonstrated not simply his understanding of Stratford's techniques, but his intention to define himself and his reign in terms of a chivalry that he then went on to construct.

Construct is to be taken literally, for in the two structures finished during the middle period of Edward's reign he articulated a concept of chivalry that emanated from the crown. Both of these are ghost structures: St. Stephen's Chapel in Westminster was destroyed by fire in 1834, and St. George's Chapel, Windsor, was extensively rebuilt by Edward IV and Henry VII. Edward himself completed and thus altered buildings that had been begun by Henry III and continued by Edward I.[74] The dating for both chapels cannot be separated from the political and social history of the 1340s, when Edward recouped the losses of the affair with Archbishop Stratford by ensuring the loyalty of his magnates and isolating Stratford and by creating the Order of the Garter, which celebrated the prowess of those most closely associated with the king.[75] Edward's political astuteness can be registered in his three building campaigns, each of which was designed to link his reign mythically to chivalric enterprise. In January 1344, at Windsor, he held a tournament that announced the formation of the Round Table and ordered the erection of a building ("una nobilissima domus") made to hold a large round table.[76] On 23 April, St. George's Day, 1349, he held a tournament to celebrate the Order of the Garter, though the College of St. George, to which the chapel was turned over, was founded in August 1348.[77] Edward's founding of the College of St. Stephen in 1348 was also accompanied by an elaborate building campaign, completing a structure begun by his grandfather, Edward I, and decorating it to magnify his own ideology of dynastic kingship.[78]

The Windsor tournament of 1344 looks forward to the founding of the two colleges and of the Order of the Garter with which it was frequently confused, even by contemporary commentators like Froissart. According to Adam Murimuth, after three days of jousting, Edward made a great feast at which he announced the Table, to be celebrated at the Feast of Pentecost, the traditional date of notable events in King Arthur's court. Jean le Bel, from whom Froissart drew much of his information about the early years of Edward's reign, says that King Arthur had originally built the castle of Windsor, which Edward rebuilt before forming the Round Table to honor the knights who served him so well.[79] This initial attempt to define his reign within the framework of Arthurian myth linked Edward to his grandfather, who had chosen to emphasize his chivalry and that of his knights and canceled Mortimer's earlier attempt to insert himself into Arthurian lineage in his own tournament of the Round Table. However, Edward's Round Table was to some extent canceled by his founding of the Order of the Garter and by his endowment of the two colleges of St. George and St. Stephen, in Windsor and Westminster. Richard Barber notes that in 1344 John, the future king of France, established a collegiate church, along with an order that would gather on 23 April, St. George's Day, and on 15 August, the Feast of the Assumption. As Barber suggests, both John and Edward in their competitiveness sought to tie their orders to a concept of nation centered on the king.[80] Here John would have the advantage, since Saint George and the Virgin Mary enjoyed a spiritual status far beyond anything King Arthur, whose very existence was questioned, could command. By abandoning the Round Table for colleges devoted to Saint George, Saint Stephen, and the Virgin Mary, Edward located his own reign within sanctified space, space the French kings had long inhabited.[81]

The chapels belonging to each college serve as more elaborate definitions of nobly sanctified space. According to accounts of the construction of the Chapel of St. George, there were pews for the royal family, along with newly built stalls for the knights of the order, above which were crooks to hang the distinctive helm and sword of each knight. Newly glazed and painted windows were installed; however, we have no idea of their content or the decorative program for the chapel.[82] The prominent position given to helms and swords suggests that the chapel was oriented around themes of Christian chivalry and kingship, meant to establish a concept of nation as a godly and loyal confraternity of knights. More is known of the Chapel of St. Stephen at Westminster because it lasted long enough for eighteenth-century antiquarians to describe and make copies of what had not been previously destroyed when the chapel, which became the site for parliamentary Commons during the reign of Edward VI, underwent "renovations" until it was eventually destroyed by fire. The chapel, which was dedicated to Saint Stephen and the Virgin Mary, had been "in progress" since the time of Edward I, but it was during the reign of Edward III that it was finished, in a manner that was intended to mark it as the English answer to the Sainte-Chapelle in Paris. Like the Sainte-Chapelle, St. Stephen's had two floors, the lower one probably for the court and the upper reserved for Edward and Philippa and their family.

The upper chapel, more private than the Chapel of St. George at Windsor, reveals both Edward's dynastic ambitions and his estimation of the perils of his place in history. The decoration of the east wall of the upper chapel on either side of the altar proclaims Edward's family in relation to images of sanctified kingship.[83] To the north Edward and his sons kneel, along with Saint George, who directs them to the Virgin and Child. To the south kneel Philippa and her daughters. All members of the royal family are dressed richly and fashionably. In the upper register above Edward and his sons is a depiction of the Magi adoring the Virgin and Child, while above the queen and her daughters are the Angels Appearing to the Shepherds, the Adoration of the Shepherds, and the Purification.[84] Paul Binski has noted that the Magi were connected to the lineage of the French royal house, a connection that Edward, claiming the French throne, would certainly wish to adopt as his own.[85] Howe has analyzed the east wall as evincing Edward's attempt to create images of cultic kingship rivaling those of the French kings. Thus Edward and his family, divided by gender, knelt worshiping the Virgin and Child directly below biblical scenes of adoration: the contemporary thereby becomes iconic, participatory in the mysteries of the Word made flesh. There are, of course, numerous medieval donor portraits in books of hours where patrons are inserted into scenes of the Nativity or the Passion as kneeling figures of penance or adoration. The person using the book for devotions thus sees himself or herself in the sacred scenes that accompany the texts. St. Stephen's Chapel offered something grander to Edward and those who worshiped in the upper chapel, for he and his family would be kneeling in a place that depicted them kneeling, their piety reflecting and reflective of the pious figures on the east wall of the chapel. In its reflexiveness, the wall seems to look forward to the Wilton Diptych, a portable altar, in which Richard would, kneeling, see himself kneeling before the Virgin and Child, flanked by his patron saints and hailed by the Child in a gesture that matched his own. Just as Richard is depicted frozen in eternal youth in the Wilton Diptych, so Edward and Philippa and their sons and daughters are frozen in their own beauty, vigor, and rich display, protected by Saint George, whom Edward had made an Englishman.[86]

The prominence of the Virgin in the program for the east wall is both conventional and reflective of Edward's own devotions.[87] As Miri Rubin has recently demonstrated, devotion to the Virgin was universal in western Europe in the late Middle Ages, and she was frequently employed to magnify the ideals of sovereignty and chivalry.[88] The site on which St. Stephen's Chapel was built was part of the complex of buildings that included Westminster Hall, in which was the Painted Chamber, and the Privy Palace (see fig. 4), along with a private oratory for the king, the Chapel of the Pew, which contained a golden image of the Virgin donated by Henry III.[89] This oratory was finished by Edward III and is associated with his deep devotion to the Virgin. J. J. Alexander's suggestion that an image in a psalter from the 1340s indicates that already by that time Edward had figuratively presented England to the Virgin is, as Howe remarks, underlined by the charter for the College of St. Stephen, in which the king states that Mary has never abandoned us with her patronage but has protected us in various dangers and been to us a better mother ("melior mater nostra"), dedicating the college and the chapel in honor of Saint Stephen, protomartyr, and of God and especially his blessed mother.[90] The intimate and familial language of the charter anticipates the wall paintings, which were executed between 1351 and 1363.[91]

Along the walls on either side of the altar and below the windows there were paintings of biblical scenes that seem to evoke the crowded panorama of the Painted Chamber while also suggesting Edward's recognition that his reign brought distinctive responsibilities.[92] The Old Testament illustrations crowded in ascending registers along the walls of the Painted Chamber, which Binski has extensively analyzed as augmenting the martial prowess and ambitions of Edward I, depict scenes of war and conquest drawn from the Books of Kings, Judges, and Samuel, as well as the narrative of Judus Macabeus from the first nine chapters of I Maccabees.[93] He speculates that the meaning of the program, specific to Edward I, was lost by 1307–8, only a few years after the completion of the paintings, when the murals were referred to as *diversae historiae*, later seen simply as warlike narratives.[94] Nonetheless, the Painted Chamber was considered one of the wonders of medieval Westminster, and Edward III's decision to decorate St. Stephen's Chapel, while certainly signaling his intention to create a place in Westminster as splendid as the Sainte-Chapelle, also indicates his awareness that murals could serve as instructive texts, especially when pictures were accompanied by inscriptions.[95] Andrew Martindale has noted that the paintings in St. Stephen's would seem more appropriate as stained-glass windows. However, the window glazing was completed by 1351, and, from the chamfering of the stones on which the surviving fragments are painted, the paintings appear to be an afterthought, set within a preexisting design. He speculates that the paintings may express ideas from within Edward's circle.[96] The two surviving fragments, both now in the British Museum, depict the destruction of Job's children (Job 1:18–19) and scenes from the Book of Tobit. The scene from Job shows the sons and daughters of Job feasting at an elaborate medieval banquet table while a hairy devil looks through the window behind them (see fig. 5). The scene from the Book of Tobit depicts the marriage of Sarah and Tobias, accompanied by a text describing them as praising and obediently magnifying God. There were eighty pictures in all, illustrating "the history of Jonah, the martyrdom of the Apostles, the history from Joseph to Joshua, the history of Daniel, Jeremiah, the Israelites, Tobit, Judith, Susannah, Bel and the Dragon, Samuel to Solomon and the Miracles of Our Savior."[97]

The sequence is usually seen as jumbled, its program not easily recoverable; however, the histories suggest a focus on heavenly redemption and favor for the faithful. The fragment depicting Job's children feasting and the opening page of the sumptuous BL Royal MS. 20 D IV, depicting Arthur's court at table, both describe noble luxury and hint at coming disaster in the devil's grinning face behind the one table and the dalliance of Lancelot and Guinevere at the other (see fig. 6).[98]

If such a scene might remind Edward of the insecurities of worldly fortune, the story of Tobit would assure him of heavenly favor for the devout, as would the stories of Susannah, Daniel, and Jonah. The latter example is especially interesting since sometimes Nineveh's penance was mentioned in prayers asking for the cessation of the pestilence.[99] Though Ormrod has demonstrated ways in which Edward and his administrators managed to come through the terrible disruptions of the plague with more economic stability than most countries, responding to its fiscal stresses by safeguarding revenues and regulating trade, and Binski has argued against reading the stories of Job and Tobit in St. Stephen's as traceable to consciousness of the plague, the relationship between the east wall with its kneeling royalty and the north and south walls with their examples of salvific history seems manifest.[100] The very good fortune of the kneeling devotees demands the reminders of disaster that are opposed to them—grinning demons, lions' dens, false charges of adultery, a city's threatened destruction, martyred innocence—averted through faith in God. The paintings were not begun until after the first devastation of the plague and were continued for eleven more years. More important yet, the chapel embodies a king's piety and obedience to God, a king who, along with his family, knelt in a place made as a reliquary to hold a golden image of Mary and, when present, that king and his family depicted on either side of its altar. Richard II might take the Wilton Diptych with him and turn each place in which he prayed into a mirror of himself hailing the Virgin and Child, but Edward constructed a place and left himself there to pray perpetually.

(The same precinct once contained another hallowed place. Midway between St. Stephen's and the Painted Chamber in the king's alley, on a site once identified with the Chapel of the Pew, was the first Cotton Library (ca. 1622). Kevin Sharpe speculates that by siting his library, which had a sign-out system and was an important center for research, in the precincts of Westminster, Cotton signified his understanding of its national importance. Cotton's collection became politically significant at the end of the decade when parliamentary calls for rights and liberties appealed to the past and an understanding of England's history. Charles I closed down the library, as earlier kings had foreclosed places of dangerous sacrality, and never returned it to Cotton during his lifetime, though he had access to his collection, which now resides in another temple of devotion, the British Library. The famous fire in the Cotton library occurred in 1731, when the collection had been moved to Ashburnham House.)[101]

St. Stephen's Chapel, like the Chapel of St. George at Windsor, defined kingship as dynastic, divinely ordained, chivalric, and mediatory. What came to Edward from the mediation of Saint George and the Virgin was then passed on to family and loyal companions through the mediating powers of Edward. Like St. George's Chapel, St. Stephen's was decorated with coats of arms; it also contained depictions of some key members of Edward's inner circle. Both chapels were nested within royal complexes. Windsor was far more private and exclusive to the king and his court. Westminster was a center for royal business, but both St. Stephen's and the king's oratory, the Chapel of Our Lady of the Pew, sometimes described as a "closet," were distinct from the Abbey, the Painted Chamber, the Privy Palace, and Westminster Hall and, from what is known, reserved for those in the court's inner circle. Place, where royalty intersects with heavenly favor, is boundaried, distinct, set apart in its own sovereign sphere, whose accoutrements are fittingly splendid and historically charged with associative meanings. The golden and jeweled image of the Virgin that occupied the Chapel of Our Lady of the Pew, Edward's "closet," was originally given by Henry III and used devotionally by subsequent kings.[102] However, it was also possibly a pilgrimage site, proximate enough to St. Stephen's Chapel for both to have been viewed by those outside the king's intimate circle.[103] The images, of the Virgin and of those on the walls of the chapel, would have offered circumscribed perspectives on sovereignty and piety, to some extent reminding the viewer of the immediate access to divinity enjoyed and mediated by princes. Place, and implicitly nation, is thus concentrated in divine kingship.

PLACE AND PLAGUE TIME

Other attempts during this same period to imagine place suggest that the 1348 outbreak of the pestilence had complicated a rhetoric already complex in the 1340s. The poet of *Wynnere and Wastoure* imagines nation in terms of a place set off by earthworks, bounded by armies and armorial banners, and centered on the king but also a place infected by post-plague economic problems and social tensions.[104] The debate he stages is played out before the king, who is crowned in gold, sumptuously dressed in a garment embroidered with golden falcons carrying garters in their beaks, and wearing a blue belt, embroidered with ducks and drakes that appeared to tremble in the presence of the falcons (lines 90–98). The poet provides a picture of England as a place where the impulses of winning and wasting are ordered by a focal point, the "comliche" king (90), in much the same way that the later and royally commissioned *Le songe du vergier* stages a debate before Charles V of France. The frontispiece for that manuscript depicts Charles sitting in judgment, his figure at the center and apex of the miniature balancing and focusing the entire composition of figures below him.[105]

Edward's ability to focus the nation through his own regality is underscored by *Wynnere and Wastoure*, which both Ralph Hanna and Vance Smith have related to the household of the realm.[106] The semi-populist concerns in some of the lyrics copied into MS Harley 2253 are, in *Wynnere and Wastoure*, narrowed, along with their implied audience. Thus poems like "Against the King's Taxes" (1338–39), "Trailbaston" (1302), and the "Song of the Husbandman" all raise issues pertinent to a broadly conceived notion of the commonwealth, ones to be found sometimes in preaching manuals, as Richard Newhauser has suggested. In contrast, *Wynnere and Wastoure* purports to speak not with the voice of the people but with the voice of the magnates. The evidence for the dire vision of contemporary England is adduced by the narrator from "boyes of blode" who wed "ladyes in londe" "with boste and with pryde." If Doomsday seems imminent, it is because a western man dare not send his son southward, where wit and wiles predominate. The narrator falls asleep and awakens in a beautiful landscape, where he sees two armies arraigned with their banners, awaiting the arrival of the king, who is described in loving and lavish detail, crowned with gold, sitting on a silken bench with a scepter in his hand, wearing elaborately embroidered clothing and a blue garter, the sign of his new order. In other words, from the beginning the debate between Wynnere and Wastoure is presented as of significance to the king, and the debate is, in the end, judged by the king, who sends Wynnere to Rome and Wastoure to London, where both can serve him, the one financing his wars and the other encouraging commerce.

In contradistinction to these places, enclosed, sacralized, bejeweled, and privileged, Langland makes place the question, not the answer. For example, *Wynnere and Wastoure* after its account of England's confusion of degree then describes the narrator as having a dream:

> Als I went in the weste, wandrynge myn one,
> Bi a bonke of a bourne; bryghte was the sone
> Undir a worthiliche wodde by a wale medewe:
> Fele floures gan folde ther my fote steppede. (32–35)

The poet here employs the conventions of dream visions: a wandering narrator with an unresolved problem and a pastoral setting. When the narrator sits down amid the flowers and lays his head upon a hill, the dream that will explore the problem, in this case the social disruptions of the present day, is bound to ensue. That dream presents the world as circumscribed by what are magnatial concerns and thus by a courtly ethic.

The opening lines of the A-text of *Piers Plowman* at once evoke those conventions and transform them:

> In a somer sesoun whanne softe was the sonne
> I shop me into a shroud as I a shep were;
> In abite as an Ermyte, vnholy of werkis,
> Wente wyde in þis world wondris to here.
> But on a may morwenyng on maluerne hilles
> Me befel a ferly, of fairie me þouȝte:
> I was wery [for] wandrit & wente me to reste
> Vndir a brood bank be a bourn[e] side,
> And as I lay & lenide & lokide on þe watris
> I slomeride into a slepyng, it swiȝede so merye. (1–10)

As Derek Pearsall points out, by the time Langland writes the C-text of the poem, he has shorn these lines of their pastoral detail.[107] However, in their earliest incarnation they nod to the conventions of dream vision, perhaps to *Wynnere and Wastoure* whose narrator also wanders in the west and has a dream in which he thinks he is in a strange part of the world. But Langland's narrator is dressed to deceive and wanders "wide in this world" to hear wonders. He slides into a dream in which he sees a field but hardly a field populated by armies and banners and a king decorated with golden falcons. The "fair field full of folk," though bounded by the tower of Truth and the pit of hell, is as indeterminate as the battlefield in *Wynnere and Wastoure* is determined by the king, its focal point. Likewise, rather than the debate carried out by two opponents before that king, Langland's narrator hears the babble of the world in all its noise, self-interest, and confusion.

Langland also marks this place, whose confusions in relation to its professed ideals are the grounds of the narrator's own search for meaning, as a place now scarred by pestilence and continues to do so through the B- and C-texts of the poem. Of Langland's several explicit references to the plague, only one suggests the plague as a boundary between what was and what is and shall be. The reference is maintained through the three texts. In A: 10 (191) Wit castigates the unnatural marriages being made between old men and young women and between widows and fortune hunters, saying that such marriages bring no fruit but jangling. He marks what he implies are unnatural couplings by saying, "Manye peire siþen [þ]e pestilence han p[l]iȝt hem togidere," the glue for such plighting of troths not truth but covetousness. In all the texts (and in some C manuscripts, *pestilence* is amplified by making of it a phrase, *pestilence tyme*), Langland sets the plague within the continuum of postlapsarian history, the devolution from Cain to Noah, and, afterward, the fresh world falling further into uncharity, the sign of which is covetous marriage. In C: 5 Langland also underlines the immediacy of *pestilence time* when he uses Will's dialogue with Conscience, what Pearsall has called his *apologia*, as the prelude to his dream wherein Reason, preaching before the king, proves that *this pestilence* is the result of sin. In A, Conscience is the preacher; in B, Reason preaches alone; in C, Conscience stands with the cross before the king while Reason preaches. The configuration in C, together with the effect of the *apologia*, in which Will locates himself in Cornhill with a wife named Kit and goes on to interrogate himself about the nature of the work he performs, links his private conversation with Conscience with a more general picture of the commonwealth. For both man and nation, Conscience is the necessary interlocutor, the medium before whom Reason itself must be judged. What Langland continues to mark with this reference to the plague is a specific place: this scene, with its evocation of a London neighborhood, another place called "vp londe," a "cot," the outlines of a young man's education, as well as the sketches of actual labor, anchors the plague reference to "real time," lifting it from the more general prophetic use of pestilence as one of the signs of God's wrath, which Langland employs in his two other references to the pestilence, one of which is only in C. Here, "this pestilence" is our pestilence, the one that now exists and has altered our understanding of the world as we know it, and that world is England. Or, as Hanna says, "through this reference, Langland creates a readily assimilable memorial space within which one might apprehend normative social relations, a space extending back to the blush of Edwardian triumph, Crécy in 1346."[108] It is in A: 10 and Wit's description of mercantile marriages, marriages whose relation to sacrament seems clearly tenuous, made *since* the pestilence that we have a greater understanding of what *pestilence time* in fact means.

Langland's *pestilence time* also domesticates what the chroniclers originally described as an arrival from distant lands, thereby turning a foreign invader into a local season as identifiable and evocative as *harvest time* or *Lenten tide*. Like those early Saxons or Danes who arrived to slaughter and stayed to farm, the pestilence, once having penetrated England's boundaries, has taken up residence.[109] Higden's *Polychronicon* and its continuations indicate the difficulties of bringing the realities of this new order into focus with an earlier image of nation. In the last paragraph of his *Polychronicon*, Higden follows an account of Edward returning to England from a subdued Calais with one of unceasing rain and *Magna mortalitas*.[110] In fact, his account of the deaths of people throughout the world is the last bit of history he records. One of his continuators describes the plague of 1361 that killed more men than women.[111] The writer then goes on to recount an ensuing state of moral chaos, for the women, now in surplus, took as husbands foreigners, imbeciles, and madmen, in their bestiality copulating with their inferiors.

The writer's description of the plague certainly is meant to suggest the overturning of a natural sexual hierarchy, but, and more important in terms of England's own myths, it suggests a return to an unnatural primordial state, one according to the *Brut* set to rights by Brutus. Following Gildas in inscribing the fallen garden onto the map of England, the *Brut* begins with the story of Dioclisian's thirty-three daughters, who murder their husbands and flee to Britain, where they lie with devils and engender giants; their new land is called Albion after the eldest daughter, Albina (3–4). These are the giants of Albion, whom Brutus must conquer before he can repopulate and civilize the island, which he calls Britain. (One account from the cathedral priory of Rochester remarks that Gog and Magog have returned from hell with the plague.)[112] The *Brut* continues to emphasize the monstrous as it affects the nation, whether through outbreaks of extreme barbarism or as barbarism is subdued or, at best, harnessed by key figures, the mythic Brutus and Arthur, and the kings of England. In what Friedrich Brie refers to as the first Continuation of the *Brut*, from 1333 to 1377, the author describes the plague after an account of Geoffrey of Charney's treachery to Edward in the twenty-fourth year of his reign (1350): "And in þis same ȝere, and in þe ȝere afore, & also in þe ȝere aftir, was so grete a pestilences . . . þis pestilence lasted in London fro Michelmasse into Auguste next followyng . . . & in þes dayes was deþ wiþoute sorwe, weddyng wiþoute frendship, wilful penaunce, and derþe wiþout scarste, and fleyng wiþoute refute or socour . . . and in þe same ȝere bygan a wonder þing þat al þat euere were born after þat pestilens hadden ij. chekteth in her heed lasse þan þey had afore." The author includes the chaos of the 1361 plague, wherein the wives of the many dead men were "out of gouernance" and "token husbondes, as wel straungers as oþere lewed and symple peple, þe whiche, forȝetyng her owne wurschip & berthe, coupled & married hem with hem þat were of lowe degre & litel reputacion."[113] What is foregrounded is monstrosity as it is manifested in alliances and affiliations. Even as the chroniclers catalog Edward's new Order of the Garter, the deeds accompanying his war with France, the tournaments celebrating England's chivalry, from 1348 onward all events occur since pestilence time. In the midst of such chivalric triumph, in 1348, Ralph Stratford, bishop of London, purchased a piece of ground called No Man's Land, enclosed it with a brick wall, and dedicated it for the burial of the many dead. Next to that graveyard were the thirteen-plus acres that Walter Manny, knight of the Garter, purchased, also for burial of the dead, and later in 1371 on the same site founded the London Charterhouse.[114] Those graveyards, or plague pits, for London's poor and felonious, for its plague victims, marked the urban landscape, just as the barren fields, the lost animals, and the deserted villages served as markers of a newly inscribed regional topography whose fissures were signs of the monstrous at work in the land.

The A-text of *Piers Plowman* should be seen as broadening a conversation that *Wynnere and Wastoure* occludes. If collections like MS Harley 2253 suggest the ways in which poems relevant to public concerns can coexist with poems seemingly more suitable for those who could afford to create such a manuscript, the A-Text of *Piers Plowman* likewise suggests a far more ambiguously conceived audience, a broadening that is certainly manifest in the poem's use in the 1381 Rising.

Let me return briefly to the debate between Stratford and Edward, or to Archbishop Stratford, who seems also to have envisioned a debate, not between magnatial personae on a battlefield where a king sat in judgment, but a debate made available to an ambiguously conceived audience, to those at Mass in Canterbury, to those in Parliament, and to his bishops. Pieces of that debate still exist as documents; the debate in Parliament was sidelined and further muffled by the panoply of chivalry as it was institutionalized through the founding of the Order of the Garter shortly thereafter. The sign of that order is immediately apparent in *Wynnere and Wastoure*, but it is not in *Piers*. Langland includes a king and courtiers in his poem, but he also includes a half acre and a croft. In exchange for the noble chivalric order with its sumptuous chivalric ideals and furnishings, devoted to the Blessed Virgin and focused on the king, Langland proffers the peasant's holding, whose need for knightly protection is explicit but which is not identified with or seen as an appendage to noble privilege. Langland then quickly assimilates that image (which stands as a corrective to tournament fields, battlefields, and aristocratic excess) to the spiritual demands of Will's quest for understanding and meaning.

The A-text of *Piers Plowman* is contemporaneous with the conception of the decorative program of St. Stephen's Chapel, and both are constructions of place, of English place. One is beautiful, decorated, compact, and focused, containing pictures, statues, and texts, meant to serve as a reliquary not simply for the relics Edward had, but for Edward himself, or for his divinely sanctioned kingship. The other is neither compact nor focused, frequently confusing, and often quite beautiful, but its aesthetic is as expansive and sometimes as tortured as that of another much later poet, Walt Whitman, who anchored his poetry in a different understanding of place and what that might mean

for an American poetics. Langland's contemporary, the poet who perhaps best understood the implications of *Piers Plowman* for English
poetry, Geoffrey Chaucer, to some extent marks the evolutionary spiral from Edwardian space to Langlandian with his own poems. The
enclosed reliquaries, the closets and bedrooms and gardens of doomed
Troy, open onto the map of England, the shires, the cities where plague
bells are heard, where apprentices run amok, where place is "now and
England," and the ground of the search.

CHAPTER FOUR

SUSANNA AND HER GARDEN

The previous chapters explored the master narrative of England's terms of self-definition as it was created by monastic historians and developed by later writers. Their accounts of that isolated but permeable island garden provided the terms for a subtle probing of national identity during and after the reign of Edward III, with William Langland initiating a contestation of images for England that emerged from Edwardian political events and retained its dialogic force during the early modern period. This chapter isolates and analyzes one narrative, the story of Susanna and the Elders, found in the apocryphal thirteenth chapter of Daniel, part of the Greek version of the Book of Daniel. Susanna's story as it was recounted by English writers from the early thirteenth to seventeenth centuries offers a remarkable commentary on the authority of the law as it pertains to individual privacy and to communal prerogatives. Those same terms that are key to England's self-definition are central to the story of Susanna, whose enclosed garden functions as a sign of her enclosed marital chastity, a space whose sanctity is potentially violated by the elders who seek to turn public law to their private purposes. In these texts, both the space and the law are recognizably English. While Edward III set Susanna in the exclusive royal space of St. Stephen's Chapel as one story among many illustrating God's care for the faithful sovereign, these accounts of that same story use it to raise questions about injustice, about the law's protection for the individual, and about the degree to which the private and the communal intersect. Moreover, that space is not conceived of as sacrosanct because it is royal but because it is individual and under the protection of the law. That Susanna is also a chaste woman with a chaste garden makes her story apposite to the literature of virgin enclosure exploited by those who wrote the story of England, as well as by those who adapted the language associated with the Virgin to its late-sixteenth-century Virgin Queen. Though the narrative inevitably reflects the religious and social language of particular periods, not simply the terms of the narrative, but the persistent emphasis on competing systems of authority offer an unusual range of reference, beginning with those found in an early-thirteenth-century Latin poem of Cistercian provenance and ending with the four significant early modern retellings of Susanna, three during the reign of Elizabeth and one in the period before England's garden would become a battlefield. In their shared concern with the nature of privacy and the sanctity of law designed to protect individual rights and property, these texts serve to illustrate the ways in which those questions regarding isolation and enclosure that characterize the terms in which England explored its historic identity can anchor a biblical narrative in a national and ongoing discourse. To this degree localized, the story of Susanna becomes an account of England's fissured but triumphant achievement.

Daniel 13 is set during the Babylonian Captivity and recounts events concerning the Jewish community in Babylon. Susanna is the beautiful and chaste wife of a wealthy man, Joachim, whose home serves as a seat of justice for his fellow Jews. While bathing in their garden, Susanna is spied on and accosted by two judges of Israel who frequent her husband's house. They invite her to satisfy both of them or suffer the penalty for a charge of adultery, which they will bring against her. She refuses, saying that she would rather fall into their hands than sin in the sight of God. She is tried, unveiled, before the people. Led off to execution, Susanna calls out to God, who stirs up the spirit of the young Daniel. Daniel's skill in separating the elders before asking for details of their evidence against Susanna reveals their perjury, and they are put to death by the crowd. The tale is certainly courtroom drama, but it is also a narrative of transgressions—of female chastity and modesty, of the household and property, of justice itself.

Throughout the Middle Ages, the narrative was used to illustrate many types of lessons. The very early church put Susanna in the *Commendatio animae*, where she is invoked in a petition asking salvation from false witnesses. She was also used "as a locus around which exegetes formulated positions regarding marital chastity." Images of Susanna circulated among upper-class Romans.[1] Ambrose, Tertullian, Augustine, and Abelard, who addresses his treatment of Susanna to the nuns of the Paraclete, all use her as an example of chastity, and sometimes her story can be found in manuscripts associated with nuns.[2] Daniel 13 is the epistle for the Saturday before the third Sunday in Lent, where Susanna is linked with the woman taken in adultery, both illustrations of God's just and humane judgment. These same two examples are also linked to the Annunciation and questions about Mary's virginity.[3] Following Saint Ambrose (see note 2), some commentators associate her with Joseph, also falsely accused of and unjustly persecuted for sexual crimes. Hildegard of Bingen compares herself to Susanna as one whom God has liberated from false testimony.[4] Even Henry VIII likened himself to Susanna when seeking to emphasize his fidelity to his conscience in the matter of divorcing Catherine, his dead brother's wife.[5] Ambrose and others praise Susanna for her silence and thus her faith and trust in heavenly justice (here, she can become a type of Christ), and some praise her for calling out in a loud voice, first in horror at the elders' demands, then, later in court, to God. Susanna also appears as the subject of several Latin poems and in poems to the Virgin.[6]

However there are treatments of Daniel 13 that are focused not exclusively on Susanna's piety or God's justice but on the evils of unjust judgment and on legal processes.[7] Genevra Kornbluth argues that Lothar II employed such interpretations to laud himself as a patron of justice and to justify his far from just treatment of his wife in his quest for divorce. Philippe Buc notes a similarly regal attempt to control Susanna's story in the *Postilla Litteralis* of Nicholas of Lyra. Since Nicholas can be placed close to French ruling circles, his attempts to conceptualize power must be considered when contemplating Valois kingship.[8] Nicholas of Lyra focuses on the relationship between the king of Babylon and his Jewish subjects, whose judicial power was delegated to them by the king and thus derived from him. Hence their stoning of the unjust judges cannot be seen as a validation of popular justice. On the other hand, Sir John Fortescue emphasizes due process, saying that the case of Susanna underlines the dangers when law allows proof only by witnesses: "Who, then, can live secure of himself or his own under such a law—a law that offers assistance to anyone hostile to him?"[9] Fortescue, of course, survived well into print culture. Although there are not a large number of medieval English treatments of Susanna, there are enough to warrant looking at her and at the uses to which she is put in political systems where ideas about the nature of power are being debated.

For example, by focusing only on Susanna's modesty, authors can preclude the more dangerous questions about false authority that are embedded in her story. The authors of *The Knight of Tour Landry* and *Le Menagier de Paris* both employ Susanna as an example of chastity and thus as a model for wifely behavior, a concept that has a particular political resonance in the France of Charles V, with its pronounced emphasis on stable marriage and patriarchal control.[10] The Knight of Tour Landry prefaces his account of Susanna with the caption, "De Suzanne, la femme Joachim."[11] He ends the chapter, wherein Susanna is saved by the miraculous intervention of the five-year-old Daniel, with the moral, "And thus by cause of her bounte god saued bothe her body and sowle. And therfor euery good lady ought to haue her trust in god and for his loue to kepe trewely her maryage and also absteyne her of synne."[12] Though Susanna is praised for her chastity and faith, neither she nor Daniel is granted much agency in this version of Daniel 13. God causes Daniel to cry out that innocent blood should not be shed, admonishing the judges to examine each of the elders alone. The author of *Le Menagier de Paris* situates Susanna in a chapter warning his wife to live chastely.[13] His account is more elaborate than that of the Knight of Tour Landry, paying great attention to Susanna as a good wife, beloved of her husband, parents, and friends, and faithful to the law of Moses; but the details are similar. He ends his account by praising Susanna for preferring death to the physical defilement of adultery. Philippe de Mèziéres does not tell her story in *Le Livre de la Vertu du Sacrement de Mariage,* though it would have fit nicely with his emphasis on wifely submission, especially if he, like many commentators, were to regard her as both chaste and silent.[14] Pierre Bersuire, also close to Valois circles, allegorizes Susanna as the soul, the water as a fountain of devotion, Daniel as a priest, and the old men as the world and the devil. The moment Susanna sends away her maids for soaps and unguents, she is vulnerable because she is alone and hence without attendant virtues. Daniel "liberates her" from the dangers of solitude.[15] Boccaccio links her story to an account of the chaste Dido, instructing women to remain silent, modest, and faithful because God will rescue them: "Lower your eyes to the ground, close your ears, and like a rock hurl back the oncoming waves; be still and let the winds blow. You will be saved."[16] In *The Book of the City of Ladies*, Rectitude uses Susanna as an example of chastity. Christine de Pizan, however, removes anything controversial from this account. Susanna is relaxing, not bathing, in her garden, and Daniel is, again, a child in arms, who cries out at the sight of Susanna being led away unjustly and whose voice prompts a reexamination of the evidence against her.[17]

Susanna occupies a subtly different range of meanings in English texts, possibly because of the different English attitude toward law and, later, because of the challenge to patriarchal control offered by heterodoxy. English regal power had been and was tested, scrutinized, and demythologized by baronial forces in ways that French regal power had not.[18] Moreover, by the late fourteenth century, in challenging ecclesiastical authority and the doctrine of transubstantiation, John Wyclif had implicitly raised the broader and more dangerous issue of civil authority. Though Wyclif himself averred the need to disendow the church's wealth and the transfer of worldly power to the secular realm, nonetheless his emphasis on moral worthiness as concomitant with true authority opened the possibility of challenges to more than priestly power.[19] These English accounts of Susanna's story oppose the authority of the law to the power of judges, underlining the law's ability to protect what is private, enclosed, and yet vulnerable, drawing a distinction between isolation and enclosure that serves as a gloss to the myth of England as it was first written by Bede.

A CISTERCIAN SUSANNA

The "Tractatus metricus de Susanna per fratrem Alanum monachum de Melsa de Beverlaco" is the work of a Yorkshire Cistercian who was clearly aware of traditional ways of using the story of Susanna but focused his account, first, through a prefatory conversion narrative, which can be linked to the Cistercian language of conversion during the order's early period, and, second, through a profound emphasis on law that seems germane to conditions in England during the late twelfth and early thirteenth century. Alan of Melsa's urgent focus on law, as well as his elaborate descriptions of Susanna's garden and home, to some extent encapsulate the emphasis she received in English versions of her story. Alan's poem, I believe, provided the anonymous fourteenth-century author of *A Pistel of Susan* with a way of creating his own urgent narrative, this one securely located in English gentry space, as later treatments of Susanna would also be located. Alan constructs a story that, like subsequent re-creations of Daniel 13, asks particular questions about the conditions of English justice and individual rights under the law.

Alan of Melsa's poem exists in one manuscript in the British Library, Harley MS 2851, written about 1300, where it is in the fifth item in the first group in a large collection of Latin prose tales and poems, some of which concern Cistercian monks.[20] Alan was Geoffrey Archbishop of York's clerk and chaplain, provost of Beverley (ca. 1204–ca. 1212), and a canon of Ripon. The provost of the college of canons at Beverley was the officer in whom the temporalities of the church were vested and saw to the distribution of tithes coming from the parishes in the East Riding of Yorkshire and to the division of the annual proceeds among the canons.[21] The collegiate church of Beverley was not far from Melsa, a daughter house of Fountains Abbey.[22]

The early history of the English Cistercian movement, particularly of the Yorkshire Cistercians, as I suggested in the first chapter, cannot be separated from the history of England itself. Following its founding in 1098 in Burgundy, the Cistercian order grew rapidly in the twelfth century, largely because of the promotion and influence of Saint Bernard, abbot of Clairvaux. The White Monks arrived in England in 1128, founding their first house at Waverley in Surrey.[23] However, the founding that resonates in English accounts of Cistercian

FIGURE 1. Detail of Wilton Diptych, left panel. Orb of the angel's banner. Infrared image. By permission of the National Gallery, London.

FIGURE 2. Wilton Diptych. Richard II presented to the Virgin and Child by his patron saint John the Baptist and saints Edward and Edmund. By permission of the National Gallery, London.

FIGURE 3. Walter Milemete, *De nobilitatibus, sapientiis et prudentiis*, f. 5a. Image © The Governing Body of Christ Church, Oxford.

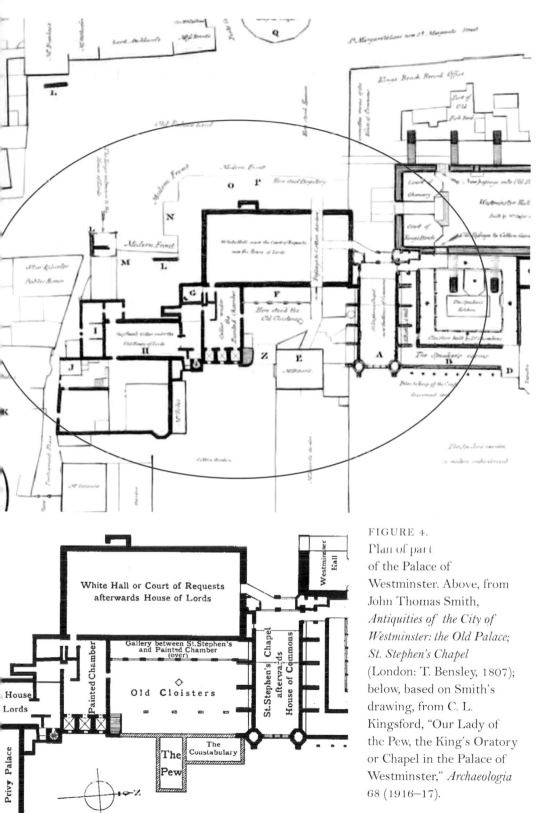

FIGURE 4.
Plan of part of the Palace of Westminster. Above, from John Thomas Smith, *Antiquities of the City of Westminster: the Old Palace; St. Stephen's Chapel* (London: T. Bensley, 1807); below, based on Smith's drawing, from C. L. Kingsford, "Our Lady of the Pew, the King's Oratory or Chapel in the Palace of Westminster," *Archaeologia* 68 (1916–17).

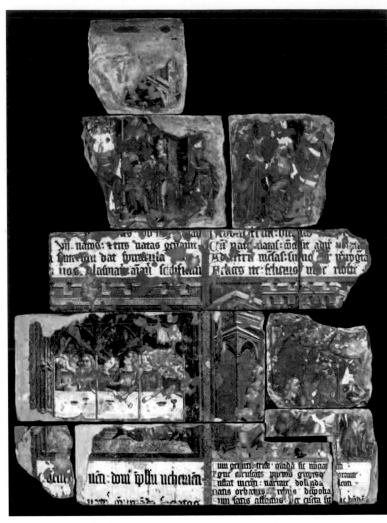

FIGURE 5.
Wall paintings,
St. Stephen's Chapel,
mural of the story of
Job (ca. 1350–63).
Detail, Job's children
feasting (Job 1:18–19).
By permission of the
British Museum. Image
© The Trustees of the
British Museum. All
Rights Reserved.

FIGURE 6. Lancelot du Lac (ca. 1360–80, England, Pleshey Castle), BL Royal MS. 20 D IV, f. 1r. By permission of the British Library. Image © The British Library Board. All Rights Reserved.

FIGURE 7. Map of New England. Cotton Mather, *Magnalia Christi Americana*. Image courtesy of the Division of Rare and Manuscript Collections, Cornell University Library.

foundations is that moment in 1131 when "oon Walter Espek brouȝt þat ordre of white monkes into Engelond, and made at Ryval an abbay of the ordre of Cisterciens."[24] Though the rapid growth of the Cistercian order certainly owed a good deal to the rigor of its ideals and to the tightness of its international organization, in England, its growth was also linked to conditions directly related to England's political and demographic chaos and the efforts of the feudal nobility to establish their own networks of power.[25] From 1135 to 1154, throughout the civil war of Stephen's reign, the number of Cistercian houses in England grew, from five to forty. Some were founded in Yorkshire, which had been left a wasteland after the Conquest. Bennett D. Hill suggests that the English baronage found Cistercian houses attractive investments because they were relatively inexpensive to endow, posed no threat to baronial ambitions but extended their own feudal networks, and offered the added bonus of instruction in new agricultural methods. After the accession of Henry II in 1154, Cistercian patrons tended to be knights involved in the work of the government.[26]

Owing both to too rapid expansion (particularly in the case of Melsa) and the difficulties of King John's reign (1199–1216), English Cistercians fell on hard times in the early thirteenth century.[27] John, faced with a debt of 30,000 marks to Philip Augustus of France, empty coffers, and a papal interdict (1208–14) for his having refused to acknowledge Stephen Langton archbishop of Canterbury, took the opportunity to mulct the clergy, especially the Cistercians. Those who tried to oppose him, like the abbot of Melsa, found themselves in even worse conditions, their lands seized and their abbeys temporarily dispersed.[28] During much of this time (1191–1212), John's half brother, Geoffrey Plantagenet, was archbishop of York; he did little to stabilize the situation in Yorkshire, though he did resist John's incursions on the clergy.[29] Geoffrey's clerk would have been in the thick of conflicts concerning ecclesiastical rights, property rights, taxation, and the administration of justice.[30] He would also have been aware of the events and struggles that led to the signing of the Magna Carta in 1215, which succeeded John's raising the interdict by signing over as feudal fiefs Ireland and England to Pope Innocent III. After 1214, when the interdict was lifted, John employed his newly made Roman alliance as leverage against baronial power.[31] Baronial liberties underwrote the Magna Carta, which set limits to regal power in guaranteeing their rights, as well as those of the church, English knights, merchants, freemen, and peasants.[32]

Rather than provide a simple solution to Alan of Melsa's "Tractatus . . . de Susanna," the above sketch suggests the sorts of questions Alan's poem might ask and allows us to make guesses about conflicts germane to it. The poem owes its urgency to its irresolutions, which attach themselves tenuously to the biblical story of Susanna but seem to belong to the likely concerns of an early-thirteenth-century Yorkshire author with ties to both the secular clergy and the Cistercian order. Though Susanna was used at least twice in the thirteenth century in texts associated with female devotion, Alan of Melsa does not seem to be writing for nuns (see note 2). His initial testimony of conversion resonates with Cistercian language, as, possibly, does his focus on space in his long description of the garden belonging to Joachim and Susanna. His overriding concern with legality and judicial corruption might reflect similar concerns to be found in northern circles during Angevin rule.

CONVERSION

The originary language of the Cistercian order is the language of conversion, and it serves as the rhetorical backbone for its early documents. These primitive Cistercian documents, which provide accounts of the foundation of Citeaux, the constitution of the Cistercian order, and the record of disciplinary decrees in the annual Great Chapter of the Cistercians, served to authorize the order, especially in light of the charges of apostasy brought against them by the Cluniacs. The documents themselves have occasioned much critical scrutiny, since to some they suggest careful editorial arrangement by the early members of the order, including Saint Bernard, arrangement, or editing, designed to create an unimpeachable textual record of the earliest Cistercian intentions and origins.[33] Those origins are encapsulated in the conversion moments of Robert Molesme, who first abandoned Cluny for Citeax and a stricter rule, though he later was pressured to return; and of the Englishman Stephen Harding, who came and stayed, providing the order with its true founding figure. Harding's experience, like the later experiences of Bernard and Aelred in Yorkshire, was one of radical conversion. These conversions were radical in the sense that the order described itself as returning to the roots of the cenobitic movement, to the original simplicity of Benedict, thus as a type of reformation. In part, as Martha G. Newman has pointed out, since the Cistercians accepted only adults into the order (they did not take oblates, nor did they have schools for boys), they were interested in the process of conversion, in the psychological transformation that propelled one into the novitiate.[34]

Evidence for this interest comes, of course, from the language the Cistercians used about themselves. One collection of poems and letters by Matthew of Rievaulx, written in about 1216 and copied by a scribe of St. Victor, contains three such letters of vocation. The collection, which certainly demonstrates the erudition and literary polish of Matthew, forms the second part of a manuscript that begins with the *Tobit* of Matthew of Vendôme.[35] In addition to these letters of vocation, there are poems whose topicality (on the interdict, on King John, on England, on Fountains Abbey, on Aelred) demonstrates Matthew's deep involvement in the realities of early-thirteenth-century Yorkshire. Considered as belonging to a set of conversations among Yorkshire Cistercians, Alan of Melsa's poem and the anthology of Matthew of Rievaulx help us understand some of the complicated concerns of those who had removed themselves from the world but could not deny its claims on them.

The letters, which succeed one another in the manuscript, are all addressed to a "brother" at Beverley, whom Matthew urges to convert to the Cistercian way.[36] He begins by employing the intense language of monastic friendship.[37] He uses the first paragraph to assure his love for and delight in his brother and to assert their brotherhood and oneness in charity ("Sumus duo ex carne una: quinimmo non duo iam, sed idem, identitate caritatis, non carnis"). He then urges his brother not to linger in Egypt among the cucumbers and fleshpots but to seek true plenty, the manna that God sends down from the sky, going on to urge him not to tarry, "Ne tardas conuerti ad Dominum," not to defer conversion, for in the world there is no true justice. He offers his hesitant brother the example of Abraham, who left Ur at God's command for a land flowing with milk and honey. The milk and honey are spiritual, for he extols the stringency of the way of John the Baptist, the abstinence of Daniel and his friends, the simplicity of

Elijah. He uses the crow, who chose to eat flesh rather than return to Noah, as a negative example. The end of the letter is a paean to Melsa, which is a short way from Beverley ("Est uia compendiosa de Beuerlaco ad Melsam; uade ad domum istam, quia uere Dominus est in loco isto . . . "), parsing the name Melsa by reference to the honey of the promised land, "A melle enim dicitur Melsa," where abounds true spiritual delight and sweetness.

In the next two letters, Matthew enlarges on the nature of the Cistercian paradise. In the second, he asserts that the Cistercian order provides a true home in Christ, a singular refuge, a gate for the destitute and orphaned, a true mother and nurse ("nutrix"). The eye is blind, the foot is lame; the pilgrim should not stay behind out of doors ("Oculus est ceco, pes claudo . . . foris non remanet peregrinus").[38] The refuge he offers to his dearest brother ("amantissimo fratri") is one of holy poverty and work, where Leah and Rachel, Mary and Martha are reconciled, for he who does not work does not eat. In the third, Matthew focuses on spiritual benefits, telling his brother that wisdom is not found in the world, but that the fear of God is the beginning of wisdom, urging him to be converted from the vain conversation of the world to God.[39] He mentions the vanity of the world and the certainty of death only to heighten the security, the quiet, the light, and the spiritual delight of the Cistercian way. He tells him to hasten to the gate of paradise, to the "hortus deliciarum," where the woman does not seduce, or the serpent deceive. In this garden, whose prototype is that in Canticles 4:12–15, are to be found roses and lilies of the valley, cyprus, nard, crocus, cinnamon, balsam, myrrh, and aloe, with all their oils. By coming into the reclaimed garden, his brother will be protected by angels as Joseph was in Egypt, Daniel in the lions' den, and the three children in the fiery furnace. Matthew employs this same pastoral imagery, which characterizes many early Cistercian accounts of their houses, in a poem in the same manuscript describing Fountains Abbey as a font of living water, healing, nourishing, sealed, sister to Rievaulx.[40] Matthew also writes of the security of living in God in another letter in the manuscript, calling on the examples of Moses in the Red Sea, the journey of Tobit, Daniel, Susanna falsely accused, Peter in chains, Paul in dangers, Lawrence in fire, and Catherine in prison to emphasize God's saving care.[41] Matthew of Rievaulx's subject, language, and exemplary method can likewise be found in Alan of Melsa's "Tractatus . . .

de Susanna," but where Matthew sees a clear line dividing the spirit and the flesh, the closed garden and the world, the lives of the just and the unjust, Alan provides a more complicated narrative, one whose parts do not exactly cohere.

The first twenty-four lines of the "Tractatus" are a conversion narrative, testifying to the speaker's self-awareness and to his radical Pauline experience of change. He begins with the arresting, "Cum mea mens loquitur mecum, fantasma uidetur/ Que prius addidici, que scio nulla scio" (When my mind speaks with me, what I previously learned seems a ghost, and I know I know nothing); "sum reor alter ego" (I am, I suppose, another self) (lines 1–2, 4). He continues to play on this sense of his own doubleness, describing what he was previously taught to honor (indulgence, impiety, the things and values of the world), comparing himself to a drunken follower of Dionysus (14). He then uses language similar to that Matthew employs, describing himself as not knowing he was naked, blind, and needy and his conversion as an act of grace: "Gracia sola Dei squamas detersit ocellis" (Only the grace of God removed the scales from my eyes) (19). He goes on, "Cecus eram, uideo: nudus, modo uestior; eger, / Conualui" (I was blind, I see, naked, now clothed, ill, healthy) (21–22). The scene is as familiar as the dark room in Damascus, where the scales come away from Paul's eyes, and he goes out to preach the very Christ he formerly persecuted (Acts 9). After this staging of the psychology of conversion where the mind sees itself dimly as it formerly was and testifies to its own reformation, the narrator says that, considering the treacheries of the flesh, the story of Susanna occurred to him as an important lesson and warning.

Alan of Melsa's preface to the story of Susanna and the Elders frames the narrative in ways other medieval renderings of it do not. Exegetical treatments of Daniel 13 do not link it to the theme of conversion. Though conversion was a common theme in early Cistercian writings and Cistercian authors sometimes employ Susanna as an example of chastity, virtue, or faith, as does Matthew of Rievaulx, the two were not brought together in a single work.[42] There are two noteworthy Latin poetic treatments of Susanna and the Elders, by Peter Riga (d. 1209) and by a Willetrudis (possibly either the German abbess of Hohenvart [fl. 1090] or the Anglo-Norman abbess of Wilton [d. ca. 1122]).[43] These three poems are sufficiently different to point up some of the possible ways in which Susanna's story appealed to monastic communities.[44]

Peter Riga's description of Susanna heightens the implicit sensuality of the narrative.[45] The heat of summer and the playful stream in the garden invite Susanna to bathe ("Illic inuitant Susannam balnea") (21). He goes on "Temptat aquam, laudat temptatam, nuda subintrat/ Laudatum, nudam uidit ueterque senum" (23–24), implying that Susanna's testing ("temptat") of the water is also a test of her, since she praises the results of her test, goes into the water nude, and is then seen by both old men, who become heated at the sight ("Vidit et incaluit") (25). In the elders' false account of Susanna's crime, or what they "saw," Peter Riga provides a sensual account of the rich fertility of the garden and the beauty of Susanna herself. He does not actually blame her for being alone and naked, but he suggests that by her actions she becomes an object of temptation.[46] Willetrudis's Susanna, as Stevenson points out, is normally surrounded by her serving women and may bathe, but we are treated to a vicarious sight of her removing her clothing. Rather than subtly complict in her own predicament, this Susanna is the innocent victim of others' lechery. Willetrudis ends the poem by using Susanna as a model for both virtuous wives and career virgins, an association possibly also important to William de Brailes of Oxford, whose Hours contain a sequence of depictions of the story of Susanna made about 1240 for a lady named Susanna.[47]

Alan of Melsa's version of the account of Susanna differs in its opening emphasis. After recounting the story of his conversion, the narrator states the benefits of telling this particular story, which renders the chastity of the woman, the wickedness of the judges, the wisdom of the man, presumably Daniel, the lasciviousness of the old. Alan refers to the story as a case ("causa"). He underlines that the work honors Susanna's "manliness" and her skill: "Pretitulatur opus Susanne causa uirilis;/ Femina que uicit scribitur arte senes" (39–40). As he sets up the story, Susanna, beautiful, chaste, and intelligent, triumphs over the old, corrupt, and lecherous. However, there is another important detail to Alan's proem to the narrative. Unlike Peter Riga who consistently refers to the elders as old men ("senes"), Alan calls them judges and points out that the story teaches true justice: "Discat in hac causa iudex procedere recto/ Tramite" (It teaches in this case a judge to proceed according to the right path) (33). Unlike either Willetrudis's or Peter Riga's, Alan's account is, from the beginning, a commentary on the workings of justice, a theme that he introduces in the opening section on conversion where he notes that he had earlier been taught to serve money ("seruire lucris") (5), to pursue cases ("insistere causis") (5), not to consider wickedness but to speak silently ("nil reputare nephas:/ Doctus eram reticenda loqui") (6–7). It is that worldly teaching and worldly self that is cast away with the scales from his eyes. The narrator thus links his former self to self-interested behavior that can only result in injustice and implies that the story of Susanna is meant to refute that early teaching, and his account of it, because it serves as a sign of his conversion.

THE GARDEN AND THE WORLD

Though sometimes Susanna is invoked in interpretations of the Canticles and the *hortus deliciarum*, Joachim's garden rests uneasily beside other notable biblical gardens, Eden, the garden of Canticles, the garden of Easter morning, and the garden of the heavenly Jerusalem. Where Eden certainly has a serpent willing to deceive, it also has an Eve, a role Susanna does not play, despite Peter Riga's attempt to associate her with the idea of temptation. Matthew of Rievaulx's description of the Cistercian order as a garden without a temptress is clearly meant to describe Melsa as a redeemed Eden. The garden of the Canticles is the site of the love play between the heavenly bridegroom and the bride and was used to describe the purity of the Blessed Virgin, where Christ joined with human flesh. The garden of Easter morning is the site of the Resurrection of Christ, the sign of the resurrection of the flesh in Christ. Heaven's garden is without mutability, unceasing in its reflection of the Lamb. The garden of Daniel 13 does not contain a temptress, is not the locus for spiritual searching or resurrection, and is certainly time-bound; in fact, it is located in Babylon and is a testimony to Joachim's prosperity. What is more important in relation to England's language of self-definition, Joachim's garden contains the world, or is penetrated by the world. Any attempt to tell the story of Susanna must come to terms with the garden itself, or must decide how that garden means. Alan of Melsa gives an enormous amount of space to this garden and, in so doing, underlines the ways in which it can and cannot mean. What is more, before he lets us into the garden, he introduces us to the world that surrounds it.

Alan's praise of Susanna is punctuated by his account of the false practices of the world around her:

> In Babilone fuit, sed nil Babilonis habebat;
> Sed male persuadent ocia, luxus, amor.
> Uxor erat Joachim; quos non petulancia sed Lex
> Uniit et legis sanctio, castus Himen. (51–52)
> [She was in Babylon, but had nothing of Babylon,
> But leisure, wealth, and love are badly persuasive.
> She was the wife of Joachim; not lust but law
> united them and the sanction of law, chaste Hymen.]

This opposition between laxity and law guides Alan's description of the marriage between Joachim and Susanna (whom he compares to Penelope) (69), as well as his account of Joachim himself, in whose house law and justice thrived and gifts to clients were not given (79, 80). However, Alan's insistence on Joachim's legal ethics sets Joachim apart from the old men, who are corrupt judges for whom the judicial forum is a marketplace (89–106). He goes on to suggest that in his own age, power too often corrupts those who were once humble (109–10), linking the biblical narrative with contemporary complaints about corrupt and greedy judges.[48] He then returns briefly to Susanna, following the account in Daniel of her early education in the law by her parents and of the way in which Joachim's house served as a forum for legal proceedings according to the laws of equity. At no point does he ignore the secular and pragmatic world of just and unjust practices.

Alan's description of Joachim and Susanna's garden is long and elaborate, but it is not a picture of Eden or of heaven's garden. Nor is it simply a garden of fleshly delight, since it contains things for both use and beauty. In Alan's description, the gallery of the house, which murmurs with clients, opens onto a distinguished courtyard, where the old men deliberate. Joachim's house, though it is ruled according to the law of justice, contains at its heart the unjust judges. Alan describes the grounds as containing a barn, a mill, a storehouse, a kitchen, and a place for the storage of food (" Horrea, pistrinum, zeta, coquina, penu") (142). He could easily be describing a Cistercian foundation, as the

Cistercians created self-sufficient estates that redefined their environment.[49] The garden is attached to these grounds and contains a sumptuous variety of flowers, herbs, fruits, and birds: white pepper, cumin, lilies, roses, violets, nard of cardamon, hyacinth, all mixed with decency or good taste ("mixta decenter erant") (146). An orchard blooms near the bedchamber, bringing in sweet smells. There, there are palms, grapes, oaks, apple trees, pear and Syrian fig, and two kinds of cherry trees. At this point Alan shifts away from the picture of great plenty to a more mythic reference, for in the garden it is perpetual spring ("Ver ibi perpetuum") (153), a type of Edenic landscape removed from time, having at its heart a clear fountain, whose water was like ambrosia. However, ominously, the water is shaded by a laurel and frequented by blackbirds, nightingales, and parrots. Both the laurel and the nightingale recall the violent Ovidian tales of Daphne and Philomena, while the parrot is one more reminder of the luxuries within Joachim's house. This garden is at once an ordered, fruitful, beautiful space and a *locus amoenus*, whose beauty conceals its threat.

To this fountain and shade comes Susanna to avoid the heat, while the old men with their cold blood and withered members ("marcida membra") (182) excited by Venus are also drawn by the possibility of seeing her. Alan then pauses to decry the way the eye can seize the mind, can drive it into a fury ("Mens oculo rapitur, mentem furatur ocellus") (183), stressing the dangerous windows the senses provide and going on to contrast the crow who left the ark and did not return with the dove, who returned bearing an olive branch (an example likewise employed by Matthew of Rievaulx), and prudent Judith who left in order to kill Holofernes with incautious Dinah, who left her home for her own ruin. His warning about the dangers of sins of the eye, the avarice that he has already linked to the corrupt judges, is related to his proem and his contemporary understanding of the nature of the world and its justice. The examples of Judith's prudence and Dinah's lack of caution suggest something more thoroughly worldly, a validation of experience, for Dinah was blameless but ignorant of the evils of the world around her. By attaching the adjective *vaga* (wandering) to Dinah (191), a word also frequently used to describe the monk out of his cloister, he suggests an identification with Susanna, who, like Eve, finds a serpent in her garden (194), in this case elders for whom love triumphs over law ("Vicit amor legem") (201).

Alan stages the confrontation between Susanna and the elders as though it were a debate about the nature of the law. Before she is accosted, Susanna is vulnerable, like Dinah, incautious. Her hair is loose ("resoluta coma") (214); she is lightly clothed in muslin ("fuit induta sindone nuda fere") (213), relaxing in the shade of her garden, waiting for her attendants to bring unguents, a lamb among wolves (221). As they do in Daniel 13, the elders acknowledge their desire for her, but Alan expands this into an argument. They describe themselves as magistrates of the people, learned in laws. However, they then say, "Maiestas sub amore iacet" (Majesty lies under love) (235), converting the word *censores* (magistrates) into *maiestas* (majesty), thereby suggesting their interest in public status rather than public duty. They then attempt to woo Susanna by flattery, recalling the examples of Sampson, David, and Solomon, all figures of might who were laid low by love. She is doubly valuable to them because she has revived their dead virility (242). When they tell her she will not be charged with adultery for her act, but if she refuses they will be witnesses against her, Susanna's response is a stirring question about their law:

> O noua res, inquit, noua lex, nouus improbat actor
> Quod deus et ueteres instituere patres. (253–54)[50]
> ["O new thing," she said, "a new law, a new advocate condemns what God and the ancient fathers established."]

She reminds them of the sanctity of marriage, recalling the example of Lucretia, then returning to the biblical script in Daniel 13 by affirming that God sees all, and it is better for her to be condemned by men than to sin in God's eyes. Their flattery has meant nothing to this Susanna; instead, she has argued against them about the very principles of the "law" they follow, this new law that supports injustice and operates against the innocent. When the elders bring their charges against her, they again employ the language of law, this time the law of Moses, which they say condemns her (331). Susanna is less eloquent publicly than in private, saying, as she does in Scripture, that she is innocent in the eyes of God. Alan returns to the biblical text for the final courtroom drama wherein Daniel brings the case to true justice by questioning the two judges separately and proving their lies. This part of the story, which takes place in a real courtroom, is given far less space than the debate in the garden, where Susanna argues for the true law against the corrupt judges. Alan drives home the lesson in justice he perceives the story to have at the end, saying that the narrative teaches judges and witnesses to love the law, women to be chaste, old men to behave themselves, and the young to be wise like Daniel. Despite his remarks about chaste living, which encapsulate a more conventional reading of the story, his emphasis throughout the poem has been on the law and the ways in which law can be twisted to further self-interest.[51]

Alan of Melsa's "Tractatus . . . de Susanna" reworks the biblical story to capture and reformulate the language of Cistercian vocation during the early thirteenth century, insisting on the need to think of the cloister as inextricably (for good or ill) joined to a world that could not be described in any but the most realistic language. The great abbeys of Rievaulx and Fountains and their daughters employed the timeless language of conversion and redemption to describe both the monks' experience and their construction of new abbeys. For example, Hugh of Kirkstall's history of the founding of Fountains Abbey begins with a narrative dictated by the abbey's oldest monk, Serlo, to Hugh.[52] Serlo refers to his entry into the Cistercian order as a conversion and to the nascent abbey as like a vine planted in the wilderness.[53] Matthew of Rievaulx's letters to the brother in Beverley suggest how resonant a language it was. Though Alan of Melsa seems to echo the Cistercian tropes of the *hortus conclusus*, the redeemed Eden, his choice to use the story of Susanna as illustrative of conversion is fraught with difficulty. The garden is hardly enclosed. In fact, like the Cistercian order itself, it is permeated by the world.

This is not to say that by the thirteenth century the Cistercians had become lax or corrupt, but it is to say that the reality was not as simple as the founding myths present. Cistercian prosperity and success rested on technical ingenuity, agricultural innovation, and careful land deals, all traits that won the order both admiration and scorn from its arrival in England. They refused to house boys and maintain schools, take tithes, exact manorial fees, or have serfs. Instead, they created a land-based self-sufficient economy, where lay brothers occupied and farmed granges close to the abbey. Though they chose isolated sites, they were nonetheless not far from main roads and were diligent in reclaiming old, worn-out land and stitching together parcels that could form compact estates.[54] In the twelfth century, soon after they arrived, Walter Map, like his friend Gerald of Wales, satirized them for what he perceived as their covetousness. He accused them of turning Mary into Martha (contemplation into labor), of being solely interested in prosperity, and of appropriating surrounding lands as the children of Israel "despoiled" the Egyptians.[55] On the other hand, Ranulf Higden, following William of Newburgh, reports that their early industry was admirable: "Þat ordre encresede so þat tyme þat þe monkes of Cisterciens were spied of alle monkes [þe] myrour of hem þat were goodliche besy, and reproof and chastisynge of slewþe."[56] They were famous for altering the environments around them, creating water mills, metal works, and breeding methods that put them in the forefront of what was a depressed English agricultural economy. They may have arranged their boundaries to keep out the world, but they also served the world in the scutage they owed their baronial patrons, in the legal scholarship and advice they provided, and in their service as papal judges-delegate.[57] During the reign of John, particularly during the interdict when John ruthlessly confiscated property and demanded ever-greater payments for "justice" in the king's courts (which always traveled with him), the Cistercians could hardly have kept themselves from knowing something of the dangers to which an unprotected garden was exposed, or their own covert or overt involvement in a world ruled by exigency.[58] There are several poems in Matthew of Rievaulx's collection that concern contemporary issues: a work on the interdict, on the Discord of the English, and on King John. Each of these proclaims the need for true justice, for honesty, for devotion to the church.[59]

When juxtaposed to Matthew of Rievaulx's letters, or other Cistercian self-descriptions, Alan of Melsa's poem asks, or begs us to ask, questions rather than to accept conventional images and ideas. In large part, these questions arise from the fissures in the poem itself. For example, if the story of Susanna seems a good narrative to tell after conversion, what does the narrative illustrate? Since he presents Susanna as dangerously innocent, not as an Eve whose curiosity and vanity are aroused by the serpent, but as chaste *and* vulnerable, is he implying that the very unworldliness that was fundamental to the Cistercian self-description cannot be sustained because there are no safe places for solitude? Is he questioning the very ideal of the solitary life as incautious? Is he exploring the two different worlds he has inhabited, one in Beverley as part of Geoffrey, archbishop of York's extended household, the other in Melsa, which was not a safe haven during the first fifteen years of the thirteenth century? Is he underlining the need for a knowledge of and an adherence to the law, law that was severely tested during the reign of King John? The end of the poem, with its morals and classical modesty statements, implicitly disclaims the severity of the questions embedded in the body of the poem, but it cannot muffle them entirely. Alan builds the "Tractatus . . . de Susanna" upon the idea of reflection, that moment when the mind observes itself as having one self in the past and another in the present, a self-scrutiny that does not resolve into soothing accounts of the peace to be had in the enclosed garden. It seems a rejoinder to Matthew of Rievaulx, an elegant tale of innocence lost, transformed into experience. Alan narrates the poem as a wiser Susanna, and, in so doing, he relates the narrative not simply to the realities of Cistercian life, but to the realities of the island, England, whose garden was neither inviolable nor isolated though enclosed by the surrounding sea.

TEXTUAL TRANSMISSIONS

Alan of Melsa's "Tractatus . . . de Susanna" also, I believe, provided a fourteenth-century Yorkshire poet with material for an arresting poem on the subject of Susanna and the elders. In making such a suggestion, I inevitably intervene in the wide-ranging arguments about the provenance and origins of English alliterative poetry. The work of Elizabeth Salter and, more recently, Michael Bennett, Ralph Hanna, David Lawton, and Susanna Fein has sketched in a wider geography for alliterative poets, confining neither them nor their work to northern or midland locales and audiences.[60] Not only were the holdings of magnates spread throughout England and monastic orders equally widespread, but texts traveled along the same roads, from monastic library or copying center to other copying centers, libraries, or great houses. Textual transmission is one aspect of the incessant mobility of medieval life.[61]

During the Middle Ages, Yorkshire, networked by ecclesiastical foundations, allowing for a good deal of textual cross-fertilization, was a center for vigorous vernacular literary production, as well as for Latin writing.[62] If we look simply at the Cistercian houses, the evidence for literary activity and interest is great. Though the Cistercians did not give prominence to the arts, the writings of Aelred of Rievaulx and Roger of Byland in the twelfth century; of Matthew of Rievaulx, Alan of Melsa, and Stephen of Sawley (d. 1252) in the thirteenth; and of John of Hovedon (d. 1322), poet and abbot of Sawley, and William of Rymynton (d. 1372), prior of Sawley, in the fourteenth suggest both scholarly acumen and attention to literary style.[63] David Bell's work on the libraries of the Cistercians, while underscoring their conservative character, evinces the care Cistercian houses took to acquire volumes that served both their everyday liturgical needs and their continuing pedagogic and scholarly aims.[64] Though the catalog for what must have been an extensive library at Fountains Abbey is no longer extant, those for Rievaulx and Melsa are rich in exegetical and homiletic texts, with a smattering of classical and historical. The organization of Cistercian houses into families is also suggestive of possible textual transmission, especially since the Cistercians valued homogeneity among houses. Thus Fountains was the mother house for Melsa, Kirkstall, and Newminster, which was, in turn, the mother house of Sawley, all associated with literary activity. Sawley, founded by the Percy family and situated in Craven near the border of Yorkshire and Lancashire, was very close to the abbey of Whalley, whose chronicle, probably of Lancastrian provenance, is important to late-fourteenth-century Ricardian history.[65]

Suggestive of later, and possibly more mundane, literary activity are the late-fourteenth-century records of expenses incurred from hospitality for both Sawley and Fountains, as well as evidence for Cistercian associations with important manuscript collections. By this time, Cistercian houses were more like other monastic foundations, thus far more open to the world than during the early days of the order. Sawley in 1381 paid 27 shillings for minstrels, and Fountains on various occasions paid for minstrels, a fool from Byland (where there was another Cistercian abbey), players from Thirsk, a fool, players, a fabulist, and the king's minstrels.[66] The Cistercian house, Bordesley Abbey, in Worcestershire, was given by Guy de Beauchamp in 1306 a vast collection of romances, including a *Tresor* by Brunetto Latini, a Lancelot, *Titus and Vespasien*, a Grail, an Amidis, and a death of Arthur.[67]

Bordesley is also loosely associated with the Vernon and Simeon manuscripts, large anthologies of devotional and instructional vernacular texts. Though there is no hard evidence that these manuscripts are of Cistercian provenance, there are hints of possible involvement or filiation. In his introduction to the facsimile of the Vernon manuscript A. I. Doyle notes that one of the paid scribes, who was probably from Lichfield or Coventry, was also responsible for some later copying in the chronicle and cartulary of the Cistercian abbey of Stoneleigh in Warwickshire, which was affiliated with Bordesley Abbey. Doyle also remarks that the historiated initial of the *Prick of Conscience* in the Vernon manuscript contains a male religious, probably a Cistercian. The cost of employing two copyists for four years, the time it would take to produce both books, would have been beyond the resources of either Stoneleigh or Bordesley, but Doyle speculates that perhaps several persons, lay or religious, supplied contents and expenses. Or possibly the manuscripts were made for a wealthy convent.[68] The manuscripts, which were copied in the last decade of the fourteenth century, contain the two earliest copies of *A Pistel of Susan*. The poem itself was probably written a decade or two earlier in southern Yorkshire or by a writer from that area.[69] None of this is intended as an argument for the Cistercian provenance of *A Pistel of Susan* but to sketch in ways in which one thirteenth-century Latin poem might have come to the attention of a late-fourteenth-century poet. Texts were frequently transmitted along ecclesiastical routes. Monasteries owed hospitality to travelers, indeed had rooms for guests, and with guests of means came clerks, who must have been interested in the texts owned by their hosts and to whom we may owe much thirteenth- and fourteenth-century vernacular literature.[70] We are used to thinking about the great Benedictine houses as centers of culture and hospitality, less so the Cistercian. Alan of Melsa's poem, though now unique, could well have traveled along the southern routes of the Fountains family, which included Melsa, Kirkstall, Sawley, and Roche.[71] Similarly, the *Pistel of Susan*, which is Edwardian, was copied into Ricardian anthologies, suggesting that it enjoyed a certain amount of popularity in later reading circles. What is more, there are significant references to Susanna in Wycliffite texts that underline her relevance to issues pertaining to individual conscience and to the interpretation and administration of the law.

SUSANNA IN LATER MEDIEVAL ENGLISH TEXTS

The first of these fourteenth-century texts is the *Pistel*, which possibly influenced later English treatments of Susanna, such as those by Chaucer, William Thorpe, Walter Brut, and Thomas Wimbledon. *A Pistel of Susan* shares with the "Tractatus . . . de Susanna" more than a Yorkshire provenance and more than a possible link to the English Cistercian houses. Like the Latin poem, *A Pistel* devotes an extraordinary amount of space to a description of Joachim and Susanna's garden and contains some details found, to my knowledge, only in Alan of Melsa's poem. Moreover, *A Pistel* suggests that its author found in the Latin poem an emphasis on law, or on justice under the law, as it pertains to individual rights. The affinities between the two poems point up the types of questions each poem seems to prompt in its audience. Where Alan of Melsa explores the very idea of a cloistered safety and its relationship to the world, the author of *A Pistel*, in locating his poem in a contemporary English world, queries the security of the gentry household in a world of potentially unjust legal practices.

A Pistel of Susan begins not with Susan but with her husband, Joachim.[72] The poet focuses the first four stanzas of the poem through him, or through our appreciation of Joachim's status as a just man, a rich man, and a husband protected by his righteousness and wealth. He is introduced in the first stanza, which begins by saying he is rich (1), of gentle blood (2), a Jew living in Babylon, loyal to his law (3), properly arrayed (4), and, to some extent, separated from the city in which he lives by the hill on which his home is built and by the moat surrounding it (5–6). The emphasis on Joachim as householder continues into the next stanzas, which detail what he "has": he "hed" a wife, Susan, and he "hed" an orchard, open to his privileged circle, among which are two judges of the law, whom the poet reveals to be powerful as priests and governors (33) but known by God to be unjust. That the poet intends us to link Joachim's wife with his garden is apparent in the opening lines of the second and third stanzas, which are similarly constructed: "He hed a wif hiȝt Susan, was sotil and sage" (14) and "He hedde an orchard newe þat neiȝed wel nere" (27). However, from the beginning it is clear that this orchard is not so much an extension of his private life as open to him and to his friends, a feature of his great house and of his hospitality and generosity. By inference,

what the judges will transgress is the hospitality of his household,
which is based on honorable wealth ("For he was real and riche of
rentes to rere, / Honest and auenaunt and honorablest aye") (29–30).
Where Alan of Melsa emphasizes the openness of Joachim's household, which functions as a hall of justice, and the privacy of the orchard, which is proximate to the bedchamber, the author of *A Pistel*,
like the biblical author, links the orchard to the broader concept of
the secular household.

Where Daniel 13 does not describe this garden or orchard, the
author of *A Pistel* presents an elaborate account of its delights. As a
locus amoenus, this garden is affiliated with those to be found in Genesis and the Song of Songs, as well as with the garden of the *Roman de
la Rose*.[73] However, it is more directly affiliated with the garden in Alan
of Melsa's "Tractatus . . . de Susanna, sharing with it details not to be
found in other accounts of Susanna and the Elders. For example, in
addition to other birds, it has parrots, which the poet mentions twice
(75, 81), once, as Alan does, in conjunction with nightingales.[74] Like
Alan of Melsa, the *Pistel*-author catalogs in loving detail the many
types of herbs, flowers, and fruits growing in the garden: grapes, apples,
cherries, cinnamon, pears, figs, pomegranates, chive, chervil, parsley,
peonies, sage, and many more. More important, it is under a laurel
tree that Susan washes:

> Forþi þe wyf werp of hir wedes vnwerde,
> Vnder a lorerc ful lowe þat ladi gan leende
>   So sone. (124–26)

Alan describes the fountain as shaded or overshadowed by a laurel,
"Laurus obumbrat aquam" (165), a tree that does not occur in other
accounts of the story. The laurel and the nightingale, signifiers of the
fates of Daphne and Philomena, remind both audiences of the dangers
the garden presents to the unaware. Just as Alan compares Susanna
to heedless Dinah, the author of the *Pistel* says that she is "unwerde"
(unguarded) in removing her clothing. Again, like Alan of Melsa, he
amplifies that remark by describing her as only taking off her "kelle,"
her headdress (128).[75]

In its wealth of florescent detail, as well as in some of its par-
ticulars, the account of the garden in *A Pistel* strongly suggests that

its author had come across Alan of Melsa's poem and read it closely enough to understood ways in which the garden itself was central to Alan's use of the narrative of Susanna and the Elders. They are not, however, the same poem; nor, despite their mutual emphasis on law, do they have the same focus. The topical concerns I adduce in Alan of Melsa's poem suggest his awareness of judicial corruption in the early thirteenth century as it can be filtered through the idealized Cistercian language of pastoral inclaustration. The author of *A Pistel* speaks from another place—from an England now far more urbanized, possessing a different set of conditions and judicial conflicts and from (or to) an audience whose values are those of the Christian secular community.

The furniture of that society is everywhere in the poem. Joachim and Susan's Babylon is recognizably English: their home is moated (5); Susan is thrown into a dungeon (174); her father has an "affinité"; she is brought before justices at the bench (183), brought back to the guild hall (293) for Daniel's examination of the elders, who are referred to throughout as judges. The scene at the end, while nodding to the biblical account of the people's capital justice on the unjust judges (Daniel 13:60–62), describes an English scene: "Þei trompe bifore þis traiters and traylen hem on tres/ Þorwout þe cité bi comuyn assent" (356–57).[76] Dragged around the city as exemplars of particularly dreadful crimes, the judges are subjected to derision as part of their punishment. The term *"comuyn assent"* is likewise important to Chaucer's construction of community, for the twenty-nine pilgrims assembled at the Tabard agree with "oon assent" to their host's plans for the trip. *Assent* meant agreement or approval, necessary in seeking to understand the degree to which covenants were binding; "comuyn assent" is the mutual agreement of two or more parties. The term thus would have possessed a certain resonance for an English audience and could be associated with the civil need to present crimes against neighbors in iconic and mnemonic ways.

The author of *A Pistel of Susan* is not concerned about regal power but constructs the poem to focus on the judicial abuse of power and hence on the processes by which injustice is redressed. Like other fourteenth-century English texts, such as *Athelston* and *The Tale of Gamelyn, A Pistel* explores judicial abuses to the property and status of those gently or nobly born.[77] *A Pistel* is without the explicit violence of the other two works, but Daniel 13 describes the inherent violence of the judges that the poem brilliantly captures. Surprised in her own garden, she is asked by the two judges, "Wolt þou, ladi, for loue on vre lay lerne, / And vnder this lorere ben vr lemmone?" (135–36). "Lay" is richly suggestive. A "lai" could be a short narrative poem about love, such as the lais of Marie de France, or it might designate the laws, either civil or ecclesiastical, that govern communal life, the practices by which that life is ordered. Though Alan of Melsa does not have the judges say this to Susanna, they do preface their attempted seduction by reminding her that they are judges and can manipulate the law to their benefit. Susanna replies to them with the scornful, "O noua res," which I have already discussed. *A Pistel*'s author quite possibly exploits those legal references by having the judges offer to teach Susan their "lay" under the laurel tree. And what kind of law would Susan learn from two men under a tree? The grotesqueness of their demand suggests the violence of the law they will turn on her.

Where *The Tale of Gamelyn* depicts a protagonist who is perfectly capable of meeting violence with violence and *Athelston* the violence and suffering produced by betrayal and treachery, *A Pistel* concentrates on Susan herself, whose space, privacy, and physical integrity are compromised and threatened by the judges. The poem shares with *Athelston* an acute sense of the vulnerabilities of the household to injustice and of the feminine as a marker for household inviolability. *Athelston*, however, concerns the household of the realm and treachery in high places; *A Pistel*, a noble or gentry household threatened by an unjust use of legal power. Here, the poet's treatment of Susan is central to his presentation of violence.

He epitomizes the rough handling of Susan by continuing to focus on her head covering as a sign of her modesty. The people of her own court find her unveiled or uncovered when they come on hearing her cries, "Whon kene men of hir court comen til hir cri, / Heo hedde cast of hir calle and hire keuercheue" (156–57). The poet embellishes the biblical account by describing Susan as put in a dungeon, manacled and without food, while her father with all his "affinité" (180) is helpless in the face of judicial falsehood. She appears in court as the great lady she is, "sengeliche arayed/ In a selken schert, with scholdres wel schene" (196–97). Her regal appearance notwithstanding, when she appears the judges lay familiar hands on her head: "Homliche on hir heued heor hondes þei leyed" (200). The poet echoes the biblical narrative, which says that Susanna is ordered to remove her veil in court, but, by substituting a head covering for the heavy veiling of the Middle Eastern wife, he translates the poem into the language of fourteenth-century fashion and marital chastity. Like the garden, Susan is violated by the public intrusion into her physical privacy. While this may be a poem of female chastity and faith, it is also a sharp critique of a legal and social system wherein false witnesses can malign and doom the vulnerable. Nor does the poet allow any grounds for antifeminist criticism of her behavior: she is not described as bathing in her garden; all she takes off is her head covering. The poet has expanded the biblical story in ways that locate it within a secular world of violated households, of precarious prosperity, and of uncertain justice. Moreover, *A Pistel* is not a poem that lauds regal power or wifely submission. Susan is articulate in her own defense. The poet describes her as "brouȝt . . . to the barre" (189), where the false judges accuse her of adultery with a large, bold young man. Surrounded and supported by her "kynred and cosyn" (238), as well as by her husband, Susan is not silent.

The poet's handling of her voice is far more nuanced than that of the author of the biblical account, for he breaks up her speech into three distinct addresses. In public, to the community and to her extended family, she says:

> 'I am sakeles of syn . . .
> Grete God of his grace þis gomes forgeue
> Þat doþ me derfliche be ded and don out of dawen
>   Wiþ dere.
>   Wolde God þat I miht
>   Speke wiþ Joachim a niht
>   And siþen to deþ me be diht
>   I charge hit not a pere.' (240–47)

She asserts that she is guiltless of sin while also signifying her charity by asking God to forgive those who wish with evil intent to deprive her of day's light. She then asks to speak to her husband, Joachim.

Her meeting with Joachim at once evinces the conventions of marital hierarchy, in that she falls down before him, *and* the companionate and almost egalitarian nature of their marriage:

Heo fel doun flat in þe flore, hir feere whon heo fand,
Carped to him kyndeli as heo ful wel couþe:
'Iwis I wrapþed þe neuere, at my witand,
Neiþer in word ne in werk, in elde ne in ʒouþe.'
Heo keuered vp on hir kneos and cussed his hand:
'For I am dampned, I ne dar disparage þi mouþ.' (247–53)

The first two lines suggest both her submissive approach to her husband ("feere") and her normally natural and loving way with him ("as she ful well knew how"). Her statement that she has never angered him in word or in work seems to look forward to Walter's demand that Griselda and/or his people neither "grucche" nor "stryve" against him in Chaucer's Clerk's tale (*CT* 4: 169–76, 351–57). Susan thus presents herself as a good subject, but at the same time she signals her normally familiar conversation with him. Though she rises to her knees and kisses his hand, her final sentence, again, suggests her wanted intimacy with him: damned, she dare not kiss his mouth as she is used to do. While this is a scene between husband and wrongly accused wife, it is also a scene between a figure of sovereignty and his falsely accused subject.[78] Joachim is far less articulate than his wife and less powerful than the false judges. He can only kiss her, presumably on the mouth, and say, "'In oþer world schul we mete'"; the poet adds, "Seide he no mare" (259–60). Whereas Susan is often praised for her silence and faith, here Joachim is silent and faithful, Susan outspoken.

Susan's prayer before she is led off to judgment accosts God's privacy:

'Þou Maker of Middelert þat most art of miht,
Boþe þe sonne and þe see þou sette vppon seuene.
Alle my werkes þou wost, þe wrong and þe riht;
Hit is nedful nou þi names to neuene.
Seþþe I am deolfolich dampned and to deþ diht,
Lord hertelich tak hede and herkne my steuene
        So fre.
        Seþþe þou maiʒt not be sene
        Wiþ no fleschliche eyene,
        Þou wost wel I am clene.
        Haue merci on me.' (263–73)

Susan here gives full evidence of her learning and wisdom. In introducing Susan (14–26), the poet goes beyond both the references to her training in the law in Daniel 13:3, and Alan of Melsa's poem, in reiterating the degree to which she has been taught the law of Moses, which he ascribes to the Trinity (l.21), in order that she might both read and understand it. Her prayer here elaborates upon that in Daniel 13:42–43: "Lord God, without bigynnyng and ende, that art knowere of hid thingis, that knowist alle thingis bifore that tho ben don; thou wost, that thei han bore fals witnessyng aȝens me, And lo! Y dye, whanne Y haue not do ony of these thingis, whiche these men han maad maliciously aȝens me."[79]

Where in the Book of Daniel Susanna's speech captures the necessary dignity with which one addresses God, in *A Pistel* Susan prays to a God who is both majestic and intimate, and her words are beautifully balanced between the demands of spiritual devotion and courtly address. She reminds God of his power, by which he created the world in seven days, of his knowledge of her most intimate self, saying that it is now necessary to call upon God's names, inevitably suggesting that she knows them. She then states her helplessness and her innocence, as she does in the Book of Daniel, but asks God to listen to her, stating that since he cannot be seen with the eye, he must see that she is pure, and asks not for justice but for mercy. Again, this is the approach of an obedient and loving subject to a sovereign power. It is respectful, but it also gives evidence of a previously familiar and loving relationship between them. If it is a model for faith, it also, as does her speech to Joachim, provides a model for political relationships and discourse between lords and subjects.

However, that relationship and discourse depend on a credible legal system whose checks and balances protect the individual, whose vulnerability is well figured in the virtuous Susanna. Possibly for this reason, the author of *A Pistel* devotes a good deal of space to Daniel, not as a prophetic child, but as an able lawyer, whose skills are related to the proper deposition of witnesses. Those anxieties about false witnessing that can be seen in both the *Parson's Tale* and Fortescue's *De Laudibus Legum Angliae* invigorate the last section of *A Pistel*, where Daniel predominates. Hence, though God certainly plays a part in the action, there is no sense of miraculous salvation as there is in some other medieval treatments of the tale. As she is led forth to death:

Grete God of his grace, of gyftes vngnede,
Help with þe Holi Gost and herde hir preyere.
He directed þis dom and þis derf dede
To Danyel þe prophete, of dedes so dere;
Such ȝiftes God him ȝaf in his ȝouþehede.
ȝit failed him of fourten fullich a ȝere,
    Nouht to layne.
    Þo criede þat freoly foode:
    'Whi spille ȝe innocens blode?' (276–84)

These lines are subtly balanced between fidelity to the more conventional treatments of Susanna and a more nuanced reading of Daniel
as having God-given gifts that he uses wisely. The chain of events the
poet adumbrates links Susanna's voice and faith to a bounteous God
who hears her prayer and directs this terrible judgment to Daniel, who
has received God's gifts in his youth, though he is not yet fourteen.
Though young, Daniel is not the five-year-old he is in *The Knight of
Tour Landry* or the "petit enfant" he is in *Le Menagier de Paris* or even
the "ȝonge child" of the Wycliffite Bible.[80] Miracle is downplayed in
favor of faith, intelligence, and due process. His cry, "Why do you spill
innocent blood?" sets a legal inquiry into motion. Though the latter
part of Daniel 13 certainly outlines such a legal inquiry, the author of
A Pistel and Alan of Melsa are among the few medieval authors to give
it such emphasis.

In *A Pistel* Daniel's complaint against the false judges takes the
form of a complaint against the unjust use of power. First these "mais-
terful men" (287) cry out against him. Daniel then calls them fiends,
saying, "Vmbiloke ȝou, lordes, such lawes ben leiþ, / Me þinkeþ ȝor
dedes vnduwe such domes to dele" (291–92). Daniel's accusation seems
doubly directed: first, at the foulness of laws by which an innocent
woman can be put to death for an uncommitted crime, and, second, at
judges whose own deeds render them unworthy to bestow such judgments. He then calls for a return to the "guildhall," where he will "be
proces apert disprouc þis apele" (294). His wording here is precise in
its attention to legality: by proper legal procedure he will disprove this
appeal. He goes on to do exactly that, providing a model for the proper
deposition of witnesses and the workings of true (and popular) justice. If Susan seems to disappear, the processes of the law by which the

community is upheld take her place. In fact, the final lines of the poem describe not her restoration to house and home but the punishment of the false judges, referred to as "traiters" (356), who are dragged through the city before being put to death. The author of *A Pistel* is certainly not unfaithful here to the last section of Daniel 13, but in privileging legal process over divine intervention he shifts the focus of the story from the picture of silent female chastity to a more provocative interest in civil proceedings and the moral worthiness of figures of judicial authority. The poem was copied into five manuscripts dating from the early 1390s to the first third of the fifteenth century, so it clearly spoke to its audience in ways that go beyond appreciation for a simple tale of meekness and miraculous intervention.[81]

Chaucer's two explicit references to her suggest both the simple and the problematic aspects of her story. Custance in the *Man of Law's Tale* prays to God in Susanna's name when she lacks a champion to defend her from false charges of murder, "She sette hire doun on knees, and thus she sayde: / 'Immortal God, that savedest Susanne" (*CT* 2: 638–39). Custance so moves King Alla that he calls for a "Britoun book, written with Evaungiles" (*CT* 2: 666), a sign of England's prior Christianity, on which the false knight can swear. When he perjures himself, a hand smites him down and a voice is heard to say, "Thou hast desclaundred, giltelees, / The doghter of hooly chirche in heigh presence" (*CT* 2: 674–75).[82] Though justice is done, like his passive heroine, Custance, the Man of Law's Susanna is beauty wronged and rescued by divine aid.[83] Neither she nor, by extension, Susanna or even Daniel, the lawyer, has a voice in the juridical system; instead, God both acts and speaks. Law, such as it is, is dependent on the king's pity for a beautiful and pious plaintiff. The Parson is blunter, citing Susanna under false witnessing, which is a subset of avarice, since it is her good name that was taken from her:

> Of Avarice comen eek lesynges, thefte, fals witnesse, and false othes. . . . Fals witnesse is in word and eek in dede. In word, as for to bireve thy neighebores goode name by thy fals witnessyng, or bireven hym his catel or his heritage by thy fals witnessyng. . . . Ware yow, questemongeres and notaries! Certes, for fals witnessyng was Susanna in ful gret sorwe and peyne, and many another mo. (*CT* 10: 794–96)

The Parson here locates Susanna in a worldly (and potentially false) system of justice on which the English community rests. Fundamental to that system is a procedure for elucidating the truth of a situation by calling and deposing witnesses; when our "neighbors," for whatever self-serving reasons, speak against us, the community itself is in jeopardy. Where the Man of Law offers a miraculous event, the Parson suggests the murkiness of our world, where abound theft, false witness, and false oaths, all present in the *Man of Law's Tale* but unpunished by any except higher powers. Indeed, in this tale there appears no established process by which the truth might be ascertained. Though the Parson admits the possibility of falsity, he rests his account of the Seven Deadly Sins within the realities of the English community, a community that may not be perfect but whose institutions attempt to uphold the common good.

It is impossible to say whether Chaucer knew the alliterative *Pistel*, the most extended treatment in Middle English of Susanna's story, but it may explain why he chose to tell the stories of Custance and Virginia, both of which concern legal redress for the innocent. *A Pistel* certainly offers a rich and complex use of Daniel 13 that Chaucer would have appreciated.[84] Moreover, though the poem itself predates English Wycliffite treatises, and the manuscripts into which *A Pistel* was copied are not associated with Lollardy, the poem, as David Lyle Jeffrey has pointed out, seems to beg for a Lollard pedigree, or, at least, an affinity.[85] It is Susanna herself who, when appearing in later English texts, speaks for the rights of the individual under the law, rights that were consistently invoked both by those who ran afoul of orthodox practice, from the Wycliffites to those involved on both sides of sixteenth-century religious conflict.

Susanna's outcry to the false judges becomes that of the victim before the bench, crying out in the name of individual conscience and rectitude. The words she says when she is first propositioned by the elders are, "Angwischis ben to me on ech side" (Dan. 13:22). In *The Testimony of William Thorpe* (ca. 1407), Thorpe repeats those words when Archbishop Arundel demands that he abjure his Wycliffite beliefs, forsake his former associates, and silence his preaching and speaking voice: "And I heerynge þese wordis þouȝte in myn herte þat þis was an vnleeful askynge, and I demed mysilf cursid of God if I consentid herto; and I þouȝte how Susanne seide 'Angwysschis ben to me on euery side,' and forþi þat I stood stille musynge and spak not."[86] Like Susanna, he claims to fall silent in anguish. Except he does not. This reference comes early in Thorpe's *Testimony* and serves as a preface to a long argument that ultimately questions Arundel's spiritual and civil authority. Directly after Thorpe quotes Susanna's words to the false elders, the archbishop orders that he respond to his demand that he recant. Thorpe, again, echoes Susanna, who follows up her statement of anguish with one of personal integrity: "But it is betere for me to falle in to ȝoure handis without werk, than to do synne in the siȝt of the Lord." Thus Thorpe:

> 'Sere, if I consentid to do þus as ȝe haue here rehersid to me, I schulde become apelour (accusor), eiþir euery bischopis aspie or sumnour of þis lond. . . . I schulde hereinne be cause of þe deeþ boþe of men and of wymmen, ȝhe, boþe bodili and as I gesse goostli. . . . But sire, I fynde nouȝwhere in holi writ þat þis office þat ȝe wolden enfeffen me now herewiþ acordiþ to ony preest of Cristis sect, neiþer to ony oþer cristen man; þerfor to do þus it were to me a ful noyous bonde to be tied wiþ, an ouer greuous charge.' (35)

Thorpe here superimposes the language of legal process ("apelour," "enfeffen" [legally bind], "bonde," and "charge") on that of the individual conscience. Were he to accept Arundel's charge, he would place not only the physical safety of others in jeopardy but their spiritual safety as well. He explains that the terrors of confinement and persecution could cause those who "stonden now in truþe" to abjure that truth, linking his sense of personal truth with his vision of a community of like-minded Christians. He ends by implying that Arundel seeks to seduce him, like one of the false elders: "Forþi, ser, if I consentid to ȝou to do hereinne ȝoure wille. . . . I deme in my consience þat I were worþi to be cursid of God and so of all seyntis" (36). Similarly, Susanna argues that to do the elders' will would mean spiritual death to her.

This interchange comes early in the *Testimony*, which comprises over two thousand lines of text, and leads into a careful examination of the basis for the authority of the church. Each of the topics about which Thorpe is questioned concerns the relationship between individual belief and communal practice. The Archbishop asks Thorpe about preaching to the people regarding the nature of the sacrament and the use of images, about pilgrimage, about tithes and the authority of a possibly unworthy priest to curse those who do not pay tithes, about the swearing of oaths when ordered to do so, and about auricular confession. Each of these issues is, of course, central to the theological struggle between orthodox practice and the Wycliffite challenge to it. Moreover, in each set of questions, Arundel is described as focusing on Thorpe's preaching, on his ability or intention to influence the community. Like Susanna, Thorpe ends in prison, a prison in which he thanks God for keeping him from his adversaries and from despair. It is from prison that he says he writes. Near the end of his *Testimony* he returns to the picture of himself as a silent victim of injustice:

> And þanne I was rebukid and scorned and manassid on ech side. And ȝit after þis dyuerse persoones crieden vpon me to knele doun to submytte me. But I stood stille and spak no word. And þanne þere weren spoke of me and to me many greete wordis; and I stood and herde hem curse and manasse and scorne me, but I seide no þing. (92–93)

The obvious reference here is the trial of Christ.[87] Typologically, that New Testament trial provides a reference for the Old Testament trial of Susanna, whose silence under menace had been described as Christ-like by Saint Ambrose. However, though Thorpe's examination by Arundel (or Arundel's examination by Thorpe) is framed by references to Susanna and her silent faith, Thorpe has, in effect, given Susanna the articulate voice with which the author of *A Pistel* also endows her. Thorpe uses that voice to speak to his adversaries and to an English community he perceives as silenced by the powers of the institutions of church and state. Thorpe's reference to and use of Daniel 13 may owe something to two previous references to Susanna: the written testimony of Walter Brut, the erudite layman called before the bishop of Hereford in 1391 for his heterodox views and Thomas Wimbledon's Paul's Cross Sermon of 1388.[88] As Thorpe does in the *Testimony*, Brut and Wimbledon locate the faithful individual in a nation whose injustice undermines its security.

Brut's text is a carefully coded use of Susanna, presented not as the silent and suffering victim but as the articulate accuser of false

systems of power. It teases, begs for a quotation from or reference to
Daniel 13. Instead, Brut employs the Book of Daniel apocalyptically as
an index of the state of temporal institutions. He begins the Latin defense he was required to write in answer to the charges against him,
first, by manifesting who he is (a layman, an Englishman, latinate)
and, second, by claiming Scripture as his authority. He then provides a
credal statement of his faith, specifying the nature of Christ that
closely follows the Nicene Creed in its doctrinal purity. Moving directly from the pristine orthodoxy of credal statement, which signals
his oneness with the body of believers, Brut refers to the papacy and
the idolatry residing in the temple of God, citing the Book of Daniel
as evidence for the abomination and desolation of the present age
(287). In comparing Rome to the Whore of Babylon, Brut quotes from
Daniel 12:11. He returns in a more apocalyptic way to the trope of
Babylon, quoting from the Books of Revelation and Isaiah (288–89).
He employs Nebuchadnezzar's questioning of Daniel to suggest the
necessary relationship between power and prophetic wisdom in times
that seem to augur the imminence of Antichrist (291–92). In illustrating the lack of true mercy to be found in the pope or in canon law, he
recounts the story from John 8 of the woman taken in adultery (317),
the text with which Daniel 13 is paired during the season of Lent, and
follows it by recalling Nebuchadnezzar's dream of the statue whose
head is gold, chest and arms silver, stomach and thighs iron, and feet
some part iron and some part clay (Dan. 2:31–45). This dream was
commonly used to diagnose historical devolution and, about the same
time as Brut's trial, was described by John Gower in the prologue to
the *Confessio Amantis*. After what is a long and frankly apocalyptic
warning to his nation, Brut ends by reinserting himself into the role
of the submissive plaintiff, assuring his accusers of his simplicity, plain
style, and obedience to a church whose authority his testimony constantly questions (358). Though he does not explicitly cite the story of
Susanna, he cites around it in such a way that the explicit reference
seems almost unnecessary. Like her, he is a citizen of the true Israel
living within Babylon, falsely accused by members of his own nation
but faithful to his beliefs and assured that the laws of God super-
sede those of man.

The analogy he continually draws between Babylon and the present age leads Brut to stress the special, and chosen, status of England

itself. He locates this in the nation's conversion during the time of King Lucius, who, hearing of a new faith, believed and sent to Rome, to Pope Eleutherius, for men who could inform him of it. He rejoiced when they arrived and was baptized with all his kingdom ("In quorum adventum gavisus et baptizatus est cum toto regno suo") (294). Brut goes on to note, as does Bede, that after accepting this faith the kingdom never deserted it. Hence their elect status: "et sic videtur michi Britones inter omnes alias gentes quasi ex Dei eleccione specialiter fuisse ad fidem vocatos et conversos" (294). Among all other people, the Britons seem elected by God, called and converted, implicitly a second Israel living in the midst of a Babylonian Captivity, that of the Roman church. In tracing England's faith, not to Pope Gregory's decision to send missionaries to convert the "angels" he saw in the Roman marketplace, but to Lucius's willingness to listen to the rumor of the new faith being preached in Rome (294), to believe in it, and to send for Christian teachers, Brut severs English Christianity from Roman or papal power and locates it in the heart of an English king.[89]

Thomas Wimbledon uses Susanna in an argument about the deficiencies of his age that is, to some degree, consistent with Brut. This sermon has a long history in both manuscript and print. There are fifteen extant manuscripts in which it is included; their contents are mainly devotional, and some are clearly of Wycliffite provenance. The sermon was also carried over into Foxe's *Acts and Monuments*, as well as printed separately and included in both Anglican and Puritan collections.[90] Wimbledon, tellingly, begins the sermon with the Parable of the Vineyard from Matthew 20, which he describes as the story of a "householder." Though Wimbledon follows exegetical tradition in linking the household to the church (14), his use of it is focused on the English household, the community, and the skewed values he perceives there. He puts forward several related and schematic ways of conceiving of this realm: he categorizes the laborers in the vineyard as having different offices, priesthood, knighthood, and laborer (38–39); different estates into which men are called by God, servant, bondman, merchant, justice, priest; or three "bailiffs," spiritual lords, temporal lords, and every Christian man (140–44) who shall answer to three questions. The questions themselves link personal intentionality with the realities of public office: how have you entered into your position;

how have you ruled, and how have you lived? These will be the questions each must answer before entering into heaven. He castigates fathers who send sons to study law or to the king's court in order that they may "make hem grete in þe world" (192) and mothers who attend to the bodies of their children and not their souls (196–97), as well as churchmen who have adopted the mercantilism of the secular world. He devotes great attention to judicial inequities, asking those who rule how they have treated the poor: "Þou þat hast ben a juge in causis of pore men, how hast þou keped þis hest of God?" (349–50), complaining "O Lord God, what abusioun is þer among officeres of here boþe lawes nowadayes" (356–57). Here Wimbledon says that a poor man cannot bring a case against a rich man, that shire-reeves and bailiffs "wolleþ retorne pore mennes writis wiþ *tarde venit* but þey felen mede in her handes" (364–65).[91]

Wimbledon cites Susanna when he comes to the final question those in civil authority shall answer on their last day: "How hast þou liued, þou þat demest and punysschist oþer men for her trespas?" (373–74). He quotes Saint Gregory from the *Moralia*, who says that he who cannot govern himself should not govern others:

'He schal not take gouernayl of oþere þat cannot go byfore hem in good lyuynge.' And whan any man stant byfore hym in dom, he most take hede tofore what Juge he shal stonde hymself to take his dom aftir his dedis.

   But it is to drede þat many fareþ as þe tweye false prestis þat wolde haue dampned to deþ holy Susanne, for sche nolde nouȝt assente to here lecherie. Of whiche it is writen: 'Þey turneden awey here eiȝen, for þey wolde not se heuene ne haue mynde of ryȝtful dom.' (381–90) [92]

Here Wimbledon securely anchors the quotidian processes of civil justice to the awesome realities of heavenly judgment. As Brut does a few years later, Wimbledon holds his own time up to the day of doom, to the coming of Antichrist, suggesting like Brut that the righteous few are still citizens of Babylon. Wimbledon sees his own age as dominated by covetousness, which has infected society in ways that enervate efforts at reform.[93]

John Foxe's handling of these three medieval figures is telling.[94] Thorpe's testimony occurs in all editions of the *Acts and Monuments*; Brut's is added with the 1570 edition. Wimbledon's sermon, which was printed independently during the sixteenth century, occurs in all editions. However, in the 1563 edition Foxe added a paragraph to the beginning of the second part in which he exploits Wimbledon's reference to the "householder": "How haste thou gouerned thy wife, thy children, and seruants? haste thou brought them vp after the laues of God, and continued them there in, as much as lyeth in thy pouer?"[95] Foxe here offers a reading of Wimbledon's late-fourteenth-century sermon as addressed to the household of the realm, in which the father and husband, the figure of civil and spiritual authority, shall answer for the godliness of those in his charge. It is this question that is in the narratives of Protestant England increasingly attached to the story of Susanna, who cannot be separated from the household, whose sanctity is violated and safety nullified.

There are other early modern references to Susanna that are likewise intended to undermine or to examine the powers of church or state. In *A Spiritual Consolation written . . . to hys sister Elizabeth* (1578), written when he awaited his death in the tower, John Fisher used Susanna as an example of someone wrongly accused by those in power. (Here, ironically, Fisher, supporting the doctrines of the Roman Catholic Church against a still-Catholic but determined king, assumes the stance of heterodoxy, a position he had formerly and vigorously persecuted when those dissenters were Protestants. His defense of both his own conscience and Christian doctrine is as staunch as any Wycliffite's defense of Christ's law.) On the other hand, in *An Account of a Disputation at Oxford, anno dom. 1554, with A Treatise of the Blessed Sacrament* (London, 1685), Nicholas Ridley cited the Elders as false witnesses, comparing them to those who insist on the truth of transubstantiation. Thomas Bilney, the Norwich martyr credited with converting Hugh Latimer, likened the courtroom proceedings against him to those against Susanna.[96] In *The English Mirror* (1586), George Whetstone raised the provocative issue of magistrates, saying that law was needed to "bridle" unjust magistrates, referring to the false justices in Daniel 13, as did Jeremy Taylor much later.[97] Sir Walter Raleigh in his own defense invoked Susanna by way of Fortescue when arguing about proof and the dangers of miscarriage of justice.[98] Each of these references concerns the workings of English justice as it affects the safety of members of England's household, a household potentially vulnerable to abuses of the powers vested in kings and magistrates.

The question of justice invigorates *A Pistel*, a poem dated to the last years of the reign of Edward III, and may well bear some relation to its reappearance in the five later manuscripts into which it was copied. There were, of course, issues relating to the administration of justice in the later years of Edward III, as there were during the 1390s when the poem was copied into both the Vernon and Simeon manuscripts. In the 1360s, a good deal of attention was paid to the administration of local justice. The Statute of 1361 gave local judicial authorities determining power in local law enforcement, in effect putting justice in the hands of county gentry, a move that reflected the tug-of-war between magnate and local power and that was reversed again in 1368.[99] Richard Kaeuper notes that the *Tale of Gamelyn* could be reproduced from court records of the period, suggesting that the evidence indicates frustration with a justice potentially at the mercy of money or force and the impulse for a serious inquiry into what might serve as an acceptable way of maintaining the King's Peace.[100] That peace was, of course, directly threatened not simply by violence, but by perjury and corruption.[101]

A Pistel of Susan seems designed to ask particular questions about justice as it pertains to landed gentry. The early emphasis on Joachim's status and the openness of his house and grounds underline the ways in which the narrative depicts an assault on a secular household that is vulnerable to the greed of the judges and possibly contributed to the relative popularity of *A Pistel of Susan*. Only one of the five manuscripts into which *A Pistel* was copied does not contain a mix of religious and secular texts.[102] The two earliest manuscripts, though later than the poem, are the important Vernon and Simeon manuscripts, dated to the last decade of the fourteenth century. These are large and related anthologies of Middle English writing, containing mainly devotional and instructional texts but some romances. The Simeon manuscript has two words that might be "Joan Boun" written in a margin.[103] Joan Bohun, daughter of Richard Fitzalan, earl of Arundel, sister of Thomas Arundel, bishop of Ely, archbishop of York and Canterbury, and widow of Humphrey Bohun, earl of Hereford,

Essex, and Northampton, mother-in-law of both Henry Bolingbroke and Thomas of Woodstock, was wealthy, powerful, pious, and long-lived. As Doyle notes, she was the sort of woman for whom the manuscript would have been appropriate. Both manuscripts would have been costly, and if they were intended for a secular household rather than a religious house it must have been a large and pious one, such as those formed by powerful widows in the late Middle Ages.[104]

If Joan Bohun ever owned or had anything to do with the making of the Simeon manuscript, texts like *A Pistel* would have had a variety of appeals. First, and most obviously, Susanna is an example of a prominent, wealthy, devout, and chaste wife, an example that might mean much to other women. The narrative's legal ramifications might have added to its appeal for a secular woman, especially during the last decade of Richard II's reign when false witnesses were numerous. Both Richard Fitzalan, earl of Arundel, Joan's brother, and Thomas of Woodstock, her son-in-law, were murdered by Richard in a sham of due process in 1397.[105] Thomas, in fact, was taken from his own Essex seat, Pleshey, by the king himself and his henchmen. Since they were convicted of treason, their goods were technically forfeit to the crown, though much of his property was held in right of his wife, Eleanor, Joan's daughter.[106] The Simeon manuscript, which is shorter and possibly subsequent to the Vernon, cannot so simply be attached to Joan Bohun because it contains *A Pistel*, but the poem raises some of the concerns Joan Bohun or other landed families certainly experienced when contemplating the security of their households and the likelihood of being able to defend their interests. Similarly, in the political instabilities of Tudor England, with their dangers for individual rights and property, Susanna and her garden would stand as powerful reminders of the need for laws that served the common, not the private, good. In those moments when Catholic or Protestant stood helpless before power, by invoking Susanna the accused at once claimed his innocence and accused power of its own lapses. In the four extended early modern treatments of the story of Susanna, three during the reign of Elizabeth and one near the end of the reign of James I, there is evidence of a use of the narrative that goes far beyond simple invocation. These texts, like the "Tractatus" and *A Pistel*, offer detailed examinations of the very language of enclosure out of which the English household made itself.

EARLY MODERN SUSANNA

There are four lengthy retellings of Daniel 13 in the early modern period: Thomas Garter's *The Commody of the moste vertuous and Godlye Susanna* (1578), Robert Greene's *The Myrrour of Modestie* (1584), Robert Roche's *Evstathia or the Constancie of Susanna* (1599), and Robert Aylett's *Svsanna: or The Arraignment of the Two Vnjvst Elders* (1622). All four share an emphasis on Susanna's chastity and describe her as an educated and gentle wife. Daniel 13 describes her as trained in the law, which medieval accounts of her likewise underline, but in these early modern versions Susanna becomes the eloquent, educated, and tireless Protestant wife. Moreover, each of these retellings at once assimilates the narrative to England by means of references or place-names *and* conveys a Protestant queasiness about Susanna's beauty as potentially iconic and thus dangerous to the beholder. She is thus a marker for chaste femininity, a subject with a good deal of relevance for the three Elizabethan retellings, but also for the dangers posed by images, which were the object of a good deal of English Protestant violence. Similarly, each of these works debates the subject of enclosure, again, a subject linked to the medieval vowed life of the nun and to England's self-definition as the enclosed but not isolated garden. Though none is "great literature," all help to illuminate what was a continuing and sometimes ambivalent exploration of the terms of national identity, for which Marvell's "Appleton House" serves as a kind of summary statement. Each text evinces its author's awareness of traditional or medieval treatments of Daniel 13 but at the same time the author's desire to translate Susanna into the terms and anxieties of contemporary English life.

For example, *The Commody of . . . Susanna* is generically a morality play with vices, a devil, his son Ill Reporte (who refers to the Devil as "Dad"), and a protagonist who is the object of severe testing. The judges are given generic names, Voluptas and Sensualitas. The play is early enough for the author to be fully aware of the conventions of both morality and mystery plays, and, in fact, there was a vigorous tradition of early modern Protestant biblical drama that would have been written and possibly produced in private settings at the same time the Catholic mystery plays continued to be read, produced, and, in some cases, rewritten. *The Commody of . . . Susanna* could be read as a rewriting of hagiographic drama like the Digby *Mary Magdalene*, whose references to the Roman religion would have been anathema to pious Protestant writers. Figures like King David, Susanna, and other biblical heroes could be used to offer entertaining and moral lessons for Protestant readers and audiences, especially since such figures need not be connected to Catholic theology and practices. In 1568–69 Thomas Colwell paid for a license to print "the playe of Susanna," but it was not until a decade later that Hugh Jackson, who married Colwell's widow, printed *The Commody . . . of Susanna*.[107] Its author, Thomas Garter, is unknown except for this play, though there was a Bernard Garter who composed the text for Elizabeth's 1578 progress in Norwich.[108] The play, which seems to belong to the first decade of Elizabeth's reign, presents its heroine as under threat by Ill Report, who seeks to ruin Susanna's reputation. Indeed, M. Lindsay Kaplan has suggested that Garter's handling of Susanna's exemplary virtue and vulnerability to slander should be seen in relation to contemporary concerns for and depictions of Elizabeth I, the learned and godly head of England's own beleaguered Protestant household.[109] The other two Elizabethan texts are related to Shakespeare's *Lucrece*, which may have drawn on Greene's *Myrrour* and which, in turn, influenced Roche, who mentions both *Lucrece* and Spenser's Colin Clout in his "To the Reader."[110] Like these Elizabethan treatments of Susanna, Aylett's *Susanna*, which also nods to Edmund Spenser, describes Susanna by reference to the ekphrastic description of the bride in the Song of Solomon, language that had been used throughout the Middle Ages to praise the Virgin Mary, as well as to praise the beauty of England, and, in the Elizabethan period, the beauty and virtue of Elizabeth herself. In other words, the four works constitute a dense network of intertextual references between Catholic and Protestant culture and among themselves and other significant early modern texts that suggests just how fraught the effort at national self-description was in a period when evidence for the rupture with past practices lay everywhere.

These four Susannas inhabit an England whose geography and judicial ideals are noticeable throughout; the vulnerability of both to incursion and corruption is manifest in each author's depiction of Susanna and her enclosed garden. Garter anchors his play of Susanna to England, first, in the prologue by suggesting that the story is a "myrour," whose good example is "meete in these oure dayes" (20, 22), and, second, by giving Vice a jingle in which he outlines a geography of England in which place-names are attached to public houses and public women, a landscape of poverty and chicanery, where the miles are enumerated between towns or between nodes of dubious commerce (461–86).[111] Ill Report refers to the needs of a "commonwealth" (582); Susanna's maid laments the strictness of her "court," which is far more sober in dress and habits than she had hoped (611–39, 708–19), and the Judge tells Susanna that even if she were a "Queene" (1054) she must be attentive to his sentence. Garter thus translates the Babylon of the biblical story into the terms of contemporary England, complete with its dangers to the innocent.

The three other treatments of Susanna leave aside the vices and comic gestures of the morality play tradition on which Garter drew and assimilate her and her household to the judicial and social values of England. Robert Greene's *Myrrour of Modestie* is dedicated to Margaret, countess of Derby, the mother of Ferdinando Stanley, Lord Strange, noted patron of the arts. His wife, Alice Spencer, whom he married in 1579/80 likewise encouraged acting companies and took over Lord Strange's Men when her husband died in 1594; she was celebrated by Thomas Nash and Edmund Spenser, as well as by Greene.[112] Greene's Joachim desires to "linke himselfe in the holie league of Matrimonie" (Ai) and searches for a wife as assiduously as any Protestant magnate, finding an educated and virtuous woman of a good and pious family. He takes her as his wife, hoping that the "grafting" of their two stocks should prove fruitful and beneficent. Greene expands the account in Daniel of the legal processes the young lawyer Daniel invokes. Daniel, in chastising the Israelites for condemning Susanna, gives them a lesson on proper evidence, asking them (Cii) how a judge can also be a witness. He lectures the judges on their duties to "measure all things in the ballance of equitie" (Ciii) and excoriates them for their sins against Joachim:

> art thou so deuoide of humanitie as thou wilt repaie the good will that Ioachim sheweth thee, with such guilefull treacherie, is thy conscience such as to requight his curtesie with wilfull crueltie, hath he fostered thee as a frend, and wilt thou abuse him as a foe. (Ciiiii)

The standards Daniel raises are those of the private household, whose chaste wife, private garden, and hospitality have been violated by false justice masquerading as friendship. The scene of the popular uprising against such justice at the end of the narrative has a peculiar force, since Daniel has just described a type of self-interested justice that has nothing to do with equity or with divine law Greene thus removes the law from the sole purview of magistrates and sovereigns and attaches it to God and the people or to a judge's accountability to both.

In *Eustathia*, published during the last and somewhat fraught years of Elizabeth's reign, Robert Roche, who graduated from Magdalene Hall, Oxford, in 1599 and occupied the vicarage of Hilton in Dorset from 1617 to 1629, locates law in the household, specifically in Joachim and Susanna's. Roche establishes the poem's relevance to contemporary England not simply by his allusions to Shakespeare and Spenser, but by a prefatory poem, "Coricæus to the Author," which raises the issue of censors, warning the author of the possibilities of public enmity but complimenting him on his poetry in this, his "Firstling." Near the end of the poem, Susanna, now on her deathbed, counsels her children, "Plaie not the cowards in your countries good, / Spend in her canse [*sic*], your deerest breath and wealth" (H5), advice that cannot apply to Jews held captive in Babylon but to Englishmen of the late sixteenth century. Moreover, the households depicted in this poem are those of Protestant England, and, indeed, Roche praises marriage as a type of law (C4 ff.), drawing on the Aristotelian analogy between the hierarchical and ordered household and the orderly state.[113] Susanna's mother "With rod in hand, to keepe her babe in awe" (B2), instructs her child in the law, and Susanna's father educates her in biblical history. Once Susanna has attained womanhood, Roche stages a debate in her mind between "barren mayden-head, and bearing wife" that rejects marriage based on lust and virginity but embraces chaste marriage as the basis for social order. Roche's account of the perils of marriage echoes the virginity literature of the Middle Ages, especially *The Letter on Virginity*, a key early-thirteenth-century West Midland text written for women that describes the physical hardships of marriage and the damage marriage and pregnancy do to the female body, in effect undoing the body once celebrated for its beauty.[114] Thus Roche catalogs "nibled teates," the "tortured" bowels, the "weakned backe," and the "swelling" feet and the horrors of birth and the disappointments

of marriage itself (B8). Where medieval virginity literature then espoused the true married pleasures of the vowed life with Christ as
husband, Roche describes the single life as frequently deceptive, hiding secret sins and, in fact "canonizing" a maidenhead (C4). In contrast, he describes marriage as an "Academie royall" (C6), containing all Christian virtues as well as the liberal arts, with Good Order
as usher and Justice as the sovereign authority. In his long description of marriage as an expression of bountiful social harmony, Roche
is, of course, able to suggest that the harmonious and pious nation
ruled over by sovereign justice is a household. At the end of this account he does commend the "mayden life" where there is "command,"
as a sign of God's grace, acknowledging the sacredness of Elizabeth's
chaste life *and* praising her for having engendered a bountiful household. Like the Virgin Mary, whom he does not mention, Elizabeth
embraces paradox: she is both enclosed and fruitful. He returns then
to the young Susanna, who chooses marriage to Joachim out of all
her suitors because he is well regarded, wealthy but munificent, of
great repute, and his life "an obiect, worthie contemplation" (D1).
Susanna's choice is thus based in reason and rooted in her own regard
for community.

When the judges begin to speak of their understanding of the
law, it becomes clear that Roche intends to juxtapose the rational and
godly law that reigns in Susanna's household to the selectively applied
and self-interested law exploited by the judges in their governance of
Israel-in-Babylon. He compares the latter to treason (D5), a term with
little relevance for Jewish Babylon but much for Elizabethan England.[115]
Similarly, he pauses to excoriate the judges for abusing their office:

> So sovereignes oft, come subiectes to their sin,
> Whilst those that should not, soonst are slaues to lust,
>
> .   .   .   .
>
> When rulers are (as yron worne with rust)
>   Consum'd with loue, then countries fall to sinne,
>   As heere you see these iudges doe beginne. (D7)

The judges compound their sin by admitting to one another (E)
that one law should be applied to all and that rulers are the looking

glasses and the books "In which all subiects eies, doe reade and looke," but they then acknowledge that their desire prevails over law and reason and look to God for mercy for their "venial" sin even before they commit it (E2). Since Roche has earlier linked Susanna's knowledge of biblical history and her obedience to divine law with the orderly nature of her household, the judges' corruption of the doctrines of penance and divine mercy constitutes a corruption of the community that they purport to rule justly. As Susannas before her have argued, Roche's Susanna condemns them in the name of the law and of the history that encodes that law. Daniel steps forward to second Susanna's eloquent defense of her innocence and submission to God's will with a stirring explanation of due process that has been violated by "periurie" and "false witnesse" as they appealed to the "multitude": "Thus carelesse commons, right or wrong support. / When they are swayd, as sovereignes do exhort" (H).

Popular hatred of Susanna for her alleged adultery turns to hatred of the false judges, and "To yeeld those reprobates, their due desertes, / The happiest man, doth hurle the heviest stone." Once justice is satisfied, Roche moves forward to Susanna's old age in which she exhorts her children to love virtue, remember their parents' precepts, honor wedlock's "bande," and recognize the "waverying" world for what it is.

This ending, which is Roche's invention, like Alan of Melsa's "Tractatus," validates experience. Though the final stanza of *Eustathia* offers a simple moral promising God's help to the righteous, the poem itself offers a scathing picture of worldly dangers for the innocently ignorant righteous. Susanna, after all, lives in Babylon and comes to see and attempts to pass on the uncertainties of life as she has experienced them. The principle by which she steers is law, the law of the individual before God that produces the bountiful and godly, but never secure, household. Her recognition that she and her household belong to a greater community united by law is nonetheless one with her recognition that communities and the individuals within them are vulnerable to those who abuse the law. With its picture of a populace too easily swayed by the wiles of those possessing authority, *Eustathia* maintains a faith in sovereignty *if* that sovereign is ruled by God's law. The very concept of a household as Aristotle explained it is hierarchical,

since a household depends on a householder and on those who live obediently according to certain rules. Though Joachim is husband and
householder, these Elizabethan writers emphasize Susanna's importance to and within the household as features of her vulnerability and,
by extension, that of her household, as befits writers whose own queen
was vulnerable to gossip, libel, treason, and sometimes vanity, which
might place her nation/household in jeopardy.

Robert Aylett (1582–1655) published *Susanna* in 1622 when the
nation's householder was a king, and a king feeling the stresses of Puritan resistance.[116] Aylett was an ecclesiastical lawyer, whose patron
was John King, bishop of London, and who was a supporter of Anglicanism as defined by Archbishop Laud. Curiously, Aylett dedicated
Susanna to Robert Rich, second earl of Warwick, whose mother, Penelope, sister to Robert Devereux, or the second earl of Essex, was
the "Stella" to whom Sir Philip Sidney addressed *Astrophil and Stella*.
Robert Rich, who was thoroughly involved in political life, began as
a king's man but came to oppose Laud and ended by supporting the
Puritans, securing the patent for the Plymouth colony and later help-
ing with the patent for the Massachusetts Bay colony.[117] In 1622 Aylett praised him as "another Daniel for iudging right" and his wife,
Frances Hatton, who died a year later, as "a Susan of this age." Aylett
states in the Argument to the poem that Susanna should be understood as "Right, or Justice," which the false elders seek to corrupt. He
links the people to the judges, since they are "prone to imitate" vice,
not virtue. He compares Joachim to a king (10), praises him for maintaining his estate, for choosing not to hold public office (14), and when
Susanna kneels before him, likens Joachim to Solomon, before whom
the queen of Sheba knelt (16). Law, then, at once upholds order in the
person of the sovereign and, as administered by Daniel, restrains
the impulse to vice. In, to some extent, displacing Susanna in favor of
Joachim, Aylett reinforces the role of law as a hedge against disorder.
Significantly, he begins the fourth book of the poem by addressing all
judges, describing them as husbandmen:

> You Iudges; that on earth Gods people wield,
> As husbands trees and bushes in a field,
> Crop which you list, and which you list let grow,
> And are as Gods Vicegerents here below. (35)

He then shifts the metaphor, comparing these bad judges of Israel to "handballs," which Ambition has thrown against the ground, watching them bounce high, then leaving them on the ground in dust. Those who should have been careful gardeners, working, like the beekeeper in *Mum and the Sothseggar* who squashes drones for the good of the hive, have abandoned justice for ambition and have been themselves abandoned "all in the Dust in equall sort." Having eschewed the garden, they are left with the infertile ground of the playing field.

Susanna, however, like other English Susannas, has her say, again speaking for the law. When accosted by the judges, she reminds them that she must obey "laws iudiciall," which specify death *"without exception"* for adultery and the laws of God that bring guilt to the sinner. The judges deny any connection between religion and law:

> Dame, said the Iudge; art thou yet so vnwise,
> Thou knowst not Polititians did deuise
> Religion, onely to represse the base,
> And hold the Noble in the peoples grace? (20)

With this stunningly modern argument that religion is the opiate devised to keep the people in line, the judges go on to redefine the laws by which community is maintained, including the law of matrimony, which they describe as *ceremony*, insisting that judges have the power to dispense with laws and urging her not to restrain her flesh but to "delight" it (21). Threatened by rape, Susanna cries out and is turned over to the engine of justice, which eventually works because Daniel knows the law.

Aylett's judges share with their Elizabethan forebears an attraction to and violence toward female beauty, the dangerous image that harbors in the mind, inspiring the gazer to idolatry, or, conversely, to iconoclasm.[118] The judges diagnose their own disease by their ekphrastic account of Susanna's beauty, which, in all four works, echoes the descriptions in the Canticles of the bride's beauty, language with a long history in the medieval and early modern poetry of desire, sacred and profane. Thus one of Garter's judges describes Susanna from top to toe in a series of trite similes and bad poetry (which Shakespeare mocks in Sonnet 130), concluding with, "Her middle small, her body long, her buttockes broade and round, / Her legges so straight, her foote so small, the like treades not on ground/ I thinke that Nature which made her, cannot make like agayne" (417–19). He then decides she may not be a made thing but a goddess. The other judge responds to this rhetoric by exclaiming, "By God I would spende my best cote to fish within her poole" (427). The transgressive violence and vulgarity of their desire is likewise apparent in the courtroom scenes, which underline the statement in Daniel 13:32 that Susanna is ordered unveiled in court so that the judges "might feast their eyes upon her beauty." Thus Garter: "though we could not touch/ Yet pleasing our eyes with this her sight shall serue our lust as much" (991–92). Greene's and Roche's judges refer to Susanna as a "saint" who has enchanted them. In Roche's *Eustathia* they go so far as to peer through the crack in the garden door to see their saint and describe their frequent presence at this door as a "pilgrimage." Here, they appear as devotées staring through the garden door/rood screen at the source of their desire. Where the Book of Daniel simply says that Susanna faces execution, these narratives underline the violence with which the judges turn on their former saint by emphasizing that the law of Moses specifies death by stoning as the penalty for adultery. Where Roche's judges wished to enclose her in their own secret desire and, in fact, surround her with their "clasped armes" in the garden as "the harmlesse deere" is "Beset with greedie curres, and eagre houndes" (E6), now Susanna awaits another violating weight from the "multitude" that will "presse her downe, with stones til she were dead" (G4). Once the judges are proved guilty, they reap the justice they would have visited upon her.

The violence with which the judges approach Susanna is concomitant with their entry into and thus violation of her garden, which in each of these texts is a sign of her married chastity. For Susanna, the garden or orchard is an extension of the bond of marriage, which is at once private and bound into community. In *Eustathia*, Susanna walks in her garden to "avoide the presse . . . and shun the gaze, of every glauncing eie"; "when the presse was past," she returns to her home, where Joachim confers with the judges, his "good friendes" (D5). In Aylett's *Susanna*, the garden is an orchard that Susanna has planted and where she and Joachim walk and talk together and where Susanna goes to read and pray. What has been created as *private* the

judges evaluate as *secret* and thus as a place where sin may be committed apart from and unknown by the "presse." As the judges say in
Greene's *Mirrour of Modestie*, "That sinne which is secretlie committed is alwaies halfe pardoned" (A10). Roche emphasizes their trespass
on private space by saying they "sneake in at the gate" and hide like
"sly foxes" (E3). It is, of course, the foxes in the vineyard that the Canticle bemoans as potentially spoiling the grapes. Both Greene's and
Roche's judges invoke David's secret sin with Bathsheba as precedent
for their own.

The distinction between privacy and secrecy also governs the
ways in which Susanna and the judges invoke the law. Susanna applies
a law handed down communally and mandated by God, who sees the
secrets of the heart and through garden walls. The judges acknowledge one law for the community and another for those who operate in
secrecy, thereby violating the concept of privacy, which is protected
by the laws of the community. For Susanna, her garden or orchard,
like her marriage, exists within the community and its laws and is enclosed but not closed off. For the judges, the garden is to be entered
as a separate world with its own set of rules that have nothing to do
with the law of Moses. The Old Testament example of Ahab's seizure
of Nabaoth's vineyard is used either as a warning on Susanna's part
or as a precedent for their action by the judges, who say that the law
of Moses could not restrain Ahab's desire.[119] If in their fascination for
and worship of Susanna's beauty as an image, they seem to evoke the
iconophilia of England's old religion, in their willingness to mutilate
that same image, they seem to bring to their tasks a puritan iconoclasm, in both guises acting as agents of destruction within the community of Babylonian Jews.[120] However, there is a good deal more here
than gynophobia: the feminine is manifested in a space that belongs
to both Joachim and Susanna but is also, because it is private, linked
to Susanna herself. As she stands naked before the intruders, her body
is violated by their gaze just as the garden is violated by their entry.
If the garden is the sign of Susanna's loving, rational, publicly celebrated marriage, it, like Edenic England, is at the mercy of those who
would use the law for their own secret purposes. The references in each
text suggesting the contemporary relevance of this particular narrative link it to England, the island enclosed by the sea, the rights of

whose citizens are guaranteed by their historically worked out laws of community, their common law.

◼   These English retellings of the biblical story of Susanna share an interest in the household—whether monastic or secular—that positions it in relation to a concept of justice as protecting the common good. Though *A Pistel* is contemporary with the A-text of *Piers Plowman* and employs the language of enclosure, it looks forward and presents that common good as a gentry estate, not as a croft. More tellingly, none of these accounts of Susanna locates justice in the person of the sovereign but in a concept of law that can be twisted by a corrupt judge but also used knowledgeably by a good lawyer to protect the innocent. What is privileged in each of these accounts is a household described in language also used to describe England in the traditions of Bedan history—Edenic, enclosed, potentially vulnerable or permeable or hospitable. Those final terms capture the anxieties of enclosure where hospitality can become vulnerability because it allows in what might threaten the sanctity of space. It is with that final term *sanctity* that I would like to close this chapter, sanctity that applies not to anointed kings but to spaces that depend on an understanding of law to ensure that enclosure and hospitality are not mutually exclusive. Just as Ben Jonson's Lady Sidney has her linen ready for the sudden guest, so that linen and the cupboard that holds it depend on a law that protects Penshurst against unjust incursion, its walled openness serves to remind the sovereign of his own status under the law. On the other hand, the story of Susanna also serves as a harsh reminder of the need to recognize evil, validating both innocence and experience as fundamental to any concept of law that holds a household, a garden, or a nation in hospitable enclosure.

CONCLUSION

Island Discourse

For just over one thousand years treatments of England the island paradise served not simply to express but also to debate and construct an identity for an English nation before ideas of nationalism or of nation-states were subjects of either inquiry or urgency. Integral to this discourse is the ideological tension between enclosure and isolation as defining the status of a nation described, first, as a discrete geographic unit, a tension also inherent in the medieval and early modern language of selfhood. Bede's carefully crafted correction or extension of Gildas's original depiction of Britain is likewise a characterization of England's monastic vitality as depending on its affiliations with the culture and practices of Catholic Christendom, as both nourished by and nourishing an ongoing and collaborative process of invasive acculturation. However, as writers subsequent to Bede attest, the notion of a collaborative process of invasive acculturation could also be a noxious oxymoron threatening infestation rather than growth. It is the tension embedded in the conceptualization of a nation as geographically or spatially enclosed that has held together the four chapters of this book as four periods of thought belonging to an extended exploration of medieval and early modern metaphoric confabulation. Each chapter reveals similar patterns that, in turn, evince the ways in which the language describing enclosed geographic space and the images for it carry over into what appear unrelated texts and offer perspectives on a historical process and set of conditions that this discourse does not so much reflect as shape and, in so doing, offers ways of exploring the implicit links between constructions of nation and of a self belonging to that nation.

For example, to move from the concept of the virgin garden/ bride/nation defiled by her own beauty to Cistercian enclosed space to the anchoress walled securely in place to the nation secure behind its seawall to the nation returned to waste by enclosure to the wife safe or unsafe within her walled orchard to the alarming and alluring openness of an estate built within and upon a past now dissolved is to confront at each turn a set of considerations that link constructions of space and the self to those of nation and constructions of its history. Embedded in these same considerations is the question of safety: who or what guards the garden, the bride, the self, the nation? And here, the thirteenth-century voice of Alan of Melsa serves to encapsulate or anticipate an ongoing conversation whose semantics depend on his understanding of the languages of gender and metaphor and the ways in which they functioned within monastic thought. In wedding his enclosed and unsafe cloister/garden to the justness of the law as interpreted by Daniel, he inevitably links that chaste space to a nation whose own inviolability is ensured not by persons or institutions but by a law properly and dispassionately administered. The "chastity" of the monastic garden and of those who inhabit it is not the result of ignorance but of experience. Alan suggests the fundamental dangers inherent in isolation, dangers likewise suggested by other authors of Susanna's story but also by the host of poets, essayists, ecclesiastics, and historians chronicled in these chapters, who debate the relative merits or dangers of the enclosed island garden.

The subject of isolation as it relates to private space was freighted with those anxieties articulated by Gildas for his potentially vagrant bride, as they were also fundamental to directions for religious enclosure and its chosen strictures. For example, when John Stratford was bishop of Winchester, he presided over the enclosure of Christina Carpenter as anchorite at Shere in 1329. Carpenter was deemed morally worthy, neither promised nor joined in marriage, and spiritually pious enough to reward her desire to separate herself from the world, to keep her heart "pure, away from the world," and her thoughts focused on God.[1] However, subsequently abandoning her anchor hold, then peti tioning to be readmitted to her reclusion, John Stratford presided over a far more punitory reenclosure designed to prevent Carpenter from "gadding about [*evagando*] for longer through the world"; she was threatened with either excommunication or death should she fail to present herself to her bishop.[2] Like Gildas's island/bride, Carpenter needs to be girdled:

> Nor should the said Christina wander from the laudable purpose which otherwise she solemnly assumed and, pulling in different directions throughout the world, be torn to pieces by the bites of the Waylayer, for which, heaven forbid, on repeated occasions, conciliators and rebels in this matter have been curbed by the statutes and censures of the church.[3]

The language here associates Christina's vagrancy with other acts of rebellion, *curbed* by the laws of the church, as Christina herself is to be "thrust down" into her reclusory and subjected to "competent vigilance." Ironically, nine years later, as archbishop of Canterbury, John Stratford was accused by Edward III of withholding needed funds and thus thwarting his own outward forays into France, a war waged by Edward for his feudal rights, and a war for which, according to Roy Martin Haines, Stratford was not alone in lacking enthusiasm.[4]

The feudal rights that Edward and his advisers understood as placing him in direct line to the French throne and thus expanding Edward's borders well beyond those of Henry II at the same time prompted the king to construct the Round Table, to institute the Order of the Garter, and to complete the Chapel of St. Stephen's in Westminster, all moves to create exclusive spaces proclaiming the sanctity of Edwardian chivalry, spaces whose self-enclosure prompted, in turn, the pointed and subtle quizzings of Langland and Chaucer. In fact, John Stow in his *Annales* recounted the French king complaining in 1349 of Edward's quartering the arms of France on his shield *and*

placing them after those of England: "making apparent to the behold-
ers, that the little Island of England is to be preferred before the great
Kingdome of France." Sir John Shorditch soothed French vanity by
saying that it was English custom to privilege the male line.[5] France's
"great Kingdome," not geographically enclosed or defined, took second place to the "little Island" and its regal sanctuaries from which Edward launched his war. The space enclosed but hardly exclusive was
the vast plague pit funded by John Stratford's nephew, Ralph, bishop of
London (see chap. 3). Where by leaving her reclusory and wandering
about, Christina Carpenter evinced the difficulties of enclosing (female)
vagrancy and the need to contain what is either pure or impure, subjects germane to Gildas's account of Britain and its history, King Edward in his expansive movements across the Channel and his careful
positioning of royal private spaces underscored both his liberties and
the boundaries between royal space and all other space. It is clear from
his letters patent that Edward recognized the need for more burial
spaces because of the plague, a plague that both threatened the English
economy and altered England's topography by usurping land formerly
used for commercial purposes for the unusual and immediate need for
graves. Thus even as the king was arranging for work on the elaborate and exclusive interior of St. Stephen's Chapel, he was also granting pardons to parishioners who had acquired land to expand church-
yards without the king's license and confronting the ongoing need for
taxation of a demographically stressed nation in order to "defend" England from French invasion.[6]

There is more here, however, than the ironies of metaphoric discourse. Borders, boundaries, and enclosures remained subjects whereby
issues pertaining to the self and its spiritual needs could be linked to
a nation that from Gildas on was described as a bounded and perilous
self, a nation that adopted the island garden as a sign for the politically dominant section of a much larger and more various island. The
deep suspicion with which Wyclif vested the word *private*—"fals pri-
uat religioun," "pryvat prioures," "Þis asse and hir fole ben comen to
þes pryvat ordris but not to alle Cristene men"—located ecclesiastical foundations like monasteries, friaries, and chantries in sequestered
spaces dangerously lacking in moral scrutiny. Chaucer, to different
effect, suggests the potential hazards of the private, playing on the

words *pryve, pryvee, pryvete*. In his many vignettes of private space—
the bedrooms, gardens, garderobes, and letters that enclose and shield
who (or what) is therein from public scrutiny—he depicts isolation
as encouraging illusion at best, vice at worst. Troy is, of course, enclosed by its walls, but it is also isolated by the surrounding Greek
army and, in fact, triply enclosed by its civic architecture, its military
situation, and the chivalric rhetoric with which it justifies itself.[7] On
the other hand, as I note in the first chapter, when in the sixteenth
century the heirs to Wyclif, the Protestant reformers, have the upper
hand, *they* are accused by Catholic Christians of cutting England off
from its continental history by sequestering the island in religious
and ideological insularity. In accusing the Protestants of sequestering England, adherents of the old religion employ the same terms
once used by Wycliffites to criticize Rome's "private religion" and its
deleterious effects on society and on the souls of the English. It is this
isolation, the determination to recognize only a particular insular line
of descent for England's church, to count as a vast blip the thousand
years of Roman Catholic practice, that is carefully and somewhat co-
vertly corrected by those sixteenth- and early-seventeenth-century
antiquarians who begin to piece back together a picture of an enclosed
garden whose identity nonetheless depends on a more inclusive history and variegated practice.

A differently directed willingness to acknowledge porous boundaries is evidenced in Hugh Latimer's second sermon before Edward VI,
where the very Protestant bishop of Worcester urged the crown to
listen to the voices of the poor. He describes himself as seeking to escape from the endless petitions that come to him by walking in the
garden of the archbishop of Canterbury in order to spend some time
with his book:

> I cannot go to my book, for poor folks come unto me, desiring me
> that I will speak that their matters may be heard. I trouble my lord
> of Canterbury; and being at his house, now and then I walk in the
> garden looking in my book, as I can do but little good at it. . . .
> I am no sooner in the garden, and have read awhile, but by-and-by
> cometh there some or other knocking at the gate. Anon cometh my
> man, and saith: "Sir, there is one at the gate would speak with you."[8]

Latimer uses this picture of the breached garden to "beseech your Grace that ye will look to these matters. Hear them yourself. View your Judges, and hear poor men's causes." Latimer here, as he does in his Sermon of the Plough, aligns himself with Langland in recasting England's ancient monastic language of Edenic self-description as political or social critique. Upon the scene of a garden of privacy and privilege, Latimer superimposes a Langlandian scene, a gentlewoman in need, a poor woman "that liveth in the Fleet, and cannot come, by any means she can make, to her answer, and would fain be bailed, offering to put in sureties worth a thousand pounds; and yet she cannot be heard." Like William of Pagula before him (see chap. 3), Latimer has an eye for detail that in vivifying the need for royal care, breaks down the boundaries of privileged privacy and inscribes the poor woman, the Fleet prison, the hard-hearted judges in the king's own space.

The joined issues of personal and national identity for which the enclosed island garden can provide a point of access, as the second chapter argues, are integral to the enclosure controversies, which are, in turn, refigured in Tusser's books of husbandry and Ben Jonson's "To Penshurst." However, Marvell's "Upon Appleton House," along with "The Garden" and the Mower poems, all linked to Marvell's time at Nun Appleton, refuse to allow for anything as simple as debate along binary lines.[9] Marvell blurs his depiction of Nun Appleton, its history, its present, and its future, as indeed Thomas Fairfax, its owner, blurred his own position in the history of which he was a part. Thomas Fairfax, third Lord Fairfax of Cameron (1612–71), was the son of Ferdinando Fairfax, second Lord Fairfax of Cameron. He followed his father into a military career, fighting, first, for Charles I and, second, for Parliament from 1642 to 1645, for the last year as commander in chief. For the next two years, he was plunged into political machinations, for which he was temperamentally unsuited. He returned to the field for the second civil war, but after the capture and trial of the king, Fairfax worked against regicide, resigning from the army in 1650 and retiring to Nun Appleton, where he wrote and made translations. He worked for the restoration of Charles II and was instrumental in bringing this about without bloodshed.[10] For most of his life, despite his physically demanding military career, Fairfax seems to have battled ill health, but some of the writing he left suggests also that he was torn between his avowedly active life as a soldier and landowner and a private life whose intense solitude lured him. His translation of "La Solitude" by Antoine Girard, sieur de Saint-Amant (1594–1661), evokes the pleasures of solitude in the original but muffles the exquisite sense of pleasure to be found in the French poem, pleasures that Marvell himself suggests in "The Garden" with the squashed melons and the surfeited narrator lying prone on the grass, exhausted by the pleasures of his own company. For example, for Saint-Amant's "Que j'ayme la solitude!" Fairfax translates the "I love" but substitutes "These Solitudes," going on to praise the picturesque rather than emphasize the sensuous and solitary pleasures avowed by Saint-Amant's narrator who describes the places "sacrez à la nuit" where banished are the world and its clamor, places that "Plaisent à mon inquietude!" Fairfax omits the reference to sacrality or consecration and tones down the sense of personal pleasure and psychological involvement with nature by saying that he loves the places "silent as the night / Ther wher noe thronging multituds / Disturbe wth noyse ther sweet delight." Fairfax also leaves out the reference to the French narrator's anxiety ("inquietude"). For the "espine fleurie" that in the spring is "amoureux," Fairfax describes this flowery thorn as "Springs delightfull plant the Cheife."[11] Marvell, of course, picks up the amorousness of natural solitude in his own, much more sophisticated poem "The Garden," perhaps written over fifteen years later but nonetheless still resonant with the language of the poems he wrote during his period with Fairfax.[12]

More intimate is Fairfax's memoir, which was published in 1699 by Brian Fairfax, a descendant of Henry Fairfax, brother to Ferdinando.[13] In the Epistle Dedicatory, which is written to his son, Brian Fairfax asserts that the memoir was written in Thomas's own hand and left in his study at Denton, going on to say, "the retired part of his life gave him greater satisfaction . . . when he lived quietly at his own House at Nun Appleton in Yorkshire." The *Short Memorials* is divided into two parts. The first part recounts northern action from 1642 to 1644 and is a straightforward military record. The second part, of decidedly penitential cast, which bears the heading, "Short Memorials of Some Things to be cleared during my Command in the Army," is a personal accounting for those private eyes that might find and read what Thomas Fairfax had left in his desk. Fairfax notes that "under Parliament Authority many injuries have been done" (125), identifying the chief injury as the execution of the king, whom he refers to as "the Golden Ball cast before the two Parties, the Parliament and the Army . . . the Army having the greater Power, got the King again into their Hands, notwithstanding all endevors to hinder it" (118). He does not hesitate to voice his guilt: "Thus have I given you the Sum of the most considerable Things, for which the world may Censure me, during this unhappy War; and I hope in all my Weakness and Failings, there shall not be found Crimes of that Magnitude to make me be numbered with those who have done these things through Ambition and Dissimulation" (128). Both the *Short Memorials* and the biblical translations, proverbs, and moral and philosophic verse that occupied him after his military career suggest that Fairfax did not see his retirement to Nun Appleton as a plunge into the delights of solitude but as a form of reclusion whereby he might come to terms with and repent the mistakes of an active life. Protestantism may have cast aside the formal ceremonies belonging to the reclusory, but the landed gentry might build their own and supply their own rules and justifications for the semisolitary life.

Fairfax's life, in fact, traces out in reverse the trajectory Marvell assigns to Cromwell in "An Horatian Ode upon Cromwell's Return from Ireland," written in 1650 after Charles's death in 1649.[14] In a poem that has been the subject of debate since its first publication, Marvell describes Cromwell as moving from "his private gardens" (29) and "the inglorious arts of peace" (10), donning the armor hanging unused and "burning through the air" like lightning to rend "palaces and temples" (22), conquering, first, Charles and, now, taming the Irish. Marvell underlines the distinction between Cromwell and Charles *and* heightens the ambiguities of his portrayal of both by describing Cromwell with active verbs that suggest his energy as well as his destructiveness. If Cromwell is like Jove's lightning tearing through the clouds, hyper-masculine and unstoppable, Charles and those "ancient rights" (38) belonging to kingdoms ruled by divinely appointed monarchs are both feminized and dignified in death:

> Nor called the Gods with vulgar spite
> To vindicate his helpless right;
>> But bowed his comely head
>> Down, as upon a bed. (61–64)

These perfectly poised lines, balancing Charles's comeliness and breeding against the vulgarity—in the truest sense—of the armed and
bloody hands of the actor/spectators in this play (55–56), and allowing
the "comely head" to retain its bow until the next line, when genuflec-
tion becomes execution and repose, may suggest Charles's inability to
counter Cromwell's force, but they also suggest how terrible a force
Cromwell unleashed on the state whose foundation consequently rests
on a "bleeding head" (69). Marvell's deployment of the language of
gender, which both enhances Cromwell's capacities and his destructiveness and points up Charles' powerlessness and his innate authority,
is carried over to the final lines of the ode where he forecasts, "the same
arts that did gain / A pow'r must it maintain" (119–20). In contrast,
Fairfax moved from that same action that rended a state to the retreat
of Nun Appleton. He describes the army as purging Parliament, in
order to make way for the king's trial. Maria, to whom the use of the
estate passed for her lifetime, in 1657 married the royalist George Villiers, second duke of Buckingham, whom Fairfax arranged to have
released from prison after Cromwell's death and for whom he paid
£20,000 bail. At the end of the *Short Memorials* Buckingham's epitaph
for Fairfax joins in Fairfax what Marvell had separated in the "Ode":

> Both Sexes Vertues were in him combin'd,
> He had the fierceness of the Manliest mind,
> And all the meekness too of Womankind.

Buckingham goes on to praise Fairfax for his modesty, describing Nun
Appleton as his "private last Retreat."

Fairfax's retreat into solitude and absorption with his Yorkshire
estate appears far less radical when juxtaposed to the georgic concerns of Abraham Cowley, John Evelyn, and Samuel Hartlib, whose desire to relandscape an England ravaged by civil war and espousals of
the virtues of agrarian life look forward to the elaborate estate and garden planning of the eighteenth century.[15] These seventeenth-century
garden designers sought to break down the enclosed gardens of great
houses and, instead, blur the boundaries between gardens and parks,
using carefully designed plantations of trees to blend what were formerly sharply defined spaces. As D. C. Chambers has noted, Marvell's

celebration of such an open landscape in "Upon Appleton House" reflects the aesthetic of Evelyn who recommended the extensive landscape of the *Georgics*, which brought art and nature together in a seamless whole.[16] Cowley's essays such as "Solitude," "Of Agriculture," and "The Garden" (dedicated to John Evelyn) and his translations from Virgil and Horace on country life do more than sing the pleasures of removal from the world or the court; they emphasize the conjunction between agriculture or country life and philosophy and between solitude and cognition.[17] They thus suggest, as indeed Fairfax's own writings suggest, that retreat might be considered *labor* rather than *otium*, and the admonishment of Contemplation in book I of *The Faerie Queene* that sends Red Crosse on to his duties in Gloriana's wars before he may think of retiring to Contemplation's mountain falls silent within the spaces of a natural world that demand both physical and spiritual labor and that is consequently remedial rather than indulgent. What in the Middle Ages was cast in the language of religious devotion, the *work* of the hands, of the soul, and of the mind outlined in the *Benedictine Rule*, is now justified in the philosophical and classical language belonging to the educated gentry.

As in George Wheler's *The Protestant Monastery or Christian OEconomicks containing Directions for the Religious Conduct of a Family*, removed from its Catholic affiliations, the daily round is sacralized.[18] Wheler defends his use of the potentially offensive term *monastery* by modifying it with "protestant." He does outline the history of monasteries and monastic life but states that now there are ample alms-houses, hospitals, and colleges for widows sponsored by the church, and "the pious conduct of private Families shall be the Monasteries" (19). Having returned us to the "private" realm, despite the Protestant emphasis on the dangers of "private religions," Wheler specifies how a family should be ordered: the father is "like an abbot"; the day is divided into certain forms of prayer and hymns for the times of the day, and it is incumbent on this family to offer alms and hospitality to the poor (21, 168, 172). As the secondary title suggests, Wheler drew on the Aristotelian language found in the *Economics*, whereby the head of the household is like a prince and responsible for the orderly system of the whole.[19] Where Christina Carpenter was returned to her reclusory and immured in private space, now the gardeners, scientists, and clergy-scholars of this new age recommend the home as the new monastic foundation. Wheler, who was also a botanist and an antiquarian travel writer whose account of his journey through Greece in 1682 remains a valuable witness, in the Protestant monastery he constructs codifies the values of Robert Roche's early modern Susanna, who lives justly according to a law she has internalized and, having come through her own trial, can pass on wisdom to her children. The law that maintains the home and that is itself limited by the laws of England,[20] maintains also the individual in a private domicile whose borders open to the world through hospitality and charity.

Translated into an even later age and stripped of her (and her garden's) associations with private and public law, Susanna throbs in the violated privacy of her beauty in Wallace Stevens's "Peter Quince at the Clavier."[21] Stevens prefaces the account of Susanna surprised in her bath with a first-person account of desire, likened to the artlessness and crudity of Shakespeare's rustic, Peter Quince, making music, or attempting to, at the clavier. Like the elders, the speaker vibrates in "pizzicati of Hosanna" as he contemplates the beauty to whom he addresses the poem. The Susanna of the second section sighs with pleasure in the water, stands spent and naked on the grass, walks, clothed by the winds, enjoying her own body, the warm night, and her solitude until she is recalled to the world by the elders. Where the speaker relishes the rude music set off by his desirous gaze, Susanna's music comes from her own body:

> In the green water; clear and warm,
> Susanna lay.
> She searched
> The touch of springs,
> And found
> Concealed imaginings.
> She sighed,
> For so much melody.

Stevens's Susanna has more in common with the speaker in Marvell's "Garden" and his delight in "delicious solitude." Stevens, like Marvell, maintains both Susanna and her garden in evanescence: her music vanishes but is immortal in her memory:

Susanna's music touched the bawdy strings
Of those white elders; but, escaping,
Left only Death's ironic scraping.
Now, in its immortality, it plays
On the clear viol of her memory,
And makes a constant sacrament of praise.

Stevens achieves here a sort of virtual string trio, where Susanna touches off music in the elders, whose own bawdy pluckings call up the ironies of death, both their own and the death that comes to all, and which touches off the final movement played by the viol of memory, constant, immortal, but circumscribed by time's own limits, the Death's Head that grins in the distance. So, too, does Marvell end "The Garden" with a sundial made of herbs and flowers, whose thyme is counted by the bees, but reckoned, nonetheless, as time that urges the bees to labor though the speaker glories in leisure, ignoring the larger warning of the natural world.[22]

Moreover, the sanctity here violated by the elders' gaze is personal. Stevens has removed Joachim, the householder, and Daniel, the spokesman for the principles of a law that links private to public and establishes limitations for self-interested action and standards for adjudication. Where in the context of England the island garden Susanna's garden derives its status and its significance from its relationship to the law that serves as a guardian for private rights, in twentieth-century America there is no such construction to anchor Susanna within an enclosed space other than that of her own mind. Stevens notes and celebrates the temporality of beauty's music, but Marvell's bees have a harsher warning, implicitly reminding the reader—if not the speaker—of the winter that falls upon gardens, killing melon vines and blighting unripened fruit. If Marvell's garden looks back to Penshurst, with its bounteous and fruitful productivity and life of hierarchical interconnection, it also looks forward and across the Atlantic, where the image and its freight of meanings yield to a world where the idea and anxieties of enclosure could not be so minutely expressed by such a trope.

As an image both expressing and constructing an identity of nation, the island garden was jettisoned by those who crossed the Atlantic to America. In the *Magnalia Christi Americana: or the ecclesiastical history of New England, from its first planting in the year 1620,* Cotton Mather says that they were driven from the "best island in the universe" to wilderness. In writing his account of the ecclesiastical history of New England, Mather drew on those of John Winthrop and William Bradford, both of whom had described the vastness of the American wilderness where a nascent fruitfulness demanded the hardihood of those sent to turn a "planting" into a garden. The language of enclosure, however, did not apply to this new garden whose expanded boundaries were inhabited and worked by those who built "a new English Israel."[23] By following the English reformers who described Protestant England as a new Israel and recasting the story of the Exodus to describe their experiences in a new land, these early American Englishmen constructed a nation/church not as Bede had made it but as an embattled and disciplined corps of Christians whose identity was inseparable from the physical exodus needed to claim and redeem a savage land. Both Bede and Mather write a geography that can shape an emerging identity. In the 1702 edition of *Magnalia,* there is "An Exact Map of New England and New York," picturing Long Island, part of eastern New Jersey, Connecticut, Massachusetts, and portions of New Hampshire (see fig. 7). To the north and west, the place-names are fewer, the spaces between those names empty of identifying features. The only boundary is the ocean to the east, and the settlers themselves had breached that boundary with their ships and constantly pushed at the western borders of the "garden." Bede ends the *History* suggesting both the vitality of England's church and culture and the dangers of ignoring potential savagery, especially in the lands to the north. Mather ends the *Magnalia* by recounting the recent Indian wars and an ensuing period of peace, counseling moral vigilance lest corruption and conflict return to New England. However, New England is not an island garden but a settlement whose boundaries are expansive and indeterminate. As Mather notes, "the earth is the Lord's garden" to be "tilled and improved" (65). Where the author of *Havelok* (see chap. 3) has Havelok describe the dream of his long body enclosing both England and Denmark before giving them to his English bride, Walt Whitman in the 1855 preface to *Leaves of Grass* builds on the language of this new nation and offers another picture whereby self is identified with nation and both are described as infinite, as without boundary or stricture, as stretching out indefinitely.[24] Whitman proclaims the United States the greatest poem, its largeness matched by the "corresponding largeness and generosity of the spirit of the citizen" (436). American poets are "to enclose old and new" (437) and to remold, creating "new free forms" (445), commensurate with the new vistas inherent in the geography of the nation.

The constitutive force of those terms of national and personal identity reverberates in the history of Thomas Fairfax's own family holdings. In his statement to the king in 1537, Robert Aske, who led the Yorkshire Pilgrimage of Grace in 1536, mourned the loss of religious houses in the north during the sixteenth century as returning England to an ancient savagery, drawing on the fear of waste inherent in this language of national self-description. However, and ironically, his family, a large and important Yorkshire family, kept at least one of them, Nun Appleton. The Fairfaxes married at least three times with Askes, and Ellen Aske was Thomas Fairfax's grandmother.[25] The specter of the wasteland so prominent in Aske's lament for a landscape bereft of its ancient abbeys is met by the Fairfax reclamation of Nun Appleton, as Marvell describes it, newly sacralized by Christian marriage and attentive estate management, whereby what was immured in false chastity is now enclosed but open to the world and to history. Thomas Fairfax's scholarly and agricultural retreat passed to his uncle Henry Fairfax's heirs after Maria's death. The sixth Lord Fairfax of Cameron was Thomas, who had to sell the Yorkshire estates to cover the debts his father, the fifth Lord Fairfax, had accrued, but he inherited from his mother's family, the Culpeppers, vast holdings in Virginia, as well as Leeds Castle in Kent. In 1745 he won a suit against the crown and doubled his Virginia holdings to five million acres, moving there in 1777 and dying in 1781 one of the richest men in America with friends on both sides of the Atlantic: Bolingbroke, Addison, Steele, and General Washington. The language of the bounded and enclosed garden is markedly absent from the case presented to the Privy Council in his name; instead, it speaks of great spaces, stream heads that go well back into the "Blue Mountains," and "a vast Extent of Country." The crown presented arguments for "restraining Lord Fairfax's bounds," but Lord Fairfax's petition was granted. He died a Virginia landowner known for his hospitality.[26]

What was far more than a metaphor retained a currency in England as a term of analytic discourse. The subjects for which the island garden was a sign gained an added urgency as England itself expanded throughout the world and as its industrial growth brought further changes to its landscape so that the image itself became resonant with nostalgia for a lost and idealized country past.[27] What the island garden offered its speakers for its first thousand years was a carefully nuanced and surprisingly elastic debate about the nature and constitution of the enclosed space that was called England, about the identity of those who called themselves English, about relations among its inhabitants and with the world outside its sea boundary, and about who or what served as the guardian of this identity. Was England an elite space belonging to kings or a space protected by a law that kings, too, must observe? And if the latter, what must be held sacred is the degree to which the law allows for the hospitable enclosure of the conditions of the daily. To go forward is to go into an England where the island colonized other lands and brought back the riches of the world, which were then parsed out and merchandised by companies acting as extensions of England's increasingly mercantile and self-consciously national identity, thus to a set of new conditions. What was a medieval and early modern language of self-identity was inevitably altered and expanded by those seeking to incorporate the present into the past, or to construct a present. The urgency of that early identity—the island garden—came very much alive in Churchill's June 1940 speech to the House of Commons where he repeats the word *Island* again and again. The threat of the island breached, the promise of the island (now the node of an empire) honoring the needs of embattled liberty throughout the world, the hope of the island whose people's native valor moves the world to fight with them owe their power to a discourse created by England's early monks who knew well that history was made by those who wrote it, and the language of nations is also the language of its peoples.

Introduction

1. Gildas, *The Ruin of Britain and Other Works*, ed. and trans. Michael Winterbottom (Totowa, NJ: Rowman and Littlefield, 1978), 2. All citations to the *De Excidio* are by section number, which correspond to Winterbotten's English and Latin texts. Though later medieval writers gave it its title, Gildas referred to his treatise as a letter. Michael Lapidge has argued for the epistolary and rhetorical aim of the work, evidence of Gildas's education in Latin rhetoric. See Michael Lapidge, "Gildas' Education and the Latin Culture of Sub-Roman Britain," in *Gildas: New Approaches*, ed. Michael Lapidge and David Dumville (Woodbridge: Boydell Press, 1984), 27–50. For more recent work, see Karen George, *Gildas's "De Excidio Britonum" and the Early British Church* (Woodbridge: Boydell Press, 2009), 10–13. For essays on the many associations between biblical and medieval actual and literary gardens, see Elisabeth B. MacDougall, ed., *Medieval Gardens*, Dumbarton Oaks Colloquium on the History of Landscape Architecture 9 (Washington, DC: Dumbarton Oaks Research Library and Collection, 1986), esp. Paul Meyvaert, "The Medieval Monastic Garden," 25–53.

2. R. R. Davies, *The First English Empire: Power and Identities in the British Isles, 1093–1343* (Oxford: Oxford University Press, 2000), 2. Sarah Foot argues for an even earlier process of Anglicization in "The Making of *Angelcyn*: English Identity before the Norman Conquest," *Transactions of the Royal Historical Society*, 6th ser., 6 (1996): 25–49.

3. The classic investigation is that of Raymond Williams, *The Country and the City* (New York: Oxford University Press, 1973), which, though it

refers to classical, medieval, and early modern texts, is primarily concerned with postindustrial British literature. For a consideration of Williams in relation to current scholarship, see Gerald MacLean, Donna Landry, and Joseph P. Ward, *The Country and the City Revisited: England and the Politics of Culture, 1550–1850* (Cambridge: Cambridge University Press, 1999).

4. Working with different materials, R. R. Davies picks 1343 as the point when English power in the British Isles was beginning to contract, necessitating a reorientation of ambitions and of conceptions of national identity. See *The First English Empire*, 177–78.

5. Lynn Staley, *Languages of Power in the Age of Richard II* (University Park: Pennsylvania State University Press, 2005).

6. I do not mean to imply that I am the first to distinguish between English and French understandings of constitutional thought, simply to suggest ways in which this project has grown out of my earlier work. For a careful probing of the distinctions between constitutionalism and continental views of sovereignty, see Brian Tierney, *Religion, Law, and the Growth of Constitutional Thought, 1150–1650* (Cambridge: Cambridge University Press, 1982), esp. 29–53, as well as the citations assembled in my earlier book.

7. James Simpson, *Reform and Cultural Revolution, The Oxford English Literary History*, vol. 2: 1350–1547 (Oxford: Oxford University Press, 2002).

8. In his conclusion to *Religion, Law, and the Growth of Constitutional Thought*, Tierney quotes Christopher Hill from *God's Englishmen* on medieval–early modern continuities: "The seventeenth century is the decisive century of English history, the epoch in which the Middle Ages ended" (103).

9. Lynn Staley Johnson, *The "Shepheardes Calender": An Introduction* (University Park: Pennsylvania State University Press, 1990). David Aers has moved between the medieval and early modern periods throughout his career. See, for example, David Aers, Bob Hodge, and Gunther Kress, eds., *Literature, Landscape, and Society in England, 1580–1680* (Totowa, NJ: Barnes and Noble, 1981); David Aers, ed., *Culture and History, 1350–1600: Essays on English Communities, Identities, and Writing* (Detroit: Wayne State University Press, 1992); David Aers, *Community, Gender, and Individual Identity: English Writing, 1360–1430* (London: Routledge, 1988).

10. See, for example, Perry Curtis and John Watkins, eds., *Shakespeare and the Middle Ages* (Oxford: Oxford University Press, 2009), esp. Sarah Beckwith, "Shakespeare's Resurrections"; and Elizabeth Fowler, "Towards a History of Performativity: Sacrament, Social Contract, and *The Merchant of Venice.*"

11. Lee Patterson, *Chaucer and the Subject of History* (Madison: University of Wisconsin Press, 1991); Paul Strohm, *England's Empty Throne: Usurpation and the Language of Legitimation, 1399–1422* (New Haven: Yale University Press, 1998). The bibliography for the Reformation is vast, but see Felicity Heal, *Reformation in Britain and Ireland* (Oxford: Oxford University

Press, 2003); and John N. King, *English Reformation Literature: The Tudor Origins of the Protestant Tradition* (Princeton: Princeton University Press, 1982).

12. James Simpson, *Burning to Read: English Fundamentalism and Its Reformation Opponents* (Cambridge: Belknap Press, 2007); Anne Hudson, *The Premature Reformation: Wycliffite Texts and Lollard History* (Oxford: Oxford University Press, 1988); Margaret Aston, *England's Iconoclasts* (Oxford: Oxford University Press, 1988).

13. Eamon Duffy, *The Stripping of the Altars: Traditional Religion in England, 1400–1580*, 2nd ed. (New Haven: Yale University Press, 2005).

14. See Staley, *Languages of Power in the Age of Richard II*.

15. For David Wallace's plan for a new way of writing the history of medieval literature and culture, see www.english.upenn.edu/~dwallace/regeneration/.

For the studies suggested above, see Ralph Hanna, *London Literature, 1300–1380* (Cambridge: Cambridge University Press, 2005); Ralph Hanna, "Yorkshire Writers," Sir Israel Gollancz Memorial Lecture, *Proceedings of the British Academy* 121 (2003): 91–109; Robert W. Barrett, *Against All England: Regional Identity and Cheshire Writing, 1195–1656* (Notre Dame: University of Notre Dame Press, 2009); Christopher Cannon, *The Grounds of English Literature* (Oxford: Oxford University Press, 2004); Sarah Beckwith, *Signifying God: Social Relation and Symbolic Act in the York Corpus Christi Plays* (Chicago: University of Chicago Press, 2001); Theresa Coletti, *Mary Magdalene and the Drama of Saints: Theater, Gender, and Religion in Late Medieval England* (Philadelphia: University of Pennsylvania Press, 2004); Gail McMurray Gibson, *The Theater of Devotion: East Anglian Drama and Society in the Late Middle Ages* (Chicago: University of Chicago Press, 1989).

16. Thorlac Turville-Petre, *England the Nation: Language, Literature, and National Identity, 1290–1340* (Oxford: Clarendon Press, 1996); Ardis Butterfield, *The Familiar Enemy: Chaucer, Language, and Nation in the Hundred Years War* (Oxford: Oxford University Press, 2009); Jocelyn Wogan-Browne, *Language and Culture in Medieval Britain: The French of England, c. 1100–c. 1500* (York: York Medieval Press, 2009).

17. For a vigorous investigation of those acts of occlusion and of the consequent early modern awareness of fragmentation, see John Kerrigan, *Archipelagic English: Literature, History, and Politics, 1603–1707* (Oxford: Oxford University Press, 2008).

18. I have co-opted R. R. Davies's useful Anglocentric term here.

19. Catherine A. M. Clarke, *Literary Landscapes and the Idea of England, 700–1400* (Cambridge: D. S. Brewer, 2006), 7–35, for the pleasurable island as defining trope, which carries over to the founding stories of the fenland monasteries of Ely and Ramsey, 79–84. For a study of England as possessing a special status because of its isolation, see Kathy Lavezzo, *Angels on the*

Edge of the World: Geography, Literature, and English Community, 1000–1534 (Ithaca: Cornell University Press, 2006). For Æthelthryth and Ely, see Virginia Blanton, *Signs of Devotion: The Cult of St. Æthelthryth in Medieval England, 695–1615* (University Park: Pennsylvania State University Press, 2007), esp. chap. 3 and p. 138. See also Monika Otter's analysis of historians embedding an account of the Conquest as rupture into other narratives: Monika Otter, "1066: The Moment of Transition in Two Narratives of the Norman Conquest," *Speculum* 74 (1999): 565–86.

20. Antonia Gransden, *Historical Writing in England: c. 550 to c. 1307* (Ithaca: Cornell University Press, 1973); and *Historical Writing in England II: c. 1307 to the Early Sixteenth Century* (Ithaca: Cornell University Press, 1982).

21. Paul Binski, *Westminster Abbey and the Plantagenets: Kingship and the Representation of Power, 1200–1400* (New Haven: Yale University Press, 1995); and *The Painted Chamber at Westminster* (London: Society of Antiquaries of London, 1986).

ONE   *Writing in the Shadow of Bede*

1. S. D. [Samuel Daniel], *The Collection of the Historie of England* (London: Nicholas Okes, 1618), 1. The metaphor also appears in Sir Walter Raleigh, *A Breviary of the History of England* (London: S. Keble and D. Brown, 1693), which Gottfried sees as a copy of a first sketch of Daniel's *Historie* found among Raleigh's papers after he died. See Rudolf B. Gottfried, "The Authorship of *A Breviary of the History of England*," *SP* 53 (1956): 190. The source is William Harrison's "Historicall Description of the Islande of Britayne," the opening section of Raphael Holinshed's *Chronicles*.

2. John Milton, *History of Britain*, ed. French Fogle, vol. 5 of *Complete Prose Works of John Milton* (New Haven: Yale University Press, 1971).

3. For Bede's familiarity with Gildas, see M. Miller, "Bede's Use of Gildas," *English Historical Review* 90 (1975): 241–61; Robert Hanning, *The Vision of History in Early Britain: From Gildas to Geoffrey of Monmouth* (New York: Columbia University Press, 1966), 70. There is copious scholarship on both Gildas and Bede. For the most recent, see George, *Gildas's "De Excidio Britonnum" and the Early British Church*; George Hardin Brown, *A Companion to Bede* (Woodbridge: Boydell Press, 2009); Vicky Gunn, *Bede's "Historiae": Genre, Rhetoric, and the Construction of Anglo-Saxon Church History* (Woodbridge: Boydell Press, 2009). These studies locate both authors historically and critically in relation to those scholarly issues pertinent to Anglo Saxon studies. Here I am concerned, not with the historical accuracy of either Gildas or Bede, or with the relationship between Bede's *Historia* and his other works, but with the impact each history had on later historians.

4. See Gransden, *Historical Writing in England II*, 436; Timothy Graham, "Matthew Parker's Manuscripts: An Elizabethan Library and Its Use," in *The Cambridge History of Libraries in Britain and Ireland*, vol. 1, ed. Elisabeth Leedham-Green and Teresa Webber (Cambridge: Cambridge University Press, 2006), 322–44; Jennifer Summit, *Memory's Library: Medieval Books in Early Modern England* (Chicago: University of Chicago Press, 2008); Colin G. C. Tite, *The Early Records of Sir Robert Cotton's Library* (London: British Library, 2003); J. P. Gilson, "The Library of Henry Savile of Banke," *Transactions of the Bibliographical Society* 9 (1906–8): 127–210.

5. Gildas, ed. and trans. Winterbottom, *The Ruin of Britain*, 3. Hereafter, in-text citations by section number correspond to Winterbotten's English and Latin texts.

6. Hanning, *Vision of History*, 44–62. For a study of the work's internal structure, see C. E. Stevens, "Gildas Sapiens," *EHR* 56 (1941): 353–73.

7. Though Bede uses *Brittannia* when describing the actual island, he recounts the story of England, the word I will use hereafter. For studies of the trope of this *locus amoenus*, see Clarke, *Literary Landscapes and the Idea of England*. In chapter 1 Clarke discusses Bede's use of the pleasurable island as defining trope, which carries over to the founding stories of the fenland monasteries of Ely and Ramsey (79–84). For these, see Janet Fairweather, trans., *Liber Eliensis: A History of the Isle of Ely from the Seventh Century to the Twelfth* (Woodbridge: Boydell Press, 2005); E. O. Blake, ed., *Liber Eliensis* (London: Royal Historical Society, 1962); W. D. Macray, ed., *Chronicon Abbatiae Rameseinsis*, Rolls Series 83 (London: Longman and Co., 1886).

8. For remarks about Bede's progressive historical perspective in relation to those of the Anglo-Saxon poets, see Renée R. Trilling, *The Aesthetics of Nostalgia: Historical Representation in Old English Verse* (Toronto: University of Toronto Press, 2009), 3–27. For an alternate view of Bede as articulating difference by his reference to the five languages, see Jeffrey Jerome Cohen, *Hybridity, Identity, and Monstrosity in Medieval Britain: On Difficult Middles* (New York: Palgrave Macmillan, 2006), 48–49. The reading I offer in the following pages is designed to suggest the overarching unity of Bede's historical perspective as guiding his rhetorical principles in the *Historia*. For a richly evocative reading of Gildas's and Bede's use of Britain's geographic and cultural relation to Rome, see Nicholas Howe, *Writing the Map of Anglo-Saxon England: Essays in Cultural Geography* (New Haven: Yale University Press, 2008), 106–9.

9. As J. M. Wallace-Hadrill noted, for Bede the British church was revealed in the lives of its saints, notable figures such as Alban and Æthelthryth; see J. M. Wallace-Hadrill, *Bede's "Ecclesiastical History of the English People": A Historical Commentary* (Oxford: Clarendon Press, 1988), xxviii.

10. For Bede's use of the word *English* and his role in defining national identity, see Patrick Wormald, "The Venerable Bede and the 'Church of the

English,'" in *The English Religious Tradition and the Genius of Anglicanism*, ed. G. Rowell (Nashville, TN: Abingdon Press, 1992), 13–32. See also the important essay by Foot, "The Making of *Angelcyn*," in which Bede's influence on Alfred's perspective on nation is reiterated (41). In Scott DeGregorio, ed., *The Cambridge Companion to Bede* (Cambridge: Cambridge University Press, 2010), see Clare Stancliffe, "British and Irish Contexts," 69–83, for contextual remarks about Bede's attitude toward the Irish; and Alan Thacker, "Bede and History," 170–90, for comments about the providential and historical focus Bede effects on the English.

11. See Howe, *Writing the Map of Anglo-Saxon England*, "Rome as Capital of Anglo-Saxon England," 101–24.

12. See, *HE*, 136 n., for an explanation of the two ways of calculating the date of Easter.

13. On book IV as focused on the world mission of the English church, see Benedicta Ward, *The Venerable Bede* (London: Continuum, 1998), 124–27; Scott DeGregorio, "Literary Contexts: Caedmon's Hymn as a Center of Bede's World," in *Caedmon's Hymn and Material Culture in the World of Bede*, ed. Allen J. Frantzen and John Hines (Morgantown: West Virginia University Press, 2007), 51–79. In *The Old English Bede* (*Proceedings of the British Academy* 48 [1962]: 57–90), Dorothy Whitelock presents a *History* whose focus is more national, English, in contrast to Bede's locating England within a providential world order. For the Old English, see Thomas Miller, ed. and trans., *The Old English Version of Bede's "Ecclesiastical History of the English People,"* EETS 95, 96 (London: Trübner & Co., 1890).

14. Cædwalla and Ine become ill and die in Rome, while Cenred and Offa give up their claims to secular power and take the tonsure in Rome and die there. See *HE*, 472 n., for remarks about the popularity of pilgrimages to Rome during the seventh and eighth centuries.

15. *HE*, 534 n.: this is Bede's free version of a letter to which he probably contributed. As Henry Mayr-Harting points out, Bede was writing the *History* simultaneously with his commentary on the Temple of Solomon, which is an allegory of the construction of the universal church. See Henry Mayr-Harting, *The Coming of Christianity to Anglo-Saxon England* (University Park: Pennsylvania State University Press, 1972), 9; *De Templo Salomonis Liber*, PL 91: 735–807.

16. For more information on the dating for Easter and for Bede's knowledge of the relevant astronomy, see Faith Wallis, trans., *Bede's The Reckoning of Time* (Liverpool: Liverpool University Press, 1999), introd.

17. As Colgrave and Mynors note (*HE*, 560 n.), Bede here refers to what he sees as the abuses of contemporary monasticism, which he deals with more fully in his *Letter to Egbert*, a mission statement for his time and nation. For the *Letter*, see Dorothy Whitelock, *English Historical Documents*, vol. 1 (London: Eyre & Spottiswoode, 1955), 735–45, esp. 741–42.

18. Thomas Stapleton, trans., *The History of the Church of England compiled by Venerable Bede Englishman* (Antwerp, 1565). Stapleton was, of course, up against adversaries whose rhetorical and historical skills were formidable. For an exploration of sixteenth-century uses of the past, see Felicity Heal, "Appropriating History: Catholic and Protestant Polemics and the National Past," *Huntington Library Quarterly* 68 (2005): 109–32. Heal's survey is a valuable one; however, the distinction she draws between Protestant and Catholic histories as apocalyptic or universal is less valuable since those same distinctions can be found in medieval histories, as this chapter suggests.

19. For Bede's influence on the Anglo-Saxon *Chronicle* and its increasing articulation of national interest, which, in turn, influenced Anglo-Norman chroniclers like Florence of Worcester and Symeon of Durham, see Gransden, *Historical Writing in England*, 31–41. For another consideration of pre-Conquest constructions of nation, see Kathleen Davis, "National Writing in the Ninth Century: A Reminder for Postcolonial Thinking about the Nation," *JMEMS* 28 (1995): 611–37.

20. For an astute study of Orderic's sense of place in relation to world geography, see Amanda Jane Hingst, *The Written World: Past and Place in the Work of Orderic Vitalis* (Notre Dame: University of Notre Dame Press, 2009). In chapter 3, pp. 51–69, Hingst focuses on Orderic's employment of the term *Albion* as a concept identified with the realm of the English king.

21. See Elisabeth M. C. van Houts, ed. and trans., *The Gesta Normannorum Ducum of William of Jumièges, Orderic Vitalis, and Robert of Torigni,* 2 vols. (Oxford: Oxford University Press, 1992); Marjorie Chibnall, ed. and trans., *The Ecclesiastical History of Orderic Vitalis,* 6 vols. (Oxford: Clarendon Press, 1969). For discussion of these authors, see Gransden, *Historical Writing in England,* 94–97.

22. In-text citations of William of Malmesbury and Henry of Huntingdon refer to R. A. B. Mynors, R. M. Thomson, and M. Winterbottom, eds. and trans., *William of Malmesbury. Gesta Regum Anglorum,* 2 vols. (Oxford: Clarendon Press, 1998) [cited hereafter as *GRA*]; Diana Greenway, ed. and trans., *Henry, Archdeacon of Huntingdon, Historia Anglorum* (Oxford: Clarendon Press, 1996) [cited hereafter as *HA*]. See, for example, William of Malmesbury's account of King Alfred's attention to learning, pp. 181 ff. For relationships among these writers, see Gransden, *Historical Writing in England,* 166–75, 198–200; Andrew Galloway, "Writing History in England," in *The Cambridge History of Medieval English Literature,* ed. David Wallace (Cambridge: Cambridge University Press, 1999), 255–83. For remarks about the Welsh and the Scots, whom William of Malmesbury links with the Danes as peoples controlled by Alfred, see *GRA* 125.1; see also *GRA* 196.3, 199.7, 155, for remarks about the Welsh as either barbarous or rebellious. For Henry of Huntingdon, see *HA* 314/315, 262/263. On this Anglocentric historical tradition, which predominated from the twelfth century on, see Davies, *The First English Empire,* 2.

23. Henry refers to Gildas but ascribes the *Historia Brittonum* to him (Greenway, *HA*, lx, xc–xci).

24. For Henry of Huntingdon and Bede, see Greenway, *HA*, lxxxvi–lxxxix; for William of Malmesbury and Bede, see Mynors, Thomson, and Winterbottom, *GRA* I.62–63; II.xxxix–xli.

25. On this theme, see Greenway, *HA*, lix; Nancy Partner, *Serious Entertainments: The Writing of History in Twelfth-Century England* (Chicago: University of Chicago Press, 1977), 22–25.

26. On William's attempt to create order from the disorder of England's history, see Robert M. Stein, "Making History English: Cultural Identity and Historical Explanation in William of Malmesbury and Laȝamon's *Brut*," in *Text and Territory: Geographical Imagination in the European Middle Ages*, ed. Sylvia Tomasch and Sealy Gilles (Philadelphia: University of Pennsylvania Press, 1997), 97–115. On the larger issue of England's relationship to Normandy much has been written. For an account of relevant scholarship, as well as a thorough quizzing of John Le Patourel's thesis that the two formed, or were intended to form, a single political unit, which he expounded in *The Norman Empire* (1976), see David Bates, "Normandy and England after 1066," *English Historical Review* 413 (1989): 851–80. Bates argues for further investigation into the complex relationship between what remained separate entities, increasingly so during the twelfth century.

27. For this account, see *GRA* 28/28, as well as the commentary on this section in vol. 2.

28. Interestingly enough, the editors speculate in their notes to this section (vol. 2) that William is drawing on Asser here, but Asser does not call Athelney an island. By turning it into an island, William creates a scene whereby Alfred is pushed further into isolation, which is, in turn, relieved by the conversations he has with Saint Cuthbert, a key figure of pre-Conquest sanctity.

29. For a far less adulatory picture of William the Conqueror, see Henry T. Riley, ed. and trans., *The Annals of Roger de Hoveden*, 2 vols. (London, 1853; rpt. New York: AMS Press, 1968), 143.

30. See also Partner, *Serious Entertainments*, 23.

31. On the subject of Henry of Huntingdon and the English monarchy, see Greenway, *HA*, lx.

32. For a consideration of William's career as a historian, see Gransden, *Historical Writing in England*, 166–85; Rodney M. Thomson, *William of Malmesbury* (Woodbridge: Boydell Press, 2003), 14–39.

33. For a rich study of Bede as both historian and exegete and, consequently, of his Christian perspective and reformist agenda, see Scott DeGregorio, "Bede's *In Ezram et Neemiam* and the Reform of the Northumbrian Church," *Speculum* 79 (2004): 1–25.

34. All in-text citations of this work refer to Geoffrey of Monmouth, *The History of the Kings of Britain*, Latin text ed. Michael D. Reeve, trans.

Neil Wright (Woodbridge: Boydell Press, 2007). For Geoffrey's sources, see J. S. P. Tatlock, *The Legendary History of Britain: Geoffrey of Monmouth's "Historia Regum Britanniae" and Its Early Vernacular Versions* (Berkeley: University of California Press, 1950), 3–6. Geoffrey used the histories of both William of Malmesbury and Henry of Huntingdon, as well as Gildas, the *Historia Brittonum*, and Bede. In turn, Henry of Huntingdon draws on Geoffrey at points in the *HA*. See Greenway, clxviii, lxxii, cl–cii, 558–83. Robert, earl of Gloucester, to whom William of Malmesbury dedicates the *GRA*, was also Geoffrey of Monmouth's patron. For remarks about the relationship between the two works, see Mynors, Thomson, and Winterbottom, *GRA*, 2:5,10, 17, 21, 121, 397. In book 1.8, William famously disparages the "fables" that recount tales of Arthur, suggesting that they need to be investigated in the context of "reliable *(ueraces)* history." For an argument detailing Geoffrey's more secular understanding of history in relation to the Christian interpretation of Gildas, as well as his debts to earlier historians, see Robert W. Hanning, *Vision of History*, 92–120. For a study of the *HRB* in relation to its contemporary political valences, see John Gillingham, "The Context and Purposes of Geoffrey of Monmouth's *History of the Kings of Britain*," *Anglo Norman Studies* 13 (1990): 99–118. For the influence of the *HRB*, see Julia C. Crick, *The "Historia Regum Britannie" of Geoffrey of Monmouth IV: Dissemination and Reception in the Later Middle Ages* (Cambridge: D. S. Brewer, 1991).

35. Francis Ingledew, *Sir Gawain and the Green Knight and the Order of the Garter* (Notre Dame: University of Notre Dame Press, 2006), 25–26.

36. Greenway, *HA*, lix.

37. See David N. Dumville, *The Historia Brittonum. The "Vatican" Recension* (Cambridge: D. S. Brewer, 1985). See also John Morris, *Nennius: British History and the Welsh Annals* (Totowa, NJ: Rowman and Littlefield, 1980); Greenway, *HA*, lviii, xc–xci. The *Historia Brittonum* was also among William of Malmesbury's sources; see *GRA*, 12.

38. On these figures, see Tatlock, *Legendary History of Britain*, 117–70.

39. Gildas, c. 25; Morris, *Nennius*, c. 56. The "Vatican" recension of the *HB* does not contain the story of Arthur's campaigns; see Morris, *Nennium*, 4–5. On references to Arthur before Geoffrey, see Tatlock, *Legendary History of Britain*, 178–206; *Geoffrey of Monmouth*, ed. Reeve, trans. Wright, lxviii–lix. For Arthur, see also Michelle R. Warren, *History on the Edge: Excalibur and the Borders of Britain, 1100–1300* (Minneapolis: University of Minnesota Press, 2000), 25–59.

40. Gildas, c. 23; Bede, *IIE* i.14–15.

41. Tatlock, *Legendary History of Britain*, 135–38.

42. The Latin is even more blunt: "Quia ergo regnum tuum in se diuisum fuit, quia furor ciuilis discordiae et liuoris fumus mentem tuam hebetauit, quia superbia tua uni regi oboedientiam ferre non permisit, cernis

iccirco patriam tuam ab impiissimis paganis desolatam, domos etiam euis-
dem supra domos ruentes" (*HRB* XI.185), where terms like *furor* and *desola-
tum* link Britain's state to that of Virgilian Carthage.

43. Roger of Wendover, whose *Flores Historiarum*, much of which is a
history of the world, draws on a wide variety of historians, including William of Malmesbury, Henry of Huntingdon, and Geoffrey of Monmouth, in his
compilation. His work was edited and continued from 1235 by the thirteenth-
century Matthew Paris of St. Albans in his *Chronica Majora*. The *Chronica* is
punctuated by Matthew Paris's maps, keyed to his historical texts, that underline the largeness of the world of which England is a part. See Gransden,
Historical Writing in England, 356–79; Suzanne Lewis, *The Art of Matthew
Paris in "The Chronica Majora"* (Berkeley: University of California Press, 1987);
Daniel K. Connolly, *The Maps of Matthew Paris: Medieval Journeys through
Time, Space, and Liturgy* (Woodbridge: Boydell Press, 2009). For a study of
the cultural riches of St. Albans and its continued vitality into the fourteenth
century, see James G. Clark, *A Monastic Renaissance at St. Albans* (Oxford:
Clarendon Press, 2004).

44. For both the text and an account of William's sources, see Richard
Howlett, ed., *Chronicles of the Reigns of Stephen, Henry II, and Richard I*, Rolls
Series 82 (London, 1884–89; Weisbaden: Kraus Reprint, 1964). In the preface Howlett gives an account of William's unacknowledged and acknowledged reliance on reliable contemporary sources, praising him, if not for his
originality, for his impartiality and keenness of perception.

45. See L. G. D. Baker, "The Genesis of English Cistercian Chronicles:
The Foundation History of Fountains Abbey," 2 pts., *Analecta Cisterciensia* 25
(1969): 14–41; 31 (1975): 179–212.

46. In *De Pontificibus et Sanctis Ecclesiae Eboracensis*, Alcuin describes Britain as "fecund" and Yorkshire as beautiful, fertile, and healthy. Pope Gregory, in
sending Augustine to Britain, is the cultivator of the fields of Christ. Likewise,
Cuthbert filled "the wastelands with flowering greenness, / watering the dry
meadows with eternal fountains." Alcuin's poem on the York church recounts
Bede's narrative of Britain's conversion, then goes on to detail the ways in
which Yorkshire offered its own civilizing gifts to a barbaric world. See Peter
Godman, ed. and trans., *Alcuin: The Bishops, Kings, and Saints of York* (Oxford:
Clarendon Press, 1982), lines 21, 30–34, 78–82, 646, 652–53.

47. Howlett, ed., *Chronicles of the Reigns*, 82 n. 6. For rich interpretations
of twelfth-century attempts to come to terms with the hybridity of English,
see Cohen, *Hybridity, Identity, and Monstrosity in Medieval Britain*, esp. 11–76.
For another interpretation of the green children as exemplifying William of
Newburgh's uneasiness regarding England's cultural diversity, see Jeffrey
Jerome Cohen, "Green Children from Another World, or the Archipelago in
England," in *Cultural Diversity in the British Middle Ages: Archipelago, Island,
England* (New York: Palgrave Macmillan, 2008), 75–94.

48. On early national identity, see Gillingham, *The English in the Twelfth Century,* 6–7, 9. Roger of Wendover also suggests that the Normans represent part of a greater cycle of invasion, acculturation/conversion, lapse, fall, and new invasion, suggesting a vision of Britain's history as process. See Henry G. Hewlett, ed., *The Flowers of History by Roger de Wendover,* 3 vols. (London: HMSO, 1887), vol. 1, pt. 2, p. 335.

49. For a study of Cistercian historians, see Elizabeth Freeman, *Narratives of a New Order. Cistercian Historical Writing in England, 1150–1220,* Medieval Church Studies 2 (Turnholt: Brepols, 2002). For the Cistercian environmental impact, see G. G. Astil, *A Medieval Industrial Complex and Its Landscape: The Metalworking Watermills and Workshops of Bordesley Abbey* (York: Council for British Archaeology, 1993).

50. A. Campbell, ed., *Æthelwulf: "De Abbatibus"* (Oxford: Clarendon Press, 1967), 48. Later, contemplating other forms of barbarism, Leland called attention to this poem (xi).

51. Paul Meyvaert, "The Medieval Monastic Garden," in MacDougall, *Medieval Gardens,* 45.

52. For the Cistercians and their extensive social networks, see Emilia Jamroziak, "Making and Breaking the Bonds: Yorkshire Cistercians and Their Neighbors," in *Perspectives for an Architecture of Solitude: Essays on Cistercians, Art, and Architecture in Honour of Peter Fergusson,* ed. Terryl N. Kinder (Turnholt: Brepols, 2004), 63–70; and *Rievaulx Abbey and Its Social Context,* Medieval Church Studies 8 (Turnholt: Brepols, 2005).

53. Charles Quest-Ritson, *The English Garden: A Social History* (Boston: David Godine, 2003), 37, 34. In *The History of Bordesley Abbey* (London: J. H. & J. Parker, 1866), 56, J. M. Woodward notes that large and varied orchards were always associated with the monastery. For a study of the ways in which the Cistercians' farming practices had an impact on the English climate, see Kenneth Addison, "Changing Places: The Cistercian Settlement and Rapid Climate Change in Britain," in *A Place to Believe In: Locating Medieval Landscapes* (University Park: Pennsylvania State University Press, 2006), 211–38.

54. See E. Margaret Thompson, *The Carthusian Order in England* (London: Macmillan, 1930), 32, 519, for a discussion of the Carthusian focus on solitude rather than community.

55. See David N. Bell, "Chambers, Cells, and Cubicles: The Cistercian General Chapter and the Development of the Private Room," in Kinder, *Perspectives for an Architecture of Solitude,* 187–98.

56. The classic text here is Jean LeClercq, *The Love of Learning and the Desire for God: A Study of Monastic Culture,* trans. Catherine Misrahi (New York: Fordham University Press, 1977).

57. Bruno Griesser, ed., *Exordium Magnum Cisterciense,* Corpus Christianorum 138 (Turnholt: Brepols, 1994); Giles Constable, "The Vision of a Cistercian Novice," in *Petrus Venerabilis, 1156–1956: Studies and Texts*

Commemorating the Eighth Centenary of His Death, ed. Giles Constable and James Kritzeck, Studia Anselmiana 40 (Rome: Herder, 1956), 95–98; Martha G. Newman, *The Boundaries of Charity: Cistercian Culture and Ecclesiastical Reform, 1098–1180* (Stanford: Stanford University Press, 1996), 67, 90–91; Freeman, *Narratives of a New Order*, 142–44.

58. Lawrence C. Braceland, trans. and ed., *The Works of Gilbert of Hoyland: Sermons on the Song of Songs* (Kalamazoo, MI: Cistercian Publications, 1978), 3: 428, 433, 457–65. See also vol. 4 (1981), Epistle 3, 99–105, where he employs the language in an attempt to dissuade another Cistercian from service to the court.

59. See, for example, the "Carmen Rythmicum in Laudem Cistercii," from MS. Univ. Coll., Oxford, J, i, ad finem, which comes after a charter for the founding of a Cistercian college at Oxford, in J. R. Walbran, James Raine, and J. T. Fowler, *Memorials of the Abbey of St. Mary at Fountains*, 3 vols., Surtees Society 42, 67, 130 (Durham: Andrews and Co., 1863–1918), 42:85–86.

60. Walbran, Raine, and Fowler, *Memorials of the Abbey of St. Mary*, 1:2 and n. 7; 5.

61. F. M. Powicke, trans., *The Life of Aelred of Rievaulx by Walter Daniel*, introd. Marsha Dutton (Kalamazoo, MI: Cistercian Publications, 1994), 98.

62. On Cistercian founding narratives, see Constance Berman, *The Cistercian Evolution: The Invention of a Religious Order in Twelfth-Century Europe* (Philadelphia: University of Pennsylvania Press, 2000); Christopher Norton, "Richard of Fountains and the Letter of Thurstan: History and Historiography of a Monastic Controversy, St. Mary's Abbey, York, 1132," in Kinder, *Perspectives for an Architecture of Solitude*, 9–31.

63. Because of the number of extant manuscripts (180) and wide availability, I refer to the Middle English prose *Brut*. For a lucid and scrupulous guide through the thicket of *Brut* manuscripts in English, Anglo-Norman, and Latin, see Lister M. Matheson, *The Prose "Brut": The Development of a Middle English Chronicle* (Tempe, AZ: Medieval & Renaissance Texts and Studies, 1998). All in-text citations of both works refer to the following editions: Friedrich W. D. Brie, ed., *The Brut or The Chronicles of England*, pt. 1 EETS 131 (Oxford: Oxford University Press, 1906); pt. 2, EETS 136 (Oxford: Oxford University Press, 1908); Joseph R. Lumby, ed., *Polychronicon Ranulphi Higden . . . with English Translations of John Trevisa and of an Unknown Writer of the Fifteenth Century*, 9 vols. (London: HMSO, 1871; Weisbaden: Kraus Reprint, 1964). For other important considerations of these works, see John Taylor, "The French Prose *Brut*: Popular History in Fourteenth-Century England," in *England in the Fourteenth Century: Proceedings of the 1985 Harlaxton Symposium*, ed. W. M. Ormrod (Woodbridge: Boydell Press, 1986), 247–54; Gransden, *Historical Writing in England II*; John Taylor, *English Historical Literature in the Fourteenth Century* (Oxford: Clarendon Press, 1987); John Taylor, *The Universal*

Chronicle of Ranulf Higden (Oxford: Clarendon Press, 1966). In *Angels on the Edge of the World*, Lavezzo devotes a chapter to Higden (71–92), focusing on his adroit use of Britain's geographic marginality, its natural plenty, and thus its self-sufficiency and supremacy.

64. Matheson, *The Prose "Brut"* (2), notes that this prologue was drawn from an Anglo-Norman poem, *De Grantz Beanz*, which was, in most Anglo-Norman texts, added to the beginning of the *Brut*. In the texts that formed the basis for the Middle English translations of the *Brut*, the poem was reduced to prose and serves as a preface.

65. Ingledew, *"Sir Gawain and the Green Knight" and the Order of the Garter*, 3.

66. See Galloway, "Writing History in England," 278, for comments on Higden's Middle English translator John Trevisa's opposing view on the veracity of Arthur.

67. On the importance of the *Polychronicon* in literary history, see Emily Steiner, "Radical Historiography: Langland, Trevisa, and the *Polychronicon*," *SAC* 27 (2005): 171–212.

68. It is obviously impossible and undesirable in a single chapter to survey the histories that Gransden has already discussed with such care, or even the fourteenth-century histories that John Taylor has analyzed. For two more recent explorations of England and its histories, see Andrew Galloway, "Writing History in England"; and Galloway, "Laȝamon's Gift," *PMLA* 121 (2006): 717–34. On the subject of royal criticism, see chapter 3 of this book.

69. On historians of the reign of King John, see Gransden, *Historical Writing in England*, 318–55, as well as her remarks about Matthew Paris and his debt to Roger of Wendover whose history he glossed (367–68). For Roger of Wendover on King John, see Hewlett, *The Flowers of History by Roger de Wendover*, 2:38–48; and Robert Fabyan, *The New Chronicle of England and France*, pref. Henry Ellis (London: F.C. & J. Rivington, 1811). Fabyan drew on a number of earlier historians, providing an entertaining and multivalent account of England's history. His account of the reign of John is negative and weaves the history of the Magna Carta into John's disastrous reign (320–23).

70. Carole Levin, "A Good Prince: King John and Early Tudor Propaganda," *Sixteenth Century Journal* 11 (1980): 23–32.

71. John Bale, *Kynge Johan*, ed. J. Payne Collier, Camden Society 2 (London: J. B. Nichols, 1838); Simon Fish, *A Supplicacyon for the Beggers* (Antwerp: Johannes Grapheus, 1524), 3v.

72. J. C. Holt, *Magna Carta and Medieval Government* (London: Hambledon Press, 1985), 265.

73. *The Boke of Magna Carta with diuers other Statutes . . . translated into Englyshe* (London, 1534).

74. On the centrality of Magna Carta to the imagination of England, see Holt, *Magna Carta*, 289.

75. See Bale, *Kynge Johan*, 84–85; Polydore Vergil, *Anglicae Historiae* (Basel, 1555; facsimile ed. Menston: Scholar Press, 1972), 281. For his sources, see Denys Hay, *Polydore Vergil: Renaissance Man of Letters* (Oxford: Clarendon Press, 1952), 85–95. For another discussion of Bale, see F. J. Levy, *Tudor Historical Thought* (San Marino, CA: Huntington Library, 1967), 93.

76. On Henry's interest in effacing Beckett, see Simpson, *Reform and Cultural Revolution*, 386–87. For an analysis of Henry's own centrality to the drive to reform Britain's ecclesiastical history, see G.W. Bernard, *The King's Reformation: Henry VIII and the Remaking of the English Church* (New Haven: Yale University Press, 2005).

77. John N. King, "Bale, John (1495–1563)," in *DNB*. For Tyndale's remarks about King John, see David Daniell, ed., *William Tyndale: The Obedience of a Christian Man* (London: Penguin Books, 2000), 187–88.

My in-text citations refer to Fish, *A Supplicacyon for the Beggers.*

78. For remarks about Simon Fish, see J. S.W. Helt, "Fish, Simon (d. 1531)," in *DNB*. In *Obedience of a Christian Man,*, 188, Tyndale also suggests that England was invaded by the church.

79. See *The Defence of Peace: lately translated out of laten in to englysshe* (London: Robert Wyer for Wyllyam Marshall, 1535); Alan Gewirth, ed. and trans., *Marsilius of Padua: The Defender of Peace*, 2 vols. (New York: Columbia University Press, 1951–56), 1:310–12.

80. *SR* 3:492.

81. *Hall's Chronicle containing the History of England during the Reign of Henry the Fourth and the succeeding monarchs to the end of the Reign of Henry the Eighth* (London, 1809; rpt. New York: AMS Press, 1965), 816.

82. For this reason, Tudor historians lauded Edward III for supporting an earlier statute of Praemunire in 1353, by which the wealth of the church was prevented from leaving the country for the coffers of alien priories or of Rome. According to Foxe, Edward was "the greatest bridler of the pope's usurped power" (*A&M* 5:806).

83. For both the Latin and the English texts, see William Mead, ed., *The Famous Historie of Chinon of England . . . to which is added The Assertion of King Arthure translated by Richard Robinson from Leland's Assertio Inclytissimi Arturii*, EETS 165 (London: Oxford University Press, 1925). For Tudor reactions to Polydore Vergil, see Hay, *Polydore Vergil*, 157–58.

84. Claire Cross, "Excising the Virgin Mary from the Civic Life of Tudor York," *Northern History* 39 (2002): 279–84; Roy Strong, *The Cult of Elizabeth: Elizabethan Portraiture and Pageantry* (London: Thames and Hudson, 1977), 114–28; Helen Hackett, *Virgin Mother, Maiden Queen: Elizabeth I and the Cult of the Virgin Mary* (New York: St. Martin's Press, 1995).

85. Henry the Eight, *Answere Unto a Certaine Letter of Martyn Luthr* (London, 1528; New York: Theatrvm Orbis Terrarvm, 1971), n.p. Henry published his Latin answer to Luther in 1522, which was translated into English and published in 1527 and 1528.

86. Denys Hay, ed. and trans., *The Anglica Historia of Polydore Vergil, A.D. 1485–1537*, Camden Series, vol. 74 (London: Offices of the Royal Historical Society, 1950), 332/333.

87. Hay, *Anglica Historia* (1950), 334/335.

88. Though the first editions of Vergil's history end in 1509, he wrote a continuation that he did not publish until 1555, after he had left England. See Gransden, *Historical Writing in England II*, 432−33, where she also discusses Vergil's changes in his earlier portrait of Henry VII, whom he came to value more as he became disenchanted with the reign of Henry VIII.

89. Sir Henry Ellis, ed., *Polydore Vergil's English History from an early translation . . . the period prior to the Norman Conquest*, Camden Society vol. 36 (London: John Bowyer Nichols and Son, 1846), 25−26.

90. For detailed studies of Tudor historians, see Levy, *Tudor Historical Thought*; John N. King, *Foxe's "Book of Martyrs" and Early Modern Print Culture* (Cambridge: Cambridge University Press, 2006); Annabel M. Patterson, *Reading Holinshed's "Chronicles"* (Chicago: University of Chicago Press, 1994).

91. George Townsend, ed., *The Acts and Monuments of John Foxe*, 8 vols. (New York: AMS Press, 1965), 1:313, 323, 355; 2:bk. 3: 105−6, 85−89.

92. *Grafton's Chronicle; or, History of England*, 2 vols. (London: J. Johnson, 1806), 1:2:154−55, 167. This is Grafton's *Chronicle at large* (1569).

93. For both the texts of Holinshed's *Chronicles*, see www.english.ox.ac.uk/holinshed/.

94. For remarks about other differences between Harrison's two "Descriptions" and his growing reformist and critical stance, see Patterson, *Reading Holinshed's "Chronicles,"* 61−70.

95. See Wyman H. Herendeen, "Camden, William (1551–1623)," in *DNB*, accessed 23 Apr. 2010 from www.oxforddnb.com/view/article/4431; John Pitcher, "Daniel, Samuel (1562/3–1619)," in *DNB*.

96. See Kevin Sharpe, *Sir Robert Cotton, 1586–1631: History and Politics in Early Modern England* (Oxford: Oxford University Press, 1979), 49; Benedict Scott Anderson, "'Darke Speech': Matthew Parker and the Reforming of History," *Sixteenth Century Journal* 29 (1998): 1061−83. As Kevin Sharpe notes, Cecil supported scholars of Matthew Parker's circle, among whom were Cotton and Camden, in research into the Saxon past because it revealed the English independence from Roman jurisdiction. Notwithstanding, I am here suggesting that these texts also indicate that there might be a way of understanding England's history as richly interdependent with the histories of

other nations. Anderson stresses Parker's "anxiety about foreign influence" (1064–65), but antiquarianism, of which both Camden and Cotton are prime examples, inevitably prompts a more latitudinarian view of the past. Citations to the *Britannia* refer to Philemon Holland's translation, *Britain, or a Chorographicall Description of the Most flourishing Kingdomes, England, Scotland, and Ireland* . . . (London, 1610), which I have used because it is readily accessible in the database *Early English Books Online*.

97. Herendeen remarks on Camden's fruitful and acknowledged use of Leland, whose *Laborious Journey* was likewise strung on a topographic chain.

98. Camden published the *Remaines*, unsigned but dedicated to Robert Cotton, in 1605, and it went through many editions and two enlargements after that (Herendeen). For the above passage, see William Camden, *Remaines concerning Britaine* (London: Iohn Legatt, 1614), 371. For an analysis of John Leland and John Bale and their divided perspectives on the past and antiquarianism, see Simpson, *Reform and Cultural Revolution*, 7–33.

99. For the texts themselves, see S. D., *The Collection of the Historie of England*; John Milton, *The History of Britain*, in *Complete Prose Works of John Milton*, vol. 5, ed. French Fogle (New Haven: Yale University Press, 1951). See also Pitcher, "Daniel, Samuel (1562/3–1619)"; Nicholas von Maltzahn, *Milton's "History of Britain": Republican Historiography in the English Revolution* (Oxford: Clarendon Press, 1991).

100. For example, see Milton, *History of Britain*, 230, 252, 275. These are, of course, not the sum of Milton's references to earlier historians, especially Gildas and Bede. For discussion, see von Maltzahn, *Milton's "History of Britain*," 82–83, and chap. 2, which discusses Renaissance historiography.

101. Daniel's account of the reign of Edward III includes his quarrel with Archbishop Stafford, which he describes dispassionately, noting Edward's necessary compromise (*The Collection of the Historie of England*, 193–95). Daniel's refusal to demonize Stafford, or the church, is unusual, since most reformed historians praise Edward for checking the power of Rome in the statute of Praemunire.

102. Von Maltzhahn, *Milton's "History of Britain*," 118–40.

103. On this episode in relation to William's Norman lineage, see also Galloway, "Writing History in England," 265.

104. The editors point out that William's reference here is to *Georgics* ii.51.

105. Felicity Heal, *Hospitality in Early Modern England* (Oxford: Clarendon Press, 1990), 8, 22.

106. William Lambarde, *A Perambulation of Kent* (London: H. Middleton, 1576), 6–7.

107. John Stow, *Chronicles of England* (London: Ralphe Newberie, 1580), 150–51.

T W O   *The Island Garden and the Anxieties of Enclosure*

1. William Shakespeare, *King Richard II*, ed. Charles R. Forker (London: Arden Shakespeare, 2002), 2.1.40–50). See Forker's notes to the passage, which cite Peele, DuBartas, Greene, Daniel, Sylvester, and Lodge.

2. For the most recent work on the Wilton Diptych, see Dillian Gordon, *Making and Meaning: The Wilton Diptych* (London: National Gallery Publications, 1993); Dillian Gordon, Lisa Monas, and Caroline Elam, eds., *The Regal Image of Richard II and the Wilton Diptych* (London: Harvey Miller, 1997), especially Nigel Morgan's "The Signification of the Banner in the Wilton Diptych," 179–88, and Gordon's introduction, 22–23, which describes and discusses the orb. I would like to thank Matthew Storey, documentation assistant at the National Gallery, for making it possible for me to use the files on the painting in the Gallery's archives.

3. Dillian Gordon, "A New Discovery in the Wilton Diptych," *Burlington Magazine* 134 (1992): 662–67. As Gordon points out, there were earlier suggestions linking the painting to the *dos Mariae*. The letter of 17 March 1905 from Everard Green to Captain Neville Wilkinson in the National Gallery Archives argues that the diptych commemorates Richard's dedication of England to the Blessed Virgin. See also Edmund Waterton, *Pietas Mariana Britannica* (London, 1879), 13–44; C. Coupe, "An Old Picture," *The Month* 84 (1895): 229–42.

4. David Wilkins, *Concilia Magnae Britannicae* (London, 1737) 3:246. See also Waterton, *Pietas Mariana Britannica*, 13–14; Dillian Gordon, "The Wilton Diptych," in Gordon, Monas, and Elam, *The Regal Image of Richard II and the Wilton Diptych*, 329–30 n. 40.

5. See Gordon, *Making and Meaning*, 82, for the provenance of the diptych, the earliest record of which is in the collection of Charles I.

6. For an exploration of Langland's achievement in investing significance in Piers the Plowman, see Elizabeth Kirk, "Langland's Plowman and the Recreation of Fourteenth-Century Religious Metaphor," *Year Book of Langland Studies* 2 (1988): 1–21.

7. Lumby, ed., *Polychronicon Ranulphi Higden*, vol. 8, p. 344/345. This is Trevisa's translation.

8. For dating, see Ralph Hanna, *William Langland* (Brookfield, VT: Ashgate, 1993), 11–12. The priority of A has been argued against; see Jill Mann, "The Power of the Alphabet: A Reassessment of the Relation between the A and B Versions of *Piers Plowman*," *Yearbook of Langland Studies* 8 (1994): 21–50. For a recent study of A's priority and importance, see Lawrence Warner, *The Lost History of "Piers Plowman"* (Philadelphia: University of Pennsylvania Press, 2011). For the rhetoric of agriculture, see Stephen A. Barney, "The Plowshare of the Tongue," *Mediaeval Studies* 35 (1973): 261–93;

Michael Camille, "Labouring for the Lord: The Ploughman and the Social Order in the Luttrell Psalter," *Art History* 10 (1987): 423–55; Nevill Coghill, "The Character of Piers Plowman," *Medium AEvum* 2 (1933): 108–35; Hanna, *William Langland*, 11; Kirk, "Langland's Plowman and the Recreation of Fourteenth-Century Religious Metaphor."

9. Derek Pearsall, ed., *William Langland: Piers Plowman, a New Annotated Edition of the C-Text* (Exeter: University of Exeter Press, 2008), 156; Christopher Dyer, *Lords and Peasants in a Changing Society: The Estates of the Bishopric of Worcester, 680–1540* (Cambridge: Cambridge University Press, 1980), 331; Christopher Dyer, *An Age of Transition? Economy and Society in England in the Later Middle Ages* (Oxford: Clarendon Press, 2005), 58, 75–77; Joan Thirsk, *The Rural Economy of England: Collected Essays* (London: Hambledon Press, 1984), 59–64. See the *Middle English Dictionary* for the use of word in legal documents.

10. David Aers, *Piers Plowman and Christian Allegory* (London: Edward Arnold, 1975), 114. In-text citations refer to the A-text unless otherwise indicated: George Kane, ed., *Piers Plowman: The A Version* (London: Athlone Press, 1988).

11. See Saint Bernard, *Sermones in Cantica*, PL 183: cols. 1081, 1084, 1086; D. W. Robertson Jr., *A Preface to Chaucer* (Princeton: Princeton University Press, 1962), 251–52. On hunting and the Law of the Forest, see William Perry Marvin, *Hunting Law and Ritual in Medieval England* (Cambridge: D. S. Brewer, 2006).

12. Jonathan J. G. Alexander, "Labeur and Paresse: Ideological Representations of Medieval Peasant Labor," *Art Bulletin* 72, no. 3 (1990): 436–52; Michael Camille, *Mirror in Parchment: The Luttrell Psalter and the Making of Medieval England* (Chicago: University of Chicago Press, 1998).

13. For the magnatial implications of wasting as it applies to household economies, see D. Vance Smith, *Arts of Possession: The Middle English Household Imaginary* (Minneapolis: University of Minnesota Press, 2003), 72–107.

14. Jacobus de Cessolis, *The Game of the Chesse by William Caxton*, reproduced in facsimile (London: J. R. Smith, 1860), Tractate 3.

15. In-text citations of the poem refer to Warren Ginsberg, ed., *Wynnere and Wastoure*, in *Wynnere and Wastoure and The Parlement of the Thre Ages* (Kalamazoo, MI: Medieval Institute Publications, 1992). See also Stephanie Trigg, ed., *Wynnere and Wastoure*, EETS 297 (Oxford: Oxford University Press, 1990). As Trigg notes (18), the author of the *incipit* is unknown, but in placing the poem with the *Parlement of the Thre Ages* Thornton categorized it as ethical. For Thornton, see Ralph Hanna, "The Growth of Robert Thornton's Books," *Studies in Bibliography* 40 (1987): 51–61; George R. Keiser, "Lincoln Cathedral Library MS 91: Life and Milieu of the Scribe," *Studies in Bibliography* 32 (1979): 158–79. For the classic study of the circulation of books through London, see Ralph Hanna, "Sir Thomas Berkeley and His

Patronage," *Speculum* 64 (1989): 878–916. For the need to see *Piers Plowman* in relation to texts like *Wynnere and Wastoure*, see Hanna, *William Langland*, 11.

For an exploration of the poem's relation to the economy and politics of the early years of the 1350s, see John Scattergood, "'Winner and Waster' and the Mid-Fourteenth-Century Economy," in *The Writer as Witness: Literature as Historical Evidence*, ed. Tom Dunne (Cork: Cork University Press, 1987), 39–57. For a study linking the poem more precisely to conditions in Chester, see Britton J. Harwood, "Anxious over Peasants: Textual Disorder in *Winner and Waster*," *JMEMS* 36 (2006): 291–319.

16. A ploughpot was a long-handled spade used to remove earth adhering to a plow or to chop roots. See the *Middle English Dictionary*.

17. Hanna, *London Literature, 1300–1380*, 262. On the language of the royal or national household that governs the poem, see Smith, *Arts of Possession*, 72–107.

18. On the realities of peasant life and food supply, see William Chester Jordan, *The Great Famine: Northern Europe in the Early Fourteenth Century* (Princeton: Princeton University Press, 1996).

19. For a subtle and suggestive argument regarding the economic and nationalistic argument that drives *Wynnere*, see Lois Roney, "*Winner and Waster*'s 'Wyse Wordes': Teaching Economics and Nationalism in Fourteenth-Century England," *Speculum* 69 (1994):1070–1100. For further remarks on the poem's Englishness, see Harwood, "Anxious over Peasants," 303–4.

20. In addition to the entries listed in the *Middle English Dictionary*, see the language of two early charters included in the appendix to the works of Bede in *PL* 95: 376, 383, and of a charter of Hugh of Lincoln in *PL* 153: 1119.

21. Sherry L. Reames, ed., *The Legend of Mary Magdalene, Penitent and Apostle*, in *Middle English Legends of Women Saints* (Kalamazoo, MI: Medieval Institute, 2003), lines 557–60.

22. Martin Stevens and A. C. Cawley, eds., *The Towneley Plays*, 2 vols. (Oxford: Oxford University Press, 1994), Play 30, "Judgment," lines 515–20.

23. W. Nelson Francis, ed., *The Book of Vices and Virtues*, EETS, o.s. 217 (London: Oxford University Press, 1942): 34/24.

24. Carl Horstmann, ed., *Proprium Sanctorum*, *Archiv* 81 (1888): 83/36–41.

25. See James M. Dean, ed., *Medieval English Political Writings* (Kalamazoo, MI: Medieval Institute Publications, 1996), 243–46. On the process of transformation that Langland effects in what is a larger dialectical process wherein initial meanings are superseded by later events in the poem, see David Aers, *Salvation and Sin: Augustine, Langland, and Fourteenth-Century Theology* (Notre Dame: University of Notre Dame Press, 2009), 103–7.

26. "Friar's Tale," in *The Canterbury Tales* 3:1581, in *The Riverside Chaucer*, ed. Larry D. Benson (Boston: Houghton Mifflin, 1987). All quotations

from the works of Chaucer are taken from this edition and will be cited in the text by fragment and line.

27. For the sources, see Thomas J. Farrell and Amy W. Goodwin, "The Clerk's Tale," in *Sources and Analogues of "The Canterbury Tales,"* ed. Robert M. Correale and Mary Hamel (Cambridge: D. S. Brewer, 2002), 114/115, 144/145.

28. Edward Wheatley, "The Nun's Priest's Tale," in Correale and Hamel, *Sources and Analogues of the "Canterbury Tales,"* 456/457, 474/475. Marie de France's version, 454/455, only places the rooster on a dungheap. For a discussion of the tale in relation to its sources, see Jill Mann, *From Aesop to Reynard: Beast Literature in Medieval Britain* (Oxford: Oxford University Press, 2009), 250–61.

29. Robertson, *A Preface to Chaucer,* 251–52; Larry Scanlon, *Narrative, Authority, and Power: The Medieval Exemplum and the Chaucerian Tradition* (Cambridge: Cambridge University Press, 1994), 230. See especially *Le Roman de Renart Contrefait,* in Correale and Hamel, *Sources and Analogues of the "Canterbury Tales,"* lines 31511–33180. See also the picture of the preaching fox/friar in G. R. Owst, *Preaching in Medieval England: An Introduction to Sermon Manuscripts of the Period* (Cambridge: Cambridge University Press, 1926), 86.

30. Elizabeth Salter, "Medieval Poetry and the Visual Arts," *Essays and Studies* 22 (1969): 19; Derek Pearsall, *The Nun's Priest's Tale. The Variorum Edition of the Works of Geoffrey Chaucer* 2, pt. 9 (Norman: University of Oklahoma Press, 1984), 150–51; Lynn Staley Johnson, "'To Make in Som Comedy': Chauntecleer, Son of Troy," *Chaucer Review* 19 (1985): 226–44; Staley, *Languages of Power in the Age of Richard II,* 142–44.

31. See Nigel Saul, *Richard II* (New Haven: Yale University Press, 1997), 340–58, for an analysis of the mannerisms of Richard's court.

32. For a learned reading of the many ways in which Chaucer asks questions through this tale, see Peter W. Travis, *Disseminal Chaucer: Rereading the Nun's Priest's Tale* (Notre Dame: University of Notre Dame Press, 2010), and for this scene in particular, see 263–66.

33. See B: 10.465–69; C: 11.292–97, which gives the passage to Recchelessnesse. See also Pearsall, *Piers Plowman . . . a New Annotated Edition of the C-Text,* 214–15, notes.

34. See Aers, *Piers Plowman and Christian Allegory,* 113; *Piers Plowman* B: 19; C: 21.

35. James M. Dean, ed., *Richard the Redeless and Mum and the Sothsegger* (Kalamazoo, MI: Medieval Institute Publications, 2000). In *Languages of Power in the Age of Richard II,* 323–24, I relate *Mum* to the concerns of the georgic.

36. George Warner, ed., *The Libelle of Englyshe Polycye: A Poem on the Use of Sea-Power, 1436* (Oxford: Clarendon Press, 1926), lines 1092–95.

37. Rosemary Horrox, trans. and ed., *The Black Death* (Manchester: Manchester University Press, 1994), 72–73, 76, 116. Geoffrey of Monmouth ends

the *History of the Kings of Britain* with famine and plague, which come to Britain after the illness of Cadwallader. The inhabitants leave for Brittany, and Britain is deserted for eleven years until the Saxons repopulate it. The Saxons, who cultivate the fields, then begin another cycle.

38. See Bertha Putnam, *Enforcement of the Statute of Laborers* (New York: Columbia University Press, 1908). For the relationship between *Piers Plowman* and the Statute, see David Aers, "Justice and Wage Labor after the Black Death," in *Faith, Ethics, and Church Writing in England, 1360–1409* (Cambridge: D. S. Brewer, 2000), 56–75. For a study of labor in relation to the idea of the common profit, see Kellie Robertson, *The Laborer's Two Bodies: Literary and Legal Productions in Britain, 1350–1500* (New York: Palgrave Macmillan, 2006), 78–116.

39. Edward died in his Jubilee year, 21 June 1377. For the Statute, see *SR*, 1:396–97.

40. For this history, see W. G. Hoskins, *The Making of the English Landscape* (London: Hodder and Stoughton, 1955).

41. See Christopher Dyer's many studies: "Deserted Medieval Villages in the West Midlands," *Economic History Review*, n.s., 35 (1982): 19–34; *Making a Living in the Middle Ages: The People of Britain, 850–1520* (New Haven: Yale University Press, 2002); and *An Age of Transition?* See also R. H. Tawney, *Religion and the Rise of Capitalism* (New York: Harcourt, Brace and World, 1926), 118–28; Mavis Mote, "The East Sussex Land Market and Agrarian Class Structure in the Late Middle Ages," *Past and Present* 139 (1993): 46–65; Rosemary Hopcroft, "The Social Origins of Agrarian Change in Late Medieval England," *American Journal of Sociology* 99 (1994): 1559–95; Gregory Clark and Anthony Clark, "Common Rights to Land in England, 1475–1839," *Journal of Economic History* 61 (2001): 1009–36.

Though histories of enclosure controversies take medieval land use and the medieval land market into account, discussions of enclosure and its relevance to literary texts usually focus on the sixteenth century. See the essays collected in Richard Burt and John Michael Archer, eds., *Enclosure Acts: Sexuality, Property, and Culture in Early Modern England* (Ithaca: Cornell University Press, 1994), especially James R. Sieman, "Landlord Not King: Agrarian Change and Interarticulation," 17–33; and William C. Carroll, "'The Nursery of Beggary': Enclosure, Vagrancy, and Sedition in the Tudor-Stuart Period," 34–47.

I am pushing this set of concerns, and the language used to express it, back into the mid-fifteenth century.

42. For Bishop Russell, see Thomson, "Russell, John A. F. (c.1430–1494)," in *DNB*. Russell had a reputation for learning and had a substantial library, which included Matthew Paris's *Historia Anglorum*. For the sermons, see J. G. Nichols, ed., *Grants etc. from the Crown during the Reign of Edward the Fifth*, *Camden Society*, o.s., 60 (1854): xxxv–lxii.

43. In addition to Nichols's comments about the fragments, see S. B. Chrimes, *English Constitutional Ideas in the Fifteenth Century* (Cambridge: Cambridge University Press, 1936), 166.

44. For another draft of the same passage, see p. lix.

45. *SR* 2:542.

46. John Rous, *Historia Regum Angliae* (London, 1716); available at Galenet.galegroup.com. Rous wrote this between 1480 and 1486. For discussions of Rous, see the *DNB* and Gransden, *Historical Writing in England II*, 308–27. Leland mentioned Rous in his *Itinerary* (Gransden, *Historical Writing in England II*, 310). The manuscript of the *Historia*, according to its editor (p. iv) was a Cotton manuscript and linked to the circle of Matthew Parker. For remarks about the agricultural depression of the period 1430–70, which inevitably affected villages, particularly in the north of England, see E. B. Fryde, *Peasants and Landlords in Later Medieval England* (New York: St. Martin's Press, 1996), 154–56.

47. See Gransden, *Historical Writing in England II*, 310, as well as her discussion of the passages relating to enclosure in the *Historia*.

48. A few years later, in 1517–18, there was an inquiry into enclosures. The commission was called, fittingly, the Domesday of Inclosures. See the edition by I. S. Leadam, Royal Historical Society (1897).

49. *SR* 3:127. In 25 Henry VIII, Statute 14 addresses the issue of pasturage and tillage, again in an attempt to protect tillage, but does not use the evocative language of the earlier statute. Twice in Elizabeth I's reign the balance between pasturage and tillage was addressed by statute, each time by reference to the history of statute law on the subject (5 Elizabeth I, c.2; 39 Elizabeth I, c. 2). In 21 James I, Statute 28, these statutes were repealed.

50. Dean, *Medieval English Political Writings*, "Gode Spede the Plough," 254–56. See Dean's comments on the links between this poem and Langland's plowman.

51. Thomas More wrote his *Utopia* in Latin, and it was published in four continental Latin editions. See Thomas More, *Utopia*, trans. George M. Logan and Robert M. Adams, Cambridge Texts in the History of Political Thought (Cambridge: Cambridge University Press, 1989), xxix. The above is the first translation into English, done by Raphe Robynson, *A frutefull pleasaunt, [and] wittie worke, of the best state of a publique weale and of the newe Yle, called Vtopia*, 2nd ed. (London, 1556). The marginal gloss to this passage (p. 14 v) reiterates the content, "English shepe deuourers of men."

52. "templo duntaxat stabulandis ovibus relicto." Thomas More, *Utopia*, in *The Complete Works of St. Thomas More*, vol. 4, ed. Edward Surtz and J. H. Hexter (New Haven: Yale University Press, 1963), 66.

53. See F. J. Furnivall, ed., *Ballads from Manuscripts*, 2 vols. (London: Ballad Society, Taylor and Co., 1868–73), 1:32–37. One epigram ends with

the lines, "Till now I thoughte the prouerbe did but iest, / Which said 'a blacke sheepe was a biting beast.'"

54. John Fitzherbert, *Here begynneth a ryght frutefull mater: and hath to name the boke of surueyinge and improuentes* (London: Rycharde Pynson, 1523). On authorship, see Reginald H. C. Fitzherbert, "The Authorship of the 'Book of Husbandry' and the 'Book of Surveying,'" *EHR* 12 (1897): 225–36. For discussion of his *Book of Husbandry*, see Andrew McRae, *God Speed the Plough: The Representation of Agrarian England, 1500–1660* (New York: Cambridge University Press, 1996), 137–38.

55. Furnivall and Cowper, *Four Supplications*, 96. For petitions, complaints, and bills regarding enclosure, see C. H. Williams, ed., *English Historical Documents, 1485–1558* (New York: Oxford University Press, 1967), 761–812, 926–53.

56. Elizabeth Lamond, ed., *A Discourse of the Common Weal of this Realm of England* (1581) (New York: Burt Franklin, [1971] 1993). Though Lamond and others assigned this treatise to John Hales, it is now thought to be the work of Sir Thomas Smith (1513–77), who was affiliated with Protector Somerset and had a distinguished, if controversial, political career. Smith was learned, and *A Discourse* is, according to Ian Archer, "the most impressive piece of economic analysis produced in the sixteenth century." See Archer's entry for Sir Thomas Smith in the *DNB*.

57. Mary Bateson and Thomas Cromwell, "Aske's Examination," *EHR* 5 (1890): 550–73. See also Mary Bateson, "The Pilgrimage of Grace," *EHR* 5 (1890): 330–45.

58. For exploration of the landscape of dissolution, see Margaret Aston, "English Ruins and English History: The Dissolution and the Sense of the Past," *JWCI* 36 (1973): 231–55; Philip Schwyzer, "The Beauties of the Land: Bale's Books, Aske's Abbeys, and the Aesthetics of Nationhood," *Renaissance Quarterly* 57 (2004): 99–125; Philip Schwyzer, *Literature, Nationalism and Memory in Early Modern England and Wales* (Cambridge: Cambridge University Press, 2004), 49–76; Simpson, *Reform and Cultural Revolution*, chap. 1; Jennifer Summit, "Leland's *Itinerary* and the Remains of the Medieval Past," in *Reading the Medieval in Early Modern England*, ed. Gordon McMullan and David Matthews (Cambridge: Cambridge University Press, 2007), 159–76; Sarah Stanbury, *The Visual Object of Desire in Late Medieval England* (Philadelphia: University of Pennsylvania Press, 2007), 1–5.

59. See Thomas Wright, ed., *Three Chapters of Letters Relating to the Suppression of Monasteries*, Camden Society, 26 (London: John Bowyer Nichols and Son, 1843).

60. John Donne, "A Hymne to the Saynts and To the Marquesse Hamilton," lines 20–24, in *The Variorum Edition of the Poetry of John Donne*, gen. ed. Gary A. Stringer (Bloomington: Indiana University Press, 1994–), 6:220.

Thanks to my colleague Margaret Maurer for bringing these lines to my attention.

61. Printed in Lamond, *A Discourse on the Common Weal of this Realm of England*, xlv–liii.

62. See also the charges leveled by Philemon in Thomas Becon's *Jewell of Joy* (1550). See Williams, *English Historical Documents, 1485–1558*, 953. See also "Materials concerning enclosures," 926–53.

63. For Sherbrooke, see A. G. Dickens, ed., *Tudor Treatises, Yorkshire Archaeological Society Record Series* 125 (1959). Dickens feels Sherbrooke composed the treatise from about 1567 to 1591 (29–32). See also Colin Platt, *The Abbeys and Priories of Medieval England* (New York: Fordham University Press, 1984), 231–34. Francis Trigge, *An apologie, or defence of our dayes, against the vaine murmurings & complaints of manie wherein is plainly proued, that our dayes are more happie & blessed than the dayes of our forefathers* (London: John Wolfe, 1589). Enclosure was also one of the grievances listed by the Norfolk Rebels in 1549, whose unrest was occasioned by Protector Somerset's mandate against it, and is given extended treatment in the poem, *Vox Populi Vox Dei*. See Furnivall, *Ballads from Manuscript*, 108–51.

64. Greg Walker, *Plays of Persuasion: Drama and Politics at the Court of Henry VIII* (Cambridge: Cambridge University Press, 1991), 104, 110. For the play, see W. W. Greg, ed., *A New Enterlude of Godly Queene Hester* (Louvain: A. Wystpruyst, 1904), esp. lines 950–69.

65. Thomas Wright, *The Disposition or Garnishment of the Soule To Receive worthily the Blessed Sacrament* (Antwerp, 1596), in John Roberts, ed., *A Critical Anthology of English Recussant Devotional Prose, 1558–1603*, Duquesne Studies Philological Series 7 (Pittsburgh: Duquesne University Press, 1966), 244.

66. See Barbara D. Palmer, "'Towneley Plays' or 'Wakefield Cycle' Revisited," *Comparative Drama* 21 (1987–88): 318–48; Barbara D. Palmer, "Recycling the Wakefield Cycle," *Research Opportunities in Renaissance Drama* 41 (2002): 88–130; Theresa Coletti and Gail McMurray Gibson, "The Tudor Origins of Medieval Drama," in *A Companion to Tudor Literature*, ed. Kent Cartwright (Oxford: Blackwell, 2010), 228–45; Peter Happé, *The Towneley Cycle: Unity and Diversity* (Cardiff: University of Wales Press, 2007), 4–19.

67. On the north, see R. R. Reid, *The King's Council in the North* (London: Longmans, Green, and Co., 1921), 122–23; Heal, *Reformation in Britain and Ireland*, 224.

68. For the text, see Stevens and Cawley, *The Towneley Plays*. For a rich study of the play in relation to the enclosure controversy, see Lisa Kiser, "'Mak's Heirs': Sheep and Humans in the Pastoral Ecology of the Towneley *First* and *Second Shepherds' Plays*," *JEGP* 108 (2009): 336–59. For further remarks on the playwright and his interest in social dissonance, see Ruth

Nissé, *Drama and the Politics of Interpretation in Late Medieval England* (Notre Dame: University of Notre Dame Press, 2005), 75–98.

69. On these "gentlery-men," see Stevens and Cawley, *The Towneley Plays*, 2:496.

70. For medieval horticultural language, see Staley, *Languages of Power in the Age of Richard II*, 291–303. On the subject of early modern husbandry and agrarian reform, see McRae, *God Speed the Plough*; Joan Thirsk, "Plough and Pen· Agricultural Writers in the Seventeenth Century," in *Social Relations and Ideas: Essays in Honour of R.H. Hilton*, ed. T.H. Aston, P.R. Cross, Christopher Dyer, and Joan Thirsk (Cambridge: Cambridge University Press, 1983), 295–318; Wendy Wall, "Renaissance National Husbandry: Gervase Markham and the Publication of England," *Sixteenth Century Journal* 27 (1996): 767–85. On the subject of the private garden, estate, or great house, see Kari Boyd McBride, *Country House Discourse in Early Modern England: A Cultural Study of Landscape and Legitimacy* (Burlington, VT: Ashgate, 2001); William A. McClung, *The Country House in English Renaissance Poetry* (Berkeley: University of California Press, 1977); Roy Strong, *The Renaissance Garden in England* (London: Thames and Hudson, 1979); Don E. Wayne, *"Penshurst": The Semiotics of Place and the Poetics of History* (Madison: University of Wisconsin Press, 1984). For essays relevant to the entire field, see Michael Leslie and Timothy Raylor, eds., *Culture and Cultivation in Early Modern England: Writing and the Land* (Leicester: Leicester University Press, 1992).

71. See Simpson, *Reform and Cultural Revolution*, chap. 1; Summit, "Leland's *Itinerary* and the Remains of the Medieval Past."

72. "To the Reader," in John Bale, *The laboryouse iourney [and] serche of Iohan Leylande, for Englandes antiquitees geuen of hym as a newe yeares gyfte to Kynge Henry the viij. in the. xxxvij. yeare of his reygne, with declaracyons enlarged* (London: Printed by S. Mierdman for John Bale, 1549), Biir.

73. Gervase Markham, *The English Husbandman* (1613) (New York: Garland, 1982), Epistle to the Reader.

74. Hugh Latimer, "Sermon of the Plough," in *Sermons* (London: J.M. Dent, 1926), 54–71.

75. Rebecca Bushnell, *Green Desire: Imagining Early Modern English Gardens* (Ithaca: Cornell University Press, 2003), 30. On Hartlib, see Timothy Raylor, "Samuel Hartlib and the Commonwealth of Bees," in Leslie and Raylor, *Culture and Cultivation*, 91–129.

76. Ralph Austen, *A Treatise of Fruit Trees* (Oxford, 1653), Epistle. Austen is pro-enclosure, going so far as to recommend setting aside spots for the poor, "their share," thus enclosing waste and common ground. "Anglia Hortus" is the title of a poem by Mildmay Fane, second earl of Westmoreland, in which he draws on the idea of England as a garden. See Alexander B. Grosart, ed., *The Poems of Mildmay, Second Earl of Westmoreland (1648)* (privately

printed, 1879), 133. For associations between Mildmay and Marvell, see Rosalie L. Colie, *My Ecchoing Song: Andrew Marvell's Poetry of Criticism* (Princeton: Princeton University Press, 1970), 225; McClung, *The Country House in English Renaissance Poetry*, 154. On the loss of horticultural knowledge with the Dissolution, see Quest-Ritson, *The English Garden*, 37, 34.

77. Andrew McRae, "Husbandry Manuals and the Language of Agrarian Improvement," in Leslie and Raylor, *Culture and Cultivation*, 45. See also McRae's entry for Tusser in the *DNB*.

78. Thomas Tusser, *Fiue hundreth pointes of good Husbandrie* (London: Henrie Denham, 1585), 14.

79. McRae, "Husbandry Manuals," 45–51.

80. On the traditions of the country house poem, see G. R. Hibbard, "The Country House Poem of the Seventeenth Century," *JWCI* 19 (1956): 159–74; Williams, *The Country and the City*, 27–34; McClung, *The Country House in English Renaissance Poetry*; Heather Dubrow, "The Country-House Poem, a Study in Generic Development," *Genre* 12 (1979): 153–79; Wayne, *"Penshurst"*; Maurice Howard, *The Early Tudor Country House: Architecture and Politics* (London: George Philip, 1987).

81. All in-text citations of "To Penshurst" refer to George Parfitt's edition, *Ben Jonson: The Complete Poems* (New Haven: Yale University Press, 1982), 95–98.

82. See Gordon Kipling, *Enter the King: Theatre, Liturgy, and Ritual in the Medieval Civic Triumph* (Oxford: Clarendon Press, 1998), 163–67, 234–36; George Kernodle, *From Art to Theatre: Form and Convention in the Renaissance* (Chicago: University of Chicago Press, 1944), 73; Strong, *The Cult of Elizabeth*, 114–63.

83. C. Paul Christianson, *The Riverside Gardens of Thomas More's London* (New Haven: Yale University Press, 2005), 6–7, 83, 200; A. L. Rowse, ed., *A Man of Singular Virtue: being a Life of Sir Thomas More . . . and a selection of More's letters* (London: Folio Society, 1980), 44; Sir Francis Bacon, "Of Gardens," in *The Essayes or Counsels, Civill and Morall*, ed. Michael Kiernan (Cambridge, MA: Harvard University Press, 1985), 139–45.

84. Holinshed, *Chronicles of England, Scotland, and Ireland* (1587, 1.17, p. 108), /www.english.ox.ac.uk/holinshed/texts.php?text1=1587_0072. Holinshed was dead by this time and had no hand in this edition. For remarks about Harrison, see Patterson, *Reading Holinshed's "Chronicles,"* 58–70.

85. For "The Description of Cooke-ham," see Susanne Woods, ed., *The Poems of Aemilia Lanyer* (New York: Oxford University Press, 1993), 130–38. On the poem, see Barbara K. Lewalski, "The Lady of the Country-House Poem," in *The Fashioning and Functioning of the British Country House*, ed. Gervase Jackson-Stops, Gordon J. Schochet, Lena Cowen Orlin, and Elisabeth Blair MacDougall (Washington, DC: National Gallery of Art, 1989), 234–41; Susanne Woods, *Lanyer: A Renaissance Woman Poet* (New York: Oxford Uni-

versity Press, 1999), 115–25. Woods suggests that we look at Lanyer's poem, which preceded Jonson's, as providing him with material to create a genre linked, tellingly, to him and not to Lanyer.

86. The play mentions *horbery shrogys*. The Cawley and Stevens edition capitalizes the term and designates it as a place-name. Gordon Epp has speculated that *horbery* might be a variation of *herbery*, meaning "shelter," thus brush for sheep. Nonetheless, the proximity of shrogs, of waste space to Bethlehem, allows place to exist within an associational geography.

87. All in-text citations to the works of Andrew Marvell refer to Nigel Smith, ed., *The Poems of Andrew Marvell*, rev. ed. (New York: Pearson/Longman, 2007). For information about provenance, dating, and influence, see 152–55.

88. All quotations from "Upon Appleton House" refer to Smith, *The Poems of Andrew Marvell*, 216–41. For evidence of Marvell's historic and political consciousness as it is manifested here, see Annabel Patterson, *Marvell and the Civic Crown* (Princeton: Princeton University Press, 1978), 95–110; Patsy Griffin, "'Twas no Religious House till now': Marvell's 'Upon Appleton House,'" *SEL* 28 (1988), 61–76; Smith's copious notes and introduction, 210–16.

89. Tite, *The Early Records of Sir Robert Cotton's Library*; Gilson, "The Library of Henry Saville of Banke."

90. See the *DNB* for both Dugdale and Ashmole. For Dodsworth, see N. Denholm-Young and H. H. E. Craster, "Roger Dodsworth and His Circle," *Yorkshire Archaelogical Journal* 32 (1934): 5–32.

91. Annabel Patterson and Martin Dzelzainis, "Marvell and the Earl of Anglesey: A Chapter in the History of Reading," *Historical Journal* 44 (2001): 703–27. For Thomas Fairfax's books, see F. Madden, H. H. E. Craster, and N. Denholm-Young, eds., *A Summary Catalogue of Western Manuscripts in the Bodleian Library at Oxford*, vol. 2, pt. 2 (Oxford: Clarendon Press, 1937), 770–87. For Henry Fairfax, see the book list in BL, Sloane MS 1872, fol. 60–81b. Thanks to Nigel Smith for generous answers to my questions about these libraries.

92. See Stephanie Trigg, "The Vulgar History of the Order of the Garter," in McMullan and Matthews, *Reading the Medieval in Early Modern England*, 91–105.

93. All references to *Cooper's Hill* (1642 edition) are drawn from Theodore Howard Banks Jr., ed., *The Poetical Works of Sir John Denham* (New Haven: Yale University Press, 1928), 63–89. See William Rockett, "'Courts Make Not Kings, but Kings the Court': *Cooper's Hill* and the Constitutional Crisis of 1642," *Restoration: Studies in English Literary Culture, 1660–1700*, 17 (1993): 1–14; Rufus Putney, "The View from Cooper's Hill," *University of Colorado Studies Series in Language and Literature* 6 (1957): 13–22.

94. Thomas Fairfax, *Short Memorials of Thomas Lord Fairfax* (London: Ri. Chiswell, 1699).

95. Colie, *"My Ecchoing Song,"* 222–24; George W. Johnson, *The Fairfax Correspondence: Memoirs of the Reign of Charles the First,* 2 vols. (London: Richard Bentley, 1848), 109.

96. See T. E. Bridgett, *Our Lady's Dower or How England gained and lost that title* (London: Burns and Oates, 1875); London, BL, MS Harley 360, fol. 98v, where a marginal note to this anti-Catholic tract reads, "England of long time hath bin said to be our Ladyes Dowrie."

THREE   *The Fourteenth Century and Place*

1. For a study of the Edwardian literature of political and social critique, including many of the texts considered in this chapter, see David Matthews, *Writing to the King: Nation, Kingship, and Literature in England, 1250–1350* (Cambridge: Cambridge University Press, 2010).

2. M. A. Michael, "The Iconography of Kingship in the Walter of Milemete Treatise," *JWCI* 57 (1994): 35–47. For the manuscript, see M. R. James and Albert Van de Put, eds., *The Treatise of Walter de Milemete De Nobilitatibus, sapientiis, et prudentiis regum,* reproduced in facsimile (Oxford: Oxford University Press, 1913). For a translation, see Cary J. Nederman, trans., *Political Thought in Early Fourteenth-Century England: Treatises by Walter of Milemete, William of Pagula, and William of Ockham* (Tempe: Arizona Center of Medieval and Renaissance Studies, in collaboration with Brepols, 2002), 24–61.

3. For the reign of Edward III, see W. M. Ormrod, *The Reign of Edward III: Crown and Political Society in England, 1327–1377* (New Haven: Yale University Press, 1990); J. S. Rothwell, ed., *The Age of Edward III* (York: York Medieval Press, 2001).

4. The manuscript is Vienna, Österreichische Nationalbibliothek cod. 1826*. See Lucy Freeman Sandler, "Political Imagery in the Bohun Manuscripts," in *English Manuscript Studies 1100–1700,* vol. 10, ed. A. S. G. Edwards (London: British Library, 2002), 114–153. See also Lucy Freeman Sandler, "Rhetorical Strategies in the Pictorial Imagery of Fourteenth-Century Manuscripts: the Case of the Bohun Psalters," in *Rhetoric beyond Words: Delight and Persuasion in the Arts of the Middle Ages,* ed. Mary Carruthers (Cambridge: Cambridge University Press, 2010), 96–123.

5. C. Johnson, ed. and trans., *Richard Fitz Nigel: Dialogues de Scaccario,* rev. ed., Oxford Medieval Texts (Oxford: Oxford University Press, 1983), 6/7.

6. For Horn, see Henry Thomas Riley, ed., *Munimenta Gildhallae Londoniensis: Liber Albus, Liber Custumarum et Liber Horn* (London: Longman, Brown, Green, Longmans and Roberts, 1859), vol. 2. *The Mirror of Justices,* which is attributed to Horn, characterizes the Britons as offending God by their use of force, so the kingdom was delivered to its humbler neighbors,

the Saxons, who changed the name to England, then divided it into districts, thus reconfiguring its topography. See William Joseph Whittaker, ed., *The Mirror of Justices* (London: Bernard Quaritch, 1895), 6. I have written about Horn in *Languages of Power*, 34–36, 304–5. For commentary on Horn's achievement, see J. Catto, "Andrew Horn: Law and History in Fourteenth-Century England," in *The Writing of History in the Middle Ages: Essays Presented to R.W. Southern*, ed. R. H. C. Davis and J. M. Wallace-Hadrill et al. (Oxford: Oxford University Press, 1981), 367–92. For a study of the Horn manuscripts, see Hanna, *London Literature, 1300–1380*, esp. 67–79.

7. Michael, "The Iconography of Kingship," 35.

8. See Jane H. M. Taylor, "*Le Roman de Fauvain:* Manuscript, Text, Image," 569–90, in the important collection *Fauvel Studies: Allegory, Chronicle, Music, and Image in Paris, Bibliothèque Nationale de France, MS franc*ais 146*, ed. Margaret Bent and Andrew Wathey (Oxford: Clarendon Press, 1998). It is outside the scope of this study but worth noting that, as Taylor points out, *Fauvel* is significant for more than its satire and occupies a special place in the history of music. See Ardis Butterfield, "The Refrain and the Transformation of Genre in the *Roman de Fauvel*," in Bent and Wathey, *Fauvel Studies*, 105–60. Thus there are additional affinities between the motets in BN fr.571, which concern royal duty, and the *Fauvain*, which provides an obverse picture of royal responsibility.

9. See Michael, "The Iconography of Kingship." See also M. A. Michael, "A Manuscript Wedding Gift from Philippa of Hainaut to Edward III," *Burlington Magazine* 127 (1985): 582–99.

10. Michael Camille, "Hybridity, Monstrosity, and Bestiality in the *Roman de Fauvel*," in Bent and Wathey, *Fauvel Studies*, 161–74.

11. Robert Steele, ed., *Lydgate and Burgh's Secrees of old philisoffres: A version of the "Secreta secretorum*," ed. from the Sloane MS 2464, with introduction, notes, and glossary, EETS 65–66 (London: K. Paul, Trench, Trübner & Co., 1894).

12. All in-text citations of the *Regiment* refer to Charles R. Blyth, ed., *The Regiment of Princes / Thomas Hoccleve* (Kalamazoo, MI: Medieval Institute Publications, 1999). For a study of the first section of the *Regiment* that explores the laicization of confession, see Katherine C. Little, *Confession and Resistance: Defining the Self in Late Medieval England* (Notre Dame: University of Notre Dame Press, 2006), 112–28.

13. Blyth, *Regiment*, 201. Derek Pearsall in "Hoccleve's *Regement of Princes*: The Poetics of Royal Self-Representation," *Speculum* 69 (1994): 386–410, argues that Henry saw the darkness of the *Regiment* as allowing him to appear a king who encouraged sober advice, suggesting that Henry's strategies of self-representation at a crucial moment in his career underlie this poem. For other noteworthy studies of those issues of vernacularity and Hoccleve's own self-representation in the *Regiment*, see David Lawton, "Dullness

and the Fifteenth Century," *ELH* 54 (1987): 761–99; Larry Scanlon, "The King's Two Voices: Narrative and Power in Hoccleve's *Regiment of Princes*," in *Literary Practice and Social Change in Britain, 1380–1530,* ed. Lee Patterson (Berkeley: University of California Press, 1990), 216–47; Robert J. Meyer-Lee, *Poets and Power from Chaucer to Wyatt* (Cambridge: Cambridge University Press 2007), 88–123. For a study of the ways in which history and intellectual, political, and cultural traditions are represented and refigured in the *Regiment,* thus creating a space for advisory discourse, see Nicholas Perkins, *Hoccleve's "Regiment of Princes": Counsel and Constraint* (Cambridge: D. S. Brewer, 2001).

14. For *Rechelessness,* see *Piers Plowman,* C-text, Passus 11–13; and the commentary in Derek Pearsall's edition, *William Langland: Piers Plowman,* beginning at 11.193.

15. For an exploration of the contemporary meaning of textual labor, see Ethan Knapp, "Poetic Work and Scribal Labor in Hoccleve and Langland," in *The Middle Ages at Work: Practicing Labor in Late Medieval England,* ed. Kellie Robertson and Michael Uebel (New York: Palgrave Macmillan, 2004), 209–28.

16. *Favel* means "flattery" in Middle English, but it was also a proper noun, denoting a flatterer or a deceiver. In *Piers Plowman* A: 2.23, Langland credits Favel, who of course, is related to the French courtier/horse, with making the marriage between Meed and False. See R. D. Cornelius, *"Piers Plowman* and the *Roman de Fauvel," PMLA* 47 (1932): 363–67; T. A. Yunck, *The Lineage of Lady Meed: The Development of Medieval Venality Satire* (Notre Dame: University of Notre Dame Press, 1963), 221–26.

17. Ethan Knapp (*The Bureaucratic Muse: Thomas Hoccleve and the Literature of Late Medieval England* [University Park: Pennsylvania State University Press, 2001], 80), sees the poem as a hybrid, the first part a begging poem, the second a mirror of princes. See pp. 83–93 for a discussion of the actual labor of scribal employment.

18. See Blyth, *Regiment,* 98, for a plate of the page that comes at the stanza beginning at 2017. In *Later Gothic Manuscripts, 1390–1490,* 2 vols. (London: Harvey Miller, 1996), 2:159, Kathleen L. Scott argues that this is a gift-giving scene rather than a donor portrait. Based on the arms depicted in this picture, the kneeling figure probably represents John Mowbray, Lord Mowbray and Segrave, later second duke of Norfolk. (Scott draws here on Kate Harris, "The Patron of BL MS Arundel 38," *Notes and Queries,* n.s., 31 [1984]: 462–63.) Pearsall, "Hoccleve's '*Regiment of Princes,'*" suggests that Henry himself was the patron for the *Regiment,* having the two extant deluxe copies of it made and sent to key figures he was courting for his own political legitimacy. Thus the "gift-giving" depicted in the miniature would entail Henry's receiving the homage of the recipient of a gift that, in turn, depicted Henry as the wise and sober king needed in such grave times.

19. Robert Avesbury remarks about the damage done to the French countryside by Edward III's invasion of September 1339. See Edward Maunde Thompson, ed., *Robertus de Avesbury de Gestis Mirabilibus Regis Edwardi Tertii*, Rolls Series 93 (London: HMSO, 1889; Wiesbaden: Kraus Reprint, 1965), 303.

20. On *PF* 211–94, see Robert A. Pratt, "Chaucer's Use of the *Teseida*," *PMLA* 62 (1947): 606.

21. For a study of Parliament in the late fourteenth century and its relevance to the literature of the same period, see Matthew Giancarlo, *Parliament and Literature in Late Medieval England* (Cambridge: Cambridge University Press, 2007), esp. 151–64.

22. On the *Knight's Tale*, see particularly Patterson, *Chaucer and the Subject of History*, 165–230; R. W. Hanning, "The Struggle between Noble Designs and Chaos: The Literary Tradition of Chaucer's Knight's Tale," in *Geoffrey Chaucer's "The Canterbury Tales": A Casebook*, ed. Lee Patterson (Oxford: Oxford University Press, 2007), 49–69; Robert R. Edwards, *Chaucer and Boccaccio: Antiquity and Modernity* (New York: Palgrave, 2002), 31–43.

23. Pratt, "Chaucer's Use of the *Teseida*," 613–20.

24. The two classic studies of medieval sermon literature are those of G. R. Owst: *Preaching in Medieval England*, esp. 222–78; and *Literature and Pulpit in Medieval England: A Neglected Chapter in the History of English Letters and of the English People* (Cambridge: Cambridge University Press, 1933). More recently, the work of Siegfried Wenzel has defined the field; see especially his edited volume, *Fasciculus Morum: A Fourteenth-Century Preacher's Handbook* (University Park: Pennsylvania State University Press, 1989); and *Macaronic Sermons: Bilingualism and Preaching in Late-Medieval England* (Ann Arbor: University of Michigan Press, 1994).

25. For discussion of the two texts and their author, see L. E. Boyle, "William of Pagula and the *Speculum Regis Edwardi III*," *Mediaeval Studies* 32 (1970): 329–36; James Tait, "On the Date and Authorship of the 'Speculum Regis Edwardi,'" *EHR* 16 (1901): 110–15. For the texts themselves, which Moisant labels Recension A and Recension B, see Joseph Moisant, *De Speculo Regis Edwardi III* (Paris: A. Picard, 1891). For a translation, see Nederman, *Political Thought in Early Fourteenth-Century England*, 73–139. In *Writing to the King*, 108–12, Matthews suggests that William intended to raise the specter of revolt as a means of chastening power. See also Wendy Scase, *Literature and Complaint in England, 1272–1553* (Oxford: Oxford University Press, 2007), 24.

26. Moisant here cites John of Salisbury, Thomas Aquinas, Bracton, and the *Song of Lewes*.

27. In *Literature and Complaint in England*, 31, Scase also notes William's use of *rapina*.

28. Cary J. Nederman, "Property and Protest: Political Theory and Subjective Rights in Fourteenth-Century England," *Review of Politics* 58 (1966): 323–44, esp. 334, 336, 338.

29. See Lynn Staley, "The Penitential Psalms: A Lexicon of Conversion from the Medieval to the Early Modern Period," *Journal of Medieval and Early Modern Studies* 37 (2007): 221–70. King John was made to say them by Innocent III.

30. Sandler, "Political Imagery in the Bohun Manuscripts." To John of Bridlington (1320–79) was attributed a collection of prophetic verses, to which was attached a prose commentary (ca. 1364) by John Ergome, which was dedicated to Humphrey of Bohun. See A. G. Rigg, "John of Bridlington's *Prophecy:* A New Look," *Speculum* 63 (1988): 596–613; Michael J. Curley, "John of Bridlington (c. 1320–1379)," in *DNB*. For both prophecy and commentary, see Thomas Wright, *Political Poems and Songs relating to English History . . . from the Accession of Edward III to that of Richard III* (London: HMSO, 1839; Nendeln: Kraus Reprint, 1965), 123–214. For a reference linking Edward to David, see pp. 171–72.

31. On the incident, see Roy Martin Haines, *Archbishop John Stratford: Political Revolutionary and Champion of the Liberties of the English Church, ca. 1275–1348* (Toronto: Pontifical Institute of Medieval Studies, 1986), 278–327. Haines provides a careful sequencing of events, which I follow below. For other important studies, see T. F. Tout, *Chapters in the Administrative History of Mediaeval England,* 6 vols. (Manchester: Manchester University Press, 1929; rpt. New York: Barnes and Noble, 1967), 3:100–112, 119–34; G. L. Harriss, *King, Parliament and Public Finance in Medieval England to 1369* (Oxford: Oxford University Press, 1975), esp. 266–304; W. M. Ormrod, *Edward III* (New Haven: Yale University Press, 2011), 229–39. See also Ormrod, *The Reign of Edward III,* 121–44, on Edward's relations with the clergy. In *Literature and Complaint,* 60–61, Scase considers these events from the perspective of the legal skirmishing by Stratford and the king, both of whom employed the written complaint as a rhetorical strategy.

32. H. Wharton, ed., *Anglia Sacra,* 2 vols. (1691; rpt. Westmead: Gregg International, 1969), 1:23–36; Edward Maunde Thompson, ed., *Robertus de Avesbury de Gestis Mirabilibus Regis Edwardi Tertii,* Rolls Series 93 (London: HMSO; Wiesbaden: Kraus Reprint, 1965), 323–39; Thomas Rymer, ed., *Foedera,* searchable text ed. (London, 1821; Ontario, CA: Tanner Ritchie, 2006), vol. 2, pt. 2, 1143–55; *The Parliament Rolls of Medieval England,* ed. C. Given-Wilson, Scholarly Digital Editions and the National Archives (Leicester, 2005), v. Edward III; G. G. Aungier, *Croniques de London,* Camden Society 28 (1845): 84–90. See also W. M. Ormrod, "Avesbury, Robert (d. 1359)," in *DNB*. As Ormrod notes, Avesbury had access to original texts. There is also a provocative account in Fabyan's *Chronicle,* 447–54.

33. Wharton, *Anglia Sacra,* 21.

34. Wharton, *Anglia Sacra,* 22.

35. Thompson, ed., *Robertus de Avesbury de Gestis Mirabilibus Regis Edwardi Tertii,* 324–27; Rymer, *Foedera,* vol. 2, pt. 2, 1143.

36. In Wharton, *Angli Sacra*, 23–27; Thompson, ed., *Robertus de Avesbury de Gestis Mirabilibus Regis Edwardi Tertii*, 330–36; Rymer, *Foedera*, vol. 2, pt. 2, 1147–48. See Chris Given-Wilson's analysis of the April 1341 Parliament in *The Parliament Rolls of Medieval England*.

37. Wharton, *Anglia Sacra*, 23.

38. Wharton, *Anglia Sacra*, 27–36.

39. For the letter to Stratford, see Wharton, *Anglia Sacra*, 36–38; for that to the pope, see Rymer, *Foedera*, vol. 2, pt. 2, 1152–53.

40. Haines, *Archbishop John Stratford*, 323–24.

41. A. K. McHardy, "Some Reflections on Edward III's Use of Propaganda," in *The Age of Edward III*, ed. J. S. Bothwell (York: York Medieval Press, 2001), 171–92.

42. Thompson, ed., *Adam of Murimuth, Continuatio Chronicarum*, 119–20. For discussion, see Harriss, *King, Parliament, and Public Finance*, 300–308; Given-Wilson, *The Parliament Rolls of Medieval England*, introduction, for 1341.

43. Nancy Mason Bradbury has argued that we should see romances like *Havelok* as having a prior and vigorous existence in oral tradition, or in the legends that make up local tradition, thus as not necessarily having written "source texts." For her very careful argument, see "The Traditional Origins of *Havelok the Dane*," *SP* 90 (1995): 115–42. See also Derek Pearsall, "The Development of Middle English Romance," *MS* 27 (1965): 98.

44. Diane Speed, "The Saracens of *King Horn*," *Speculum* 65 (1990): 564–95. For a study of both poems in relation to England's history and baronial ideology, see Susan Crane, *Insular Romance: Politics, Faith, and Culture in Anglo-Norman and Middle English Literature* (Berkeley: University of California Press, 1986), 13–52. All in-text citations from both poems refer to Ronald B. Herzman, Graham Drake, and Eve Salisbury, eds., *Four Romances of England: King Horn, Havelok the Dane, Bevis of Hampton, Athelston*, TEAMS Middle English Texts (Kalamazoo, MI: Medieval Institute Publications, 1999). See also Mildred Katharine Pope, ed., *Thomas, The Romance of Horn*, *ANTS* 9, 10, 12, 13; G. V. Smithers, ed., *Havelock* (Oxford: Clarendon Press, 1982). For further manuscript information about both texts, see Ruth J. Dean, *Anglo-Norman Literature: A Guide to Texts and Manuscripts* (London: Anglo-Norman Text Society, 1999), 88–89. For the Auchinleck manuscript, see http://digital.nls.uk/auchinleck/.

45. See Herzman, Drake, and Salisbury, *Four Romances of England*, 72.

46. For a study of *King Horn* in relation to Horn's psychological development, see J. M. Hill, "An Interpretation of *King Horn*," *Anglia* 75 (1957): 157–72.

47. Crane, *Insular Romance*, 40. For another study of the integrity of *Havelok*'s construction, see R. W. Hanning, "*Havelok the Dane*: Structure, Symbols, Meaning," *SP* 64 (1967): 586–605. Smithers (*Havelok*, lvii) links

Havelok to the Danish Cnut by the poem's emphasis on Havelok's lawful right to rule England as Goldeboru's husband.

48. See Alexander Bell, ed., *Le Lai d'Haveloc and Gaimar's Haveloc Episode* (Manchester: Manchester University Press, 1925), Estoire, 400–432; *lai*, 193–234. See Bell's introduction for work on the relationship of the two texts, as well as on the relationship between written texts and local legends or preexisting oral traditions. Hanning discusses this change as balancing the account of Goldeboru's childhood with that of Havelok (589).

49. William of Malmesbury, *GRA*, ii.122.

50. Cnut, of course, married Emma, wife of Æthelred the Unready, the former English king. See the introduction to *Havelok* for discussion of the hero's body as a symbol of his political strength.

51. See Hanning, *"Havelok the Dane,"* 601, for discussion of the differences between the English and French versions of this dream. Hanning sees the dream as emphasizing Havelok's power. In the French versions (*Estoire*, 195–290; *lai*, 397–484) Goldeboru (Argentille) has the dream, which she does not understand, and Havelok misinterprets it as looking forward to the feast attended by the king and his barons.

52. Butterfield's assertion throughout *The Familiar Enemy* that we should see a mutually nourishing tradition of Britain's French and English texts is apposite here. For remarks regarding Bodleian MS Laud Misc.108, see Herzman, Drake, and Salisbury, eds., *Four Romances of England*, 79–80.

53. On the Auchinleck manuscript, see Turville-Petre, *England the Nation*, 134–38; Ralph Hanna, "Reconsidering the Auchinleck Manuscript," in *New Directions in Later Medieval Manuscript Studies: Essays from the 1998 Harvard Conference*, ed. Derek Pearsall (York: York Medieval Press, 2000), 91–102; Staley, *Languages of Power*, 308–9, 311–16; http://digital.nls.uk/auchinleck/editorial/importance.html. For MS Harley 2253, see Susanna Fein, ed., *Studies in the Harley Manuscript: The Scribes, Contents, and Social Contexts of British Library MS Harley 2253* (Kalamazoo, MI: Medieval Institute Publications, 2000).

54. In *English and International: Studies in the Literature, Art and Patronage of Medieval England*, ed. Derek Pearsall and Nicolette Zeeman (Cambridge: Cambridge University Press, 1988), 159, 163–64, Elizabeth Salter links "The Simonie," to *Piers Plowman*. More recently, Scase, *Literature and Complaint*, 33–62, has considered the early and mid-fourteenth-century vernacular poetry of social protest in relation to the evolution of the judicial process of complaint. Matthews, in *Writing to the King*, 116–29, analyzes these poems in terms of their imagined communities, political focus, and perceptions of England as a failed or destroyed community.

55. For discussion of "The Simonie," see Dean, *Medieval English Political Writings*, 180–82; for the text, see 193–212. Dean's edition follows the Auchinleck version, which is incomplete, supplemented by the text to be

found in Bodley 48. Dean has also regularized spelling. For the three extant versions of "The Simonie," along with comments about each text and its provenance, see Dan Embree and Elizabeth Urquhart, *The Simonie: A Parallel-Text Edition* (Heidelberg: Carl Winter, 1991). I have written about this poem in *Languages of Power*, 319–20.

56. For the "Song of the Husbandman," see Dean, *Medieval English Political Writings*, 251–53. See also Wright, *Political Poems and Songs relating to English History*, 149–52. For "Trailbaston," see Isabel Aspin, ed., *Anglo-Norman Political Songs* (Oxford: Anglo-Norman Text Society, 1953), 67–78. In addition to remarks by Scase and Matthews noted above, on these poems, see John Scattergood, "Authority and Resistance: the Political Verse," in Fein, *Studies in the Harley Manuscript*, 163–202; and Richard Newhauser, "Historicity and Complaint in *Song of the Husbandman*," in Fein, *Studies in the Harley Manuscript*, 203–18.

57. For further discussion of the poem and the abuses of Trailbaston, see Richard Firth Green, *A Crisis of Truth: Literature and Law in Ricardian England* (Philadelphia: University of Pennsylvania Press, 1999), 171–75. I am following Aspin's translation for the most part.

58. Matthews, *Writing to the King*, 117, describes the speaker of "Trailbaston" as a Robin Hood without agency.

59. For the texts and discussion, see Stephen Knight and Thomas Ohlgren, eds., *Robin Hood and Other Outlaw Tales* (Kalamazoo, MI: Medieval Institute Publications, 2000). The bibliographies in this edition are excellent, but see particularly R. H. Hilton, "The Origins of Robin Hood," *Past and Present* 14 (1958): 30–44; J. C. Holt, *Robin Hood* (London: Thames and Hudson, 1982), esp. 15–39.

60. J. R. Maddicott, "The Birth and Setting of the Ballads of Robin Hood," *EHR* 93 (1978): 276–99; Knight and Ohlgreen, *Robin Hood and Other Outlaw Tales*, 81.

61. See Colin Richmond, "An Outlaw and Some Peasants: The Possible Significance of Robin Hood," *Nottingham Medieval Studies* 37 (1993): 90–101, for an argument that as a yeoman Robin enacts a critique of chivalric values. While studies of Robin Hood see the tales as suspicious of the values of townsfolk, the many points of similarity between the world of the forest and that of the town suggest a subtler probing of identity.

62. Knight and Ohlgreen, *Robin Hood and Other Outlaw Tales*, 31, suggest that while the phrase "oure cumly kyng" (line 331) has been thought to refer to Edward IV, it was certainly used of Edward III, and the errors in copying could suggest an earlier text that had been transmitted several times.

63. See Aspin, *Anglo-Norman Political Songs*, 105–15.

64. For further background, see T. F. Tout, *The Place of the Reign of Edward II in English History*, 2nd ed. rev. Hilda Johnstone (Manchester: Manchester University Press, 1936), 28–31. Tout discusses the ways in which

Edward tried to break baronial power by summoning gentry and merchant; once begun, it was not to be undone. See also C. L. Kingsford, ed., *The Song of Lewes* (Oxford: Clarendon Press, 1890), for an argument linking the poem to a program of constitutional reform.

65. For the text, see Wright, *English Political Songs*, 125–27.

66. In Wright, *English Political Songs*, 249–50.

67. George Woodbine, ed., Samuel E. Thorne, trans., *De legibus et consuetudinibus Angliae (On the Laws and Customs of England)* attributed to Henry of Bratton, Bracton On-Line, vol. 2, p. 19: "cum legis vigorem habeat quidquid de consilio et consensu magnatum et rei publicæ communi sponsione, auctoritate regis sive principis præcedente, iuste fuerit definitum et approbatum."

68. Woodbine, ed., *On the Laws and Customs of England*, vol. 2, p. 33, "Sic ergo rex, ne potestas sua maneat infrenata."

69. Here Scase, *Literature and Complaint*, 5–41, provides excellent background.

70. McHardy, "Some Reflections on Edward III's Use of Propaganda." See, for example, Thomas Duffus Hardy, *Syllabus (in English) of the documents relating to England and other kingdoms contained in the collection known as "Rymer's Foedera,"* 3 vols. (London: Longmans, Green, 1869–85), vol. 1. On 10 February 1341, Edward ordered churchmen to cease fulminating against collectors of sheaves and to publish an account of the archbishop of Canterbury's crimes; on 31 March 1341, Edward ordered the bishop of London to publish letters justifying the king's conduct toward the archbishop of Canterbury. On 20 August 1342, Edward directed the archbishop of Canterbury to offer prayers. On 15 March 1346, Edward ordered the provincial of the Friar Preachers and the prior of St. Augustine's to explain to the people the king's title to the French crown and the reasons for the war. On 3 August 1346, the king ordered the archbishop of Canterbury and the archbishop of York to offer prayers of thanksgiving for the king's army's landing in Normandy.

71. Juliet Vale, *Edward III and Chivalry: Chivalric Society and Its Context, 1270–1350* (Woodbridge: Boydell Press, 1982), 57–75; Appendix 12, 172–74. The list stops with the year 1357. See the continuation in Julian Munby, Richard Barber, and Richard Brown, *Edward III's Round Table at Windsor: The House of the Round Table and the Windsor Festival of 1344* (Woodbridge: Boydell Press, 2007), 35.

72. For dating, see Ian Mortimer, *The Greatest Traitor: The Life of Sir Roger Mortimer, Ruler of England, 1327–1330* (New York: Thomas Dunne Books, 2006), 297.

73. See Hardy, *Syllabus*, vol. 1, for 7 December 1327; 30 April 1322; 2 June 1329; 12 July 1330; 8 October 1331; 13 February 1334; 10 October 1340; 5 February 1341; 26 May 1341; 4 November 1343; 29 January 1344; 3 May 1348; 18 July 1354. On 10 February 1344, a license was granted for

an annual tournament to be held at Lincoln on the Monday after St. John's birthday of which the earl of Derby was to be captain.

74. For the history of Windsor, see W. H. St. John Hope, *Windsor Castle: An Architectural History* (London: Offices of Country Life, 1913), 3 vols.; Nigel Saul, ed., *St. George's Chapel Windsor in the Fourteenth Century* (Woodbridge: Boydell Press, 2005); Munby, Barber, and Brown, *Edward III's Round Table at Windsor*. For St. Stephen's Chapel, see, first, Emily Howe, "Divine Kingship and Dynastic Display: The Altar Wall Murals of St. Stephen's Chapel, Westminster," *Antiquarian Journal* 81 (2001): 259–303. This essay offers a valuable history of the large literature on the chapel. For that history, see John Thomas Smith, *Antiquities of the City of Westminster: The Old Palace; St. Stephen's Chapel* (London: T. Bensley, 1807); John Topham, *An Account of the Collegiate Chapel of Saint Stephen at Westminster* (London: Simpkin & Marshall, 1834); Edward Wedlake Brayley and John Britton, *The History of the Ancient Palace and Late Houses of Parliament at Westminster* (London: John Weale, 1836); C. L Kingsford, "Our Lady of the Pew, the King's Oratory or Chapel in the Palace of Westminster," *Archaeologia* 68 (1916–17): 1–20; Maurice Hastings, *St. Stephen's Chapel and Its Place in the Development of Perpendicular Style in England* (Cambridge: Cambridge University Press, 1955); E. W. Tristram, *English Wall Paintings of the Fourteenth Century* (London: Routledge and Kegan Paul, 1955); Howard Colvin, *The History of the King's Works*, 6 vols. (London: HMSO, 1963–73), vol. 1: *The Middle Ages*, 516; Andrew Martindale, "St. Stephen's Chapel, Westminster, and the Italian Experience," in *Studies in Medieval Art and Architecture presented to Peter Lasko*, ed. David Buckton and T. A. Heslop (Dover, NH: Alan Sutton, 1994), 102–12.

75. On Edward's political victory, see Ormrod, *The Reign of Edward III*, 16–26.

76. For accounts, see Thompson, *Adam of Murimuth, Continuato Chronicarum*, 155–56 (quotation, p. 156) and 231–32; Vale, *Edward III and Chivalry*, 77; St. John Hope, *Windsor Castle*, 1:111–28. Froissart conflates the tournament of the Round Table with the founding of the Order of the Garter; see *The Chronicle of Froissart translated out of French by Sir John Bourchier Lord Berners, 1523–25*, introd. William Paton Ker, 6 vols. (London, 1901; rpt. New York: AMS Press, 1967), 1:232–33. See also Julian Munby, "Carpentry Works for Edward III at Windsor Castle," in Saul, *St. George's Chapel Windsor*, 225–38, esp 227–28; Munby, Barber, and Brown, *Edward III's Round Table*, xi, 38–43.

77. Vale, *Edward III and Chivalry*, 83. See also Dugdale, *Monasticon*, vol. 6.3:1353–54.

78. See Howe, "Divine Kingship"; Binski, *Westminster Abbey and the Plantagenets*, 182–85.

79. Thompson, *Adam of Murimuth, Continuatio Chronicarum*, 155–56; Jules Viard and Eugène Déprez, eds., *Chronique de Jean le Bel*, 2 vols. (Paris: Librairie Renouard, 1904), 2:26; Vale, *Edward III and Chivalry*, 76–77.

80. Munby, Barber, and Brown, *Edward III's Round Table*, 79.

81. On French kingship, see Colette Beaune, *The Birth of an Ideology: Myths and Symbols of Nation in Late Medieval France*, trans. Susan Ross Hudson (Berkeley: University of California Press, 1991). In Saul, *St. George's Chapel Windsor*, see D. A. L. Morgan, "The Banner-bearer of Christ and Our Lady's Knight: How God Became an Englishman Revisited," 51–62, for the invention of the English St. George; and W. M. Ormrod, "For Arthur and St. George: Edward III, Windsor Castle and the Order of the Garter," 13–34. Ormrod suggests that this was an impulsive move on Edward's part.

82. Hope, *Windsor Castle*, 2:139; W. M. Ormrod, "The Personal Religion of Edward III," *Speculum* 64 (1989): 865–66, 876.

83. See Howe, "Divine Kingship and Dynastic Display," for a detailed description. My thanks to the Society of Antiquaries for making available to me the paintings of the murals made by T. Smith, ca. 1800–1807.

84. Described by Smith, cited in Howe, "Divine Kingship and Dynastic Display," 280.

85. Binski, *Westminster Abbey and the Plantagenets*, 183; Binski also notes Edward's devotion to the Three Kings. Howe, "Divine Kingship and Dynastic Display," 283–84, links the ornamentation of the casket carried by one of the kings to metalwork associated with Edward III.

86. For Saint George, see Morgan, "The Banner-Bearer of Christ and Our Lady's Knight," in Saul, *St. George's Chapel Windsor*, 51–62; Ormrod, "The Personal Religion of Edward III," 859 n. 61.

87. Ormrod, "The Personal Religion of Edward III," 857; Howe, "Divine Kingship and Dynastic Display," 285.

88. Miri Rubin, *Mother of God: A History of the Virgin Mary* (New Haven: Yale University Press, 2009), 285–89.

89. This chapel has been the subject of a good deal of speculation. Smith (*Antiquities of Westminster*, 123) says the chapel was on the south side of St. Stephen's. Kingsford ("Our Lady of the Pew") describes it as a separate structure attached to the Chapel of St. Stephen's, the lower level of which was dedicated to the Virgin, by a cloister. Hastings (*St. Stephen's Chapel*, 74–76) identifies it with the king's pew in St. Stephen's, a pew, or closet, that contained an image of the Virgin and an altar, from which he could also see the altar in St. Stephen's.

90. See Howe, "Divine Kingship and Dynastic Display," 284. For the Latin, see Dugdale, *Monasticon*, 6.3:1349–50; Colvin, *The History of the King's Works*, 1:510–25, *Plans*, Westminster; Kingsford, "Our Lady of the Pew," 2–9.

91. The dating here is Colvin's, *History of the King's Works*, 1:518–19. Tristram dated the paintings from 1350–51, saying that large payments to painters and for materials ceased at this time. See Tristram, *English Wall Paintings of the Fourteenth Century*, 48. Martindale, "St. Stephen's Chapel, West-

minster, and the Italian Experience," 103, citing Colvin 1:522, says that the painting is documented from 1351–63.

92. Martindale, "St. Stephen's Chapel Westminster," 104.

93. Binski, *The Painted Chamber at Westminster*, 71–103.

94. Binski, *The Painted Chamber at Westminster*, 103.

95. Binski, *Westminster Abbey*, 184, makes this point also, suggesting that we might look to the page layouts of picture Bibles for precedents for the dense compositions of text and picture.

96. Martindale, "St. Stephen's Chapel Westminster," 108.

97. Another account of the windows before they were destroyed says that they were illuminated with the stories of Adam and Eve, of Noah and his family, and of Abraham. John Topham, *Some Account of the Collegiate Chapel of Saint Stephen, Westminster* (London: Society of Antiquaries, 1975 and 1811), quoted by Martindale, "St. Stephen's Chapel Westminster," 111–12.

98. Job's children in Alexander and Binski, *Age of Chivalry*, n. 680.

99. See Horrox, *The Black Death*, 112, 120, 121, for references to Nineveh in calls for prayers and a plague mass included in the Sarum rite. Millard Meiss linked the stories of Job and Tobit to a preoccupation with patience in suffering occasioned by the plague; see *Painting in Florence and Sienna after the Black Death* (Princeton: Princeton University Press, 1951), 68.

100. W. M. Ormrod, "The English Government and the Black Death of 1348–49," in Ormrod, *England in the Fourteenth Century*, 175–88; W. M. Ormrod, "The Politics of Pestilence: Government in England after the Black Death," in *The Black Death in England*, ed. W. M. Ormrod and P. G. Lindley (Stamford: Paul Watkins, 1996), 147–81; Binski, *Westminster Abbey*, 185. The Ordinance of Laborers (1349) begins with the recognition that the many deaths from the plague have made servants scarce. The Ordinance and later the Statute of Laborers attempt to meet this scarcity by seeking to freeze England in preplague economics.

101. See Sharpe, *Sir Robert Cotton*, 74, 80–83.

102. Kingsford, "Our Lady of the Pew." Hastings, *St. Stephen's Chapel*, 75–77, notes that Richard visited it before meeting Wat Tyler and gives further information about its history.

103. Ormrod, "The Personal Religion of Edward III," 876, notes that the canons of St. Stephen's considered it a pilgrimage site, as was the Sainte-Chapelle.

104. See Ginsberg, *Wynnere and Wastoure and The Parlement of the Thre Ages*, introduction, 2–3.

105. See Staley, *Languages of Power*, fig. 1 and pp. 91, 222, 302, for the frontispiece and discussion of the poem.

106. Hanna, *London Literature*, 262; Smith, *Arts of Possession*, 72–107.

107. Pearsall, *William Langland: Piers Plowman*, 43 n. 1; Pearsall also mentions *Wynnere and Wastoure*.

108. Hanna, *London Literature*, 254.

109. See the accounts of the arrival of the pestilence in England collected in Horrox, *The Black Death*, 62–82. The writers describe the pestilence as first breaking out in the East and later arriving in Europe, then in England, where it first attacked in Bristol, a port city, and spread from there. What begins as foreign becomes quickly naturalized throughout the island.

110. Lumby, *Polychonicon*, 8: 344/345.

111. Lumby, *Polychronicon*, 8: 411.

112. From the *Historia Roffensis*, cited by Horrox, *The Black Death*, 73.

113. Brie, *Brut*, pt. 2, pp. 303, 314.

114. Dugdale, *Monasticon*, VI,1:6–9; Caroline M. Barron, *London in the Later Middle Ages: Government and People, 1200–1500* (Oxford: Oxford University Press, 2004), 240.

F O U R   *Susanna and Her Garden*

1. Kathryn A. Smith, "Inventing Marital Chastity: Iconography of Susanna," *Oxford Art Journal* 16 (1993): 3.

2. See Tertullian, "De Corona," *PL* 2: 81; Ambrose, "De Joseph," *PL* 14: 652; "De Tobia," *PL* 14: 789; and "De Viduis," *PL* 16: 242; Augustine, "Sermo CCCXLIII: De Susanna et Joseph," *PL* 39: 1505–10; Abelard, "Sermo XXIX: De Sancta Susanna, ad hortationem virginum," *PL* 178: 555–64.

BL MS Additional 10596, a fifteenth-century English manuscript owned by Matilde Hoyle, a nun of Barking, contains a separate recension of the later Wycliffite version titled "A Pistle of Holy Susanna, danyell xiii c." For discussion of this manuscript, see Mary C. Erler, *Women, Reading, and Piety in Late Medieval England* (Cambridge: Cambridge University Press, 2002), 4. For another poem about Susanna, possibly of English provenance, see Jane Stevenson, *Latin Poets: Language, Gender, and Authority from Antiquity to the Eighteenth Century* (Oxford: Oxford University Press, 2005), 130–37. This poem was written by an "abbess Wiltrudis," possibly either an eleventh-century German nun or a twelfth-century English nun from Wilton. For important uses of Susanna in thirteenth-century manuscript culture, see Claire Donovan, *The de Brailes Hours: Shaping the Book of Hours in Thirteenth-Century Oxford* (Toronto: University of Toronto Press, 1991), 24, 25, 116–21. See also Marie-Louise Fabre, *Suzanne ou les avatars d'un motif biblique* (Paris: L'Harmatton, 2000).

3. See Bernard, *In Festo Annuntiationis Beatae Mariae Virginis*, Sermo III, "De muliere adultera; de Susanna; de B. Maria," *PL* 183: 393–98.

4. See Hildegard of Bingen, "Vita sanctae Hildegardis," *PL* 197, col. 113.

5. James P. Carley, *The Books of King Henry VIII and His Wives*, pref. David Starkey (London: British Library, 2004), 123.

6. For Susanna as a type of Christ, see Ambrose, "In Psalmum XXXVII Enarratio," *PL* 14: 1033; and *Expositio Evangelii Secundum Lucam*, *PL* 15: 1828; and see Catherine Brown Tkacz's informative essay, "Susanna as a Type of Christ," *Studies in Iconography* 20 (1999): 101–53. For Susanna as the subject of Latin poetry, see J. H. Mozley, ed., "Susanna and the Elders. Three Medieval Poems," *Studi Medievali*, n.s., 3 (1930): 27–52; Stevenson, *Latin Poets*, 130–38; F. J. E. Raby, ed., *Poems of John of Hoveden*, Publications of the Surtees Society 154 (1939): xlvii, 241.

7. Genevra Kornbluth, *Engraved Gems of the Carolingian Empire* (University Park: Pennsylvania State University Press, 1995), 43–48. Kornbluth's remarks apply to the Susanna Crystal, now in the British Museum.

8. Philippe Buc, "The Book of Kings: Nicholas of Lyra's Mirror of Princes," in Philip Krey and Lesley Smith, *Nicholas of Lyra: The Senses of Scripture* (Boston: Brill, 2000), 89.

9. Shelley Lockwood, ed., *Sir John Fortescue: On the Laws and Governance of England* (Cambridge: Cambridge University Press, 1997).

10. See my *Languages of Power*, chap. 4.

11. Anatole de Montaiglon, ed., *Le livre du Chevalier de la Tour Landry* (Paris: Jannet, 1854), 191. Caxton's rubric reads: "How god taketh in his kepynge them that haue fyaunce and truste in hym." See M. Y. Offord., ed., *The Book of the Knight of the Tower*, trans. William Caxton (London: Oxford University Press, 1971), 130.

12. Offord, *The Book of the Knight of the Tower*, 131. Caxton here is slightly less emphatic than the Knight of Tour Landry, who offers an even greater focus on marriage as a bond like that between the soul and God· "Et pour ce toute bonne femme doit tousjours espérer en Dieu, et, pour l'amour de lui et l'amour de son mariage, soy garder de perilz et ne de pechier si grandement ne si vilment comme enffraindre son serement et sa bonne loy" (192–93).

13. Georgine E. Brereton and Janet M. Ferrier, eds., *Le Menagier de Paris* (Oxford: Clarendon Press, 1981), 47–51.

14. For this text, see Joan B. Williamson, ed., *Philippe de Mézières: Le Livre de la Vertu du Sacrement de Mariage* (Washington, DC: Catholic University of America Press, 1993). I have discussed this work in *Languages of Power*, 282–85.

15. Pierre Bersuire, *Reductorium Morale Super Totam Bibliam* (Venice, 1633), 206.

16. Giovanni Boccaccio, *Famous Women*, ed. and trans. Virginia Brown (Cambridge, MA: Harvard University Press, 2001), 42:17. For an exploration of three late-sixteenth-century Spanish dramas recounting Susanna's story,

see Robert L. Hathaway, "Dramaturgic Variation in the Pre-Lopean Theatre: Susanna and the Elders," *Bulletin of the Comediantes* 43 (1991): 109–31.

17. Christine de Pizan, *The Book of the City of Ladies*, trans. Earl Jeffrey Richards (New York: Persea Books, 1982), II: 37.1.

18. In J. H. Burns, ed., *The Cambridge History of Medieval Political Thought, c. 350–1450* (Cambridge: Cambridge University Press, 1988), see J. Canning, "Law, Sovereignty and Corporation Theory, 1300–1450," 454–76; and Jean Dunbabin, "Government," 477–519. See also W. Ullman, *Principles of Government and Politics in the Middle Ages* (New York: Barnes and Noble, 1961), chap. 4; H. G. Richardson, "The Coronation in Medieval England: The Evolution of the Office and the Oath," *Traditio* 16 (1960): 111–203; W. L. Warren, *King John* (Berkeley: University of California Press, 1961), 174–240; Staley, *Languages of Power*, 81–95.

19. See Paul Strohm, *England's Empty Throne: Usurpation and the Language of Legitimation, 1399–1422* (New Haven: Yale University Press, 1998), 139–41; David Aers, *Sanctifying Signs: Making Christian Tradition in Late Medieval England* (Notre Dame: University of Notre Dame Press, 2004), 53–66; Staley, *Languages of Power*, 95–101.

20. *Catalogue of Romances in the Department of Manuscripts in the British Museum* (London, 1808), 2:748, 401–2, 669–71; 3:503–9. My thanks to Elaine Pordes of the British Library for her helpfulness.

21. For Alan, see Marie Lovatt, ed., *English Episcopal Acta, 27, York, 1189–1212* (Oxford: Oxford University Press, 2004), lxxxii–lxxxiv, ci; Arthur Francis Leach, ed., *Memorials of Beverley Minster: The Chapter Act Book of the Collegiate Church of St. John of Beverley, A.D. 1286–1347*, Surtees Society 98 (1898); William Page, *Victoria County History of Yorkshire*, 3 vols. (London: A. Constable and Co., 1907–13), 3:354. Mozeley, "Susanna and the Elders," 28, accepts this identification.

22. On the provostship, see Richard T. W. McDermid, *Beverley Minster Fasti, Yorkshire Archaeological Society Record Series* 149 (1993 for 1990): 1–5. The provost of Beverley received revenues from the Abbey of Melsa. For the history of Melsa, see Edward A. Bond, ed., *Chronica Monasterii de Melsa a fundatione usque ad annum 1396*, 3 vols. (London: Longmans, Green, Reader, and Dyer, 1866).

For the history of Fountains, see William Dugdale, *Monasticon Anglicanum*, vol. 5, 286–314; Hugh of Kirkstall, "Narratio de fundatione Fontanis Monasterii," in *Memorials of the Abbey of St. Mary of Fountains*, vol. 1, ed. John Richard Walbran, James Raine, and J. T. Fowler, Publications of the Surtees Society 42 (1862): 1–129. For documents recording early Cistercian ideals, see M.-Anselme Dimier, "Un Témoin Tardif Peu Connu du Conflit entre Cisterciens et Clunisiens," in *Peter the Venerable, 1156–1956: Studies and Texts Commemorating the Eighth Centenary of His Death*, ed. Giles Constable and James Kritzeck, Studia Anselmiana 40 (Rome: Herder, 1956), 81–90; David

Knowles, *Great Historical Enterprises: Problems in Monastic History* (London: Nelson, 1964), 199–224.

For Melsa, see Page, *Victoria County History of Yorkshire*, 3:135.

23. Dugdale, *Monasticon*, 5:219.

24. Lumby, *Polychronicon*, 7:400/401. Higden misdates the founding to 1135.

25. For this account, I am indebted to Bennett D. Hill, *English Cistercian Monasteries and Their Patrons in the Twelfth Century* (Urbana: University of Illinois Press, 1968), 15–64. See also R. H. C. Davis, *King Stephen, 1135–1154* (Berkeley: University of California Press, 1967), 98–106, who notes the importance of the Cistercians for the anti-Canterbury leanings of the northern church, as well as for its antiroyalist sentiments. Pierre-André Burton, "Aux origenes de l'expansion anglaise de Cîteaux. La fondation de Rievaulx et la conversion d'Aelred: 1128–1134," *Collectanea cisterciensia* 61 (1999): 186–214, argues that Bernard of Clairvaux persuaded Henry I to bring the Cistercians to England as part of an effort to pacify and Normanize the realm.

26. Hill, *English Cistercian Monasteries*, 40, 62.

27. For Melsa and its financial problems, see Bond, *Chronica Monasterii de Melsa*, 1:289, 328, 342–43, 344–46; Joan Wardrop, *Fountains Abbey and Its Benefactors*, Cistercian Studies Series 91 (Kalamazoo, MI: Cistercian Publications, 1987), 18–20.

28. See C. R. Cheney, "King John and the Papal Interdict," *Bulletin of the John Rylands Library* 31 (1948): 295–317; C. R. Cheney, "King John's Reaction to the Interdict on England," *Transactions of the Royal Historical Society*, 4th ser., 31 (1949): 129–50; J. C. Holt, *The Northerners: A Study in the Reign of King John* (Oxford: Clarendon Press, 1961), 147, 166–70; Sidney Painter, *The Reign of King John* (Baltimore: Johns Hopkins University Press, 1949), 155–202; Ralph V. Turner, *The English Judiciary in the Age of Glanvill and Bracton, c. 1176–1239* (Cambridge: Cambridge University Press, 1985), 158–62; Ralph V. Turner, *Magna Carta through the Ages* (London: Pearson, Longman, 2003), 39–49, Warren, *King John*, 173. For a contemporary account, see the *Historia Rerum Anglicarum of William of Newburgh*, in Howlett, *Chronicles of the Reigns of Stephen, Henry II, and Richard I*, 1:509, 511.

29. Holt, *The Northerners*, 204.

30. Lovatt, *English Episcopal Acta*, notes that Alan witnessed two-thirds of the *acta* of Geoffrey for which witness lists survive (ci). Under John, justice was firmly tied to the king, who could behave unspeakably when opposed. Greedy and ruthless, he gouged both the clergy and the nobility, turning in 1213 to the Jews in Yorkshire and Lincolnshire as possible sources of added income (Turner, *Magna Carta*, 43, 47; Holt, *The Northerners*, 169).

31. See Warren, *King John*, 207–16, for an analysis of the situation.

32. Peasants are mentioned, but it is, of course, a baronial document. See Warren, *King John*, 232–40; F. M. Powicke, *Stephen Langton: The Ford*

Lectures delivered in the University of Oxford in Hilary Term 1927 (Oxford: Clarendon Press, 1928), 102–27; Turner, *Magna Carta*.

33. See Knowles, *Great Historical Enterprises*, which explains the issues very well.

34. Newman, *The Boundaries of Charity*, 16–23. For contemporary accounts describing the intensity of the Cistercian vocation, see Jean LeClercq, "Lettres de vocation à la vie monastique," *Analecta Monastica*, 3rd ser., *Studia Anselmiana* 37 (1955): 172–89; "La Collection des lettres d'Yves de Chartres," *Revue Bénédictine* 56 (1945–46): 123–25; C. H. Talbot, "Letters of Vocation by Roger, Abbot of Byland," *Analecta Sacri Ordinis Cisterciensis* 7 (1951): 218–31.

35. See A. Wilmart, "Les mélanges de Matthieu Préchantre de Rievaulx au début du XIIIe siècle," *Revue Bénédictine* 52 (1940): 15–84; LeClercq, "Lettres de vocation," 173–79. The manuscript is Bibl. Nat. 15157. Wilmart (15 n.1) describes the letters of Matthew of Rievaulx as copied by one hand and corrected by two contemporary revisers, probably against an original English archtype. Wilmart notes his belief that these revisers were English, since they added a supplement (fol. 130–35), now mutilated, that contains some poems concerning Rievaulx. For these, see Wilmart, "Les mélanges," 48–51.

36. See Wilmart, "Les mélanges," 40–41, who notes that they take up folios 89v–97. In his numbering of the items in the manuscript, the letters are 63, 64, and 65. Megan Cassidy-Welch (*Monastic Spaces and Their Meanings: Thirteenth-Century English Cistercian Monasteries* [Turnholt: Brepols, 2001], 65–66), discusses Matthew of Rievaulx's letters as capturing the Cistercian language of paradisial space.

37. For this letter, see LeClercq, "Lettres de vocation," 175–77. This first letter is no. 63 in Wilmart's numbering.

38. The second letter is edited in Wilmart, "Les mélanges," 72–74.

39. LeClercq, "Lettres de vocation," 177–79.

40. See Wilmart, "Les mélanges," 69–70.

41. Wilmart, "Les mélanges," 38. Wilmart notes that this letter, whose addressee is unknown, was probably written to another monk in some sort of difficulty.

42. Bernard, *In Festo Annuntiationis*, discusses Susanna. See also Thomas the Cistercian in his commentary on the Canticles (*PL* 206: 41, 117) and Gunther the Cistercian in *De Oratione Jejunio et Eleemosyna* (*PL* 212: 169).

43. For Willetrudis, see Stevenson, *Latin Poets*, 130–37. Stevenson also mentions Peter Riga and Alan of Melsa. Her suggestion that Willetrudis might have been an Anglo-Norman nun from the Benedictine house of Wilton in Wiltshire is intriguing, particularly considering Jocelyn Wogan-Browne's work on the textual communities of Anglo-Norman nuns. See Jocelyn Wogan-Browne, *Saints' Lives and Women's Literary Culture, c. 1150–1300: Virginity and Its Authorizations* (Oxford: Oxford University Press, 2001). Peter Riga's poem

is edited by Mozley, "Susanna and the Elders," 30–41. For a more recent edition, as well as comments on Peter Riga, see Paul E. Beichner, ed., *Aurora Petri Rigae Biblia Versificata*, 2 vols. (South Bend: University of Notre Dame Press, 1965), 360–67, 371–74. Peter Riga, according to Beichner (see vol. 1, notes to lines 451–646), wrote the *Historia Susanne* as an independent poem before putting it into the *Aurora*. Aegidius of Paris, in revising the *Aurora*, destroyed the *Historia Susanne* as a debate, rearranging the parts and making additions to it so that it began in the garden and not at the trial. Mozley and Beichner print both versions of the *Historia Susanne*. Beichner also notes (p. xxix) that the *Aurora* was in the library at Melsa, though he does not say which version. This is not surprising, considering the widespread popularity of the poem.

44. Mozley, "Susanna and the Elders," 27, also notes that there are references to poems on the subject of Susanna in old library catalogs, such as those of St. Augustine's Abbey, Canterbury, Peterborough Abbey Library, and the library of the Austin Friars at York. For the Austin Friars' importance to textual dissemination, see Ralph Hanna, "Augustinian Canons and Middle English Literature," in *The English Medieval Book: Studies in Memory of Jeremy Griffiths*, ed. A. S. G. Edwards, Vincent Gillespie, and Ralph Hanna (London: British Library, 2000), 27–42.

45. Stevenson, *Latin Poets*, 132, also talks about this, noting the ways in which Peter's verbs implicate Susanna as a temptress. My quotations from the *Historia Susanne* are taken from Mozeley's edition of Aegidius's redaction, who takes this section (which belongs to Daniel's accusation of the Elders) and uses it early in the poem to describe the scene in the garden.

46. In the *Reductorium Morale*, 206, Pierre Bersuire likens Susanna to the soul and says that she should not have been alone (hence, without attendant virtues) in the garden.

47. See Donovan, *The de Brailles Hours*, 4–5.

48. Such complaints would have had a good deal of relevance for Cistercians. See Painter, *The Reign of King John*, 155, 158, 171, 183; Hewlett, *The Flowers of History*, 2:47. For legal conditions, see Turner, *Magna Carta*, 43, 158–62; David Carpenter, *The Struggle for Mastery: Britain, 1066–1284* (Oxford: Oxford University Press, 2003), 273; Warren, *King John*, 173.

49. See Hill, *English Cistercian Monasteries*, 44–45, 76, 78; Newman, *The Boundaries of Charity*, 70–72, 90–91.

50. Peter Riga likewise employs the term *res nova* (line 149), but he uses it to describe the revolutionary force of Susanna's beauty on the decrepitude of the elders.

51. Stevenson's reading of Willetrudis's account of Susanna is instructive here, for Willetrudis shapes the account, probably written for nuns, so that the emphasis is on female strength and chastity. See Stevenson, *Latin Poets*, 133.

52. For a study of the documents, composition, and reception history of this narrative, see Baker, "The Genesis of English Cistercian Chronicles"; for the history, see Walbran, Raine, and Fowler, *Memorials*, 1, *Narratio.*

53. Walbran, *Hugh of Kirkstall*, 1, p. 2. Cassidy-Welch, *Monastic Spaces*, 66–68, also discusses the pastoral language of Cistercian foundation narratives.

54. See Burton, *The Monastic Order in Yorkshire*, 217, 243; Pauline Matarasso, *The Cistercian World: Monastic Writings of the Twelfth Century* (London: Penguin, 1993), xii; F. J. Mullin, *A History of the Work of the Cistercians in Yorkshire (1131–1300)* (Washington, DC: Catholic University of America Press, 1932), 38–39, 88; Newman, *The Boundaries of Charity*, 23, 67–72, 90–91.

55. See M. R. James, ed. and trans., *Walter Map. De Nugis Curialium. Courtiers' Trifles*, rev. C. N. L. Brooke and R. A. B. Mynors (Oxford: Clarendon Press, 2002), xliv, 72–113.

56. Lumby, *Polychronicon*, 7:405.

57. Hill, *English Cistercian Monasteries*, 57–59, 137–40.

58. On justice during the reign of John, see Warren, *King John*, 168–73; Carpenter, *The Struggle for Mastery*, 273; Turner, *Magna Carta*, 41–43.

59. Wilmart, "Les mélanges," 47, 56–57, 66–67. For a study of one way in which the political issues associated with the reign of John were refracted through a literary text, see Galloway, "Laȝamon's Gift."

60. Michael Bennett, *Community, Class, and Careerism: Cheshire and Lancaster Society in the Age of "Sir Gawain and the Green Knight"* (Cambridge: Cambridge University Press, 1983); Susanna Greer Fein, "The Early Thirteen-Line Stanza: Style and Metrics Reconsidered," *Parergon* 18 (2000): 97–126; Ralph Hanna, *Pursuing History: Middle English Manuscripts and Their Texts* (Stanford: Stanford University Press, 1996); Hanna, "Sir Thomas Berkeley and His Patronage"; Ralph Hanna and David Lawton, eds., *The Siege of Jerusalem*, EETS 320 (Oxford: Oxford University Press, 2003), introduction; David Lawton, "The Diversity of Middle English Alliterative Poetry," *Leeds Studies in English* 20 (1989): 143–72.

61. See, for example, F. M. Stenton, "The Road System of Medieval England," *Economic History Review* 7 (1936): 1–21.

62. The term is Burton's (*The Monastic Order in Yorkshire*, 286–87). For vernacular production, see Ralph Hanna, "Yorkshire Writers," along with his "Contextualizing the *Siege of Jerusalem*," *YLS* 6 (1992): 109–21. Hanna, of course, follows in a tradition established by Carl Horstman's *Yorkshire Writers*, 2 vols. (London, 1895–96); and Hope E. Allen, *Writings Ascribed to Richard Rolle, Hermit of Hampole and Materials for His Biography* (New York, 1927). For Latin culture during the earlier period of Yorkshire's history, see Burton, *The Monastic Order in Yorkshire*, 277–96. For historical writing, see J. Taylor, *Medieval Historical Writing in Yorkshire*, Borthwick Institute of Historical Research (York: St. Anthony's Press, 1961).

63. See Glyn Coppack, "Sawley Abbey: An English Cistercian Abbey on the Edge of 'Stabilitas,'" *Cîteaux* 52 (2001): 319–36; J. Harland, ed., *Historical Account of the Cistercian Abbey of Salley* (London: J. Russell Smith, 1853); E. Mikkers, "Un Speculum novitii inédit d'Etienne de Salley," *Collectanea Ordinis Cisterciensium reformatorum* 8 (1946): 2–68; Talbot, "Letters of Vocation by Roger de Byland." Though just over the border from Yorkshire, Sawley had extensive ties to the Yorkshire Cistercian houses, since it was a daughter house of Newminster (Burton, *The Monastic Order in Yorkshire*, xix).

In addition, in the fourteenth century Thomas Burton, abbot of Melsa, wrote the chronicle of that abbey. Burton was affiliated with Thomas of Woodstock, who was accused of forcing Burton's election to abbot. In 1394, after the death of Queen Anne and in the same year that he founded the college of secular priests at his Essex seat of Pleshey, Thomas was granted the lordship of Holderness and thus stood in relation to the founder of the monastery of Melsa. See Bond, *Chronica Monasterii de Melsa*, 1:lxiii; Anthony Goodman, *The Loyal Conspiracy: The Lords Appellant under Richard II* (Coral Gables, FL: University of Miami Press, 1971), 76–77, 93.

Though abbot of Swineshead in Lincolnshire, Gilbert of Holland (d. 1172), who was one of the two English continuators of Saint Bernard's commentary on the Canticles, had extensive ties to the Yorkshire Cistercians, since Furness was the mother house of both Byland and Swineshead. See Lawrence C. Braceland, ed. and trans., *The Works of Gilbert of Hoyland: Sermons on the Song of Songs* (Kalamazoo, MI: Cistercian Publications, 1978).

64. David Bell, ed., *The Libraries of the Cistercians, Gilbertines, and Premonstratentians* (London: British Library, 1992), xxiii–iv.

65. M. V. Clarke, *Fourteenth Century Studies*, ed. L. S. Sutherland and M. McKisack (Oxford: Clarendon Press, 1937), 91. Hanna, "Contextualizing *The Siege of Jerusalem*," 116, also cites Whalley for its potential for literary activity. See Thorlac Turville-Petre, "The Author of the *Destruction of Troy*," *Medium Ævum* 57 (1988): 264–69, which identifies the author of the poem as a monk of Whalley.

66. Mullin, *A History of the Work of the Cistercians in Yorkshire*, 91–93.

67. For the full list, see Bell, *The Libraries of the Cistercians*, 4–5. Sometime after 1386, John Northwood, a monk of Bordesley, wrote a miscellany (BL MS ADD. 37787), fifteen of whose twenty English pieces are likewise in the Vernon manuscript. For an edition, see Nita Scudder Baugh, "A Worcestershire Miscellany compiled by John Northwood, c. 1400" (thesis, Bryn Mawr College, 1956).

68. Turville-Petre, *The Alliterative Revival*, 44–46, has suggested that the manuscripts were copied at Bordesley. However, see *The Vernon Manuscript: A Facsimile of Bodleian Library, Oxford, MS Eng. Poet.a.1*, with an introduction by A. I. Doyle (Cambridge: D. S. Brewer, 1987), esp. 13–16. For information

about Stoneleigh Abbey, see Dugdale, *Monasticon*, 5:443–45. Stoneleigh was founded in 1154 at Radmore in Staffordshire, and the monks of Bordesley helped to instruct the new monks in the Cistercian discipline. As Dugdale notes, "there grew great friendship betwixt these two monasteries" (443). Twelve years later, the monastery moved to Stoneleigh.

69. The suggestion about dating belongs to Ralph Hanna; see Staley, *Languages of Power*, 340 n. 3.

70. Derek Pearsall ("The Alliterative Revival: Origins and Social Backgrounds," in *Middle English Alliterative Poetry and Its Literary Background*, ed. David Lawton [Cambridge: D. S. Brewer, 1982], 34–53) has suggested that we might look to the monasteries themselves for the alliterative poets, whose poems might have been intended as entertainment for visiting patrons. Harland, *Historical Account of the Cistercian Abbey of Salley*, has made a similar suggestion for Sawley Abbey.

71. For a map of Cistercian monasteries in England in the twelfth century, see Peter Ferguson, *Architecture of Solitude: Cistercian Abbeys in Twelfth-Century England* (Princeton: Princeton University Press, 1984), pl. 1; see pl. 2 for the filiations of these monasteries.

72. Citations from *A Pistel of Susan* are from Thorlac Turville-Petre, ed., *Alliterative Poetry of the Later Middle Ages* (Washington, DC: Catholic University of America Press, 1989), 120–139, and are cited by line number in the text. There are two other editions of the poem, both of which contain excellent notes and commentary: Alice Miskimin, ed., *Susannah: An Alliterative Poem of the Fourteenth Century* (New Haven: Yale University Press, 1969); and *The Pistel of Swete Susan*, in Russell A. Peck, ed., *Heroic Women from the Old Testament in Middle English Verse* (Kalamazoo, MI: Medieval Institute Publications, 1991), 73–108.

73. Turville-Petre, *Alliterative Poetry*, 126 nn. 66–117. See also *The Pistel of Swete Susan*, in Peck, *Heroic Women from the Old Testament*, 73–78.

74. See "Tractatus . . . de Susanna," line 166.

75. "Tractatus . . . de Susanna," line 213. In *A Pistel*, the poet has the judges repeat the word *"lorere"* (laurel) twice more (lines 136, 143), probably to have them incriminate themselves as persecutors of the innocent, as well as to look forward to Daniel's questioning about the type of tree later in the poem.

76. In reference to this line, Turville-Petre, *Alliterative Poetry*, 139, notes that such punishment before execution was reserved for "particularly heinous crimes."

77. For these poems, see Knight and Ohlgren, eds., *The Tale of Gamelyn*, in *Robin Hood and Other Outlaw Tales*, 184–226; *Athelston*, in Herzman, Drake, and Salisbury, *Four Romances of England*, 341–84.

78. For an extended treatment of the political implications of late medieval texts dealing with marriage and the household, see chapter 4 of my *Languages of Power*.

79. *The Holy Bible . . . made from the Latin Vulgate by John Wycliffe and His Followers*, 4 vols., ed. Josiah Forshall and Sir Frederic Madden (Oxford: Oxford University Press, 1850; rpt. New York: AMS Press, 1982), vol. 3.

80. In *The Book of the City of Ladies*, he is a young child in his mother's arms. In *Wicliffe's Apology*, Daniel "ʒet a barne, jugid þe prestis"; see James Henthorn Todd, ed., *Apology for Lollard Doctrines* (Camden Society, 1842) (New York: AMS Press, 1968). See Turville-Petre, *Alliterative Poetry*, on line 281, which notes the patristic opinion that Daniel was twelve.

81. See Miskimin, *Susannah*, 20–41; Peck, *The Pistel of Swete Susan*, introd., in *Heroic Women*, 77–79; Turville-Petre, *Alliterative Poetry*, 120–21.

82. For a reading of the *Man of Law's Tale* as epitomizing the narrator's concern with an English juridical identity (as opposed to Roman), see Lavezzo, *Angels on the Edge of the World*, 98–106. In "*The Man of Law's Tale* and Rome" (*Exemplaria* 22 [2010]: 119–37), Sarah Stanbury has explored the ideological relations between late-fourteenth-century England and Rome as a center of both commerce and religion.

83. Winthrop Wetherbee has studied both Chaucer's and Gower's versions of the story of Constance and offers a trenchant reading of the *Man of Law's Tale* in terms of its passive heroine, its controlling narrator, its cultural context, and its evidence of social distress and dislocation. See Winthrop Wetherbee, "Constance and the World in Chaucer and Gower," in *John Gower: Recent Readings*, ed. R. F. Yeager (Kalamazoo, MI: Medieval Institute Publications, 1989), 65–94. For studies linking Custance to alterity through her gender, see David Raybin, "Custance and History: Woman as Outsider in Chaucer's *Man of Law's Tale*," *Studies in the Age of Chaucer* 12 (1990): 65–84; Susan Schibanoff, "Worlds Apart: Orientalism, Antifeminism, and Heresy in Chaucer's *Man of Law's Tale*," *Exemplaria* 8 (1996): 59–96; Geraldine Heng, *Empire of Magic: Medieval Romance and the Politics of Cultural Fantasy* (New York: Columbia University Press, 2003), 181–238. V. A. Kolve, in *Chaucer and the Imagery of Narrative: The First Five Canterbury Tales* (Stanford: Stanford University Press, 1984), 297–358, has considered the *Man of Law's Tale* in terms of the broader cultural context evoked in the account as a tale of conversion and its heroine as exemplary.

84. For suggestions that he did know the poem, see Alfred Kellogg, "Susannah and the *Merchant's Tale*," *Speculum* 35 (1960): 275–79, which argues that the Merchant employs a reference to the *Pistel* to expose the "moral distortion" of January.

85. David Lyle Jeffrey, "False Witness and the Just Use of Evidence in the Wycliffite *Pistel of Swete Susan*," in *The Judgment of Susanna: Authority and Witness*, ed. Ellen Spolsky (Atlanta: Scholars Press, 1996), 57–71. Though I disagree with Jeffrey's argument that *A Pistel of Susan* is a Wycliffite poem, there are indications that the Wycliffites found Susanna a compelling example. In particular, see Jeffrey's discussion of the sermon "Of Prelates," *The*

Testimony of William Thorpe (which I also discuss below), and the "Apology of Wycliffe," or *Apology for Lollard Doctrines*, which focuses on Daniel as the spokesman for true law. See Todd, *Apology for Lollard Doctrines*, 63–67, which describes Daniel's castigation of the false priests.

86. Anne Hudson, ed., *Two Wycliffite Texts: The Sermon of William Taylor, 1406, the Testimony of William Thorpe 1407*, EETS 301 (Oxford: Oxford University Press, 1993), 35. For dating, see xlv–liii.

87. See Ritchie D. Kendall, *The Drama of Dissent: The Radical Poetics of Nonconformity, 1380–1590* (Chapel Hill: University of North Carolina Press, 1986), 57, 59. On the relationship between Thorpe's *Testimony* and Margery Kempe's trials, see Lynn Staley, *Margery Kempe's Dissenting Fictions* (University Park: Pennsylvania State University Press, 1994), 139. In "False Witness and the Just Use of Evidence," 66, Jeffrey also notes the association between Thorpe's silence and that of Christ. In the Wycliffite sermon "Of Prelates," Susanna is similarly linked to Christ through silence and false testimony. See F. D. Matthew, *The English Works of Wyclif*, EETS 74 (London: Trübner & Co., 1880), 74–75. Jeffrey also discusses this reference (66).

88. For Walter Brut, see William W. Capes, *Registrum Johannis Trefnant* (London: Canterbury and York Society, 1916), 278–359. For Thomas Wimbledon, see Ione Kemp Knight, *Wimbledon's Sermon "Redde Rationem Villicationis Tue: A Middle English Sermon of the Fifteenth Century* (Pittsburgh: Duquesne University Press, 1967); Nancy H. Owen, ed., "Thomas Wimbledon's Sermon: 'Redde racionem villicacionis tue,'" *Medieval Studies* 28 (1966): 176–97. In *The Premature Reformation*, Hudson notes that in 1392 the Lollard John Belgrave "posted a pamphlet on the doors of St. Martin's Church in Leicester comparing the archdeacon's official who was due to hold court there the following day with the elders who condemned Susannah, and called him *vn jugge de deable de iniquite*" (153–54). For recent work on Brut and on the texts associated with him, see Fiona Somerset, "*Eciam Mulier:* Women in Lollardy and the Problem of Sources," and Kathryn Kerby-Fulton, "*Eciam Lollardi*: Some Further Thoughts on Fiona Somerset's "*Eciam Mulier*: Women in Lollardy and the Problem of Sources," in *Voices in Dialogue: Reading Women in the Middle Ages*, ed. Linda Olson and Kathryn Kerby-Fulton (Notre Dame: University of Notre Dame Press, 2005), 245–60, 261–78.

89. John Foxe will tackle the same question of origins in book II of the *Acts and Monuments*, where he acknowledges the story of King Lucius and Pope Eleutherius and of Pope Gregory I and Augustine of Canterbury but chooses, instead, either Joseph of Arimathea or one of the apostles, thus predating any Roman foundation. See George Townsend, ed., *The Acts and Monuments of John Foxe*, 8 vols. (New York: AMS Press, 1965), 1:305–7.

90. See Knight, *Wimbledon's Sermon*, 3–26; Hudson, *Premature Reformation*, 424.

91. Knight notes (*Wimbledon's Sermon*, 131 nn. 356–68) of this section that it echoes Isidore of Seville's castigation of corrupt judges who demand rewards and that one manuscript containing Wimbledon's sermon quotes Isidore.

92. The final sentence is a quotation from Daniel 13:9.

93. Wimbledon's apocalypticism is apparent in his references in the second part of the sermon to Joachim of Fiore (887) and to Hildegard of Bingen (841) and their prophecies of the end of the world; he also cites the prophet Daniel (880, 884) and John's account of the opening of the seals (910ff.).

94. Townsend, *Acts and Monuments*, 3. For the making of Foxe's *Acts and Monuments*, see King, *Foxe's Book of Martyrs and Early Modern Print Culture*.

95. Townsend, *The Acts and Monuments*, 3:300. This paragraph was removed from subsequent editions. For notes regarding Foxe's handling of Wimbledon's sermon, see 3:292 n. 1.

96. Townsend, *Acts and Monuments*, 4:631.

97. See Jeremy Taylor, *Ductor dubitantium, or The rule of conscience in all her general measures* (London, 1660), chap. 2, rule 8.

98. Sir Walter Raleigh, *The arraignment and conviction of Sr. Walter Rawleigh . . . on 17 November 1603* (London, 1648).

99. Bertha Haven Putnam, "The Transformation of the Keepers of the Peace into the Justices of the Peace, 1327–1380," *Transactions of the Royal Historical Society*, 4th ser., 12 (1929): 19–48, esp. 45–48; Ormrod, *The Reign of Edward III*, 23, 32, 152.

100. Richard W. Kaeuper, *War, Justice, and Public Order: England and France in the Later Middle Ages* (Oxford: Clarendon Press, 1988), 181–82, 375. Kaeuper pays particular attention to the Robin Hood tales.

101. See Green, *A Crisis of Truth*, 64, 220, 221; Tout, *Chapters*, III: 259–64.

102. Pierpont Morgan MS 818 (Ingilby MS), ca. 1425–75. According to the Pierpont Morgan notes, this manuscript is possibly from Yorkshire and possibly associated with the Cistercian abbey of Fountains. However as Ralph Hanna noted in a private communication, it is linked with Fountains because it was long owned by the Ingilbys of Ripley, who may have pillaged Fountains at the Dissolution. It contains *A Pistil*, Rolle's *Form of Living*, and the earliest known version of the A-text of *Piers Plowman*. The other two manuscripts are:

BL Cotton Caligula A.ii, part 1 (ca. 1440–60). This manuscript contains a number of romances, as well as the *Siege of Jerusalem* and moral and religious works. For a description of this manuscript, in which *A Pistel* appears in a separate booklet at the head, see Hanna and Lawton, *The Siege of Jerusalem*, xxiv–xxvi.

Huntington HM 114 (ca. 1425–50), which contains a text of *Piers Plowman* but also of *Mandeville's Travels, Three Kings of Cologne*, and Chaucer's

Troilus and Criseyde. See C. W. Dutschke, with the assistance of R. H. Rouse and Sara S. Hodson, Virginia Rust, Herbert C. Schulz, and Ephrem Compte, *Guide to Medieval and Renaissance Manuscripts in the Huntington Library* (San Marino, CA: Huntington Library, 1989), 150–52.

103. Peck, *Heroic Women,* 78, quotes Doyle's comments from his introduction to the Vernon *Facsimile,* 15–16, to which I refer. See also my remarks in *Languages of Power,* 340–45.

104. The history of the Bohun family is inevitably a history of English books and bookmaking. See, for example, Lucy Freeman Sandler, *The Lichtenthal Psalter and the Manuscript Patronage of the Bohun Family* (London: Harvey Miller, 2004). Joan and her husband, Humphrey, were important patrons of many religious foundations, especially Walden Abbey in Essex. Joan also helped found a chantry in the Cistercian abbey of Coggeshall in Essex (see Dugdale, *Monasticon,* 5:451), and her son-in-law, Thomas of Woodstock, a notorious book collector himself, was deeply involved with Melsa in Yorkshire. For books associated with both, see Sheila H. Cavanaugh, "A Study of Books Privately Owned in England, 1300–1450" (Ph.D. diss., University of Pennsylvania, 1980).

105. See Saul, *Richard II,* 373–75.

106. Anthony Goodman, "The Countess and the Rebels: Essex and a Crisis in English Society," *Essex Archaeology and History: The Transactions of the Essex Archaeological Society* 2 (1972): 274. On forfeiture, see C. D. Ross, "Forfeiture for Treason in the Reign of Richard II," *EHR* 71 (1956): 560–75.

107. Thomas Garter, *The Most Virtuous & Godly Susanna,* Malone Society Reprints (Oxford: Oxford University Press, 1937), v–vi; Lily B. Campbell, *Divine Poetry and Drama in Sixteenth-Century England* (Berkeley: University of California Press, 1959), 218–19. As Campbell remarks, this may not be the same play, but it seems likely. Campbell offers accounts of the subjects of Protestant poetry and drama throughout the book. See also Murray Roston, *Biblical Drama in England from the Middle Ages to the Present Day* (Evanston, IL: Northwestern University Press, 1968), 87–92. See "An excellent ballad, intituled, The constancy of Susanna" (1640; 1650–59; 1689–92), all available at Early English Books Online. The illustrations in the 1640 copy depict a contemporary courtroom.

108. M. Lindsay Kaplan, "Sexual Slander and the Politics of the Erotic in Garter's *Susanna,*" in Spolsky, *The Judgment of Susanna,* 80. Kaplan speculates that Bernard may be Thomas's brother. The entry for Bernard in the *DNB* begins, "Garter, Bernard (*fl.* 1565–1579), poet, who describes himself on his title-pages as citizen of London, was, according to Hunter, the second son of Sir William Garter of London, and the father of a Bernard Garter of Brigstocke, Northamptonshire. But in the 1633–5 visitation of London, 'Barnerd Garter of Brikstocke', Northamptonshire, was described as the son of Thomas Garter, the husband of Elizabeth Catelyne, and the father of

George Garter, who was living in 1634 (Visitation, 1.303). He is described as a clerk of the Blacksmiths' Company in an Elizabethan chancery suit involving the company and Joseph Preston (TNA: PRO, C Pp.8.55)." Sidney, Lee, "Garter, Bernard (*fl.* 1565–1579)," in *DNB*.

109. See note 109. See also M. Lindsay Kaplan, *The Culture of Slander in Early Modern England* (Cambridge: Cambridge University Press, 1997), which discusses slander in relation to the Elizabethan state.

110. Campbell, *Divine Poetry and Drama*, 124–27, discusses these poems, citing C. S. Lewis (122 n. 2) for the identification of the "kind" as an *epyllion*.

111. References are to Thomas Garter, *The Most Virtuous & Godly Susanna*, Malone Society Reprints, and are designated in the text by line number.

112. David Kathman, "Stanley, Ferdinando, fifth earl of Derby (1559?1594)," in *DNB*.

113. For a discussion of this construct and its importance in the medieval literature of political advice, see Staley, *Languages of Power*, 89, 268–69.

114. See Bella Millet and Jocelyn Wogan-Browne, ed. and trans., *Medieval English Prose for Women: Selections from the Katherine Group and "Ancrene Wisse"* (Oxford: Clarendon Press, 1990), 30/31–32/33.

115. Roche also draws on the comedy of withered age seeking to renew itself with cosmetics and wanton antics, possibly here glancing at the aged queen.

116. For Aylett, see Matthew Steggle, "Aylett, Robert (*c.* 1582–1655)," in *DNB*.

117. Sean Kelsey, "Rich, Robert, second earl of Warwick (1587–1658)," in *DNB*.

118. See the essays collected in Jeremy Dimmick, James Simpson, and Nicolette Zeeman, eds., *Images, Idolatry, and Iconoclasms in Late Medieval England* (Oxford: Oxford University Press, 2002).

119. Robert Aylett, *Svsanna: or The Arraignment of the Two Vnjvst Elders* (London: John Teage, 1622) 29; Robert Greene, *The Myrrour of Modestie* (London: Roger Warde, 1584), Biii.

120. For suggestions about the ways in which the Elizabethan dramatists represent and sometimes seek to redress the ruptures caused by the Reformation, see Huston Diehl, *Staging Reform, Reforming the Stage: Protestantism and Popular Theater in Early Modern England* (Ithaca: Cornell University Press, 1997). For a statement about images and their proper use, see the 1536 *Articles about Religion*, in Charles Lloyd, ed., *Formularies of Faith* (Oxford: Clarendon Press, 1825), 13–14. Aylett, *Svsanna*, 41, compares the judges to those who prepared the Gunpowder plot, thus Catholics, but they are also eager to despoil the very image they formerly venerated. Roche has the judges blame Susanna for the effect of her beauty, her image thus kindling their desire. Greene's judges accuse her of being a "saint" who enchanted them.

Conclusion

1. See the collection of letters regarding Christina Carpenter's enclosure translated by Liz Herbert McAvoy in *Rhetoric of the Anchorhold: Space, Place, and Body within the Discourses of Enclosure*, ed. Liz Herbert McAvoy (Cardiff: University of Wales Press, 2008), 221–24. The letters are recorded in the register of Bishop John de Stratford (1323–33) (Hampshire Records Office, MS 21M65/A1/5, fol. 46v and fol. 76r) and bear no special emphasis or marginal notations. In the same volume see McAvoy's essay, "Gender, Rhetoric, and Space in the *Speculum Inclusorum, Letter to a Bury Recluse* and the Strange Case of Christine Carpenter," 111–26.

2. McAvoy, *Rhetoric of the Anchorhold*, 223–24. In her essay in this volume McAvoy suggests that the language used to describe the enclosure of anchoresses was different from that used for anchorites, who, as men, were without the potentially wandering bodies and desires of women. For comments about the canonical process of reenclosure, see Miri Rubin, "An English Anchorite: The Making, Unmaking, and Remaking of Christine Carpenter," in *Pragmatic Utopias: Ideals and Communities, 1200–1630*, ed. Rosemary Horrox and Sarah Rees Jones (Cambridge: Cambridge University Press, 2001), esp. 214–16.

3. McAvoy, *Rhetoric of the Anchorhold*, 224.

4. Haines, *Archbishop John Stratford*, 245, 251, 266.

5. This, of course, begs the question of Edward's seeking the French throne by right of his mother. John Stow, *Annales, or, a generall chronicle of England. Begun by Iohn Stow: continued and augmented with matters forraigne and domestique, ancient and moderne, vnto the end of this present yeere, 1631*, by Edmund Howes (London, 1632), 236. For a discussion of these arms, see M. A. Michael, "The Little Land of England Is Preferred before the Great Kingdom of France: The Quartering of the Royal Arms by Edward III," in *Studies in Medieval Art and Architecture Presented to Peter Lasko*, ed. David Buckton and T. A. Heslop (Dover, NH: Alan Sutton, 1994), 113–26.

6. *Calendar of Patent Rolls. Edward III 1348–1350*, 27, 56, 385, 428, 441, 459. For the language used to justify taxation to support the war, see Harriss, *King, Parliament, and Public Finance in England to 1369*, 313–55.

7. See the *MED*, v. *privat*, for the above citations. For discussion, see Hudson, *The Premature Reformation*, 347–351. *Pierce Plowman's Crede*, the late-fourteenth-century Lollard poem, assigns walled, and hence private, gardens to the friars as signs of their worldliness and then goes on to compare their carved and painted chapter house to a parliament house. See James Dean, ed., *Six Ecclesiastical Satires* (Kalamazoo, MI: Medieval Institute Publications, 1991), lines 164–68, 202. For an exploration of Chaucer's use of what is private/privy, see William Robins, "Troilus in the Gutter," in *Sacred and*

Profane in Chaucer and Late Medieval Literature: Essays in Honour of John V. Fleming (Toronto: University of Toronto Press, 2010), 91–112.

8. *The Sermons of the Right Reverend Father in God, Master Hugh Latimer, . . . Many of which were preached before King Edward VI . . . on the religious and civil liberties of Englishmen, &c. To which is prefixed, Bishop Latimer's life,* 2 vols (London: J. Scott, 1758), 99–100. The spelling is modernized in Hugh Latimer, *Sermons* (London: J. M. Dent & Sons, 1926), 100.

9. For an overview of the critical commentary on these poems, see Smith, *The Poems of Andrew Marvell,* 128–30.

10. For the Fairfaxes, see Ian J. Gentles, "Fairfax, Thomas, third Lord Fairfax of Cameron (1612–1671)," and Andrew J. Hopper, "Fairfax, Henry (1588–1665)," both in *DNB;* Edward Bliss Reed, *The Poems of Thomas, Third Lord Fairfax from MS Fairfax 40 in the Bodleian Library, Oxford, Transactions of the Connecticut Academy of Arts and Sciences* 14 (1909): 241–42.

11. For the two texts, see Reed, *The Poems of Thomas, Third Lord Fairfax,* 263–70. My examples are drawn from stanzas 1 and 3. For other remarks about the poetic interaction between Fairfax and Marvell, see Smith, *Andrew Marvell,* 97.

12. For remarks about the dating of this poem and its affinities with the works of the poets Katherine Phillips and Abraham Cowley, as well as later political events, see Nigel Smith, *Andrew Marvell: The Chameleon* (New Haven: Yale University Press, 2010), 219–20.

13. Thomas, Lord Fairfax, *Short Memorials of Thomas Lord Fairfax* (London: Ri. Chiswell, 1699).

14. For the text and critical commentary regarding genre, style, Marvell's political perspectives, and the poem's modern appraisal, see Smith, *The Poems of Andrew Marvell,* 267–72. For commentary about Fairfax and Cromwell and the relationships between "Horatian Ode" and "Upon Appleton House," see Annabel M. Patterson, *Marvell and the Civic Crown* (Princeton: Princeton University Press, 1978), 66–76, 95–110. For an extended reading of the balanced antitheses of "Horatian Ode" in relation to republican and/or monarchist language, see David Norbrook, *Writing the English Republic: Poetry, Rhetoric, and Politics, 1627–1660* (Cambridge: Cambridge University Press, 1999), 243–70; Smith, *Andrew Marvell,* 82–84.

15. In *Silva* (London, 1729), John Evelyn advised the reader to plant trees in order to repair the "late impolitick waste" (ii). See also Therese O'Malley and Joachim Wolschke-Bulmahn, eds., *John Evelyn's "Elysium Britannicum" and European Gardening* (Washington, DC: Dumbarton Oaks Research Library and Collection, 1998). For studies of the politics of seventeenth-century landscaping, see James Turner, *The Politics of Landscape: Rural Scenery and Society in English Poetry, 1630–1660* (Cambridge, MA: Harvard University Press, 1979), 49–84; Annabel Patterson, *Pastoral and Ideology: Virgil to Valéry*

(Oxford: Oxford University Press, 1988), 133–63; D. C. Chambers, *The Planters of the English Landscape Garden: Botany, Trees, and the Georgics* (New Haven: Yale University Press, 1993); Rebecca Bushnell, *Green Desire: Imagining Early Modern English Gardens* (Ithaca: Cornell University Press, 2003). In Leslie and Raylor, *Culture and Cultivation,* see especially the essays by Douglas Chambers, Michael Leslie, Graham Perry, and Timothy Raylor.

For the politically freighted landscape discourse of the eighteenth century, see Anthony Low, *The Georgic Revolution* (Princeton: Princeton University Press, 1985); Rachel Crawford, *Poetry, Enclosure, and the Vernacular Landscape, 1700–1830* (Cambridge: Cambridge University Press, 2002); Tim Fulford, *Landscape, Liberty, and Authority: Criticism and Politics from Thomson to Wordsworth* (Cambridge: Cambridge University Press, 1996).

16. Chambers, "'Wild Pastorall Encounter,'" in Leslie and Raylor, *Culture and Cultivation,* 174–75; and John Dixon Hunt, "Evelyn's Idea of the Garden," 279, in O'Malley and Wolschke-Bulmahn, *John Evelyn . . . and European Gardening.* Citing Annabel Patterson's and Erica Veevers's remarks about the ways in which the mythology of Charles I's court had damaged the status of the pastoral, Chambers engages with the renewed respect for the georgic as a critique of courtly aesthetics. For an exploration of Marvell's deliberately ambiguous use of nature, see Cristina Malcolmson, "The Garden Enclosed/The Woman Enclosed: Marvell and the Cavalier Poets," in *Enclosure Acts: Sexuality, Property, and Culture in Early Modern England,* ed. Richard Burt and John Michael Archer (Ithaca: Cornell University Press, 1994), 251–69.

17. A. R. Waller, ed., *Abraham Cowley,* 2 vols. (Cambridge: Cambridge University Press, 1905), II: *Essays, Plays, and Sundry Verses,* 392–428.

18. George Wheler, *The Protestant Monastery or Christian OEconomicks containing Directions for the Religious Conduct of a Family* (London, 1698). Felicity Heal (*Hospitality in Early Modern England,* 66) cites this text as the last of the manuals of advice for gentry householders, obliging them to care for the poor.

19. See my discussion of the Aristotelian household as expressing the ideals of the medieval georgic in *Languages of Power,* 268–69.

20. Wheler, *The Protestant Monastery,* 25.

21. Wallace Stevens, *Collected Poems,* ed. John N. Serio (New York: Alfred A. Knopf, 2009), 55–57.

22. For the historical and temporal contingencies that Marvell builds into his garden poems, see Jonathan Crewe, "The Garden State: Marvell's Poetic of Enclosure," in Burt and Archer, *Enclosure Acts,* 270–89.

23. Cotton Mather, *Magnalia Christi Americana: or the ecclesiastical history of New England, from its first planting in the year 1620* (London: Thomas Parkhurst, 1702), 40, 42, 43, 65, for example. See Douglas Anderson, *William Bradford's Books: "Of Plimmoth Plantation" and the Printed Word* (Baltimore: Johns Hopkins University Press, 2003), 2.

24. Floyd Stovall, ed., *Walt Whitman: Prose Works, 1892*, 2 vols. (New York: New York University Press, 1964), 2:434–58. For an exploration of American poems of place in relation to English models, see Lawrence Buell, *New England Literary Culture from Revolution through Renaissance* (Cambridge: Cambridge University Press, 1986), 290.

25. Charles Fairfax, brother to Ferdinando, wrote the *Analecta Fairfaxiana* (Brotherton Coll. MS Yks 2) for his son Henry at Magdalene College. It is a careful—if not obsessive—account of family history and genealogy. On p. 8 he records the marriage of Thomas Lord Fairfax (the father of Ferdinando) with "Elen da: of Robt Aske. by his wife Eliz." He repeats this on pp. 27, 279. He lists other Fairfax-Aske marriages on pp. 280, 341. At the end of the volume, pp. 403–4, he records his father's and his own worries that Thomas Fairfax, "ledd much by his wife . . . will destroy his House." Charles is particularly upset that Thomas changed the entail to include a daughter or daughters and points out that his brother Henry has children and grandchildren. The estate did, after Maria's death, pass to these heirs, but Charles is careful to note his worry, a worry he apparently shared with Thomas himself.

26. See Virginia, Governor and Council, The Right Honourable Thomas Lord Fairfax,—petitioner, the Governor and Council of Virginia, in right of the Crown, Defendants. The case on behalf of the Crown. [London], [1745]. Eighteenth Century Collections Online. For the sixth Lord Fairfax's life, see Stuart E. Brown Jr., *Virginia Baron: The Story of Thomas 6th Lord Fairfax* (Berryville, VA: Chesapeake Book Co., 1965).

27. See particularly Crawford, *Poetry, Enclosure, and the Vernacular Landscape, 1700–1830*, 3–36.

WORKS CITED

Manuscripts

Analecta Fairfaxiana. Brotherton Coll. MS Yks 2.
Auckinleck manuscript. http://digital.nls.uk/auchinleck/.
Hampshire Records Office. MS 21M65/A1/5.
London, BL, MS Harley 360.
London, BL, Sloane MS 1872, fol. 60–81b.
Pierpont Morgan MS 818 (Ingilby MS).

Primary Texts

Abelard. "Sermo XXIX: De Sancta Susanna, ad hortationem virginum." *PL* 178: 555–64.
Allen, Hope E. *Writings Ascribed to Richard Rolle, Hermit of Hampole and Materials for His Biography.* New York, 1927.
Ambrose. "De Joseph." *PL* 14: 641–72.
———. "De Tobia." *PL* 14: 759–94.
———. "De Viduis." *PL* 16: 233–62.
———. *Expositio Evangelii Secundum Lucam. PL* 15: 1527–1850.
———. "In Psalmum XXXVII Enarratio." *PL* 14: 1001–1181.
Aspin, Isabel, ed. *Anglo-Norman Political Songs.* Oxford: Anglo-Norman Text Society, 1953.
Augustine. "Sermo CCCXLIII: De Susanna et Joseph." *PL* 39: 1505–10.
Aungier, G. G., ed. *Croniques de London.* Camden Society 28 (1844).

Austen, Ralph. *A Treatise of Fruit Trees.* Oxford, 1653.

Aylett, Robert. *Svsanna: or The Arraignment of the Two Vnjvst Elders.* London: John Teage, 1622.

Bacon, Sir Francis. "Of Gardens." In *The Essayes or Counsels, Civill and Morall,* ed. Michael Kiernan, 139–45. Cambridge, MA: Harvard University Press, 1985.

Bale, John. *Kynge Johan.* Ed. J. Payne Collier. Camden Society 2. London: J. B. Nichols, 1838.

————. *The laboryouse iourney [and] serche of Iohan Leylande, for Englandes antiquitees geuen of hym as a newe yeares gyfte to Kynge Henry the viij. in the. xxxvij. yeare of his reygne, with declaracyons enlarged.* London: Printed by S. Mierdman for John Bale,1549.

Banks, Theodore Howard, Jr., ed. *The Poetical Works of Sir John Denham.* New Haven: Yale University Press, 1928.

Baugh, Nita Scudder. "A Worcestershire Miscellany compiled by John Northwood, c. 1400." Ph.D. diss., Bryn Mawr College, 1956.

Bede. *De Templo Salomonis Liber. PL* 91: 735–807.

Beichner, Paul E., ed. *Aurora: Petri Rigae Biblia Versificata.* 2 vols. South Bend: University of Notre Dame Press, 1965.

Bell, Alexander, ed. *Le Lai d'Haveloc and Gaimar's Haveloc Episode.* Manchester: Manchester University Press, 1925.

Bell, David, ed. *The Libraries of the Cistercians, Gilbertines, and Premonstratentians.* London: British Library, 1992.

Benson, Larry D., ed. *The Riverside Chaucer.* Boston: Houghton Mifflin, 1987.

Bernard. *In Festo Annuntiationis Beatae Mariae Virginis.* Sermo III, "De muliere adultera; de Susanna; de B. Maria." *PL* 183: 393–98.

————. *Sermones in Cantica. PL* 183.

Bersuire, Pierre. *Reductorium Morale Super Totam Bibliam.* Venice, 1633.

Blake, E. O., ed. *Liber Eliensis.* London: Royal Historical Society, 1962.

Blyth, Charles R., ed. *The Regiment of Princes / Thomas Hoccleve.* Kalamazoo, MI: Medieval Institute Publications, 1999.

Boccaccio, Giovanni. *Famous Women.* Ed. and trans. Virginia Brown. Cambridge, MA: Harvard University Press, 2001.

The Boke of Magna Carta with diuers other Statutes . . . translated into Englyshe. London, 1534.

Bond, Edward A., ed. *Chronica Monasterii de Melsa a fundatione usque ad annum 1396.* 3 vols. London: Longmans, Green, Reader, and Dyer, 1866.

Braceland, Lawrence C., trans. and ed. *The Works of Gilbert of Hoyland: Sermons on the Song of Songs.* Kalamazoo, MI: Cistercian Publications, 1978.

Brereton, Georgine E., and Janet M. Ferrier, eds. *Le Menagier de Paris.* Oxford: Clarendon Press, 1981.

Brie, Friedrich W. D., ed. *The Brut or The Chronicles of England.* Pt. 1. EETS 131. Oxford: Oxford University Press, 1906.

―――. *The Brut or The Chronicles of England.* Pt. 2. EETS 136. Oxford: Oxford University Press, 1908.

Calendar of Patent Rolls. Edward III, 1348–1350. 16 vols. Nendeln: Kraus Reprints, 1971–72.

Camden, William. *Britannia.* Trans. Philemon Holland. *Britain, or a Chorographicall Description of the Most flourishing Kingdomes, England, Scotland, and Ireland . . .* London, 1610.

―――. *Remaines concerning Britaine.* London: Iohn Legatt, 1614.

Campbell, A., ed. *Æthelwulf: "De Abbatibus."* Oxford: Clarendon Press, 1967.

Capes, William W., ed. *Registrum Johannis Trefnant.* London: Canterbury and York Society, 1916.

Catalogue of Romances in the Department of Manuscripts in the British Museum. Vol. 2. London, 1808.

Chibnall, Marjorie, ed. and trans. *The Ecclesiastical History of Orderic Vitalis.* 6 vols. Oxford: Clarendon Press, 1969.

Christine de Pizan. *The Book of the City of Ladies.* Trans. Earl Jeffrey Richards. New York: Persea Books, 1982.

The Chronicle of Froissart translated out of French by Sir John Bourchier Lord Berners, 1523–25. Introd. William Paton Ker. 6 vols. London, 1901; rpt. New York: AMS Press, 1967.

Colgrave, Bertram, and R. A. B. Mynors, ed. and trans. *Bede's Ecclesiastical History of the English People.* Oxford: Clarendon Press, 1969.

Correale, Robert M., and Mary Hamel, eds. *Sources and Analogues of "The Canterbury Tales."* Cambridge: D. S. Brewer, 2002.

S. D. [Samuel Daniel]. *The Collection of the Historie of England.* London: Nicholas Okes, 1618.

Dean, James, ed. *Medieval English Political Writings.* Kalamazoo, MI: Medieval Institute Publications, 1996.

―――. *Richard the Redeless and Mum and the Sothsegger.* Kalamazoo, MI: Medieval Institute Publications, 2000.

―――. *Six Ecclesiastical Satires.* Kalamazoo, MI: Medieval Institute Publications, 1991.

Dean, Ruth J. *Anglo-Norman Literature: A Guide to Texts and Manuscripts.* London: Anglo-Norman Text Society, 1999.

The Defense of Peace: lately translated out of laten in to englysshe. London: Robert Wyer for Wyllyam Marshall, 1535.

Dickens, A. G., ed. *Tudor Treatises. Yorkshire Archaeological Society Record Series* 125 (1959).

Dimier, M.-Anselme. "Un Témoin Tardif Peu Connu du Conflit entre Cisterciens et Clunisiens." In *Peter the Venerable, 1156–1956: Studies and Texts Commemorating the Eighth Centenary of His Death,* ed. Giles Constable and James Kritzeck, 81–90. Studia Anselmiana 40. Rome: Herder, 1956.

Dugdale, Sir William. *Monasticon Anglicanum: a history of the abbies and other monasteries, hospitals, frieries, and cathedral and collegiate churches, with their dependencies, in England and Wales: also of all such Scotch, Irish, and French monasteries, as were in any manner connected with religious houses in England.* New ed. Ed. John Caley, Henry Ellis, and the Rev. Bulkeley Bandinel (London, 1817–30). Ann Arbor, MI: UMI Books on Demand, 2005.

Dumville, David N. *The Historia Brittonum. The "Vatican" Recension.* Cambridge: D. S. Brewer, 1985.

Dutschke, C.W., with R. H. Rouse, Sara S. Hodson, Virginia Rust, Herbert C. Schulz, and Ephrem Compte. *Guide to Medieval and Renaissance Manuscripts in the Huntington Library.* San Marino, CA: Huntington Library, 1989.

Ellis, Sir Henry, ed. *Polydore Vergil's English History from an early translation . . . the period prior to the Norman Conquest.* Camden Society vol. 36. London: John Bowyer Nichols and Son, 1846. *See also* Hay, Denys.

Embree, Dan, and Elizabeth Urquhart, eds. *The Simonie: A Parallel-Text Edition.* Heidelberg: Carl Winter, 1991.

Evelyn, John. *Silva.* London, 1729.

Fabyan, Robert. *The New Chronicle of England and France.* Preface by Henry Ellis. London: F. C. and J. Rivington, 1811.

Fairfax, Thomas. *Short Memorials of Thomas Lord Fairfax.* London: Ri. Chiswell, 1699.

Fairweather, Janet, trans. *Liber Eliensis: A History of the Isle of Ely from the Seventh Century to the Twelfth.* Woodbridge, UK: Boydell Press, 2005.

Farrell, Thomas J., and Amy W. Goodwin. "The Clerk's Tale." In Correale and Hamel, *Sources and Analogues of "The Canterbury Tales,"* 101–68.

Fish, Simon. *A Supplicacyon for the Beggers.* Antwerp: Johannes Grapheus, 1529.

Fitzherbert, John. *Here begynneth a ryght frutefull mater: and hath to name the boke of surueyinge and improuentes.* London: Rycharde Pynson, 1523.

Francis, W. Nelson, ed. *The Book of Vices and Virtues.* EETS, o.s., 217. London: Oxford University Press, 1942.

Furnivall, F. J., ed. *Ballads from Manuscripts.* 2 vols. London: Ballad Society, Taylor and Co., 1868–73.

Furnivall, F. J., and J. Meadows Cowper, eds. *Four Supplications.* EETS, e.s., 13. London: N. Trübner & Co., 1871.

Garter, Thomas. *The Most Virtuous & Godly Susanna.* Malone Society Reprints. Oxford: Oxford University Press, 1937.

Geoffrey of Monmouth. The History of the Kings of Britain. Latin text ed. Michael D. Reeve, trans. Neil Wright. Woodbridge, UK: Boydell Press, 2007.

Gewirth, Alan, ed. and trans. *Marsilius of Padua: The Defender of Peace.* 2 vols. New York: Columbia University Press, 1951–56.

Gildas. *The Ruin of Britain and Other Works.* Ed. and trans. Michael Winterbottom. Totowa, NJ: Rowman and Littlefield, 1978.

Ginsberg, Warren, ed. *Wynnere and Wastoure.* In *Wynnere and Wastoure and The Parlement of the Thre Ages.* Kalamazoo, MI: Medieval Institute Publications, 1992.

Godman, Peter, ed. and trans. *Alcuin: The Bishops, Kings, and Saints of York.* Oxford: Clarendon Press, 1982.

Grafton's Chronicle; or, History of England. 2 vols. London: J. Johnson, 1806.

Greene, Robert. *The Myrrour of Modestie.* London: Roger Warde, 1504.

Greenway, Diana, ed. and trans. *Hentry, Archdeacon of Huntingdon. Historia Anglorum.* Oxford: Clarendon Press, 1996.

Greg, W.W., ed. *A New Enterlude of Godly Queene Hester.* Louvain: A. Wystpruyst, 1904.

Griesser, Bruno, ed. *Exordium Magnum Cisterciense.* Corpus Christianorum 138. Turnholt: Brepols, 1994.

Grosart, Alexander B., ed. *The Poems of Mildmay, Second Earl of Westmoreland (1648).* Privately printed, 1879.

Gunther the Cistercian. *De Oratione Jejunio et Eleemosyna. PL* 212: 101–222.

Hall's Chronicle containing the History of England during the Reign of Henry the Fourth and the succeeding monarchs to the end of the Reign of Henry the Eighth. London, 1809; rpt. New York: AMS Press, 1965.

Hanna, Ralph, and David Lawton, eds. *The Siege of Jerusalem.* EETS 320. Oxford: Oxford University Press, 2003.

Hardy, Thomas Duffus. *Syllabus (in English) of the documents relating to England and other kingdoms contained in the collection known as "Rymer's Foedera."* 3 vols. London: Longmans, Green, 1869–85.

Harland, J., ed. *Historical Account of the Cistercian Abbey of Salley.* London: J. Russell Smith, 1853.

Hay, Denys, ed. and trans. *The Anglica Historia of Polydore Vergil, A.D. 1485–1537.* Camden Series, vol. 74. London: Offices of the Royal Historical Society, 1950. *See also* Ellis.

Henry the Eighth. *Answere Unto a Certaine Letter of Martyn Luther.* London, 1528; New York: Theatrvm Orbis Terrarvm, 1971.

Herzman, Ronald B., Graham Drake, and Eve Salisbury, eds. *Four Romances of England: King Horn, Havelok the Dane, Bevis of Hampton, Athelston.* TEAMS Middle English Texts. Kalamazoo, MI: Medieval Institute Publications, 1999.

Hewlett, Henry G., ed. *The Flowers of History by Roger de Wendover.* 3 vols. London: HMSO, 1887. 2:38–48.

Hildegard of Bingen. "Vita sanctae Hildegardis." *PL* 197: 91–130.

Holinshed, Raphael. *Chronicles.* www.english.ox.ac.uk/holinshed/.

The Holy Bible . . . made from the Latin Vulgate by John Wycliffe and His Followers. 4 vols. Ed. Josiah Forshall and Sir Frederic Madden. Oxford: Oxford University Press, 1850; rpt. New York: AMS Press, 1982.

Horrox, Rosemary, trans. and ed. *The Black Death.* Manchester: Manchester University Press, 1994.

Horstmann, Carl, ed. *Proprium Sanctorum. Archiv* 81 (1888): 83–114, 300–321.

———. *Yorkshire Writers.* 2 vols. London, 1895–96.

Howlett, Richard, ed. *Chronicles of the Reigns of Stephen, Henry II, and Richard I.* Rolls Series 82. Wiesbaden: Kraus Reprint, 1964.

Hudson, Anne, ed. *Two Wycliffite Texts: The Sermon of William Taylor 1406, the Testimony of William Thorpe, 1407.* EETS 301. Oxford: Oxford University Press, 1993.

Jacobus de Cessolis. *The Game of the Chesse by William Caxton.* Reproduced in facsimile. London: J. R. Smith, 1860.

James, M. R., ed. and trans. *Walter Map. De Nugis Curialium. Courtiers' Trifles.* Rev. ed. C. N. L. Brooke and R. A. B. Mynors. Oxford: Clarendon Press, 2002.

James, M. R., and Albert Van de Put, eds. *The Treatise of Walter de Milemete De Nobilitatibus, sapientiis, et prudentiis regum.* Reproduced in facsimile. Oxford: Oxford University Press, 1913.

Johnson, C., ed. and trans. *Richard Fitz Nigel: Dialogues de Scaccario.* Rev. ed. Oxford Medieval Texts. Oxford: Oxford University Press, 1983.

Johnson, George W. *The Fairfax Correspondence: Memoirs of the Reign of Charles the First.* 2 vols. London: Richard Bentley, 1848.

Kingsford, C. L., ed. *The Song of Lewes.* Oxford: Clarendon Press, 1890.

Knight, Ione Kemp. *Wimbledon's Sermon "Redde Rationem Villicationis Tue": A Middle English Sermon of the Fifteenth Century.* Pittsburgh: Duquesne University Press, 1967.

Knight, Stephen, and Thomas Ohlgren, eds. *Robin Hood and Other Outlaw Tales.* 2nd ed. Kalamazoo, MI: Medieval Institute Publications, 2000.

———. *The Tale of Gamelyn.* In *Robin Hood and Other Outlaw Tales.* Kalamazoo, MI: Medieval Institute Publications, 1997.

Lambarde, William. *A Perambulation of Kent.* London: H. Middleton, 1576.

Lamond, Elizabeth, ed. *A Discourse of the Common Weal of this Realm of England* (1581). New York: Burt Franklin, [1971] 1993.

Latimer, Hugh. *Sermons.* London: J. M. Dent, 1926.

Leach, Arthur Francis, ed. *Memorials of Beverley Minster: The Chapter Act Book of the Collegiate Church of St. John of Beverley, A.D. 1286–1347.* Publications of the Surtees Society 98, 1898.

Leadam, I. S., ed. *Domesday of Inclosures.* London: Royal Historical Society, 1897.

LeClercq, Jean. "La Collection des lettres d'Yves de Chartres." *Revue Bénédictine* 56 (1945–46): 123–25.

———. "Lettres de vocation à la vie monastique." *Analecta Monastica*, 3rd ser., *Studia Anselmiana* 37 (1955): 172–89.

Lloyd, Charles, ed. *Formularies of Faith.* Oxford: Clarendon Press, 1825.

Lockwood, Shelley, ed. *Sir John Fortescue: On the Laws and Governance of England.* Cambridge: Cambridge University Press, 1997.

Lovatt, Marie, ed. *English Episcopal Acta, 27, York, 1189–1212.* Oxford: Oxford University Press, 2004.

Lumby, Joseph R., ed. *Polychronicon Ranulphi Higden . . . with English Translations of John Trevisa and of an Unknown Writer of the Fifteenth Century.* 9 vols. London: HMSO, 1871; London: Kraus Reprint, 1964.

Macray, W. D., ed. *Chronicon Abbatiae Rameseinsis.* Rolls Series 83. London: Longman and Co., 1886.

Madden, F., H. H. E. Craster, and N. Denholm-Young, eds. *A Summary Catalogue of Western Manuscripts in the Bodleian Library at Oxford.* Vol. 2, pt. 2. Oxford: Clarendon Press, 1937.

Markham, Gervase. *The English Husbandman* (1613). New York: Garland, 1982.

Mather, Cotton. *Magnalia Christi Americana: or the ecclesiastical history of New England, from its first planting in the year 1620.* London: Thomas Parkhurst, 1702.

Matthew, F. D., ed. *The English Works of Wyclif.* EETS 74. London: Trübner & Co., 1880.

McDermid, Richard T.W., ed. *Beverley Minster Fasti. Yorkshire Archaeological Society Record Series* 149 (1993 for 1990).

Mead, William, ed. *The Famous Historie of Chinon of England . . . to which is added The Assertion of King Arthure translated by Richard Robinson from Leland's Assertio Inclytissimi Arturii.* EETS 165. London: Oxford University Press, 1925.

Migne, J.-P. [Jacques-Paul]. *Patrologiae cursus completus. Series Latina.* Paris: [various publishers], 1844–64.

Mikkers, E. "Un Speculum novitii inédit d'Etienne de Salley." *Collectanea Ordinis Cisterciensium reformatorum* 8 (1946): 2–68.

Miller, Thomas, ed. and trans. *The Old English Version of Bede's "Ecclesiastical History of the English People."* EETS 95, 96. London: Trübner & Co., 1890.

Millet, Bella, and Jocelyn Wogan-Browne, ed. and trans. *Medieval English Prose for Women: Selections from the Katherine Group and "Ancrene Wisse."* Oxford: Clarendon Press, 1990.

Milton, John. *History of Britain.* In *Complete Prose Works of John Milton,* vol. 5, ed. French Fogle. New Haven: Yale University Press, 1971.

Miskimin, Alice, ed. *Susannah: An Alliterative Poem of the Fourteenth Century.* New Haven: Yale University Press, 1969.

Moisant, Joseph. *De Speculo Regis Edwardi III.* Paris: A. Picard, 1891.

Montaiglon, Anatole de, ed. *Le livre du Chevalier de la Tour Landry.* Paris: Jannet, 1854.

More, Thomas. *Utopia*. Trans. George M. Logan and Robert M. Adams. Cambridge Texts in the History of Political Thought. Cambridge: Cambridge University Press, 1989.

———. *Utopia*. In *The Complete Works of St. Thomas More*, vol. 4, ed. Edward Surtz and J. H. Hexter. New Haven: Yale University Press, 1963.

Mozley, J. H., ed. "Susanna and the Elders: Three Medieval Poems." *Studi Medievali*, n.s., 3 (1930): 27–52.

Mynors, R. A. B., R. M. Thomson, and M. Winterbottom, ed. and trans. *William of Malmesbury. Gesta Regum Anglorum*. 2 vols. Oxford: Clarendon Press, 1998.

Nederman, Cary J., trans. *Political Thought in Early Fourteenth-Century England: Treatises by Walter of Milemete, William of Pagula, and William of Ockham*. Tempe: Arizona Center of Medieval and Renaissance Studies, in collaboration with Brepols, 2002.

Nichols, J. G., ed. *Grants etc. from the Crown during the Reign of Edward the Fifth. Camden Society*, o.s., 60 (1854).

Offord., M. Y., ed. *The Book of the Knight of the Tower*. Trans. William Caxton. London: Oxford University Press, 1971.

Owen, Nancy H., ed. "Thomas Wimbledon's Sermon: 'Redde racionem villicacionis tue.'" *Medieval Studies* 28 (1966): 176–97.

Page, William. *Victoria County History of Yorkshire*. 3 vols. London: A. Constable and Co., 1907–13.

Parfitt, George, ed. *Ben Jonson: The Complete Poems*. New Haven: Yale University Press, 1982.

The Parliament Rolls of Medieval England. Ed. C. Given-Wilson et al. Leicester: Scholarly Digital Editions and the National Archives, 2005.

Pearsall, Derek, ed. *William Langland: Piers Plowman, a New Annotated Edition of the C-Text*. Exeter: University of Exeter Press, 2008.

Peck, Russell, A., ed. *The Pistel of Swete Susan*. In *Heroic Women from the Old Testament in Middle English Verse*. Kalamazoo, MI: Medieval Institute Publications, 1991.

Piers Plowman. 3 vols. London: Athlone Press, 1988, 1988, 1997.

The A Version. Ed. George Kane (1988).

The B Version. Ed. George Kane and E. Talbot Donaldson (1988).

The C Version. Ed. George Russell and George Kane (1997).

Pope, Mildred Katharine, ed. *Thomas, The Romance of Horn. ANTS* 9, 10, 12, 13. Oxford: Blackwell, 1955–64.

Powicke, F. M., trans. and annot. *The Life of Aelred of Rievaulx by Walter Daniel*. Introd. Marsha Dutton. Kalamazoo, MI: Cistercian Publications, 1994.

Raby, F. J. E., ed. *Poems of John of Hoveden*. Publications of the Surtees Society 154 (1939).

Raleigh, Sir Walter. *The arraignment and conviction of Sr. Walter Rawleigh . . . on 17 November 1603*. London, 1648.

————. *A Breviary of the History of England.* London: S. Keble and D. Brown, 1693.

Reames, Sherry L., ed. *The Legend of Mary Magdalene, Penitent and Apostle.* In *Middle English Legends of Women Saints.* Kalamazoo, MI: Medieval Institute Publications, 2003.

Reed, Edward Bliss, ed. *The Poems of Thomas, Third Lord Fairfax, from MS Fairfax 40 in the Bodleian Library, Oxford. Transactions of the Connecticut Academy of Arts and Sciences* 14 (1909).

Riley, Henry T., ed. and trans. *The Annal of Roger de Hoveden.* 2 vols. London, 1853; rpt. New York: AMS Press, 1968.

————, ed. *Munimenta Gildhallae Londoniensis: Liber Albus, Liber Custumarum et Liber Horn.* 2 vols. London: Longman, Brown, Green, Longmans and Roberts, 1859.

Roberts, John, ed. *A Critical Anthology of English Recussant Devotional Prose, 1558–1603.* Duquesne Studies Philological Series 7. Pittsburgh: Duquesne University Press, 1966.

Robynson, Raphe. *A frutefull pleasaunt, [and] wittie worke, of the best state of a publique weale and of the newe Yle, called Vtopia.* 2nd ed. London, 1556.

Roche, Robert. *Evstathia, or the Constancie of Susanna.* Oxford: Joseph Barnes, 1599.

Rous, John. *Historia Regum Angliae.* London, 1716.

Rymer, Thomas, ed. *Foedera.* Searchable text ed. London, 1821; Ontario, CA: Tanner Ritchie, 2006.

Salter, Elizabeth. *English and International: Studies in the Literature, Art, and Patronage of Medieval England.* Ed. Derek Pearsall and Nicolette Zeeman. Cambridge: Cambridge University Press, 1988.

The Sermons of the Right Reverend Father in God, Master Hugh Latimer, . . . Many of which were preached before King Edward VI . . . on the religious and civil liberties of Englishmen, &c. To which is prefixed, Bishop Latimer's life. 2 vols. London: J. Scott, 1758.

Shakespeare, William. *King Richard II.* Ed. Charles R. Forker. London: Arden Shakespeare, 2002.

Smith, Nigel, ed. *The Poems of Andrew Marvell.* Rev. ed. New York: Pearson/Longman, 2007.

Smithers, G. V., ed. *Havelock.* Oxford: Clarendon Press, 1982.

Stapleton, Thomas, trans. *The History of the Church of England compiled by Venerable Bede Englishman.* Antwerp, 1565.

Statutes of the Realm. 4 vols. London, 1810–19. Searchable text edition. Burlington, ONT: Tanner Ritchie, n.d.

Steele, Robert, ed. *Lydgate and Burgh's Secrees of old philisoffres: A version of the "Secreta secretorum."* Ed. from Sloane MS 2464, with introduction, notes, and glossary. EETS 65–66. London: K. Paul, Trench, Trübner & Co., 1894.

Steggle, Matthew. "Aylett, Robert (*c.* 1582–1655)." In *DNB.*

Stevens, Martin, and A. C. Cawley, eds. *The Towneley Plays.* 2 vols. Oxford: Oxford University Press, 1994.

Stevens, Wallace. *Collected Poems.* Ed. John N. Serio. New York: Alfred A. Knopf, 2009.

Stovall, Floyd, ed. *Walt Whitman: Prose Works, 1892.* 2 vols. New York: New York University Press, 1964.

Stow, John. *Annales, or, a generall chronicle of England. Begun by Iohn Stow: continued and augmented with matters forraigne and domestique, ancient and moderne, vnto the end of this present yeere, 1631.* By Edmund Howes. London, 1632.

———. *Chronicles of England.* London: Ralphe Newberie, 1580.

Stringer, Gary A., gen. ed. *The Variorum Edition of the Poetry of John Donne.* Vol. 6. Bloomington: Indiana University Press, 1994.

Talbot, C. H. "Letters of Vocation by Roger de Byland." *Analecta Sacri Ordinis Cisterciensis* 7 (1951): 218–31.

Taylor, Jeremy. *Ductor dubitantium, or The rule of conscience in all her general measures.* London, 1660.

Tertullian. "De Corona." *PL* 2: 76–101.

Thomas the Cistercian. *Cantica Canticorum. PL* 206: 17–859.

Thompson, Edward Maunde, ed. *Adam of Murimuth, Continuatio Chronicarum.* Roll Series 93. London: HMSO, 1889; Weisbaden: Kraus Reprint, 1965.

———. *Robertus de Avesbury de Gestis Mirabilibus Regis Edwardi Tertii.* Rolls Series 93. London: HMSO; Weisbaden: Kraus Reprint, 1965.

Todd, James Henthorn, ed. *Apology for Lollard Doctrines.* Camden Society, 1842. New York: AMS Press, 1968.

Townsend, George, ed. *The Acts and Monuments of John Foxe.* 8 vols. New York: AMS Press, 1965.

Trigg, Stephanie, ed. *Wynnere and Wastoure.* EETS 297. Oxford: Oxford University Press, 1990.

Trigge, Francis. *An apologie, or defence of our dayes, against the vaine murmurings & complaints of manie wherein is plainly proued, that our dayes are more happie & blessed than the dayes of our forefathers.* London: John Wolfe, 1589.

Turville-Petre, Thorlac, ed. *Alliterative Poetry of the Later Middle Ages.* Washington, DC: Catholic University of America Press, 1989.

Tusser, Thomas. *Fiue hundreth pointes of good Husbandrie.* London: Henrie Denham, 1585.

van Houts, Elisabeth M. C., ed. and trans. *The Gesta Normannorum Ducum of William of Jumièges, Orderic Vitalis, and Robert of Torigni.* 2 vols. Oxford: Oxford University Press, 1992.

Vergil, Polydore. *Anglicae Historiae* (Basel, 1555). Facsimile ed. Menston, UK: Scholar Press, 1972.

The Vernon Manuscript: A Facsimile of Bodleian Library, Oxford, MS Eng. Poet.a.1, with an Introduction by A.I. Doyle. Cambridge: D. S. Brewer, 1987.

Viard, Jules, and Eugène Déprez, eds. *Chronique de Jean le Bel.* 2 vols. Paris: Librairie Renouard, 1904.

Virginia. Governor and Council. The Right Honourable Thomas Lord Fairfax,—petitioner, the Governor and Council of Virginia, in right of the Crown, Defendants. The case on behalf of the Crown. [London], [1745]. Eighteenth Century Collections Online.

Walbran, John Richard, ed. *Hugh of Kirkstall. Narratio de Fundatione Fontanis Monasterii* in *Memorials of the Abbey of St. Mary of Fountains.* 3 vols. Publications of the Surtees Society, 42, 67, 130 (1863–1918).

Waller, A. R., ed. *Abraham Cowley.* 2 vols. Cambridge: Cambridge University Press, 1905.

Wallis, Faith, trans. *Bede's The Reckoning of Time.* Liverpool: Liverpool University Press, 1999.

Warner, George, ed. *The Libelle of Englyshe Polycye: A Poem on the Use of Sea-Power, 1436.* Oxford: Clarendon Press, 1926.

Wenzel, Siegfried, ed. *Fasciculus Morum: A Fourteenth-Century Preacher's Handbook.* University Park: Pennsylvania State University Press, 1989.

Wharton, H., ed. *Anglia Sacra.* 2 vols. 1691; rpt. Westmead, UK: Gregg International, 1969.

Wheatley, Edward. "The Nun's Priest's Tale." In Correale and Hamel, *Sources and Analogues of the "Canterbury Tales,"* 449–90.

Wheler, George. *The Protestant Monastery; or Christian Œconomicks containing Directions for the Religious Conduct of a Family.* London, 1698.

Whitelock, Dorothy, ed. *English Historical Documents.* Vol. 1. London: Eyre & Spottiswoode, 1955.

Whittaker, William Joseph, ed. *The Mirror of Justices.* London: Bernard Quaritch, 1895.

Wilkins, David. *Concilia Magnae Britannicae.* London, 1737.

Williams, C. H., ed. *English Historical Documents, 1485–1558.* New York: Oxford University Press, 1967.

Williamson, Joan B., ed. *Philippe de Mézières: Le Livre de la Vertu du Sacrement de Mariage.* Washington, DC: Catholic University of America Press, 1993.

Wilmart, A. "Les mélanges de Matthieu Préchantre de Ricvaulx au début du XIIIe siècle." *Revue Bénédictine* 52 (1940):15–84.

Woodbine, George, ed., Samuel E. Thorne, trans. *De legibus et consuetudinibus Angliae (On the Laws and Customs of England)* attributed to Henry of Bratton. Bracton On-Line: http://hlsl5.law.harvard.edu/bracton/Framed/mframe.htm.

Woods, Susanne, ed. *The Poems of Aemilia Lanyer.* New York: Oxford University Press, 1993.

Wright, Thomas, ed. *Political Poems and Songs relating to English History . . . from the Accession of Edward III to that of Richard III.* London: HMSO, 1839; Nendeln: Kraus Reprint, 1965).

———. *Three Chapters of Letters Relating to the Suppression of Monasteries.* Camden Society, 26. London: John Bowyer Nichols and Son, 1843.

Secondary Texts

Addison, Kenneth."Changing Places: The Cistercian Settlement and Rapid Climate Change in Britain." In *A Place to Believe In: Locating Medieval Landscapes,* 211–38. University Park: Pennsylvania State University Press, 2006.

Aers, David. *Community, Gender, and Individual Identity: English Writing, 1360–1430.* London: Routledge, 1988.

———. *Faith, Ethics, and Church Writing in England, 1360–1409.* Cambridge: D. S. Brewer, 2000.

———. *Piers Plowman and Christian Allegory.* London: Edward Arnold, 1975.

———. *Salvation and Sin: Augustine, Langland, and Fourteenth-Century Theology.* Notre Dame: University of Notre Dame Press, 2009.

———. *Sanctifying Signs: Making Christian Tradition in Late Medieval England.* Notre Dame: University of Notre Dame Press, 2004.

———, ed. *Culture and History, 1350–1600: Essays on English Communities, Identities, and Writing.* Detroit: Wayne State University Press, 1992.

Aers, David, Bob Hodge, and Gunther Kress, eds. *Literature, Landscape, and Society in England, 1580–1680.* Totowa, NJ: Barnes and Noble, 1981.

Alexander, Jonathan J. G., "Labeur and Paresse: Ideological Representations of Medieval Peasant Labor." *Art Bulletin* 72, no. 3 (1990): 436–52.

Anderson, Benedict Scott. "'Darke Speech': Matthew Parker and the Reforming of History." *Sixteenth Century Journal* 29 (1998): 1061–83.

Anderson, Douglas. *William Bradford's Books: "Of Plimmoth Plantation" and the Printed Word.* Baltimore: Johns Hopkins University Press, 2003.

Archer, Ian W. "Smith, Sir Thomas (1513–1577)." In *DNB*.

Astil, G. G. *A Medieval Industrial Complex and Its Landscape: The Metalworking Watermills and Workshops of Bordesley Abbey.* York: Council for British Archaeology, 1993.

Aston, Margaret. *England's Iconoclasts.* Oxford: Oxford University Press, 1988.

———. "English Ruins and English History: The Dissolution and the Sense of the Past." *JWCI* 36 (1973): 231–55.

Baker, L. G. D. "The Genesis of English Cistercian Chronicles: The Foundation History of Fountains Abbey." 2 pts. *Analecta Cisterciensia* 25 (1969): 14–41; 31 (1975): 179–212.

Barney, Stephen A. "The Plowshare of the Tongue." *Mediaeval Studies* 35 (1973): 261–93.

Barrett, Robert W. *Against All England: Regional Identity and Cheshire Writing, 1195–1656.* Notre Dame: University of Notre Dame Press, 2009.

Barron, Caroline M. *London in the Later Middle Ages: Government and People, 1200–1500.* Oxford: Oxford University Press, 2004.

Bates, David. "Normandy and England after 1066." *EHR* 413 (1989): 851–80

Bateson, Mary. "The Pilgrimage of Grace." *EHR* 5 (1890): 330–45.

Bateson, Mary, and Thomas Cromwell. "Aske's Examination." *EHR* 5 (1890): 550–73.

Beaune, Colette. *The Birth of an Ideology: Myths and Symbols of Nation in Late Medieval France.* Trans. Susan Ross Hudson. Berkeley: University of California Press, 1991.

Beckwith, Sarah. "Shakespeare's Resurrections." In Curtis and Watkins, *Shakespeare and the Middle Ages,* 45–67.

———. *Signifying God: Social Relation and Symbolic Act in the York Corpus Christi Plays.* Chicago: University of Chicago Press, 2001.

Bell, David N. "Chambers, Cells, and Cubicles: The Cistercian General Chapter and the Development of the Private Room." In Kinder, *Perspectives for an Architecture of Solitude,* 187–98.

Bennett, Michael. *Community, Class, and Careerism: Cheshire and Lancaster Society in the Age of "Sir Gawain and the Green Knight."* Cambridge: Cambridge University Press, 1983.

Bent, Margaret, and Andrew Wathey, eds. *Fauvel Studies: Allegory, Chronicle, Music, and Image in Paris, Bibliothèque Nationale de France, MS franc*ais 146.* Oxford: Clarendon Press, 1998.

Berman, Constance. *The Cistercian Evolution: The Invention of a Religious Order in Twelfth-Century Europe.* Philadelphia: University of Pennsylvania Press, 2000.

Bernard, G.W. *The King's Reformation: Henry VIII and the Remaking of the English Church.* New Haven: Yale University Press, 2005.

Binski, Paul. *The Painted Chamber at Westminster.* London: Society of Antiquaries of London, 1986.

———. *Westminster Abbey and the Plantagenets: Kingship and the Representation of Power, 1200–1400.* New Haven: Yale University Press, 1995.

Blanton, Virginia. *Signs of Devotion: The Cult of St. Æthelthryth in Medieval England, 695–1615.* University Park: Pennsylvania State University Press, 2007.

Boyle, L. E. "William of Pagula and the *Speculum Regis Edwardi III.*" *Mediaeval Studies* 32 (1970): 329–36.

Bradbury, Nancy Mason. "The Traditional Origins of *Havelok the Dane.*" *SP* 90 (1995): 115–42.

Brayley, Edward Wedlake, and John Britton. *The History of the Ancient Palace and Late Houses of Parliament at Westminster.* London: John Weale, 1836.

Bridgett, T. E. *Our Lady's Dower or How England gained and lost that title.* London: Burns and Oates, 1875.

Brown, George Hardin. *A Companion to Bede.* Woodbridge, UK: Boydell Press, 2009.

Brown, Stuart E., Jr. *Virginia Baron: The Story of Thomas 6th Lord Fairfax.* Berryville, VA: Chesapeake Book Company, 1965.

Buc, Philippe. "The Book of Kings: Nicholas of Lyra's Mirror of Princes." In *Nicholas of Lyra: The Senses of Scripture,* ed. Philip Krey and Lesley Smith, 83–109. Boston: Brill, 2000.

Buell, Lawrence. *New England Literary Culture from Revolution through Renaissance.* Cambridge: Cambridge University Press, 1986.

Burns, J. H., ed. *The Cambridge History of Medieval Political Thought, c. 350–1450.* Cambridge: Cambridge University Press, 1988.

Burt, Richard, and John Michael Archer, eds. *Enclosure Acts: Sexuality, Property, and Culture in Early Modern England.* Ithaca: Cornell University Press, 1994.

Burton, Pierre-André. "Aux origenes de l'expansion anglaise de Cîteaux. La fondation de Rievaulx et la conversion d'Aelred: 1128–1134." *Collectanea cisterciensia* 61 (1999): 186–214.

Bushnell, Rebecca. *Green Desire: Imagining Early Modern English Gardens.* Ithaca: Cornell University Press, 2003.

Butterfield, Ardis. *The Familiar Enemy: Chaucer, Language, and Nation in the Hundred Years War.* Oxford: Oxford University Press, 2009.

———. "The Refrain and the Transformation of Genre in the *Roman de Fauvel.*" In Bent and Wathey, *Fauvel Studies,* 105–60.

Camille, Michael. "Hybridity, Monstrosity, and Bestiality in the *Roman de Fauvel.*" In Bent and Wathey, *Fauvel Studies,* 161–74.

———. "Labouring for the Lord: The Ploughman and the Social Order in the Luttrell Psalter." *Art History* 10 (1987): 423–55.

———. *Mirror in Parchment: The Luttrell Psalter and the Making of Medieval England.* Chicago: University of Chicago Press, 1998.

Campbell, Lily B. *Divine Poetry and Drama in Sixteenth-Century England.* Berkeley: University of California Press, 1959.

Canning, J. "Law, Sovereignty and Corporation Theory, 1300–1450." In Burns, *Cambridge History of Medieval Political Thought,* 454–76.

Cannon, Christopher. *The Grounds of English Literature.* Oxford: Oxford University Press, 2004.

Carley, James P. *The Books of King Henry VIII and His Wives.* Pref. David Starkey. London: British Library, 2004.

Carpenter, David. *The Struggle for Mastery: Britain, 1066–1284.* Oxford: Oxford University Press, 2003.

Carroll, William C. "'The Nursery of Beggary': Enclosure, Vagrancy, and Sedition in the Tudor-Stuart Period." In Burt and Archer, *Enclosure Acts*, 34–47.

Cassidy-Welch, Megan. *Monastic Spaces and Their Meanings: Thirteenth-Century English Cistercian Monasteries.* Turnholt: Brepols, 2001.

Catto, J. "Andrew Horn: Law and History in Fourteenth-Century England." In *The Writing of History in the Middle Ages: Essays Presented to R. W. Southern*, ed. R. H. C. Davis and J. M. Wallace-Hadril et al., 367–92. Oxford: Oxford University Press, 1981.

Cavanaugh, Sheila H. "A Study of Books Privately Owned in England, 1300–1450." Ph.D. diss., University of Pennsylvania, 1980.

Chambers, D. D. C. *The Planters of the English Landscape Garden: Botany, Trees, and the Georgics.* New Haven: Yale University Press, 1993.

———. "'Wild Pastorall Encounter': John Evelyn, John Beale and the Renegotiation of Pastoral in the Mid-Seventeenth Century." In Leslie and Raylor, *Culture and Cultivation*, 173–194.

Cheney, C. R. "King John and the Papal Interdict." *Bulletin of the John Rylands Library* 31 (1948): 295–317.

———. "King John's Reaction to the Interdict on England." *Transactions of the Royal Historical Society*, 4th ser., 31 (1949): 129–50.

Chrimes, S. B. *English Constitutional Ideas in the Fifteenth Century.* Cambridge: Cambridge University Press, 1936.

Christianson, C. Paul. *The Riverside Gardens of Thomas More's London.* New Haven: Yale University Press, 2005.

Clark, Gregory, and Anthony Clark. "Common Rights to Land in England, 1475–1839." *Journal of Economic History* 61 (2001): 1009–36.

Clark, James G. *A Monastic Renaissance at St. Albans.* Oxford: Clarendon Press, 2004.

Clarke, Catherine A. M. *Literary Landscapes and the Idea of England, 700–1400.* Cambridge: D. S. Brewer, 2006.

Clarke, M. V. *Fourteenth Century Studies.* Ed. L. S. Sutherland and M. McKisack. Oxford: Clarendon Press, 1937.

Coghill, Nevill. "The Character of Piers Plowman." *Medium Ævum* 2 (1933): 108–35.

Cohen, Jeffrey Jerome. "Green Children from Another World, or the Archipelago in England." In *Cultural Diversity in the British Middle Ages: Archipelago, Island, England*, 75–94. New York: Palgrave Macmillan, 2008.

———. *Hybridity, Identity, and Monstrosity in Medieval Britain: On Difficult Middles.* New York: Palgrave Macmillan, 2006.

Coletti, Theresa. *Mary Magdalene and the Drama of Saints: Theater, Gender, and Religion in Late Medieval England.* Philadelphia: University of Pennsylvania Press, 2004.

Coletti, Theresa, and Gail McMurray Gibson. "The Tudor Origins of Medieval Drama." In *A Companion to Tudor Literature*, ed. Kent Cartwright, 228–45. Oxford: Blackwell, 2010.

Colie, Rosalie L. *My Ecchoing Song: Andrew Marvell's Poetry of Criticism.* Princeton: Princeton University Press, 1970.

Colvin, Howard. *The History of the King's Works.* 6 vols. London: HMSO, 1963–73.

Connolly, Daniel K. *The Maps of Matthew Paris: Medieval Journeys through Time, Space, and Liturgy.* Woodbridge, UK: Boydell Press, 2009.

Constable, Giles. "The Vision of a Cistercian Novice." In *Petrus Venerabilis, 1156–1956: Studies and Texts Commemorating the Eighth Centenary of His Death*, ed. Giles Constable and James Kritzeck, 95–98. Studia Anselmiana 40. Rome: Herder, 1956.

Coppack, Glyn. "Sawley Abbey: An English Cistercian Abbey on the Edge of 'Stabilitas.'" *Cîteaux* 52 (2001): 319–36.

Cornelius, R. D. "*Piers Plowman* and the *Roman de Fauvel*." *PMLA* 47 (1932): 363–67.

Coupe, C. "An Old Picture." *The Month* 84 (1895): 229–42.

Crane, Susan. *Insular Romance: Politics, Faith, and Culture in Anglo-Norman and Middle English Literature.* Berkeley: University of California Press, 1986.

Crawford, Rachel. *Poetry, Enclosure, and the Vernacular Landscape, 1700–1830.* Cambridge: Cambridge University Press, 2002.

Crewe, Jonathan. "The Garden State: Marvell's Poetic of Enclosure." In Burt and Archer, *Enclosure Acts*, 270–89.

Crick, Julia C. *The "Historia Regum Britannie" of Geoffrey of Monmouth IV: Dissemination and Reception in the Later Middle Ages.* Cambridge: D. S. Brewer, 1991.

Cross, Claire. "Excising the Virgin Mary from the Civic Life of Tudor York." *Northern History* 39 (2002): 279–84.

Curley, Michael J. "John of Bridlington (c. 1320–1379)." In *DNB*.

Curtis, Perry, and John Watkins, eds. *Shakespeare and the Middle Ages.* Oxford: Oxford University Press, 2009.

Daniell, David, ed. *William Tyndale: The Obedience of a Christian Man.* London: Penguin Books, 2000.

Davies, R. R. *The First English Empire: Power and Identities in the British Isles, 1093–1343.* Oxford: Oxford University Press, 2000.

Davis, Kathleen. "National Writing in the Ninth Century: A Reminder for Postcolonial Thinking about the Nation." *JMEMS* 28 (1995): 611–37.

Davis, R. H. C. *King Stephen, 1135–1154.* Berkeley: University of California Press, 1967.

DeGregorio, Scott. "Bede's *In Ezram et Neemiam* and the Reform of the Northumbrian Church." *Speculum* 79 (2004):1–25.

————, ed. *The Cambridge Companion to Bede*. Cambridge: Cambridge University Press, 2010.

————. "Literary Contexts: Caedmon's Hymn as a Center of Bede's World." In *Caedmon's Hymn and Material Culture in the World of Bede*, ed. Allen J. Frantzen and John Hines, 51–79. Morgantown: West Virginia University Press, 2007.

Denholm-Young, N., and H. H. E. Craster. "Roger Dodsworth and His Circle." *Yorkshire Archaeological Journal* 32 (1934): 5–32.

Diehl, Huston. *Staging Reform, Reforming the Stage: Protestantism and Popular Theater in Early Modern England*. Ithaca: Cornell University Press, 1997.

Dimmick, Jeremy, James Simpson, and Nicolette Zeeman. *Images, Idolatry, and Iconoclasms in Late Medieval England*. Oxford: Oxford University Press, 2002.

Donovan, Claire. *The de Brailes Hours: Shaping the Book of Hours in Thirteenth-Century Oxford*. Toronto: University of Toronto Press, 1991.

Dubrow, Heather. "The Country-House Poem, a Study in Generic Development." *Genre* 12 (1979): 153–79.

Duffy, Eamon. *The Stripping of the Altars: Traditional Religion in England, 1400–1580*. 2nd ed. New Haven: Yale University Press, 2005.

Dunbabin, Jean. "Government." In Burns, *Cambridge History of Medieval Political Thought*, 477–519.

Dyer, Christopher. *An Age of Transition? Economy and Society in England in the Later Middle Ages*. Oxford: Clarendon Press, 2005.

————. "Deserted Medieval Villages in the West Midlands." *Economic History Review*, n.s., 35 (1982): 19–34.

————. *Lords and Peasants in a Changing Society: The Estates of the Bishopric of Worcester, 680–1540*. Cambridge: Cambridge University Press, 1980.

————. *Making a Living in the Middle Ages: The People of Britain, 850–1520*. New Haven: Yale University Press, 2002.

Edwards, Robert R. *Chaucer and Boccaccio: Antiquity and Modernity*. New York: Palgrave, 2002.

Erler, Mary C. *Women, Reading, and Piety in Late Medieval England*. Cambridge: Cambridge University Press, 2002.

Fabre, Marie-Louise. *Suzanne ou les avatars d'un motif biblique*. Paris: L'Harmatton, 2000.

Fein, Susanna Greer. "The Early Thirteen-Line Stanza: Style and Metrics Reconsidered." *Parergon* 18 (2000): 97–126.

————, ed. *Studies in the Harley Manuscript: The Scribes, Contents, and Social Contexts of British Library MS Harley 2253*. Kalamazoo, MI: Medieval Institute Publications, 2000.

Ferguson, Peter. *Architecture of Solitude: Cistercian Abbeys in Twelfth-Century England*. Princeton: Princeton University Press, 1984.

Fitzherbert, Reginald H. C. "The Authorship of the 'Book of Husbandry' and the 'Book of Surveying.'" *EHR* 12 (1897): 225–36.

Foot, Sarah. "The Making of *Angelcyn*: English Identity before the Norman Conquest." *Transactions of the Royal Historical Society*, 6th ser., 6 (1996): 25–49.

Fowler, Elizabeth. "Towards a History of Performativity: Sacrament, Social Contract, and *The Merchant of Venice*." In Curtis and Watkins, *Shakespeare and the Middle Ages*, 68–77.

Freeman, Elizabeth. *Narratives of a New Order: Cistercian Historical Writing in England, 1150–1220*. Medieval Church Studies, 2. Turnholt: Brepols, 2002.

Fryde, E. B. *Peasants and Landlords in Later Medieval England*. New York: St. Martin's Press, 1996.

Fulford, Tim. *Landscape, Liberty and Authority: Criticism and Politics from Thomson to Wordsworth*. Cambridge: Cambridge University Press, 1996.

Galloway, Andrew. "Laʒmon's Gift." *PMLA* 121 (2006): 717–34.

———. "Writing History in England." In *The Cambridge History of Medieval English Literature*, ed. David Wallace, 255–83. Cambridge: Cambridge University Press, 1999.

Gentles, Ian J. "Fairfax, Thomas, third Lord Fairfax of Cameron (1612–1671)." In *DNB*.

George, Karen. *Gildas's "De Excidio Britonnum" and the Early British Church*. Woodbridge, UK: Boydell Press, 2009.

Giancarlo, Matthew. *Parliament and Literature in Late Medieval England*. Cambridge: Cambridge University Press, 2007.

Gibson, Gail McMurray. *The Theater of Devotion: East Anglian Drama and Society in the Late Middle Ages*. Chicago: University of Chicago Press, 1989.

Gillingham, John. "The Context and Purposes of Geoffrey of Monmouth's *History of the Kings of Britain*." *Anglo Norman Studies* 13 (1990): 99–118.

———. *The English in the Twelfth Century: Imperialism, National Identity, and Political Values*. Woodbridge, UK: Boydell Press, 2000.

Gilson, J. P. "The Library of Henry Savile of Banke." *Transactions of the Bibliographical Society* 9 (1906–8): 127–210.

Goodman, Anthony. "The Countess and the Rebels: Essex and a Crisis in English Society." *Essex Archaeology and History: Transactions of the Essex Archaeological Society* 2 (1972): 274.

———. *The Loyal Conspiracy: The Lords Appellant under Richard II*. Coral Gables, FL: University of Miami Press, 1971.

Gordon, Dillian. *Making and Meaning: The Wilton Diptych*. London: National Gallery Publications, 1993.

———. "A New Discovery in the Wilton Diptych." *Burlington Magazine* 134 (1992): 662–67.

————. "The Wilton Diptych." In Gordon, Monas, and Elam, *The Regal Image of Richard II and the Wilton Diptych*, 19–26.

Gordon, Dillian, Lisa Monas, and Caroline Elam, eds. *The Regal Image of Richard II and the Wilton Diptych*. London: Harvey Miller, 1997.

Gottfried, Rudolf B. "The Authorship of *A Breviary of the History of England*." *SP* 53 (1956): 172–90.

Graham, Timothy. "Matthew Parker's Manuscripts: An Elizabethan Library and Its Use." In *The Cambridge History of Libraries in Britain and Ireland*, vol. 1, ed. Elisabeth Leedham-Green and Teresa Webber, 322–44. Cambridge: Cambridge University Press, 2006.

Gransden, Antonia. *Historical Writing in England: c. 550 to c. 1307*. Ithaca: Cornell University Press, 1973.

————. *Historical Writing in England II: c. 1307 to the Early Sixteenth Century*. Ithaca: Cornell University Press, 1982.

Green, Richard Firth. *A Crisis of Truth: Literature and Law in Ricardian England*. Philadelphia: University of Pennsylvania Press, 1999.

Griffin, Patsy. "'Twas no Religious House till now': Marvell's 'Upon Appleton House.'" *SEL* 28 (1988): 61–76.

Gunn, Vicky. *Bede's "Historiae": Genre, Rhetoric, and the Construction of Anglo-Saxon Church History*. Woodbridge, UK: Boydell Press, 2009.

Hackett, Helen. *Virgin Mother, Maiden Queen: Elizabeth I and the Cult of the Virgin Mary*. New York: St. Martin's Press, 1995.

Haines, Roy Martin. *Archbishop John Stratford: Political Revolutionary and Champion of the Liberties of the English Church, ca. 1275–1348*. Toronto: Pontifical Institute of Medieval Studies, 1986.

Hanna, Ralph. "Augustinian Canons and Middle English Literature." In *The English Medieval Book: Studies in Memory of Jeremy Griffiths*, ed. A. S. G. Edwards, Vincent Gillespie, and Ralph Hanna, 27–42. London: British Library, 2000.

————. "Contextualizing the *Siege of Jerusalem*." *YLS* 6 (1992): 109–121.

————. "The Growth of Robert Thornton's Books." *Studies in Bibliography* 40 (1987): 51–61.

————. *London Literature, 1300–1380*. Cambridge: Cambridge University Press, 2005.

————. *Pursuing History: Middle English Manuscripts and Their Texts*. Stanford: Stanford University Press, 1996.

————. "Reconsidering the Auchinleck Manuscript." In *New Directions in Later Medieval Manuscript Studies: Essays from the 1998 Harvard Conference*, ed. Derek Pearsall, 91–102. York: York Medieval Press, 2000.

————. "Sir Thomas Berkeley and His Patronage." *Speculum* 64 (1989): 878–916.

————. *William Langland*. Brookfield, VT: Ashgate, 1993.

————. "Yorkshire Writers." Sir Israel Gollancz Memorial Lecture. *Proceedings of the British Academy* 121 (2003): 91–109.

Hanning, R.W. "*Havelok the Dane*: Structure, Symbols, Meaning." *SP* 64 (1967): 586–605.

————. "The Struggle between Noble Designs and Chaos: The Literary Tradition of Chaucer's Knight's Tale." In *Geoffrey Chaucer's "The Canterbury Tales": A Casebook*, ed. Lee Patterson, 49–69. Oxford: Oxford University Press, 2007.

————. *The Vision of History in Early Britain: From Gildas to Geoffrey of Monmouth*. New York: Columbia University Press, 1966.

Happé, Peter. *The Towneley Cycle: Unity and Diversity*. Cardiff: University of Wales Press, 2007.

Harris, Kate. "The Patron of BL MS Arundel 38." *Notes and Queries*, n.s., 31 (1984): 462–63.

Harriss, G.L. *King, Parliament, and Public Finance in Medieval England to 1369*. Oxford: Oxford University Press, 1975.

Harwood, Britton J. "Anxious over Peasants: Textual Disorder in *Winner and Waster*." *JMEMS* 36 (2006): 291–319.

Hastings, Maurice. *St. Stephen's Chapel and Its Place in the Development of Perpendicular Style in England*. Cambridge; Cambridge University Press, 1955.

Hathaway, Robert L. "Dramaturgic Variation in the Pre-Lopean Theatre: Susanna and the Elders." *Bulletin of the Comediantes* 43 (1991): 109–31.

Hay, Denys. *Polydore Vergil: Renaissance Man of Letters*. Oxford: Clarendon Press, 1952.

Heal, Felicity. "Appropriating History: Catholic and Protestant Polemics and the National Past." *Huntington Library Quarterly* 68 (2005): 109–32.

————. *Hospitality in Early Modern England*. Oxford: Clarendon Press, 1990.

————. *Reformation in Britain and Ireland*. Oxford: Oxford University Press, 2003.

Helt, J.S.W. "Fish, Simon (d. 1531)." In *DNB*.

Heng, Geraldine. *Empire of Magic: Medieval Romance and the Politics of Cultural Fantasy*. New York: Columbia University Press, 2003.

Herendeen, Wyman H. "Camden, William (1551–1623)." In *DNB*.

Hibbard, G.R. "The Country House Poem of the Seventeenth Century." *JWCI* 19 (1956): 159–74.

Hill, Bennett D. *English Cistercian Monasteries and Their Patrons in the Twelfth Century*. Urbana: University of Illinois Press, 1968.

Hill, J.M. "An Interpretation of *King Horn*." *Anglia* 75 (1957): 157–72.

Hilton, R.H. "The Origins of Robin Hood." *Past and Present* 14 (1958): 30–44.

Hingst, Amanda Jane. *The Written World: Past and Place in the Work of Orderic Vitalis*. Notre Dame: University of Notre Dame Press, 2009.

Holt, J.C. *Magna Carta and Medieval Government*. London: Hambledon Press, 1985.

————. *The Northerners: A Study in the Reign of King John.* Oxford: Clarendon Press, 1961.

————. *Robin Hood.* London: Thames and Hudson, 1982.

Hopcroft, Rosemary. "The Social Origins of Agrarian Change in Late Medieval England." *American Journal of Sociology* 99 (1994): 1559–95.

Hope, W. H. St. John. *Windsor Castle: An Architectural History.* 3 vols. London: Offices of Country Life, 1913.

Hopper, Andrew J. "Fairfax, Henry (1588–1665)." In *DNB.*

Hoskins, W. G. *The Making of the English Landscape.* London: Hodder and Stoughton, 1955.

Howard, Maurice. *The Early Tudor Country House: Architecture and Politics.* London: George Philip, 1987.

Howe, Emily. "Divine Kingship and Dynastic Display: The Altar Wall Murals of St. Stephen's Chapel, Westminster." *Antiquarian Journal* 81 (2001): 259–303.

Howe, Nicholas. *Writing the Map of Anglo-Saxon England: Essays in Cultural Geography.* New Haven: Yale University Press, 2008.

Hudson, Anne. *The Premature Reformation: Wycliffite Texts and Lollard History.* Oxford: Oxford University Press, 1988.

Hunt, John Dixon. "Evelyn's Idea of the Garden." In O'Malley and Wolschke-Bulmahn, *John Evelyn . . . and European Gardening,* 269–88.

Hunter, Michael. "Ashmole, Elias (1617–1692)." In *DNB.*

Ingledew, Francis. *Sir Gawain and the Green Knight and the Order of the Garter.* Notre Dame: University of Notre Dame Press, 2006.

Jamroziak, Emilia. "Making and Breaking the Bonds: Yorkshire Cistercians and Their Neighbors." In Kinder, *Perspectives for an Architecture of Solitude,* 63–70.

————. *Rievaulx Abbey and Its Social Context.* Medieval Church Studies, 8. Turnholt: Brepols, 2005.

Jeffrey, David Lyle. "False Witness and the Just Use of Evidence in the Wycliffite *Pistel of Swete Susan.*" In Spolsky, *The Judgment of Susanna,* 57–71.

Johnson, Lynn Staley. *The "Shepheardes Calender": An Introduction.* University Park: Pennsylvania State University Press, 1990.

————. "'To Make in Som Comedy': Chauntecleer, Son of Troy." *Chaucer Review* 19 (1985): 226–44. *See also* Staley, Lynn.

Jordan, William Chester. *The Great Famine. Northern Europe in the Early Fourteenth Century.* Princeton: Princeton University Press, 1996.

Kaeuper, Richard W. *War, Justice, and Public Order: England and France in the Later Middle Ages.* Oxford: Clarendon Press, 1988.

Kaplan, M. Lindsay. *The Culture of Slander in Early Modern England.* Cambridge: Cambridge University Press, 1997.

————. "Sexual Slander and the Politics of the Erotic in Garter's *Susanna.*" In Spolsky, *The Judgment of Susanna,* 73–84.

Kathman, David. "Stanley, Ferdinando, fifth earl of Derby (1559?–1594)." In *DNB*.

Keiser, George R. "Lincoln Cathedral Library MS 91: Life and Milieu of the Scribe." *Studies in Bibliography* 32 (1979): 158–79.

Kellogg, Alfred. "Susannah and the *Merchant's Tale.*" *Speculum* 35 (1960): 275–79.

Kelsey, Sean. "Rich, Robert, second earl of Warwick (1587–1658)." In *DNB*.

Kendall, Ritchie D. *The Drama of Dissent: The Radical Poetics of Nonconformity, 1380–1590*. Chapel Hill: University of North Carolina Press, 1986.

Kerby-Fulton, Kathryn. "*Eciam Lollardi*: Some Further Thoughts on Fiona Somerset's *Eciam Mulier*: Women in Lollardy and the Problem of Sources." In Olson and Kerby Fulton, *Voices in Dialogue*, 261–78.

Kernodle, George. *From Art to Theatre: Form and Convention in the Renaissance.* Chicago: University of Chicago Press, 1944.

Kerrigan, John. *Archipelagic English: Literature, History, and Politics, 1603–1707.* Oxford: Oxford University Press, 2008.

Kinder, Terry N., ed. *Perspectives for an Architecture of Solitude: Essays on Cistercians, Art, and Architecture in Honour of Peter Fergusson.* Turnholt: Brepols, 2004.

King, John N. "Bale, John (1495–1563)." In *DNB*.

———. *English Reformation Literature: The Tudor Origins of the Protestant Tradition.* Princeton: Princeton University Press, 1982.

———. *Foxe's "Book of Martyrs" and Early Modern Print Culture.* Cambridge: Cambridge University Press, 2006.

Kingsford, C. L. "Our Lady of the Pew, the King's Oratory or Chapel in the Palace of Westminster." *Archaeologia* 68 (1916–17): 1–20.

Kipling, Gordon. *Enter the King: Theatre, Liturgy, and Ritual in the Medieval Civic Triumph.* Oxford: Clarendon Press, 1998.

Kirk, Elizabeth. "Langland's Plowman and the Recreation of Fourteenth-Century Religious Metaphor." *YLS* 2 (1988): 1–21.

Kiser, Lisa. "'Mak's Heirs': Sheep and Humans in the Pastoral Ecology of the Towneley *First* and *Second Shepherds' Plays.*" *JEGP* 108 (2009): 336–59.

Knapp, Ethan. *The Bureaucratic Muse: Thomas Hoccleve and the Literature of Late Medieval England.* University Park: Pennsylvania State University Press, 2001.

———. "Poetic Work and Scribal Labor in Hoccleve and Langland." In *The Middle Ages at Work: Practicing Labor in Late Medieval England*, ed. Kellie Robertson and Michael Uebel. New York: Palgrave Macmillan, 2004.

Knowles, David. *Great Historical Enterprises: Problems in Monastic History.* London: Nelson, 1964.

Kolve, V. A. *Chaucer and the Imagery of Narrative: The First Five Canterbury Tales.* Stanford: Stanford University Press, 1984.

Kornbluth, Genevra. *Engraved Gems of the Carolingian Empire.* University Park: Pennsylvania State University Press, 1995.

Lapidge, Michael. "Gildas' Education and the Latin Culture of Sub-Roman Britain." In *Gildas: New Approaches,* ed. Michael Lapidge and David Dumville, 27–50. Woodbridge, UK: Boydell Press, 1984.

Lavezzo, Kathy. *Angels on the Edge of the World: Geography, Literature, and English Community, 1000–1534.* Ithaca: Cornell University Press, 2006.

Lawton, David. "The Diversity of Middle English Alliterative Poetry." *Leeds Studies in English* 20 (1989): 143–72.

———. "Dullness and the Fifteenth Century." *ELH* 54 (1987): 761–99.

LeClercq, Jean. *The Love of Learning and the Desire for God: A Study of Monastic Culture.* Trans. Catherine Misrahi. New York: Fordham University Press, 1977.

Lee, Sidney. "Garter, Bernard (*fl.* 1565–1579)." Revised Matthew Steggle. In *DNB.*

Leslie, Michael. "The Spiritual Husbandry of John Beale." In Leslie and Raynor, *Culture and Cultivation,* 150–71.

Leslie, Michael, and Timothy Raylor, eds. *Culture and Cultivation in Early Modern England: Writing and the Land.* Leicester: Leicester University Press, 1992.

Levin, Carole. "A Good Prince: King John and Early Tudor Propaganda." *Sixteenth Century Journal* 11 (1980): 23–32.

Levy, F. J. *Tudor Historical Thought.* San Marino, CA: Huntington Library, 1967.

Lewalski, Barbara K. "The Lady of the Country-House Poem." In *The Fashioning and Functioning of the British Country House,* ed. Gervase Jackson-Stops, Gordon J. Schochet, Lena Cowen Orlin, and Elisabeth Blair MacDougall, 234–41. Washington, DC: National Gallery of Art, 1989.

Lewis, Suzanne. *The Art of Matthew Paris in "The Chronica Majora."* Berkeley: University of California Press, 1987.

Little, Katherine C. *Confession and Resistance: Defining the Self in Late Medieval England.* Notre Dame: University of Notre Dame Press, 2006.

Low, Anthony. *The Georgic Revolution.* Princeton: Princeton University Press, 1985.

MacDougall, Elisabeth B., ed. *Medieval Gardens.* Dumbarton Oaks Colloquium on the History of Landscape Architecture 9. Washington, DC: Dumbarton Oaks Research Library and Collection, 1986.

MacLean, Gerald, Donna Landry, and Joseph P. Ward. *The Country and the City Revisited: England and the Politics of Culture, 1550–1850.* Cambridge: Cambridge University Press, 1999.

Maddicott, J. R. "The Birth and Setting of the Ballads of Robin Hood." *EHR* 93 (1978): 276–99.

Malcolmson, Cristina. "The Garden Enclosed/The Woman Enclosed: Marvell and the Cavalier Poets." In Burt and Archer, *Enclosure Acts*, 251–69.

Mann, Jill. *From Aesop to Reynard: Beast Literature in Medieval Britain.* Oxford: Oxford University Press, 2009.

———. "The Power of the Alphabet: A Reassessment of the Relation between the A and B Versions of *Piers Plowman*." *YLS* 8 (1994): 21–50.

Martindale, Andrew. "St. Stephen's Chapel, Westminster, and the Italian Experience." In *Studies in Medieval Art and Architecture presented to Peter Lasko*, ed. David Buckton and T. A. Heslop, 102–12. Dover, NH: Alan Sutton, 1994.

Marvin, William Perry. *Hunting Law and Ritual in Medieval England.* Cambridge: D. S. Brewer, 2006.

Matarasso, Pauline. *The Cistercian World: Monastic Writings of the Twelfth Century.* London: Penguin, 1993.

Matheson, Lister M. *The Prose "Brut": The Development of a Middle English Chronicle.* No. 180. Tempe, AZ: Medieval & Renaissance Texts and Studies, 1998.

Matthews, David. *Writing to the King: Nation, Kingship, and Literature in England, 1250–1350.* Cambridge: Cambridge University Press, 2010.

Mayr-Harting, Henry. *The Coming of Christianity to Anglo-Saxon England.* University Park: Pennsylvania State University Press, 1972.

McAvoy, Liz Herbert. "Gender, Rhetoric, and Space in the *Speculum Inclusorum, Letter to a Bury Recluse*, and the Strange Case of Christine Carpenter." In *Rhetoric of the Anchorhold: Space, Place, and Body within the Discourses of Enclosure*, ed. Liz Herbert McAvoy, 221–24. Cardiff: University of Wales Press, 2008.

McBride, Kari Boyd. *Country House Discourse in Early Modern England: A Cultural Study of Landscape and Legitimacy.* Burlington, VT: Ashgate, 2001.

McClung, William A. *The Country House in English Renaissance Poetry.* Berkeley: University of California Press, 1977.

McHardy, A. K. "Some Reflections on Edward III's Use of Propaganda." In *The Age of Edward III*, ed. J. S. Bothwell, 171–92. York: York Medieval Press, 2001.

McRae, Andrew. *God Speed the Plough: The Representation of Agrarian England, 1500–1660.* New York: Cambridge University Press, 1996.

———. "Husbandry Manuals and the Language of Agrarian Improvement." In Leslie and Raylor, *Culture and Cultivation*, 35–80.

———. "Tusser, Thomas (c. 1524–1580)." In *DNB*.

Meiss, Millard. *Painting in Florence and Sienna after the Black Death.* Princeton: Princeton University Press, 1951.

Meyer-Lee, Robert J. *Poets and Power from Chaucer to Wyatt* (Cambridge: Cambridge University Press, 2007).

Meyvaert, Paul. "The Medieval Monastic Garden." In MacDougall, *Medieval Gardens*, 25–53.

Michael, M. A. "The Iconography of Kingship in the Walter of Milemete Treatise." *JWCI* 57 (1994): 35–47.

———. "The Little Land of England Is Preferred before the Great Kingdom of France: The Quartering of the Royal Arms by Edward III." In *Studies in Medieval Art and Architecture Presented to Peter Lasko*, ed. David Buckton and T. A. Heslop, 113–26. Dover, NH: Alan Sutton, 1994.

———. "A Manuscript Wedding Gift from Philippa of Hainaut to Edward III." *Burlington Magazine* 127 (1985): 582–99.

Miller, M. "Bede's Use of Gildas." *EHR* 90 (1975): 241–61.

Morgan, D. A. L. "The Banner-Bearer of Christ and Our Lady's Knight: How God Became an Englishman Revisited." In Saul, *St. George's Chapel Windsor*, 51–62.

Morgan, Nigel. "The Signification of the Banner in the Wilton Diptych." In Gordon, Monas, and Elam, *Regal Image*, 179–88.

Morris, John. *Nennius: British History and the Welsh Annals.* Totowa, NJ: Rowman and Littlefield, 1980.

Mortimer, Ian. *The Greatest Traitor: The Life of Sir Roger Mortimer, Ruler of England, 1327–1330.* New York: Thomas Dunne Books, 2006.

Mote, Mavis. "The East Sussex Land Market and Agrarian Class Structure in the Late Middle Ages." *Past and Present* 139 (1993): 46–65.

Mullin, F. J. *A History of the Work of the Cistercians in Yorkshire (1131–1300).* Washington, DC: Catholic University of America Press, 1932.

Munby, Julian. "Carpentry Works for Edward III at Windsor Castle." In Saul, *St. George's Chapel Windsor*, 225–38.

Munby, Julian, Richard Barber, and Richard Brown. *Edward III's Round Table at Windsor: The House of the Round Table and the Windsor Festival of 1344.* Woodbridge, UK: Boydell Press, 2007.

Nederman, Cary J. "Property and Protest: Political Theory and Subjective Rights in Fourteenth-Century England." *Review of Politics* 58 (1966): 323–44.

Newhauser, Richard. "Historicity and Complaint in *Song of the Husbandman*." In Fein, *Studies in the Harley Manuscript*, 203–18.

Newman, Martha G. *The Boundaries of Charity: Cistercian Culture and Ecclesiastical Reform, 1098–1180.* Stanford: Stanford University Press, 1996.

Nissé, Ruth. *Drama and the Politics of Interpretation in Late Medieval England.* Notre Dame: University of Notre Dame Press, 2005.

Norbrook, David. *Writing the English Republic: Poetry, Rhetoric, and Politics, 1627–1660.* Cambridge: Cambridge University Press, 1999.

Norton, Christopher. "Richard of Fountains and the Letter of Thurstan: History and Historiography of a Monastic Controversy, St. Mary's Abbey, York, 1132." In Kinder, *Perspectives for an Architecture of Solitude*, 9–31.

Olson, Linda, and Kathryn Kerby-Fulton, eds. *Voices in Dialogue: Reading Women in the Middle Ages.* Notre Dame: University of Notre Dame Press, 2005.

O'Malley, Therese, and Joachim Wolschke-Bulmahn, eds. *John Evelyn's "Elysium Britannicum" and European Gardening.* Washington, DC: Dumbarton Oaks Research Library and Collection, 1998.

Ormrod, W. M. "Avesbury, Robert (d. 1359)." In *DNB.*

———. *Edward III.* New Haven: Yale University Press, 2011.

———. "The English Government and the Black Death of 1348–49." In *England in the Fourteenth Century, Proceedings of the 1985 Harlaxton Symposium,* ed. W. M. Ormrod, 175–88. Woodbridge, UK: Boydell Press, 1986.

———. "For Arthur and St. George: Edward III, Windsor Castle, and the Order of the Garter." In Saul, *St. George's Chapel Windsor,* 13–34.

———. "The Personal Religion of Edward III." *Speculum* 64 (1989): 849–77.

———. "The Politics of Pestilence: Government in England after the Black Death." In *The Black Death in England,* ed. W. M. Ormrod and P. G. Lindley, 147–81. Stamford, CT: Paul Watkins, 1996.

———. *The Reign of Edward III: Crown and Political Society in England, 1327–1377.* New Haven: Yale University Press, 1990.

Otter, Monika. "1066: The Moment of Transition in Two Narratives of the Norman Conquest." *Speculum* 74 (1999): 565–86.

Owst, G. R. *Literature and Pulpit in Medieval England: A Neglected Chapter in the History of English Letters and of the English People.* Cambridge: Cambridge University Press, 1933.

———. *Preaching in Medieval England: An Introduction to Sermon Manuscripts of the Period.* Cambridge: Cambridge University Press, 1926.

Oxford Dictionary of National Biography (DNB). Ed. H. C. G. Matthew and Brian Harrison. Oxford: Oxford University Press, 2004. Online ed., ed. Lawrence Goldman.

Painter, Sidney. *The Reign of King John.* Baltimore: Johns Hopkins University Press, 1949.

Palmer, Barbara D. "Recycling the Wakefield Cycle." *Research Opportunities in Renaissance Drama* 41 (2002): 88–130.

———. "'Towneley Plays' or 'Wakefield Cycle' Revisited." *Comparative Drama* 21 (1987–88): 318–48.

Parry, Graham. "Dugdale, Sir William (1605–1686)." In *DNB.*

Partner, Nancy. *Serious Entertainments: The Writing of History in Twelfth-Century England.* Chicago: University of Chicago Press, 1977.

Patterson, Annabel. *Marvell and the Civic Crown.* Princeton: Princeton University Press, 1978.

———. *Pastoral and Ideology: Virgil to Valéry.* Oxford: Oxford University Press, 1988.

————. *Reading Holinshed's "Chronicles."* Chicago: University of Chicago Press, 1994.

Patterson, Annabel, and Martin Dzelzainis. "Marvell and the Earl of Anglesey: A Chapter in the History of Reading." *Historical Journal* 44 (2001): 703–27.

Patterson, Lee. *Chaucer and the Subject of History.* Madison: University of Wisconsin Press, 1991,

Pearsall, Derek. "The Alliterative Revival: Origins and Social Backgrounds." In *Middle English Alliterative Poetry and Its Literary Background,* ed. David Lawton, 34–53. Cambridge: D. S. Brewer, 1982.

————. "The Development of Middle English Romance." *Mediaeval Studies* 27 (1965): 91–116.

————. "Hoccleve's *Regiment of Princes*: The Poetics of Royal Self-Representation." *Speculum* 69 (1994): 386–410.

————. *The Nun's Priest's Tale. The Variorum Edition of the Works of Geoffrey Chaucer* 2, pt. 9. Norman: University of Oklahoma Press, 1984.

Perkins, Nicholas. *Hoccleve's "Regiment of Princes": Counsel and Constraint.* Cambridge: D. S. Brewer, 2001.

Perry, Graham. "John Evelyn as Hortulan Saint." In Leslie and Raylor, *Culture and Cultivation,* 130–49.

Pitcher, John. "Daniel, Samuel (1562/3–1619)." In *DNB.*

Platt, Colin. *The Abbeys and Priories of Medieval England.* New York: Fordham University Press, 1984.

Powicke, F. M. *Stephen Langton: The Ford Lectures Delivered in the University of Oxford in Hilary Term 1927.* Oxford: Clarendon Press, 1928.

Pratt, Robert A. "Chaucer's Use of the *Teseida.*" *PMLA* 62 (1947): 598–621.

Putnam, Bertha. *Enforcement of the Statute of Laborers.* New York: Columbia University Press, 1908.

————. "The Transformation of the Keepers of the Peace into the Justices of the Peace, 1327–1380." *Transactions of the Royal Historical Society,* 4th ser., 12 (1929):19–48.

Putney, Rufus. "The View from Cooper's Hill." *University of Colorado Studies Series in Language and Literature* 6 (1957): 13–22.

Quest-Ritson, Charles. *The English Garden: A Social History.* Boston: David Godine, 2003.

Raybin, David. "Custance and History: Woman as Outsider in Chaucer's *Man of Law's Tale.*" *Studies in the Age of Chaucer* 12 (1990): 65–84.

Raylor, Timothy. "Samuel Hartlib and the Commonwealth of Bees." In Leslie and Raylor, *Culture and Cultivation,* 91–129.

Reid, R. R. *The King's Council in the North.* London: Longmans, Green, and Co., 1921.

Richardson, H. G. "The Coronation in Medieval England: The Evolution of the Office and the Oath." *Traditio* 16 (1960): 111–203.

Richmond, Colin. "An Outlaw and Some Peasants: The Possible Significance of Robin Hood." *Nottingham Medieval Studies* 37 (1993): 90–101.

Rigg, A. G. "John of Bridlington's *Prophecy*: A New Look." *Speculum* 63 (1988): 596–613.

Robertson, D.W., Jr. *A Preface to Chaucer.* Princeton: Princeton University Press, 1962.

Robertson, Kellie. *The Laborer's Two Bodies: Literary and Legal Productions in Britain, 1350–1500.* New York: Palgrave Macmillan, 2006.

Robins, William. "Troilus in the Gutter." In *Sacred and Profane in Chaucer and Late Medieval Literature: Essays in Honour of John V. Fleming,* 91–112. Toronto: University of Toronto Press, 2010.

Rockett, William. "'Courts Make Not Kings, but Kings the Court': *Cooper's Hill* and the Constitutional Crisis of 1642." *Restoration: Studies in English Literary Culture, 1660–1700,* 17 (1993): 1–14.

Roney, Lois. "*Winner and Waster's* 'Wyse Wordes': Teaching Economics and Nationalism in Fourteenth-Century England." *Speculum* 69 (1994):1070–1100.

Ross, C. D. "Forfeiture for Treason in the Reign of Richard II." *EHR* 71 (1956): 560–75.

Roston, Murray. *Biblical Drama in England from the Middle Ages to the Present Day.* Evanston, IL: Northwestern University Press, 1968.

Rothwell, J. S., ed. *The Age of Edward III.* York: York Medieval Press, 2001.

Rowse, A. L., ed. *A Man of Singular Virtue: being a Life of Sir Thomas More . . . and a selection of More's letters.* London: Folio Society, 1980.

Rubin, Miri. "An English Anchorite: The Making, Unmaking, and Remaking of Christine Carpenter." In *Pragmatic Utopias: Ideals and Communtities, 1200–1630,* ed. Rosemary Horrox and Sarah Rees Jones, 204–23. Cambridge: Cambridge University Press, 2001.

———. *Mother of God: A History of the Virgin Mary.* New Haven: Yale University Press, 2009.

Salter, Elizabeth. Medieval Poetry and the Visual Arts." *Essays and Studies* 22 (1969): 16–32.

Sandler, Lucy Freeman. *The Lichtenthal Psalter and the Manuscript Patronage of the Bohun Family.* London: Harvey Miller, 2004.

———. "Political Imagery in the Bohun Manuscripts." In *English Manuscript Studies, 1100–1700,* vol. 10, ed. A. S. G. Edwards, 114–53. London: British Library, 2002.

———. "Rhetorical Strategies in the Pictorial Imagery of Fourteenth-Century Manuscripts: The Case of the Bohun Psalters." In *Rhetoric beyond Words: Delight and Persuasion in the Arts of the Middle Ages,* ed. Mary Carruthers, 96–123. Cambridge: Cambridge University Press, 2010.

Saul, Nigel. *Richard II.* New Haven: Yale University Press, 1997.

————, ed. *St. George's Chapel Windsor in the Fourteenth Century.* Woodbridge, UK: Boydell Press, 2005.

Scanlon, Larry. "The King's Two Voices: Narrative and Power in Hoccleve's *Regiment of Princes.*" In *Literary Practice and Social Change in Britain, 1380–1530,* ed. Lee Patterson, 216–47. Berkeley: University of California Press, 1990.

————, *Narrative, Authority, and Power: The Medieval Exemplum and the Chaucerian Tradition.* Cambridge; Cambridge University Press, 1994.

Scase, Wendy. *Literature and Complaint in England, 1272–1553.* Oxford: Oxford University Press, 2007.

Scattergood, John. "Authority and Resistance: The Political Verse." In Fein, *Studies in the Harley Manuscript,* 163–202.

————. "'Winner and Waster' and the Mid-Fourteenth-Century Economy." In *The Writer as Witness: Literature as Historical Evidence,* ed. Tom Dunne, 39–57. Cork: Cork University Press, 1987.

Schibanoff, Susan. "Worlds Apart: Orientalism, Antifeminism, and Heresy in Chaucer's *Man of Law's Tale.*" *Exemplaria* 8 (1996): 59–96.

Schwyzer, Philip. "The Beauties of the Land: Bale's Books, Aske's Abbeys, and the Aesthetics of Nationhood." *Renaissance Quarterly* 57 (2004): 99–125.

————. *Literature, Nationalism, and Memory in Early Modern England and Wales.* Cambridge: Cambridge University Press, 2004.

Scott, Kathleen L. *Later Gothic Manuscripts, 1390–1490.* London: Harvey Miller, 1996.

Sharpe, Kevin. *Sir Robert Cotton, 1586–1631: History and Politics in Early Modern England.* Oxford: Oxford University Press, 1979.

Sieman, James R. "Landlord not King: Agrarian Change and Interarticulation." In Burt and Archer, *Enclosure Acts,* 17–33.

Simpson, James. *Burning to Read: English Fundamentalism and Its Reformation Opponents.* Cambridge, MA: Belknap Press, 2007.

————, *Reform and Cultural Revolution. The Oxford English Literary History,* vol. 2: *1350–1547.* Oxford: Oxford University Press, 2002.

Smith, D. Vance. *Arts of Possession: The Middle English Household Imaginary.* Minneapolis: University of Minnesota Press, 2003.

Smith, John Thomas. *Antiquities of the City of Westminster: The Old Palace; St. Stephen's Chapel.* London: T. Bensley, 1807.

Smith, Kathryn A. "Inventing Marital Chastity: Iconography of Susanna." *Oxford Art Journal* 16 (1993): 3–24.

Smith, Nigel. *Andrew Marvell: The Chameleon.* New Haven: Yale University Press, 2010.

Somerset, Fiona. "*Eciam Mulier*: Women in Lollardy and the Problem of Sources." In Olson and Kerby-Fulton, *Voices in Dialogue,* 245–60.

Speed, Diane. "The Saracens of *King Horn.*" *Speculum* 65 (1990): 564–95.

Spolsky, Ellen, ed. *The Judgment of Susanna: Authority and Witness.* Atlanta: Scholars Press, 1996.

Staley, Lynn. *Languages of Power in the Age of Richard II.* University Park: Pennsylvania State University Press, 2005.

———. *Margery Kempe's Dissenting Fictions.* University Park: Pennsylvania State University Press, 1994.

———. "The Penitential Psalms: A Lexicon of Conversion from the Medieval to the Early Modern Period." *JMEMS* 37 (2007): 221–70.

Stanbury, Sarah. "*The Man of Law's Tale* and Rome." *Exemplaria* 22 (2010): 119–137.

———. *The Visual Object of Desire in Late Medieval England.* Philadelphia: University of Pennsylvania Press, 2007.

Stancliffe, Clare. "British and Irish Contexts." In DeGregorio, *The Cambridge Companion to Bede,* 69–83.

Stein, Robert M. "Making History English: Cultural Identity and Historical Explanation in William of Malmesbury and Laȝamon's *Brut.*" In *Text and Territory: Geographical Imagination in the European Middle Ages,* ed. Sylvia Tomasch and Sealy Gilles, 97–115. Philadelphia: University of Pennsylvania Press, 1997.

Steiner, Emily. "Radical Historiography: Langland, Trevisa, and the *Polychronicon.*" *SAC* 27 (2005): 171–212.

Stenton, F. M. "The Road System of Medieval England." *Economic History Review* 7 (1936): 1–21.

Stevens, C. E. "Gildas Sapiens." *EHR* 56 (1941): 353–73.

Stevenson, Jane. *Latin Poets: Language, Gender, and Authority from Antiquity to the Eighteenth Century.* Oxford: Oxford University Press, 2005.

Strohm, Paul. *England's Empty Throne: Usurpation and the Language of Legitimation, 1399–1422.* New Haven: Yale University Press, 1998.

Strong, Roy. *The Cult of Elizabeth: Elizabethan Portraiture and Pageantry.* London: Thames and Hudson, 1977.

———. *The Renaissance Garden in England.* London: Thames and Hudson, 1979.

Summit, Jennifer. "Leland's *Itinerary* and the Remains of the Medieval Past." In *Reading the Medieval in Early Modern England,* ed. Gordon McMullan and David Matthews, 159–76. Cambridge: Cambridge University Press, 2007.

———. *Memory's Library: Medieval Books in Early Modern England.* Chicago: University of Chicago Press, 2008.

Tait, James. "On the Date and Authorship of the 'Speculum Regis Edwardi.'" *EHR* 16 (1901): 110–15.

Tatlock, J. S. P. *The Legendary History of Britain: Geoffrey of Monmouth's "Historia Regum Britanniae" and Its Early Vernacular Versions.* Berkeley: University of California Press, 1950.

Tawney, R. H. *Religion and the Rise of Capitalism*. New York: Harcourt, Brace and World, 1926.

Taylor, Jane H. M. "*Le Roman de Fauvain*: Manuscript, Text, Image." In Bent and Wathey, *Fauvel Studies*, 569–590.

Taylor, John. *English Historical Literature in the Fourteenth Century*. Oxford: Clarendon Press, 1987.

————. "The French Prose *Brut*: Popular History in Fourteenth-Century England." In Ormrod, *England in the Fourteenth Century*, 247–54.

————. *Medieval Historical Writing in Yorkshire*. Borthwick Institute of Historical Research. York: St. Anthony's Press, 1961.

————. *The Universal Chronicle of Ranulf Higden*. Oxford: Clarendon Press, 1966.

Thacker, Alan. "Bede and History." In DeGregorio, *The Cambridge Companion to Bede*, 170–90.

Thirsk, Joan. "Plough and Pen: Agricultural Writers in the Seventeenth Century." In *Social Relations and Ideas: Essays in Honour of R.H. Hilton*, ed. T. H. Aston, P. R. Cross, Christopher Dyer, and Joan Thirsk, 295–318. Cambridge: Cambridge University Press, 1983.

————. *The Rural Economy of England: Collected Essays*. London: Hambledon Press, 1984.

Thompson, E. Margaret. *The Carthusian Order in England*. London: Macmillan, 1930.

Thomson, John A. F. "Russell, John (c. 1430–1494)." In *DNB*.

Thomson, Rodney M. *William of Malmesbury*. Woodbridge, UK: Boydell Press, 2003.

Tierney, Brian. *Religion, Law, and the Growth of Constitutional Thought, 1150–1650*. Cambridge: Cambridge University Press, 1982.

Tite, Colin G. C. *The Early Records of Sir Robert Cotton's Library*. London: British Library, 2003.

Tkacz, Catherine Brown. "Susanna as a Type of Christ." *Studies in Iconography* 20 (1999): 101–53.

Topham, John. *An Account of the Collegiate Chapel of Saint Stephen at Westminster*. London: Simpkin & Marshall, 1834.

Tout, T. F. *Chapters in the Administrative History of Mediaeval England*. 6 vols. Manchester: Manchester University Press, 1929; rpt. New York: Barnes and Noble, 1967.

————. *The Place of the Reign of Edward II in English History*. 2nd ed. rev., Hilda Johnstone. Manchester: Manchester University Press, 1936.

Travis, Peter W. *Disseminal Chaucer: Rereading the Nun's Priest's Tale*. Notre Dame: University of Notre Dame Press, 2010.

Trigg, Stephanie. "The Vulgar History of the Order of the Garter." In *Reading the Medieval in Early Modern England*, ed. Gordon McMullan and David Matthews, 91–105. Cambridge: Cambridge University Press, 2007.

Trilling, Renée R. *The Aesthetics of Nostalgia: Historical Representation in Old English Verse.* Toronto: University of Toronto Press, 2009.

Tristram, E.W. *English Wall Paintings of the Fourteenth Century.* London: Routledge and Kegan Paul, 1955.

Turner, James. *The Politics of Landscape: Rural Scenery and Society in English Poetry, 1630–1660.* Cambridge, MA: Harvard University Press, 1979.

Turner, Ralph V. *The English Judiciary in the Age of Glanvill and Bracton, c. 1176–1239.* Cambridge: Cambridge University Press, 1985.

————. *Magna Carta through the Ages.* London: Pearson, Longman, [1985] 2003.

Turville-Petre, Thorlac. " The Author of the *Destruction of Troy.*" *Medium Ævum* 57 (1988): 264–69.

————. *England the Nation: Language, Literature, and National Identity, 1290–1340.* Oxford: Clarendon Press, 1996.

Ullman, W. *Principles of Government and Politics in the Middle Ages.* New York: Barnes and Noble, 1961.

Vale, Juliet. *Edward III and Chivalry: Chivalric Society and Its Context, 1270–1350.* Woodbridge, UK: Boydell Press, 1982.

von Maltzahn, Nicholas. *Milton's "History of Britain": Republican Historiography in the English Revolution.* Oxford: Clarendon Press, 1991.

Walker, Greg. *Plays of Persuasion: Drama and Politics at the Court of Henry VIII.* Cambridge: Cambridge University Press, 1991.

Wall, Wendy. "Renaissance National Husbandry: Gervase Markham and the Publication of England." *Sixteenth Century Journal* 27 (1996): 767–85.

Wallace-Hadrill, J. M. *Bede's "Ecclesiastical History of the English People": A Historical Commentary.* Oxford: Clarendon Press, 1988.

Ward, Benedicta. *The Venerable Bede.* London: Continuum, 1998.

Wardrop, Joan. *Fountains Abbey and Its Benefactors.* Cistercian Studies, 91. Kalamazoo, MI: Cistercian Publications, 1987.

Warner, Lawrence. *The Lost History of "Piers Plowman."* Philadelphia: University of Pennsylvania Press, 2011.

Warren, Michelle R. *History on the Edge: Excalibur and the Borders of Britain, 1100–1300* (Minneapolis: University of Minnesota Press, 2000).

Warren, W. L. *King John.* Berkeley: University of California Press, 1961.

Waterton, Edmund. *Pietas Mariana Britannica.* London, 1879.

Wayne, Don E. *"Penshurst": The Semiotics of Place and the Poetics of History.* Madison: University of Wisconsin Press, 1984.

Wenzel, Siegfried. *Macaronic Sermons: Bilingualism and Preaching in Late-Medieval England.* Ann Arbor: University of Michigan Press, 1994.

Wetherbee, Winthrop. "Constance and the World in Chaucer and Gower." In *John Gower: Recent Readings,* ed. R. F. Yeager, 65–94. Kalamazoo, MI: Medieval Institute Publications, 1989.

Whitelock, Dorothy. *The Old English Bede. Proceedings of the British Academy* 48 (1962): 57–90.

Williams, Raymond. *The Country and the City.* New York: Oxford University Press, 1973.

Wogan-Browne, Jocelyn. *Language and Culture in Medieval Britain: The French of England, c. 1100–c. 1500.* York: York Medieval Press, 2009.

———. *Saints' Lives and Women's Literary Culture, c. 1150–1300: Virginity and Its Authorizations.* Oxford: Oxford University Press, 2001.

Woods, Susanne. *Lanyer: A Renaissance Woman Poet.* New York: Oxford University Press, 1999.

Woodward, J. M. *The History of Bordesley Abbey.* London: J. H. & J. Parker, 1866.

Wormald, Patrick. "The Venerable Bede and the 'Church of the English.'" In *The English Religious Tradition and the Genius of Anglicanism*, ed. G. Rowell, 13–32. Nashville, TN: Abingdon Press, 1992.

Yunck, T. A. *The Lineage of Lady Meed: The Development of Medieval Venality Satire.* Notre Dame: University of Notre Dame Press, 1963.

INDEX

Abelard, 179

Acte agaynst pullyng doun of
Tounes, 95

active life, 114

advice to princes, 123, 125, 131, 141

Aelred of Rievaulx, 47, 184–85, 196

Aers, David, 75

Æthelbert, 21, 32, 67–69

Æthelred, 36

Æthelwulf, 46

Æthethryth, 24

"Against the King's Taxes," 159,
170

Ahab, 95, 139

Aidan of Iona, 21, 23

Alan of Melsa, 182, 196–201, 205,
228

"Tractatus metricus de Susanna,"
182, 186, 189, 193–95, 199,
204, 215, 221

Alban, 20, 25, 67

Albert the Great, 96

Albina, 48–50, 65, 118, 174

Alcuin, 32–34, 45, 252n.46

Alexander, J. J., 166

Alfred, king of England, 33–35, 96,
148

alliterative poetry, 195

Ambrose, St., 179, 209

America, 8, 238–40

Amidis, 196

Anglo Saxon Chronicle, 67

Anglocentric perspective, 30

antiquarianism, 116, 231, 258n.96

Appleton House, 115, 117, 119

Arian heresy, 18, 21

Aristotle, 125, 130–31
  concept of the household, 221
  Economics, 236

Arthur, king, 40–43, 48–50, 52, 54,
57, 59, 66, 80, 148, 163, 164, 174

Arthurian history, 38, 40

Arundel, Thomas, 72, 207–8, 214

Ashmole, Elias, 116

Aske, Robert, 103–4, 107, 240

Aske family, 299n.25

Athelston, 200–201

Auchinleck manuscript, 142, 145,
151–52

Augustine, St., 16–17, 179

Augustine of Canterbury, 21–22,
    25–26, 32, 37, 68
Austen, Ralph, 109–10
Avesbury, Robert, 143
Avicenna, 96
Aylett, Robert
    *Susanna: or The Arraignment of
    the Two Vniust Elders*, 216, 217,
    222–24

Bale, John, 16, 52, 108
    Kynge Johan, 53
barbarism, 19, 31, 34, 45–46, 49,
    99, 108–9, 115, 142, 174
Barber, Richard, 164
baronial power, 183
Bathsheba, 225
Beale, John, 109
Becket, Thomas, 53, 57
Bedan history, 30, 42, 44, 51, 118,
    226
Bede
    and Christian culture, 11
    *Ecclesiastical History of the English
    People*, 2–3, 10, 16, 19–25,
    27–34, 36, 38, 40, 42–45, 48,
    50–51, 58–59, 61–62, 66–68,
    73, 90, 114–15, 120, 181, 211,
    227, 239
    historiography, 30
bees, 89
Bell, David, 196
Benedict Biscop, 24, 25, 33
Benedictine Rule, 236
Bennett, Michael, 195
Bernard of Clairvaux, St., 45, 47,
    62, 182, 184
Bersuire, Pierre, 181
Bill on Decay of Tillage, 104
Bilney, Thomas, 213
Binski, Paul, 11, 165–66, 168
BL MS Harley 2253, 142, 151–53,
    159, 160, 170, 175

Blyth, Charles, 126
Boccaccio, Giovanni, 135, 181
    Teseida, 132, 134
body politic
    and disease, 128
    and health, 127, 141
Bohun, Joan, 214–15
Bohun manuscripts, 122, 140,
    294n.104
Bolton Priory, 116
The Book of the City of Ladies, 181
The Book of the Vices and Virtues, 83
Bordesley Abbey, 196–97
    library, 196
boundaries, 18, 25, 28, 30, 33, 36,
    38, 43–44, 57, 100, 115, 136,
    150, 173, 230–32, 235
Bracton, Henry
    De Legibus, 161
Bradford, William, 239
bride
    England as, 17, 19, 47, 67
    Israel as, 19
Bridlington Prophecies, 140
Britain/England, 49
Britons, 16, 18, 20, 23, 26–27,
    39–45, 50, 59, 61–62, 65,
    66, 109
Brut, 3, 38, 48–52, 117, 173–74, 210
Brut, Walter, 198, 209, 211–13
Brutus, 38–39, 49–50, 65–66, 96,
    118, 174
Buc, Philippe, 179
Butterfield, Ardis, 9
Byland Abbey, 45

Caedmon, 22, 24
Caesar, 39–41, 69
Camden, William, 4, 61–63, 69, 116
Camille, Michael, 125
cannibal sheep, 99
Carpenter, Christina, 229–30, 236
Carthusians, 46

Cassibellaunus, 39
Castle of Perseverance, 83
Cecil, William, Lord Burghley, 62
*Certayne causes gathered together
    wherein shewed the decaye of
    England*, 101
Chambers, D. C., 235
Chapel of St. George, Windsor,
    163–65, 169
Chapel of St. Stephen, Westminster,
    163, 165–69, 175, 178, 229–30
Chapel of the Pew, Westminster,
    166, 169, 280n.89
Charlemagne, 33
Charles I, 116, 168
Charles V of France, 170, 180
chastity, 72, 111, 119, 177, 179–80,
    216, 224, 228
Chaucer, Geoffrey, 4, 28, 43, 74, 80,
    84, 87, 90, 122, 125, 127,
    130–32, 140, 176, 198, 200,
    207, 229
    Book of the Duchess, 127
    Canterbury Tales, 85, 134
    —*Clerk's Tale*, 203
    —*General Prologue*, 134–35
    —*Knight's Tale*, 132, 134–35
    —*Man of Law's Tale*, 206
    —*Nun's Priest's Tale*, 85–88, 132
    —*Parson's Tale*, 206
    gardens, 135
    Parliament of Fowls, 132, 133, 136
    Troilus and Criseyde, 43
chivalry, 162–64, 229
Churchill, Winston, 241
Cicero, 130–31
Cistercian Order, 36–37, 44–50,
    115–16, 103, 109, 182, 183,
    184, 189, 191, 193, 196
    accounts of vocation, 47, 184, 193
    founding narratives, 46, 48
    houses and entertainment, 196
    houses in England, 183

language of conversion, 182
language of identity, 46, 47, 200
libraries, 196
provenance for manuscripts, 197
Clairvaux Abbey, 47–48
Cnut, king of England, 35–36, 148
College of St. George, 163
College of St. Stephen, 163, 166
Colman, bishop, 23
common good, 73–74, 77–78,
    81–82, 89–90, 94–95, 98–101,
    106, 112, 128, 133, 135, 201,
    215, 226
community, 25, 32, 46, 55, 76, 78,
    91, 93, 96–98, 102–8, 110,
    112–14, 120, 127, 200, 206–8,
    211, 221, 223–26
Constantine, 21
contemplation, 115
conversion, 17, 21, 23, 27–28, 32,
    35, 38, 67, 68, 185, 187–89,
    193–94
Cotton, Robert, 5, 16, 62, 69, 116,
    168
country-city debate, 4
Cowley, Abraham, 235
Cranmer, Thomas, 53
croft, 74–76, 80–92, 121, 132, 152,
    175, 226
Cromwell, Thomas, 52, 55, 62, 104
Cuthbert, 21, 25

Danes, 34, 61, 64, 66, 96, 109, 173
Daniel, Samuel, 4, 15, 60–61, 63
Daniel, Walter
    Life of Aelred of Rievaulx, 47
Daphne, 199
David, king of Israel, 122, 139–40,
    225
Davies, R. R., 2, 244n.4
Death of Arthur, 196
Denham, John
    "Cooper's Hill," 116–17

Dido, 181
Digby *Mary Magdalene,* 217
Dimock, Cressy, 109
Dinah, 191–92, 199
Diocletian, 18, 20
Dioclisian's daughters, 48, 173
*A Discourse of the Common Weal of
    this Realm of England,* 102
Dissolution, 46, 62, 104–6, 108–9,
    116, 118
Dodsworth, Roger, 116
Domesday Book, 37, 59, 97
Domesday of Inclosures, 264n.48
Donne, John, 104
dos Mariae, 72, 117, 119
    as England, 83
Doyle, A. I., 197, 215
Duffy, Eamon, 9
Dugdale, William, 5, 116
Dzelzainis, Martin, 116

Easter
    date of, 23–24, 26
Eden, 1, 17, 97
Edward I, 138, 160, 163, 165, 167
Edward II, 122, 138–39, 145,
    151–53
Edward III, 5, 64, 73, 83, 87,
    90–91, 116–17, 121–24, 129,
    131, 137, 139–40, 162,
    164–70, 173–75, 177, 214,
    229–30
    chivalry, 125
    crisis of 1341, 142, 144–45
    Hundred Years War, 142
    Order of the Garter, 38, 83
    propaganda, 145, 278n.70
    tournaments, 162
    and Tudor history, 256n.82
Edward IV, 163
Edward V, 92, 95
Edward VI, 104, 165, 231
Edward the Confessor, 59, 138

elegy, 96, 98
"The Elegy on the Death of
    Edward I," 160
Eleutherius, 211
Elizabeth I, 57, 112, 178, 217, 220,
    222
    progress in Norwich, 217
    reign of, 215
enclosure, 3, 47, 51, 74, 83, 89–92,
    94–95, 97–100, 106, 110–15,
    120, 150, 177–78, 181, 195,
    215–16, 220, 224–28, 230–31,
    238–41
    Cistercian language of, 11
enclosure controversies, 232
England
    as dower of Virgin, 166
    relationship to Rome, 20, 56–57
    relationship to the world, 32, 33,
        35, 38, 42, 51–52, 59–62, 73
Espec, Walter, 50
estate management, 101
Eusebius, 19
Evelyn, John, 235

Fabyan, Robert, 52
Fairfax, Henry, 116, 240
Fairfax, Maria, 115, 119, 235, 240
Fairfax, Thomas, 114, 116, 119–20,
    232–35, 240
    Short Memorials, 233, 235
Fane, Mildmay, 267n.76
Fauvel/Fauvain, 124–29, 131–32,
    272n.16
Fein, Susanna, 195
Fish, Simon, 52
    Supplicacyon for the Beggers,
        52–54
Fisher, John, 58, 213
Fitz Nigel, Richard
    Dialogue of the Exchequer, 123
Fitzalan, Richard, earl of Arundel,
    215

Fitzherbert, John, 100–103, 110
flattery, 86, 129, 192
Florence of Worcester, 63
Fortescue, Sir John
  De Laudibus Legum Angliae, 204,
    213, 180
Fortunatus, 67
Fountains Abbey, 44, 45, 47, 62,
    182, 185–86, 193, 196–97
Foxe, John, 10, 52–53, 59, 68, 211,
    213
Froissart, Jean, 164
Fulgentius, 135

gardens
  design, 235
  enclosed, 135
  fallen, 48, 49, 60, 90
Garter, Thomas
  *The Commody of the moste vertuous
    and Godlye Susanna*, 216, 217,
    223
Geoffrey, Archbishop of York, 183,
    195
Geoffrey of Monmouth, 3, 30, 38, 40,
    42–44, 48–51, 57, 65–66, 148
georgic, 89, 116, 235
Gerald of Wales, 194
A Geste of Robyn Hode, 155
Gewirth, Alan, 55
Gilbert of Hoyland, 47
Gildas, 1, 3, 10, 16–20, 25–26,
    30–31, 33, 38–40, 42–44, 48,
    51, 57–58, 60, 64–68, 73, 90,
    108, 115, 227–28, 230
Giles of Rome, 130, 131
Girard, Antoine
  "La Solitude," 233
"Gode Spede the Plough," 98
Godly Queene Hester, 105
Gordon, Dillian, 72
Gough map, 155
Gower, John, 123, 125, 127, 132, 210

Grafton, Richard, 59
Grail romance, 196
Gransden, Antonia, 10
Greene, Robert
  The Myrrour of Modestie, 216–18,
    224–25
Greenway, Diana, 38
Gregory of Tours, 29
Gregory the Great, 21, 22, 26–27,
    32, 68
  mission to England, 66
Griselda, 85–86
Guillaume de Lorris, 135
Guy de Beauchamp, 196
gynophobia, 225

Hadrian, 22
Haines, Roy, 142, 145, 229
half-acre, 74, 75, 78, 82, 84, 87–89,
    101, 109, 121
Hall, Edward
  Chronicle, 56, 57
Hanna, Ralph, 78, 170, 173, 195,
    293n.102
Harding, Stephen, 37, 45, 50, 184
Harrison, William, 59, 112
Harriss, G. L., 142
Hartlib, Samuel, 109, 235
Havelok the Dane, 145, 148, 151, 239
Heal, Felicity, 69
Hengist and Horsa, 45, 54
Henry I, 36
Henry II, 36–37, 44, 123, 183
Henry III, 53, 138, 163, 166
Henry IV, 88, 215
Henry V, 89, 123, 127, 129–32, 141
Henry VI, 125
Henry VII, 52, 95, 97, 163
Henry VIII, 51–56, 58, 62, 97, 112,
    179
Henry of Huntingdon, 3, 16,
    30–31, 34, 36–38, 41, 44, 60,
    63, 66, 68, 123

heterodoxy, 181
Higden, Ranulf, 3, 48–52, 57, 73,
    173, 194
Hild, 21
Hildegard of Bingen, 179
Hill, Bennett D., 183
history
    Bede's view of, 19
    Gildas's view of, 17
    perspective on, 17, 31, 34, 38,
        40, 42
    as reparation, 21
Hoccleve, Thomas
    Regiment of Princes, 122, 123,
        125–32, 141
Holinshed, Raphael
    Chronicles, 4, 59, 112
Holt, J. C., 53
Horn, Andrew, 123
    The Mirror of Justices, 270n.6
horticulture, 46, 108–9
hospitality, 67–69, 197–98, 226,
    240
household, 179, 198–99, 201, 202,
    211, 213–15, 217, 219–21, 226
housewifery, 110–11
Howe, Emily, 165–66
Hugh of Kirkstall, 193
husbandmen, 91, 99, 107, 109
husbandry, 108, 110–11

iconoclasm, 223, 225
iconophilia, 225
idolatry, 223
image-making, 122
    national, 122
images, 216
    dangers of, 223, 295n.120
individual rights, 198
Ingledew, Francis, 38, 49
injustice, 200–202, 209
innocence, 226
Innocent III, 49, 51–53

insularity, 2, 117, 142
interdict, 50, 183, 194
invasion, 17, 18, 19–21, 25, 27, 29,
    38–39, 43, 45, 53–54, 56–60,
    65–66, 69, 90, 118, 146, 148,
    173
Iona, 22, 24, 26–27
Ireland, 20, 23–25
isolation, 17–18, 20–21, 25, 27–30,
    32–33, 45–46, 57–59, 65, 69,
    90, 92, 97, 99, 104, 108, 112,
    120, 151, 178, 181, 227–28,
    231
Israel, 1, 16, 18–19, 26, 43, 106,
    137, 139
    England as, 11

Jacob de Cessolis
    A Game of the Chese, 76, 130
James I, 215
Jean le Bel, 164
Jeffrey, David Lyle, 207
jeremiad, 42–43
Jezebel, 95
John, king of England, 49–50, 52,
    59, 64, 138, 183, 185, 194–95
    Tudor view of, 52–54, 57
John of Hovedon, 196
John of Salisbury, 141
Jonson, Ben
    "To Penshurst," 4, 74, 110–14,
        116–17, 120, 226, 232, 238
Judith, 191
justice, 138, 141, 189, 192, 202, 214,
    226

Kaeuper, Richard, 214
Kaplan, M. Lindsay, 217
Kendall, Ritchie D., 103
Kent, 69–70
King Horn, 145–46, 148, 151
kingship, 121, 124, 175
Kirkstall Abbey, 197

Knight, Stephen, 155
The Knight of Tour Landry, 180, 205
Kornbluth, Genevra, 179

labor, 55, 81, 98–99, 110, 128
Lambarde, William, 4, 69
Lancashire, 103, 107, 108
Lancelot, 196
landscape, 45–46, 51, 74, 79, 82, 84,
    88–92, 95–98, 100–108, 117,
    129, 132–35
Langland, William
    Piers Plowman, 4, 73–79, 81–85,
        87–88, 90, 101, 109, 122, 127,
        128, 132, 136, 142, 151–52, 155,
        171–73, 175–77, 226, 229, 232
Langton, Stephen, 50, 52
Lanyer, Aemelia
    "Description of Cooke-ham," 113
Latimer, Hugh, 109, 213, 231
Latini, Brunetto, 123, 141, 196
laurel tree, 199
law, 35, 37, 61, 70, 72–73, 89,
    91–96, 115, 136, 139, 154,
    161–62, 178, 181–82, 190–93,
    198, 200–201, 204–5, 207,
    216, 219–23, 225–26, 228, 238
Law of the Forest, 76
Lawton, David, 195
Le Menagier de Paris, 180, 205
Le Roman de Renart, 85
Le Roman de Renart le Contrefait, 85
Le songe du vergier, 170
Lear, 39
Leland, John, 16, 57, 108, 253n.50
    Laboryouse Journey, 108
The Letter on Virginity, 219
Levin, Carol, 52
Libelle of Englyshe Polycye, 89
Lindisfarne, 22, 24
locus amoenus, 199
Lollard satire, 54
Lollardy, 84, 128, 207

lordship, 140
Lud, king, 39
Luther, Martin, 58
Luttrell Psalter, 76, 135
"Lycidas," 113
Lydgate, John
    Secrees of Old Philisoffres, 125, 127

Maddicott, J. R., 155
Magi, 165
Magna Carta, 49, 52–53, 64, 138,
    143–45, 160, 183
Maltzahn, Nicholas von, 64
Manny, Walter, 174
Map, Walter, 194
Markham, Gervase, 109, 110
marriage, chaste, 219
Marshall, William, 55
Marsilius of Padua, 55
Martindale, Andrew, 167
Marvell, Andrew, 74, 114, 116
    "The Garden," 113–14, 233, 237
    "An Horatian Ode," 234–5
    Mower poems, 232
    "Upon Appleton House," 4,
        114–17, 119, 120, 216, 232, 235
Mary Magdalene, 82
Massachusetts Bay colony, 222
Mather, Cotton
    Magnalia Christi Americana, 239
Matilda of England, 36, 44
Matthew of Rievaulx, 185–87, 189,
    191, 193, 194, 196
Matthew of Vendôme, 185
Maximus, 19
McHardy, A. K., 145, 162
McRae, Andrew, 109, 110
Melsa Abbey, 196–97
memory, 96
Merlin, 38, 40, 43
Meyvaert, Paul, 46
Michael, M. A., 122, 124
Milemete, Walter, 122, 124–25

Milton, John, 63, 64, 66, 68
modesty *topos*, 126
Molesme, Robert, 184
monasteries, 29, 32, 62, 69, 73, 84,
      96, 103, 105, 107, 118
Monophysite heresy, 25
monstrosity, 125, 174–75
morality play, 216, 218
More, Thomas, 112
   Utopia, 58, 99
Mortimer, Roger, 122, 162, 164
Mum and the Sothseggar, 74, 84, 88,
      90, 141, 223
Murimuth, Adam, 145, 164
myths of origin, 15

Nabaoth's vineyard, 225
Nash, Thomas, 218
Nathan, 140
Nederman, Cary J., 140
Nennius, 66
   Historia Brittonum, 39–40
New Troy, 39
Newhauser, Richard, 170
Newman, Martha G., 185
Nicholas of Lyra, 179
nightingale, 199
Norman Conquest, 11, 34, 44, 59,
      60
Normans, 35–37, 62, 64, 70, 96,
      109
Northern Homily Cycle, 83
nostalgia, 90–91, 95–96, 98, 106
Nun Appleton, 4, 232–35, 240

Ohlgren, Thomas, 155
Order of the Garter, 5, 38, 73,
      83, 87, 116–17, 142, 162–64,
      170, 174–75, 229
Orderic Vitalis, 29
Ordinance of Laborers, 91
Ormrod, Mark, 168

Orosius, 16–17, 19, 38
Oswald, king of Northumbria, 23
Oswiu, 23–24
Ovid, 135

Pandulf, 49, 51, 53
Paris, Matthew, 53, 252n.43
Parker, Matthew, 16, 53
parliament, 94, 142, 145
pastoral, 113, 116
Patterson, Annabel, 59, 116
Patterson, Lee, 9
Pearsall, Derek, 171–72, 271n.13,
      272n.18
Pelagian heresy, 21
Penitential Psalms, 140
pestilence, 43, 90–91, 142, 172–73,
      230, 282n.109
Philippa of Hainault, 124
Philippe de Mèziéres, 181
Philomena, 199
Piers Plowman. See under Langland,
      William
Pilgrimage of Grace, 103, 105, 240
A Pistel of Susan, 182, 197–207,
      214–15, 226
Pleshey, 122, 215
plowmen, 84, 88
plows, 102, 107
Plymouth colony, 222
Pratt, Robert A., 132, 134
Prick of Conscience, 197
princely address, 129, 132
privacy, 47–48, 75, 91, 95, 100–101,
      106, 112–13, 178, 202, 224,
      225, 230, 232, 236
profit, 98, 100–101, 103, 110, 112
propaganda, 52, 55, 162
prosperity, 89, 92, 95, 102
Protestantism
   biblical drama, 216
   female virtues, 216, 218

Puritans, 222
purveyance, 107, 137, 140

Quest-Ritson, Charles, 46

Raleigh, Sir Walter, 213
Ralph of Coggeshall, 45
rechelessness, 128
regal power, 183
rhetoric of loss, 49
Rich, Robert, 222
Richard II, 72, 86, 112, 120, 168,
    215
Richard III, 92–93, 95
Ridley, Nicholas, 213
Rievaulx Abbey, 45, 48, 50, 186,
    193, 196
Riga, Peter, 187–89
Rising of 1381, 87, 175
Robert, earl of Gloucester, 36
Robertson, D.W., 86
Robin Hood, 155, 159
Robin Hood and the Monk, 155, 157,
    159
Robin Hood and the Potter, 155–56
Robynson, Raphe, 99
Roche, Robert
    Eustathia, 216, 219–21, 224–25,
    237
Roche Abbey, 105, 197
Roger Hovedon, 63
Roger of Byland, 47, 196
Roger of Wendover, 252n.43,
    253n.48
Roman de Fauvain, 124–25
Roman de Fauvel, 124
Roman de la Rose, 132, 199
Rome, 10, 39, 41, 51–52, 58, 64, 69,
    109
    England's relationship with, 25
Round Table, 163–64, 229
Rous, John, 95–97

Rubin, Miri, 166
Russell, John, 92–94, 104, 117

Saint George, 166
Sainte-Chapelle, 165, 167
Salter, Elizabeth, 195
Sandler, Lucy Freeman, 122, 140
Saracens, 27, 146
Savigniacs, 45
Sawley Abbey, 196, 197
Saxons, 18–19, 21, 25, 28, 31, 35,
    40, 42, 44, 48, 54, 59, 61–62,
    64, 66, 109, 173
Scanlon, Larry, 86
Scotland, 50
Scots, 18–19, 30–31, 34–35, 42,
    45, 65
Second Shepherds' Play, 107, 113
secrecy, 225
Secreta Secretorum, 124, 127–29,
    131, 141
sermon literature, 137
Shakespeare, William, 219
    Lucrece, 217
    Richard II, 71, 108
    Sonnet 130, 223
sheep, 97, 99, 101–2, 107
Sherbrook, Michael
    The Fall of Religious Houses,
    105–6
Sidney, Sir Philip, 222
Simeon manuscript, 197, 214–15
Simon de Montfort, 160
"The Simonie," 151–52
Simpson, James, 7, 9
Sir Gawain and the Green Knight,
    80
Smith, Vance, 170
social satire, 121
Society of Antiquaries, 69
solitude, 181, 233–34, 236
The Song of Lewes, 160

Song of Songs, 47, 189, 199, 217, 223, 225
"Song of the Husbandman," 152, 170
South English Legendary, 82
sovereignty, 95, 115, 122, 169, 203, 221, 226
Spenser, Edmund, 57, 60, 217–18
   The Faerie Queene, 236
   Shepheardes Calender, 8, 113
St. Bridget of Sweden, 131
St. George, 72, 122, 124, 164–65, 166, 169
St. Mary's of York, 47
Stapleton, Thomas, 28, 29
statutes against the pulling down of towns, 97
Statute of 1361, 214
Statute of Laborers, 91
Stephen, king of England, 36, 44–45
Stephen of Sawley, 196
Stevens, Wallace
   "Peter Quince at the Clavier," 237
Stow, John, 70, 229
Stratford, John, archbishop of Canterbury, 5, 142–45, 159–60, 162–63, 175, 228–29
Stratford, Ralph, 174, 230
Strohm, Paul, 9

Tale of Gamelyn, 200, 201, 214
Taylor, Jane H. M., 124
Taylor, Jeremy, 213
Tertullian, 179
The Testimony of William Thorpe, 207
textual transmission, 195, 197
Theodore, archbishop of Canterbury, 21–22, 24, 42, 59
Thomas à Becket, 160
Thomas of Woodstock, earl of Gloucester, 215, 289n.63
Thornton, Robert, 77

Thorpe, William, 198
   The Testimony of William Thorpe, 207–9, 213
Titus, 96
Titus and Vespasien, 196
Tobit, 185–86
tonsure, 22, 24, 26–27
tournaments, 162–63
Tout, T. F., 142
Towneley manuscript, 107
Towneley plays
   Judgment, 83
   Second Shepherds', 107–8
Trailbaston (proceedings), 157
"Trailbaston," 152–53, 155, 159, 170
treason, 220
Tres Riches Heures, 76
Trigge, Francis
   An Apologie or Defence of Our Dayes, 105–6
Troy, 176
Tudor historians, 3, 51–63
Tudor period, 8, 16
Tusser, Thomas, 74, 110–11, 113, 232
Tyndale, William, 53

Uther, 40

vagabonds, 102
Vale, Juliet, 162
Vergil, Polydore, 16, 53, 57–58
Vernon manuscript, 197, 214
Vespasian, 96
Villiers, George, 235
Virgil, 130–31
   Aeneid, 38
Virgin Mary, 47, 57, 72–73, 83, 87, 118, 119, 120, 161, 164, 166, 168–69, 175, 178, 189, 217, 220
Virginia, 240
virginity literature, 219
Vortigern, 40, 54, 66

Walker, Greg, 105
Warwickshire, 96
wasteland, 17–19, 34, 37, 43–44, 95, 97, 100, 103, 106–9, 112, 120, 131–32, 240, 138
wasters, 76, 78
Welsh, 30, 41
Westminster, 168–69
    Painted Chamber, 166, 167
Westmoreland, 103, 107
Whalley Abbey, 196
Wheler, George
    The Protestant Monastery, 236, 237
Whetstone, George, 213
Whitby, 22
Whitby, council of, 23
Whitman, Walt, 175, 239
wilderness, 239
Wilfrid, 21, 23–25
Willetrudis, 187–88
William de Brailes, 188
William of Jumiéges, 29
William of Malmesbury, 3, 16, 30, 32–33, 36, 41, 44, 57, 61–63, 66–67, 69, 149

William of Newburgh, 10, 16, 37, 44–45, 57, 62, 103, 194
William of Pagula, 137, 139–43, 160, 232
William of Rymynton, 196
William the Conqueror, 34–37, 59, 61, 63, 66, 70, 96
Williams, Raymond, 243n.3
Wilton Diptych, 72–73, 84, 86–88, 115–16, 119, 166, 168
Wimbledon, Thomas, 198, 209, 211–13
Wogan-Brown, Jocelyn, 9
Woolsey, Cardinal, 105
Wyclif, John, 181, 230–31
Wycliffism
    beliefs, 209
    Bible, 205
    texts, 197, 207
Wynnere and Wastoure, 74, 77–79, 80–82, 101, 110, 169–71, 175

Yorkshire, 5, 34, 36–37, 44–45, 62, 77, 103, 105, 107, 115–16, 182–85, 195–98

LYNN STALEY

is Harrington and Shirley Drake Professor of the Humanities

in the Department of English, Colgate University.